*The Decline
of Democratic
Politics*

POLITICS IN THE TWENTIETH CENTURY

VOLUME I
THE DECLINE OF DEMOCRATIC POLITICS

VOLUME II
THE IMPASSE OF AMERICAN FOREIGN POLICY

VOLUME III
THE RESTORATION OF AMERICAN POLITICS

The Decline
of Democratic
Politics

Hans J. Morgenthau

THE UNIVERSITY OF CHICAGO PRESS

CHICAGO AND LONDON

Standard Book Number: 226-53821-4
Library of Congress Catalog Card Number: 62-18111

THE UNIVERSITY OF CHICAGO PRESS, CHICAGO 60637
The University of Chicago Press, Ltd., London

Parts of this work were published under the title
Dilemmas of Politics
© 1958 by The University of Chicago

© *1962 by The University of Chicago. All rights reserved. Published 1962*
Third Impression 1969
Printed in the United States of America

To my mother

FRIEDA BACHMANN MORGENTHAU

*on the occasion of her
eightieth birthday,
September 24, 1962*

Every time that I have approached a question, I have found that my enquiries ended by giving rise to new problems, and the farther I pushed my investigations the more disquieting these new problems became. But philosophy is after all perhaps only the recognition of the abysses which lie on each side of the footpath that the vulgar follow with the serenity of somnambulists.

GEORGES SOREL, *Reflections on Violence*

Preface

    The essays which comprise this book were written during a period of almost twenty-five years for different publications on different occasions about different subjects. But they have been written by the same author, for whose unchanged philosophy and intellectual preoccupations they have furnished an opportunity for expression. Some of them have been brought up to date. Additions have been made primarily for the purpose of emphasizing the common concern of all these essays with the fundamental problems of politics. Certain articles, previously published in book form, have not been included.

I gratefully acknowledge the permission of the following publications and publishers to use copyrighted material: *America, American Journal of International Law, American Perspective, American Political Science Review,* Basic Books, *Bulletin of the Atomic Scientists,* Carnegie Endowment for International Peace, *Christianity and Crisis, Commentary,* Harper and Brothers, *Harvard Law Review,* Holt, Rinehart and Winston, *International Social Science Bulletin, Iowa Law Review,* Leo Baeck Institute, Meridian Books, National War College, *New Republic,* Northwestern University Press, Philosophical Library, *Review of Politics, University of Chicago Law Review, University* (of Kansas City) *Review,* University of Maryland Press, University of Notre Dame Press, University of Toronto Press, *World Politics, Yale Law Journal, Yale Review, Year Book of World Affairs.*

Contents

Introduction

The history of political thought is a dialogue between the teachings of tradition and the demands of the contemporary world. Creative political thought illuminates the political experience of the day—and of all days—by discovering within it the perennial forces, problems, and patterns of interaction, of which political life consists. Both the tradition of political thought and the contemporary experience of political life, then, contain two elements: one contingent and ephemeral, the other necessary and perennial. Each epoch of history has the task to disengage from the tradition of political thought those truths which fit its own experience and, in turn, to separate out of the welter of its own experience the perennial configurations of political life. It must test yesterday's dogmas against the facts of today and today's orthodoxies against the perennial truths. It must liberate itself from the dead hand of tradition without falling victim to new dogma or else being lost in the labyrinth of uncomprehended experience.

This task confronts political thought with an inescapable dilemma. What of the tradition is perennially true, and what is but the outgrowth of particular interests and circumstances? And what in the political experience of the contemporary world is the ephemeral product of historic accident, and what is a manifestation of the eternal verities of politics? The history of political thought is the story of the gropings with which successive generations have searched for answers to these questions. They had to beware of two temptations which are indeed the horns of the dilemma: either to smother the contemporary world with obsolescent dogma or else to exchange the wisdom of the ages for the innovations of the age.

Until the French Revolution of 1789, political thought tended to err on the side of dogma and tradition. Finding the perennial truths of politics imbedded in the shell of historic contingencies, each generation is tempted by its prideful or spiteful identification with its own times to give the contingent the appearance of the perennial. Theocracies have claimed for themselves a monopoly of truth, denying to rival theocracies any part of it. The philosophers of the Greek city-state fashioned out of their limited historic experience a model of political perfection. Imperial Rome saw in its constitution the repository of eternal truth and, hence, thought it would last forever. Both the feudal order of the Middle Ages and the absolute monarchy following it claimed to apply the truth of religion to the political sphere. In our own time, both liberal democracy and divers totalitarianisms have laid claim to being true democracies, both assuming that the truth of politics is to be found only in democracy, however defined.

While thus in the past the great source of error has been the unresisted temptation to clothe a particular political position or tradition with the dignity of absolute truth, our own time has to come to terms with the opposite temptation, that is, to throw all tradition overboard and either to deny the existence of objective political truth altogether or else to seek it in some novel political arrangement or device, apparently unencumbered by past political experience. That new temptation results from the successful attack to which the tradition of Western political thought has been exposed in the last two centuries.

In the realm of immediate experience, a succession of technological revolutions has transformed the natural and social environment of man almost beyond recognition and has radically changed man's experience of himself A succession of political revolutions opened the doors of the political arena to the masses which before the French Revolution had been excluded from active participation in political life. The Western tradition appeared to be incapable of coping in thought or deed with these novel experiences, and in the face of their novelty it appeared to be hopelessly out of date. Thus intellectual movements arose which tried to absorb these experiences by being openly or surreptitiously at odds with the Western tradition. Rousseau undermined it by substituting for the transcendent and substantive standards of the tradition an immanent and formal standard, the General Will, as the source of political truth. Marx destroyed it by making truth a function of political power.

Since in every epoch political thought is but the particular manifestation and application of a general philosophy, this destruction of the political tradition must be seen in the context of the general intellectual trend of the times. What Rousseau and Marx did to politics, Kierkegaard did to religion, Nietzsche to philosophy, and Freud to the image of man. These attacks upon the very foundations of Western civilization have left the received systems of thought empty of content and, in any event, without conviction. They live on as ritualistic incantations and ideological justifications and rationalizations, proclaiming their truth loudly but without rational vitality. Religion has become an organized social activity and the public demonstration of official piety, permeated with doubt and disbelief. Philosophy has set itself the task of proving that the very enterprise of philosophy is absurd and limits itself to clarifying the meaning of concepts. The image of man has disintegrated into a bundle of impulses with an infinite capacity for self-deception and an infinite need for expert management. And of politics nothing is left but the struggle of individuals and groups for access to the levers of power, in terms either of majority or oligarchic rule, crying out again either for expert management or else for utopian reform, oblivious of the distinction of what is desirable and what is possible and of the ineluctability of power itself.

The dilemma which confronts us today, then, is twofold. We must come to terms with the dilemma which grows from the very nature of political thought and which every epoch must try to solve anew: the tension between the political ideas which have come to us from the past, claiming to tell us the truth about ourselves, and the political experiences of the age which, at the very least, question this claim. Yet before we face this perennial dilemma of political thought we must cope with the attitude peculiar to our age which denies the value of tradition to help us understand and master the problems of contemporary politics and therefore denies the existence of the perennial dilemma itself.

This book indeed assumes, as shown in particular in the second chapter, not only the continuing value of the tradition of political thought for the contemporary world but also the need for the restoration of its timeless elements. It is especially concerned with the restoration of politics as an autonomous sphere of thought and action. Beyond this preliminary task of restoration, it subjects a number of traditional political ideas and institutions to the test of their contemporary relevance, discarding, affirming, and refashioning as the situation may require.

3

The result is bound to be tentative and fragmentary. For the disintegration of the great intellectual systems from which the Western world used to receive its meaning has not spared even our sense of reality. As modern physics has destroyed the reliability and relevance of the sensory perception of our natural environment, so do Marxism and psychoanalysis and their derivatives deny the reliability of consciousness of ourselves and of our social environment. Things natural and social are not what they seem to be. What parades as truth in matters political is but a delusion of self and of others or a pretense, masking interests of class and the desires of self. This is no doubt so, sometimes or even often. But the whole history of the race and our own inner experience militates against the assumption that it is so always. When is it so and when is it not? When is truth in matters political not a delusion or a pretense?

This is the crucial question which faces political philosophy, as it has faced general philosophy since Plato inquired into the difference between truth and opinion. Given the present state of philosophic and political thought, this question cannot be answered today in any systematic fashion. Yet from a piecemeal examination of concrete issues there might at least emerge an awareness of the dilemma in its perennial and contemporary configuration.

PART I

UNDERSTANDING

POLITICS

1 *The Intellectual and Moral Dilemma of Politics*

It is a great paradox that nature is much more unambiguously susceptible to human understanding than is society past and present. That which man has not created and which it is beyond his power to create—the macrocosm of the stars and the microcosm of the cells and atoms—man can understand with an adequacy that points to the common source of both. How else explain the affinity between the cognitive qualities of the human mind and the laws by which the universe moves? Not only is man able to retrace and project into the future the movements of the natural bodies, but by virtue of that ability he is capable of re-creating the forces of nature and harnessing them to his will. Nowhere, except in the contemplation of his suffering and hope, is man more triumphantly aware of his kinship with the Creator than in his cognitive and manipulative relations with nature.

In the world of nature, which he faces ready-made and which he leaves as he finds it, man proves himself a master of understanding, imitation, and control. How different, how frustrating and humiliating is the role he plays in understanding and controlling the social world, a world that is properly his own, which would not exist if he had not created it, and which exists the way it does only because he has given it the imprint of his nature. Of this social world man can at best have but a partial and corrupted understanding and but a partial and ultimately illusory control. For the social world being but a projection of human nature onto the collective plane, being but man writ large, man can understand and maintain control of society no more than he can of himself. Thus the very intimacy of his involvement impedes both understanding and control.

The awareness of this paradox is, if I understand its intent correctly, the moving force of Reinhold Niebuhr's new book, *The Structure of Nations and Empires*. It is the *mega thaumazein*, the "great wonderment," the shock of incongruity, which according to

From *Christianity and Crisis*, February 8, 1960.

Aristotle is at the beginning of all philosophy. That shock feeds on two basic experiences—one intellectual, the other moral—and both cast doubt on man's ability to find the truth about society. The intellectual experience is doubt about the meaning of history. What is unique and ephemeral in history and what is constantly revealing a repetitive pattern that lends itself to generalization about the past and future?

... is there any consistency, any perennial pattern or permanent force in man's search for community? Is there a permanent pattern in the anatomy of community which may be discerned in such diverse communities as the tribe, the city-state, or the ancient or modern empire?

The moral experience is doubt about man's ability to grasp what meaning there is in history, given the involvement of his pride and aspirations in the historic process.

The intellectual difficulty that stands in the way of a theoretical inquiry into the meaning of history results from the ambiguity of the material with which the observer has to deal. The events he must try to understand are, on the one hand, unique occurrences. They happened in this way only once and never before or since. On the other hand they are similar, for they are manifestations of social forces. Social forces are the product of human nature in action. Therefore, under similar conditions, they will manifest themselves in a similar manner. But where is the line to be drawn between the similar and the unique?

This ambiguity of the events to be understood by a theory of history—it may be pointed out in passing—is but a special instance of a general impediment of human understanding.

As no event and no shape [observes Montaigne] is entirely like another, so also is there none entirely different from another: *an ingenious mixture on the part of Nature. If there were no similarity in our faces, we could not distinguish man from beast; if there were no dissimilarity, we could not distinguish one man from another.* All things hold together by some similarity; every example is halting, and the comparison that is derived from experience is always defective and imperfect. And yet one links up the comparisons at some corner. And so do laws become serviceable and adapt themselves to every one of our affairs by some wrested, forced, and biased interpretation.

It is against such "wrested, forced and biased interpretation" of historic events that a theory of history must be continuously on guard.

Nor are the untoward results of this dilemma of having to distinguish between what is typical and perennial and what is unique and ephemeral in history limited to the interpretation of past events. That dilemma affects gravely, and sometimes absurdly, forecasts of and planning for the future. In 1776, Washington declared that "the Fate of our Country depends in all human probability, on the Exertion of a Few Weeks." Yet it was not until seven years later that the War of Independence came to an end.

In February, 1792, British Prime Minister Pitt justified the reduction of military expenditures and held out hope for more reductions to come by declaring: "Unquestionably there never was a time in the history of this country when from the situation of Europe we might more reasonably expect fifteen years of peace than at the present moment." Only two months later the continent of Europe was engulfed in war. Less than a year later Great Britain was involved. Thus was initiated a period of almost continuous warfare that lasted nearly a quarter of a century.

When Lord Granville became British foreign secretary in 1870, he was informed by the permanent undersecretary that "he had never, during his long experience, known so great a lull in foreign affairs, and that he was not aware of any important question that he [Lord Granville] should have to deal with." On that same day Prince Leopold of Hohenzollern-Sigmaringen accepted the Crown of Spain, an event that three weeks later led to the outbreak of the Franco-Prussian War.

The day before World War I broke out, the British ambassador to Germany disparaged the possibility of war in a report to his government. Franklin D. Roosevelt thought toward the end of his life that the great political issue with which the postwar world would have to deal would be Anglo-Russian rivalry, with the United States playing the role of mediator.

These difficulties, inherent in the nature of things, have been magnified since the eighteenth century by a philosophic tendency to identify a particular historic phenomenon with a particular social situation and to draw from this identification the conclusion that by doing away with the social situation one could eliminate an undesirable historic phenomenon. Conversely, by generalizing the social situation one could generalize a desirable historic phenomenon as

9

well. Thus the conviction arose that war was a by-product of either the autocratic or the capitalistic organization of society. Therefore the destruction of autocracy or capitalism would of necessity usher in the abolition of war; conversely, the universal triumph of democracy or of communism would usher in universal peace.

Similarly and more particularly, imperialism has been identified, and by no means only by Marxists, with capitalism, from which identification the logical conclusion was drawn that the end of capitalism would signify the end of imperialism as well. The very existence of power relations, the inequality of the strong and the weak, the mastery of the former over the latter, the differentiation between ruler and ruled was attributed by nineteenth-century liberals to autocratic government and is attributed by contemporary Marxists to the class structure of society.

All these identifications have one fallacy in common: the confusion between the perennial and the ephemeral, the typical and the unique in history. Our society in particular, with its underdeveloped sense of historic continuity and its penchant for social innovation, finds it hard to accept the underlying regularity and typicality of the historic process. If you accept these qualities of history, you must submit to its laws and try to learn from them, and you are foreclosed from treating each new historic situation *de novo* as a unique occurrence to be disposed of by one radical action similarly unique. On the other hand, if you do not accept these qualities of history and are free to transcend the limitations of tradition and disregard the counsels of ancient wisdom, your social inventiveness is limited, if it is limited at all, by nothing but elemental common sense and common prudence.

Philosophy, tradition, and individual experience have predisposed us for the latter attitude. The great problems of history with which we must come to terms tend to appear to us not as members of a chain organically tied to the past and growing into the future, but as cataclysmic interruptions of the normalcy of peace and harmony, occasioned by evil men and evil institutions. Let us do away with those men and institutions, and we will have solved not only this particular historic problem but the problem of history itself. We are, as it were, in flight from history, and whenever history catches up with us, as it did intermittently before World War II and has done continuously since, we endeavor to gain our freedom from it by obliterating in one great effort the issue that blocks our way.

The vanity of these endeavors is attested to by their consistent failures. It is one of the great contributions of Professor Niebuhr's book to demonstrate through the analysis of historic phenomena the fallacy of this approach to historic understanding and political action. The demonstration is made by fitting the imperialism, universalism, and utopianism of communism—the overriding historic phenomenon of the age—into a pattern of empire that was not established by communism but of which communism is but the latest manifestation.

The roots of that pattern reach back to ancient Persia and Babylon. The pattern is clearly visible in the character and claims of the Roman and Chinese empires and fully developed in the two Christian and the Islamic empires of the Middle Ages. The articulation of both the similarities and dissimilarities—but particularly the former—between the great empires of the past and the imperial structure and claims of communism illuminates both the historic and contemporary scene.

The tendency to disparage the perennial and typical in history and to dissolve the historic process into a series of disconnected disturbances, unique and ephemeral, disarms contemporary man in the face of a phenomenon that is truly unique: the ability for universal destruction that man has received from nuclear power. This ability has introduced into the relations among nations a radically novel factor. Qualitatively speaking, it is the only structural change that has occurred in international relations since the beginning of history. For nuclear power has radically altered the relations that have existed since the beginning of history between the ends of foreign policy and violence as a means to these ends.

These relations have traditionally been by and large of a rational nature. That is to say: the risks run and the liabilities incurred through the use of violent means were generally not out of proportion to the ends sought. A nation calculating these risks and liabilities could rationally conclude that, even if it should lose, its losses would be tolerable in view of the ends sought. A nation acted very much like a gambler who could afford to risk a certain portion of his assets and was willing to risk them in view of the chances for gain provided by taking the risk.

This rational relationship between the means of violence and the ends of foreign policy has been destroyed by the availability of nuclear power as a means to these ends. For the possibility of universal destruction obliterates the means-end relationship itself by threatening the nations and their ends with total destruction. No such radical qualitative transformation of the structure of international relations has ever occurred in history, and the radical nature of the transformation calls for correspondingly radical innovations in the sphere of policy.

Yet, paradoxically enough, a civilization that likes to see novelty in history where there is none, by dint of its distorted historic perspective seems to perceive but dimly the genuine novelty with which nuclear power confronts it. A society that is almost enamored by social innovation for innovation's sake faces in virtual helplessness a situation that requires—not for the sake of a traditional national interest but for the survival of civilization, if not of mankind itself—an extreme effort of bold, innovating imagination. Thus history threatens to avenge itself for having been misunderstood in thought and abused in action.

Faced with this mortal threat to their survival, both the United States and the Soviet Union have fallen back upon a time-honored yet thus far ineffectual remedy: disarmament. Are the chances for disarmament better now than they were in the past? The answer to that question depends again upon what one considers the perennial and ephemeral factors in history to be.

One school of thought holds that the possibility of disarmament is predicated upon the preceding or at least simultaneous settlement of outstanding political issues that have given rise to the armaments race in the first place, and that the threat of nuclear war has not materially affected this perennial functional dependence of disarmament upon a political settlement. Another school of thought assumes that the threat of nuclear war has radically altered this traditional relationship, which was perennial only in appearance but was in fact dependent upon certain ephemeral factors no longer present today. It also assumes that the desire to avoid nuclear destruction provides today an incentive for disarmament that invalidates the conditions upon which disarmament was predicated in the past. The question whether or not the novelty of the nuclear threat has actually reduced what seemed to be a perennial principle of statecraft to an ephemeral configuration poses again the dilemma that casts doubt upon our understanding of history and renders hazardous our political action.

The other great dilemma upon which Professor Niebuhr's book centers is the moral dilemma in which history involves man. That moral dilemma results from the ineradicable tendency of man to claim for his position in history more in terms of moral dignity than he is entitled to and to grant his fellows less than is their due. Hamlet implores the Queen in vain:

> . . . Mother, for love of grace,
> Lay not that flattering unction to your soul,
> That not your trespass, but my madness speaks.

For the position of the actor on the political scene is of necessity morally ambivalent, and that ambivalence, in conjunction with the logic inherent in the political act, inevitably corrupts his moral judgment.

The political actor seeks power, that is to say, he seeks to reduce his fellow man to a means for his ends. By doing so, he violates a basic tenet of Western morality: to respect man as an end in himself and not to use him as a means to an end. Both the contradiction between the political act and morality and the logic of the power relation itself compel the political actor to make it appear as though his striving for power and the exercise of it, far from violating morality, were actually its consummation. That appearance is achieved by clothing him and his act with a moral dignity they do not deserve and by depriving the object of the political act of at least some of the moral dignity he deserves.

Politics and morality are reconciled by the latter being bent to the requirements of the former. The political actor now can proceed with a good conscience, being assured of his moral superiority and the moral inferiority of the object of his power. He can also proceed with a determination maximizing his chances for political success; for he will find it hard to convince himself that, in view of the difference in moral qualities between himself and the object of his power, he has not only a moral right but also a moral duty to rule. As Tolstoi put it in the epilogue to *War and Peace:*

When a man acts alone, he always carries within him a certain series of considerations that have, as he supposes, directed his past conduct and serve to justify to him his present action and to lead him to make projects for his future activity.

Assemblies of men act in the same way, only leaving to those who do not take direct part in the action to invent consideration, justifications and projects concerning their combined activity.

For causes, known or unknown to us, the French begin to chop and hack at each other. And to match the event, it is accompanied by its justification in the expressed wills of certain men who declare it essential for the good of France, for the cause of freedom, of equality. Men cease slaughtering one another, and that event is accompanied by the justification of the necessity of centralization of power, of resistance to Europe, and so on. Men march from west to east, killing their fellow-creatures, and this event is accompanied by phrases about the glory of France, the baseness of England, and so on. History teaches us that those justifications for the event are devoid of all common sense, that they are inconsistent with one another, as, for instance, the murder of a man as a result of the declaration of his rights, and the murder of millions in Russia for the abasement of England. But those justifications have an incontestable value in their own day.

They remove moral responsibility from those men who produce the events. At the time they do the work of brooms, that go in front to clear the rails for the train: they clear the path of men's moral responsibility. Apart from those justifications, no solution could be found for the most obvious question that occurs to one at once on examining any historical event; that is, How did millions of men combine to commit crimes, murders, wars, and so on?

Professor Niebuhr lays bare the mechanism by which morality clothes politics with undeserved dignity and politics transforms morality into an instrument of political domination. It is particularly fascinating to observe how this mechanism operates in the relations between the great imperial and religious structures. The religious structures become imperial in performance and the imperial structures become religious in pretense. Typically, it is politics and imperium as its more dynamic manifestation that transform and corrupt morality and religion, and it is much rarer for morality and religion to reform and spiritualize politics and imperium.

The moral dilemma of history, like its intellectual counterpart, is existential. They can be mitigated but not resolved. Both grow out of the nature of man and of history as man's creation. In history man meets himself, and in his encounter with history he encounters again, magnified into superhuman proportions, the fallibility of his intellectual understanding and moral judgment that prevents him from completely understanding and adequately judging both history and himself.

2 *The State of Political Science*

In Plato's *Theaetetus* Socrates develops the character of the philosopher, the man of knowledge, in contrast to the atheoretical, practical man. He endeavors to demonstrate the distinctive qualities of the philosopher by emphasizing his peculiar attitude toward the political sphere.

First, the philosopher has no political ambitions, and he does not care about what is going on in the political sphere. The philosophers

have never, from their youth upwards, known their way to the Agora, or the dicastery, or the council, or any other political assembly; they neither see nor hear the laws or decrees, as they are called, of the State written or recited; the eagerness of political societies in the attainment of offices—clubs, and banquets, and revels, and singing-maidens—do not enter even into their dreams. Whether any event has turned out well or ill in the city, what disgrace may have descended to any one from his ancestors, male or female, are matters of which the philosopher no more knows than he can tell, as they say, how many pints are contained in the ocean.

Second, the philosopher is ignorant about political matters and incapable of acting effectively on the political plane. He "is wholly unacquainted with his next-door neighbor; he is ignorant, not only of what he is doing, but he hardly knows whether he is a man or an animal. . . . His awkwardness is fearful, and gives the impression of imbecility. When he is reviled, he has nothing personal to say in answer to the civilities of his adversaries, for he knows no scandals of anyone, and they do not interest him. . . ."

Third, the philosopher is morally uncommitted and indifferent to the values of politics.

When he hears a tyrant or king eulogized, he fancies that he is listening to the praises of some keeper of cattle—a swineherd, or shepherd, or perhaps a cowherd, who is congratulated on the quantity of milk which he squeezes from them; and he remarks that the creature whom they tend, and out of whom they squeeze the wealth, is of a less tractable and more

From the *Review of Politics*. October, 1955; Roland Young (ed.), *Approaches to the Study of Politics* (1958); and a book review in the *American Political Science Review*, March, 1952.

insidious nature. Then again, he observes that the great man is of necessity as ill-mannered and uneducated as any shepherd—for he has no leisure, and he is surrounded by a wall, which is his mountain-pen. Hearing of enormous landed proprietors of ten thousand acres and more, our philosopher deems this to be a trifle, because he has been accustomed to think of the whole earth; and when they sing the praises of family, and say that some one is a gentleman because he can show seven generations of wealthy ancestors, he thinks that their sentiments only betray a dull and narrow vision in those who utter them and who are not educated enough to look at the whole, nor to consider that every man has had thousands and ten thousands of progenitors, and among them have been rich and poor, kings and slaves, Hellenes and barbarians, innumerable. And when people pride themselves on having a pedigree of twenty-five ancestors, which goes back to Heracles, the son of Amphitryon, he cannot understand their poverty of ideas. Why are they unable to calculate that Amphitryon had a twenty-fifth ancestor, who might have had a fiftieth, and so on? He amuses himself with the notion that they cannot count, and thinks that a little arithmetic would have got rid of their senseless vanity.

This political indifference and incapacity is the reflection of the philosopher's positive nature. The philosopher's

outer form . . . only is in the city. His mind, disdaining the littlenesses and nothingnesses of human things, is "flying all abroad" as Pindar says, measuring earth and heaven and the things which are under and on the earth and above the heaven, interrogating the whole nature of each and all in their entirety, but not condescending to anything which is within reach. . . . He is searching into the essence of man, and busy in enquiring what belongs to such a nature to do or suffer different from any other. . . .

This commitment to the search for the truth for its own sake and, concomitant with it, his divorcement—morally and intellectually, in judgment and action—from the political sphere makes the man of theory a scandal in the eyes of the multitude. He "is laughed at for his sheepishness. . . . He seems to be a downright idiot." He "is derided by the vulgar, partly because he is thought to despise them, and also because he is ignorant of what is before him and always at a loss." Socrates tells "the jest which the clever witty Thracian handmaid is said to have made about Thales, when he fell into a well as he was looking up at the stars. She said, that he was so eager to know what was going on in heaven, that he could not see what was before his feet." And Socrates adds: "This is a jest which is equally applicable to all philosophers."

Yet the philosopher has his revenge.

But, O my friend, when he draws the other into upper air, and gets him out of his pleas and rejoinders into the contemplation of justice and injustice in their own nature and in their difference from one another and from all other things; or from the commonplaces about the happiness of a king or a rich man to the consideration of government, and of human happiness and misery in general—what they are, and how a man is to attain the one and avoid the other—when that narrow, keen, little legal mind is called to account about all this, he gives the philosopher his revenge; for dizzied by the height at which he is hanging, whence he looks down into space, which is a strange experience to him, he being dismayed, and lost, and stammering broken words, is laughed at, not by Thracian handmaidens or any other uneducated persons, for they have no eye for the situation but by every man who has not been brought up a slave.

We may well recognize in this juxtaposition of the philosopher with the practitioner the archetypes of a perennial conflict between the theoretical man who thinks for the sake of finding the truth and the practical man who thinks for the sake of finding solutions to practical problems. Yet neither can we fail to recognize the limitations of the Platonic analysis, which is too neat, too "Greek" in its classical simplicity to satisfy us. While what Plato says is true, it is not the whole truth of the matter. There is, as we shall see, in the political thinker's place within the society about which he thinks an ambiguity—intellectual and moral—of which the ancients knew—and perhaps were bound to know—nothing. Yet with all its limitations Plato's statement conveys an insight into the nature of philosophy, theory, and science which, in turn, sheds an illuminating light upon the state of political science in America.

The impulse to which American political science owes its existence was overwhelmingly practical. It was nourished from two roots, one of which it has in common with all of modern political science, while the other is peculiar to itself.

Political science as an academic discipline everywhere in the Western world owes its existence to the disintegration, after their last flowering in the early nineteenth century, of the great philosophic systems which had dominated Western thought and to the concomitant development of the empirical investigation of the social world. All the social sciences are the fruit of the emancipation of the Western mind from metaphysical systems which had made the social world primarily a subject for metaphysical speculation and ethical postulates. In certain fields, such as economics, that emancipation occurred early; in others, such as political science, it occurred relatively late (for reasons which, as we shall see, are inherent in the nature of political science).

This antispeculative and empirical tendency of Western thought, as it developed in the second half of the nineteenth century, could not but find a ready and, as it were, natural response in the propensities of the American mind. Yet, while European political thought continued to combine an antimetaphysical position with concern for theory, American political science was overwhelmed by the practical promises of the new discipline. The first departments of political science were established in America in the eighties of the last century, not for the purpose of theoretical understanding, let alone philosophic speculation, but primarily for the purpose of meeting the practical exigencies of the day.

It is illuminating in this context, and it is in a sense a moving experience, to read the address that was delivered on October 3, 1881, at the opening of the School of Political Science at the University of Michigan by its first dean, Charles Kendall Adams.[1] Of the perennial problems of politics, such as power, legitimacy, authority, freedom, forms of government, natural law, sovereignty, revolution, tyranny, majority rule, this address makes no mention. The only problems which concern it are the practical problems of the day, and the case it tries to make for political science in America rests exclusively upon the contribution the new discipline promises to make to the solution of these problems. Looking abroad, Dean Adams finds that the rapid recovery of France after 1871 was primarily due to the instruction in political science. "The close of their war was six years later than the close of ours; and yet long before we had gained our financial equilibrium, France was the most prosperous nation in Europe." In England, "political instruction . . . has been given by men, some of whom have been thought worthy of high places in Parliament, in the diplomatic service, and in the Cabinet. . . . Their pupils are all about them in Parliament and in the diplomatic service." In diplomacy and, more particularly, in economic reform the influence of university instruction has been persuasive. Dean Adams finds the same beneficial results in Germany. "Graduates of these schools [of political

[1] *The Relations of Political Science to National Prosperity* (Ann Arbor, 1881).

19

science] found their way into administration positions of influence in all parts of Germany. . . . Commissioner White . . . uses these words: 'In conversation with leading men in Southern Germany I have not found one who did not declare this and similar courses of instruction the main cause of the present efficiency in the German administration.' "

Having thus made a case for the advantages that political science has brought to the practice of European governments, Dean Adams must now dispose of the argument that American political institutions are superior to those of Europe and that, therefore, America has no need of political science. The argument is revealing in its exclusive emphasis upon the practical benefits to be expected.

Is it certain that our municipal governments are better than theirs? Are our systems of taxation more equitably adjusted than theirs? Do our public and private corporations have greater respect for the rights of the people than theirs? Can we maintain that our legislatures are more free from corruption and bribery than theirs? Was our financial management at the close of our war wiser than that of France at the close of hers? If these questions can be answered in the affirmative, and without the shadow of a doubt, I concede that an argument may be built upon them in favor of what may be called intuitive methods.

After passing in systematic review the operations of the three branches of government which are in need of improvement, Dean Adams turns to "several other fields of activity in which great influence is exerted." He singles out journalism and speechmaking, which political science can help to improve. He sums up his argument in favor of political science by saying:

It is for the purpose of aiding in the several directions that have been hinted at, and in others that would be mentioned if there were time, that the School of Political Science in the University of Michigan has been established. It finds its justification where the other schools of the University find theirs: in the good of the people and the welfare of the State.

This exclusive concern with practical improvements is by no means an isolated instance. It dominates the virtually simultaneous establishment of a School of Political Science at Columbia University. The objective of that school was as practical as that of Michigan; yet while the latter's appeal was one of boundless vocationalism, the former's practical interests were narrowly confined to a particular profession, that of the civil servant. When President

20

Barnard submitted the proposal for the establishment of the school to the trustees of Columbia University, he called it "Proposed School of Preparation for the Civil Service." Reflecting the philosophy of John W. Burgess, the driving spirit behind the proposal, we find the purpose of the school defined as "to prepare young men for public life whether in the Civil Service at home or abroad, or in the legislatures of the States or of the nation; and also to fit young men for the duties and responsibilities of public journalists."[2]

The first departments of political science in this country, then, did not grow organically from a general conception as to what was covered by the field of political science, nor did they respond to a strongly felt intellectual need. Rather they tried to satisfy practical demands, which other academic disciplines refused to meet. For instance, in that period the law schools would not deal with public law. It was felt that somebody ought to deal with it, and thus it was made part of political science. There was a demand for instruction in journalism, but there was no place for it to be taught; thus it was made part of political science. There was a local demand for guidance in certain aspects of municipal administration; and thus a course in that subject was made part of the curriculum of political science.

In other words, political science grew, not by virtue of an intellectual principle germane to the field, but in response to pressures from the outside. What could not be defined in terms of a traditional academic discipline was defined as political science. This inorganic growth and haphazard character of political science is strikingly reflected in the curriculums of the early departments of political science, such as those of Michigan, Columbia, and Harvard. In the address from which we have quoted, Dean Adams mentions the following subjects which were to form part of the curriculum of the School of Political Science: General History, The History of Political Institutions, The Recent Political History of Europe, The Political and Constitutional History of England, The Political and Constitutional History of the United States; several courses in political economy; under the general heading of "Sanitary Science": The Laws of Physiological Growth and Decay, The Varieties and

---

[2] R. Gordon Hoxie *et al., A History of the Faculty of Political Science, Columbia University* (New York: Columbia University Press, 1955), p. 13.

Adaptabilities of Foods, The Best Methods of Supplying Pure Water and Air, The Causes of Infectious Diseases, The Proper Disposal of Decomposing Matter, The Proper Functions of Boards of Health and Health Officers; under the general heading of "Social Science": The Prevalence of Crime and the Most Efficient Means of Diminishing and Preventing It, The Best Methods of Treating our Criminals, The Care of the Insane and the Management of Asylums, The Proper Treatment of the Poor and the Proper Superintendence of Almshouses, The Place and the Proper Equipment and Control of Hospitals; courses in forestry and political ethics; and finally "crowning the whole": The Idea of the State; The Nature of Individual, Social, and Political Rights; The History of Political Ideas; The Government of Cities; Theories and Methods of Taxation; Comparative Constitutional Law; Comparative Administrative Law; Theories of International Law; and The History of Modern Diplomacy. "Such," Dean Adams concludes, "in the briefest outline, is what it is the purpose of the school at present to teach. Additions to the corps and the courses of instruction will be added, from time to time, as the necessity is revealed."

While this program is but an extreme example of the practicality of early American political science, the list of courses which formed the curriculum of the School of Political Science of Columbia University from 1880 to 1887 is typical of its eclecticism. According to Burgess, the "School of Political Science" was "the collective name which we give the graduate or university courses in history, philosophy, economy, public law, jurisprudence, diplomacy, and sociology."[3] These are the courses which were then taught: Physical and Political Geography, Ethnology, General Political and Constitutional History of Europe, Political and Constitutional History of England, Political and Constitutional History of the United States, Bibliography of the Political Sciences, History of Roman Law to the Present Day, Comparative Constitutional Law of the Principal European States and of the United States, Statistical Science—Methods and Results, Comparative Jurisprudence of the Principal European Systems of Civil Law, Comparative Constitutional Law of the Several Commonwealths of the American Union,

[3] John W. Burgess, "The Study of the Political Sciences in Columbia College," *International Review*, XII (1882), 348.

History of Diplomacy, Comparative Administrative Law of the Principal States of Europe and of the United States, Comparative Administrative Law of the Several Commonwealths of the American Union, Private International Law; social sciences: Communistic and Socialistic Theories; political economy: History of Politico-Economic Institutions, Taxation and Finance; philosophy: History of Political Theories from Plato to Hegel.[4]

Similarly, the courses differentiated in 1892–93 at Harvard under the heading of "Government" comprised: Constitutional Government; Elements of International Law (which included history of diplomacy); History and Institutes of Roman Law; Federal Government—Historical and Comparative; Leading Principles of Constitutional Law—Selected Cases American and English; History of Political Theories, with particular reference to the origin of American institutions; Government and Political Methods in the United States; and International Law as Administered by the Courts.[5]

In its further development political science as an academic discipline has undergone a process of both contraction and expansion. On the one hand, new schools and departments have absorbed much of the subject matter that was formerly taught in departments of political science because there was no other place in the university to teach them. On the other hand, however, new practical interests have continued to call for the inclusion of new subjects of instruction in the curriculum.

Thus today the curriculum of political science still bears the unmistakable marks of its haphazard origin and development. To pick out at random some courses from two departments of political science with which I am familiar, what have "Plato's Political Philosophy and Its Metaphysical Foundation" and "The Politics of Conservation" in common, or "General Principles of Organization and Administration" and "International Law," or "Conduct of American Foreign Relations" and "Introduction to Jurisprudence," or "Nationalism" and "Political Behavior and Public Policy," or "Russian Political and Economic Institutions" and "Public Personnel Administration"? The only common denominator which

[4] Hoxie *et al., op. cit.,* pp. 305–6.

[5] Anna Haddow, *Political Science in American Colleges and Universities, 1636–1900* (New York: Appleton-Century, 1939), p. 175.

now ties these courses loosely together is a general and vague orientation toward the nature and activities of the state and toward activities which have in turn a direct bearing upon the state. Beyond that orientation toward a common subject matter, defined in the most general terms, contemporary political science has no unity of method, outlook, and purpose.

As concerns method, political science is split five ways, and four of these methodological positions have hardly anything in common. Their disparity is such that there is hardly even a possibility of fruitful discourse among the representatives of the different approaches beyond polemics which deny the very legitimacy of the other approaches. These approaches can be classified as philosophic theory, empirical theory, empirical science, description, and practical amelioration.

These five methodological approaches are not peculiar to political science. They have appeared in other social sciences as well—such as psychology, economics, and sociology—yet with two significant differences. First of all, the other social sciences have traditionally shown a much greater awareness of the existence, nature, and separate functions of these approaches than has political science. Second, they have been able, at least at times, to rid themselves in good measure of the ameliorative and vocational approach which has by itself only a minimum of intellectual relevance. Political science, on the other hand, has never squarely faced the methodological problem in terms of the intrinsic character of these different approaches and the functions which they are able to perform for the understanding of its subject matter. These five approaches have rather coexisted without clear distinction within the departments of political science, one to be emphasized over the others at different times and places according to the pressures of supply and demand. Here, too, the development has been haphazard and subject to accident rather than guided by certain fundamental requirements of theory.

Thus political science has not generally been able to make that distinction which is a precondition for the development of any true science: the distinction between what is worth knowing intellectually and what is useful for practice. It is this distinction which economics and sociology accomplished some decades ago when schools of business, home economics, retailing, social work, and the like took over the practical concerns which at best develop practical uses for theoretical knowledge or else have but the most tenuous connection with it. Political science has taken a similar step in some instances by organizing the practical uses of political science for the amelioration of government activities in schools of administration and the like. But not only has this separation been exceptional rather than typical, it has also been made as a matter of convenience rather than in application of a generally accepted theoretical principle. In consequence, improvement of the processes of government is still generally considered not only a worthwhile activity to be engaged in by political scientists but also a legitimate, and sometimes even the only legitimate, element of political science as an academic discipline, to be taught under any of the course headings composing its curriculum.

It should be pointed out in passing that we are dealing here not with a specific subject matter but with a particular method, a particular intellectual approach. This approach will naturally manifest itself most frequently and typically in those fields of political science which have a direct relevance to the operations of government, such as public administration, but it is by no means limited to them. The other fields of political science, such as international relations, American government, constitutional law, and parties, have at times been dominated by the practical approach seeking practical remedies for conditions regarded as being in need of amelioration.

Yet it is exactly this commitment of modern political science to practical ends which has powerfully contributed to its decline as theory. Modern political science has been largely committed to the practical goals of liberal reform. Each major achievement in the direction of one of these goals was expected to bring society that much closer to solving once and for all one of the perennial problems of politics, such as inequality, insecurity, conflict, violence, power itself—and none ever did. The old problems reappeared in a new garb, mocking the scientific pretenses and eschatological expectations of liberal political science, and yesterday's hope and today's achievement became tomorrow's illusion. To this succession of blows which liberal politics suffered at the hands of experience must be attributed in good measure its disenchantment with reform and its decline in creative thought and action. The grand ameliorative schemes of liberal political science petered out in proposals for piecemeal improvements from which no great things can be expected.

Thus description is today the method most widely used in political science. Factual information arranged according to certain traditional classifications still dominates most of the textbooks in the field. While it is unnecessary to argue the case for the need for factual information, it ought to be no more necessary to argue that factual description is not science but a mere, however indispensable, preparation for the scientific understanding of the facts. It may, however, point toward a theoretical awakening that descriptive political science tends to dress up descriptive accounts of facts in theoretical garb and to use fancy classifications and terminologies in order to conceal the mere descriptive character of its substance. While the theoretical pretense of factual accounts shows an awareness of the need for theoretical understanding, that understanding itself requires more than the demonstrative use of an elaborate apparatus of classification and terminology.

With this last type of descriptive political science which overlays its descriptive substance with theoretical pretense, we are in the borderland where description and empirical science merge. Empirical science is today the most vigorous branch of political science and tends to attract many of the abler and more inventive students. Taking its cue from the natural sciences, or what it thinks the natural sciences are, it tries to develop rigorous methods of quantitative verification which are expected in good time to attain the same precision in the discovery of uniformities and in prediction to which the natural sciences owe their theoretical and practical success.

I have argued elsewhere against this analogy between the social and the natural sciences,[6] and this is not the place to resume the controversy. It must suffice here to state dogmatically that the object of the social sciences is man, not as a product of nature but as both the creature and the creator of history in and through

[6] *Scientific Man vs. Power Politics* (Chicago: University of Chicago Press, 1946).

which his individuality and freedom of choice manifest themselves. To make susceptibility to quantitative measurement the yardstick of the scientific character of the social sciences in general and of political science in particular is to deprive these sciences of that very orientation which is adequate to the understanding of their subject matter.

The inadequacy of the quantitative method to the subject matter of political science is demonstrated by the limitation of its success to those types of political behavior which by their very nature lend themselves to a certain measure of quantification, such as voting, and the barrenness of the attempts to apply the quantitative method to phenomena which are determined by historic individuality, rational or moral choice. As concerns these phenomena, the best quantification can achieve is to confirm and refine knowledge which theory has already discovered. It will not do to argue that this limitation is due to the "backwardness" of political science which could be overcome if only more and better people would spend more time and money for quantification. For that argument to be plausible, the limitation is too persistent, and it becomes ever more spectacular as more and better people spend more time and money to make it a success.

Once quantification has left that narrow sphere where it can contribute to relevant knowledge, two roads are open to it. Either it can try to quantify phenomena which in their aspects relevant to political science are not susceptible to quantification, and by doing so obscure and distort what political science ought to know; thus much of quantitative political science has become a pretentious collection of trivialities. Or, dimly aware of this inadequacy, quantification may shun contact with the empirical phenomena of political life altogether and try to find out instead what the correct way of quantifying is. Basic to this methodological concern is the assumption that the failure of quantification to yield results in any way proportionate to the effort spent follows from the lack of a correct quantitative method. Once that method is discovered and applied, quantification will yield the results in precise knowledge its adherents claim for it.

However, it is obvious that these methodological investigations, patently intended for the guidance of empirical research, have hardly exerted any influence upon the latter. This divorce of methodology from empirical investigation is not fortuitous. For it points not only to the inadequacy of the quantitative method for the understanding of much of the subject matter of political science, an inadequacy which must become particularly striking when quantification is confronted in its pure theoretical form with the actuality of political life. That divorce also illuminates a tendency, common not only to all methodological endeavors in the social sciences but to general philosophy as well, to retreat ever more from contact with the empirical world into a realm of self-sufficient abstractions. Logical positivism and general semantics owe their existence as independent branches of philosophy to this "new scholasticism," as it has been aptly called.[7] General sociological theory is dominated by it, and it has left its impact also upon political science. The new scholastic dissolves the substance of knowledge into the processes of knowing; he tends to think about how to think and to conceptualize about concepts, regressing ever further from empirical reality until he finds the logical consummation of his endeavors in mathematical symbols and other formal relations. And it is not fortuitous that the apparent precision of his formal categories tends to go hand in hand with an often shocking imprecision of his vestigial substantive thought; for, to the extent that objective reality demands qualitative evaluation, formalism either misses the point altogether or else distorts it.

A remarkable example of this new political science—remarkable by virtue of the reputation of its authors and of its own claims—is Lasswell and Kaplan, *Power and Society: A Framework for Political Inquiry*.[8] This book claims to be "a book of political theory, not an analysis of the contemporary or impending political situation" (p. ix). Critical of the German *Staatslehre* and of De Tocqueville and Bryce, it finds itself "much closer to the straightforward empirical standpoint of Machiavelli's *Discourses* or Michels' *Political Parties*" (p. x). "The present work is an attempt to formulate the basic concepts and hypotheses of political science" (p. xi). Its purpose is "to provide a framework for political science" (p. xiii). There can

[7] Barrington Moore, Jr., "The New Scholasticism and the Study of Politics," *World Politics*, VI (1953), 122–38.

[8] New Haven: Yale University Press, 1950.

be no doubt that the authors present this work as a major contribution to political theory.

The book consists of a series of definitions and propositions, with commentary, under the following headings: persons, perspectives, groups, influence, power, symbols, practices, functions, structures, process. What do these definitions and propositions contribute to knowledge? We open the book at random and read on page 13 the following definitions: "A *personality trait* is a kind of act characteristic of a self. The *personality* is the totality of the personality traits pertaining to an actor. A person is an actor characterized as to personality." This is hardly more meaningful than Gertrude Stein's "Rose is a rose is a rose is a rose," and does not have even its primitive phonetic charm. On page 154, we read the following proposition: "Acquisition and maintenance of leadership is a function of the prestige of the leaders." On page 187, the rulers are defined as "those supreme in the body politic." On page 218, information is conveyed in the form of the following definition: "*Autocracy* is the form of rule in which the weight of power is chiefly in the hands of one person; *oligarchy*, in the hands of a group of rulers; a *republic*, distributed throughout the domain." On page 234, democracy and despotism are defined as follows: "A *democracy* is a libertarian, juridical commonwealth; a *despotism* is a nondemocratic rule." These definitions are obviously either platitudinous, circular, or tautological, and at best convey information which Aristotle would have taken for granted.

However, what vitiates this book as a major contribution to political theory is a thorough misunderstanding of the nature of political theory and of its relationship to empirical research. The authors believe that political science can be "straightforward empirical" and that Machiavelli and Michels so conceived it. We shall not deal here with the case of Michels. But do the authors not recognize the fact that Machiavelli was a political philosopher steeped in the ancient tradition, that his empirical inquiry is inclosed within a philosophical framework resting upon the pillars of *fortuna* and *virtu*, concepts which come straight from classical antiquity, and that his work, far from being "straightforward empirical," is a philosophic protest against the scholastic tradition in an attempt to reassert the political philosophy of the ancients? Are the authors unaware of the fact that in this sense Machiavelli is no more an empiricist in politics than Raphael and Michelangelo are naturalists in art? Their purpose, as that of the Renaissance as a whole, was philosophic and not merely descriptive. Are the authors unfamiliar with the literature which has uncovered the philosophic system behind the seemingly empirical surface of Machiavelli's writings?

One error, perhaps inconsequential in itself, but characteristic of the authors' method, will illustrate the point. The authors express their criticism of the metaphysical speculation of the "German *Staatslehre* tradition, so influential at the turn of the century" (p. x). As an example they quote J. K. Bluntschli and give as the date of his *Theory of the State* the year 1921. It so happens that Bluntschli was a Hegelian who died in 1881 and whose work, referred to by the authors, was published in 1851 and 1852. What the authors cite is the third edition of the English translation, the first of which appeared in 1885 (the year of the last German one), the second in 1895. Neither Bluntschli's organismic brand of Hegelianism nor metaphysical speculation in general had any considerable influence on German political thought at the turn of the century, having been replaced by the theories of social and legal historians such as Gierke, or of constitutional and comparative lawyers such as Laband, Gneist, and Jellinek. In 1921 Bluntschli and his metaphysical speculations were a mere historic recollection, and the epic struggle between Kelsen, the philosopher of the pure theory of law, and his politically oriented enemies provided the great issues in political science.

The authors are not only careless about the incontestable facts of political theory; they are also given to sweeping judgments barely supported by evidence. Let us examine the following statement: "Many of the most influential political writings—those of Plato, Locke, Rousseau, the *Federalist*, and others—have not been concerned with political inquiry at all, but with the justification of existent or proposed political structures. We say such works formulate *political doctrine* rather than propositions of *political science*" (p. xi). What is correct in this statement is that the great writings of political theory had as their ultimate purpose the justification of a certain political system. This is true of Plato and Locke, as it is of Machiavelli and Michels. There have been thinkers who were "not concerned with political inquiry at all," as there were and are those who are concerned with nothing but political science conceived in "straightforward empirical" terms; most of them for that very reason have been, and will be, forgotten. What makes it today worth reading Plato, Locke, Rousseau, the *Federalist*, and above all Aristotle (whom the authors have omitted from their list) is exactly that, within the framework of a political doctrine, they have given us the results of political inquiry in the form of propositions of political science, more profound and more illuminating by far than anything that a "straightforward empirical standpoint" has to offer. The authors are unable to see that a political science inclosed in nothing but an empirical framework is a contradiction in terms and a monstrosity. The intellectual barrenness of the present work, its logical aimlessness and diffuseness, and its excessive concern with verbal artifices are the results of this fundamental misunderstanding.

Every student approaches the political scene, whether as a thinker or as an actor, with certain intellectual and moral preconceptions regarding it. His thoughts and actions are determined by those preconceptions. In other words, he looks at the political scene from a perspective which is determined by his philosophy and which he will share with some but not with other observers. Whether or not he approves of it, whether or not he realizes it, he is a political philosopher before he is a political scientist. All observers of politics, then, bring to their observations a framework of political philosophy, however inarticulate and fragmentary it may be. It is only within such a philosophical framework that an empirical framework of political inquiry can have meaning and that empirical inquiry can become fruitful. Of the realization in theory and practice of that necessary relationship between political philosophy and empirical inquiry, Aristotle provides the unrivaled example.

Our authors have subjected Aristotle to a kind of content analysis and have found, on the basis of a sample of three hundred sentences, that the proportion of "political philosophy (demand statements and evaluations) to political science (statements of facts and empirical hypotheses)" (p. 118 n.) is 25 to 75. We shall not compete with the authors in a mechanical exercise of this kind and shall not even raise the question of whether the three hundred sentences chosen were "representative samples." We only call attention to the basic proposition that in politics empirical inquiry without a philosophic framework must needs be blind, as political philosophy without empirical verification must needs be wholly speculative. To have understood this makes Aristotle a great political scientist, regardless of the quantitative proportions of different kinds of statements in his work.

We have said that all men dealing with the political realm bring of necessity to their field of inquiry or action a political philosophy, and our authors are no exception. Their philosophy is that of freedom (pp. xiii–xxiv). Yet the difference between the layman and the dilettante, on the one hand, and the political scientist worthy of the name, on the other, is determined by whether the individual has made his political philosophy articulate and whether he has brought it into organic relationship with his empirical inquiry. In this respect all the great political thinkers of the past, from Plato and Aristotle onward, stand on one side; our authors, together with many academic political scientists of the day, stand on the other. The latter take the democratic values of freedom for granted and do not ask themselves what the content of those values and what the relations among those values and between them and other values of a non-democratic character must be under the conditions of the contemporary world. Nor are they aware—and they cannot be, in view of their preconceptions—of the necessary relationship between those questions of political philosophy and the framework and content of empirical political inquiry. As their political philosophy is inarticulate and fragmentary, so their empirical inquiry is bound to be without direction and barren of meaning.

This spectacle of two superbly endowed minds failing so thoroughly in spite of great ability and great effort contains an element of tragedy. That tragedy is not so much the tragedy of two men as the tragedy of political science and of philosophy in America. For as Mr. Lasswell is the product of a school of political science which was, if not hostile, in any case indifferent, to the necessary contribution which political philosophy must make to empirical inquiry, so Mr. Kaplan is the product of a school of philosophy which sees in the history of philosophy primarily a history of errors. These authors are among the most gifted representatives of schools which at present ride the crest of the wave. Yet in truth they represent an obsolescent point of view. This book perhaps constitutes the most extreme, and therefore self-defeating, product of the fundamental errors of those schools. It may well contribute to their demise by virtue of its own absurdity.

There is a revealing similarity, pointing to a common root in the disorders of our culture, between abstract modern political science and abstract modern art. Both retreat from empirical reality into a world of formal relations and abstract symbols, which either on closer examination reveal themselves to be trivial or else are unintelligible, except to the initiated. Both share in the indifference to the accumulated achievements of mankind in their respective fields; Plato and Phidias, St. Thomas and Giotto, Spinoza and Rembrandt have no message for them. That divorcement from reality, contemporary and historic, deprives both of that wholesome discipline which prevents the mind from indulging its fancies without regard to some relevant objective standards. Thus one fashion, intellectual or artistic, follows the other, each oblivious of what has gone before, each relegated to limbo by its successors. Both abstract political science and abstract modern art tend to become esoteric, self-sufficient, and self-perpetuating cults, clustered around a "master," imitating his "style," and conversing in a lingo intelligible only to the members. Yet common sense, trying to penetrate the mysteries of these abstractions, cannot help wondering whether even the initiated understand each other and themselves. Perhaps, common sense continues wondering, some of the "masters" are just pulling the legs of their followers, who must pretend to understand in order to remain intellectually "up to date." "Enlightened people," to quote Georges Sorel, "dare not admit that they cannot understand arguments that are presented in very sophisticated language by an illustrious writer."

With this emphasis upon theoretical abstractions which have no relation to political reality, the methodology of political science joins a school which from the beginning to this day has occupied an honored but lonely place in the curriculum of political science: political theory. Political theory as an academic discipline has been traditionally the history of political philosophies in chronological succession, starting with Plato and ending, if time permits, with Laski. As an academic discipline, political theory has been hardly more than an account of what writers of the past, traditionally regarded as "great," have thought about the traditional problems of

33

politics, with hardly a systematic attempt being made to correlate that historic knowledge to the other fields of political science and to the contemporary political world. "The danger," in the words of Sir Ernest Barker, "of some subjects of speculation—I would cite in evidence literary criticism as well as political theory—is that they may be choked, as it were, by the history of their own past."[9] Thus political theory as an academic discipline has been intellectually sterile, and it is not by accident that some of the most important contributions to contemporary political theory have been made not by professional political scientists but by theologians, philosophers, and sociologists.

Political theory remained an indispensable part of the curriculum, not because of the vital influence it was able to exert upon our thinking, but rather because of a vague conviction that there was something venerable and respectable in this otherwise useless exercise. Thus the academic concern with political theory tended to become an intellectually and practically meaningless ritual which one had to engage in for reasons of tradition and prestige before one could occupy one's self with the things that really mattered.

The awareness of this contrast between the prestige of political theory and its actual lack of relevance for the understanding of contemporary political problems has led theory closer to the contemporary political world. On the other hand, the awareness of the meagerness of the insights to be gained from strictly empirical investigations has made empirical political science search for a theoretical framework. Avoiding the limitations of the traditional approaches and fusing certain of their elements, contemporary political science is in the process of reviving a tradition to which most of the classics of political science owe their existence and influence. The intent of that tradition is theoretical: it wants to understand political reality in a theoretical manner, that is, by bringing to bear upon it propositions of both objective and general validity. These propositions claim to be objective in that their validity is not affected by the subjective limitations of the observer. They claim to be general in that their validity is not affected by the peculiar circumstances of time and place of the subject matter.

[9] *The Study of Political Science and Its Relation to Cognate Studies* (Cambridge: Cambridge University Press, 1929), pp. 25–26.

The subject matter of this theoretical concern is the contemporary political world. This branch of political science, which we call empirical theory, reflects in theoretical terms upon the contemporary political world. The political world, however, poses a formidable obstacle to such understanding. This obstacle is of a moral rather than an intellectual nature. Before we turn to the requirements of such an empirical theory and its central concept, we have to dispose of the moral problem with which political science must come to terms.

3 The Commitments of Political Science

The moral position of the political scientist in society is ambivalent; it can even be called paradoxical. For the political scientist is a product of the society which it is his mission to understand. He is also an active part, and frequently he seeks to be a leading part, of that society. To be faithful to his mission he would, then, have to overcome two limitations: the limitation of origin, which determines the perspective from which he looks at society, and the limitation of purpose, which makes him wish to remain a member in good standing of that society or even to play a leading role in it.

The mind of the political scientist is molded by the society which he observes. His outlook, his intellectual interests, and his mode of thinking are determined by the civilization, the national community, and all the particular religious, political, economic, and social groups of which he is a member. The "personal equation" of the political scientist both limits and directs his scholarly pursuits. The truth which a mind thus socially conditioned is able to grasp is likewise socially conditioned. The perspective of the observer determines what can be known and how it is to be understood. In consequence, the truth of political science is of necessity a partial truth.[1]

Upon a mind which by its very nature is unable to see more than part of the truth, society exerts its pressures, which confront the scholar with a choice between social advantage and the truth. The stronger the trend toward conformity within the society and the stronger the social ambitions within the individual scholar, the greater will be the temptation to sacrifice the moral commitment to the truth for social advantage. It follows that a respectable political science—respectable, that is, in terms of the society to be investi-

From the *Review of Politics*, October, 1955; and Roland Young (ed.), *Approaches to the Study of Politics* (1958).

[1] Cf. below, pp. 46 ff., the comment on the changing perspectives of political science. The views, expressed here necessarily in an aphoristic form, develop further what was said in *Scientific Man vs. Power Politics* (Chicago: University of Chicago Press, 1946), pp. 166–67.

gated—is in a sense a contradiction in terms. For a political science which is faithful to its moral commitment of telling the truth about the political world cannot help telling society things it does not want to hear. The truth of political science is the truth about power, its manifestations, its configurations, its limitations, its implications, its laws. Yet one of the main purposes of society is to conceal these truths from its members. That concealment, that elaborate and subtle and purposeful misunderstanding of the nature of political man and of political society, is one of the cornerstones upon which all societies are founded.[2]

In his search for truth, the political scientist is hemmed in by society in three different ways: with regard to the objects, the results, and the methods of his inquiry. In so far as the political scientist yields to these pressures, he violates his moral commitment to discovering the truth of society.

In all societies certain social problems cannot be investigated at all, or only at grave risk to the investigator. The basic philosophic assumptions by which a society lives are beyond scientific investigation. For to question them is tantamount to questioning the worth of society itself, its justice, its rationality, its very right to exist. Thus a theocratic society cannot permit the scientific investigation of its religious beliefs. A Marxist society cannot tolerate scientific inquiry into dialectic materialism. In a society based upon racial discrimination, race problems are beyond the ken of social science. The profit motive and free enterprise are taboo in capitalistic societies, and the popular control of government will be taken for granted rather than questioned in democracies.

Similarly, in all societies certain results are beyond the reach of scientific inquiry, or they can be reached only at great personal risks. No Russian economist is likely to conclude publicly that capitalism is superior to communism, nor is an American professor of economics likely to maintain the reverse position. Social scientists in monogamic societies are not likely to see virtue in polygamy, and in a scientific civilization, they will emphasize the advantages of science rather than its liabilities.

What is true of the objects and results of scientific investigation

---

[2] For an elaboration of this theme see *ibid.*, pp. 155 ff.; *Politics among Nations* (2d ed.; New York: Alfred A. Knopf, 1954), pp. 80 ff.

is true likewise of its methods. In a humanistically or religiously oriented society, quantitative methods and experimental methods in general will be at a disadvantage. The same fate will befall the methods of philosophic inquiry and rational deduction in a scientifically oriented society. Thus different societies put the stamp of social approval or disapproval upon different methods of inquiry, and the political scientist is again confronted with a dilemma between his commitment to the truth and his concern with social convenience and advancement.

No lengthy explanation is needed to show that those different pressures against which the political scientist must maintain his moral commitment are multiplied in the actual situation in which he must make his decisions. For the political scientist to be a member of a pluralistic society, such as America, means actually to be a member of a multiplicity of sectional societies of a religious, political, social, and economic character, all exerting parallel or contradictory pressures upon him. All these groups are committed to a particular social "truth," and the political scientist cannot help deviating from one or the other of these "truths," if he does not want to forego his moral commitment to discovering *the* truth of society altogether.

These pressures account for the enormous positive and negative influence which foundations exert upon the objects, results, and methods of research. They reward certain types of research by supporting them and stimulate more research of the same type by promising to support it. On the other hand, they thwart or make impossible other types of research by not supporting them. The political scientist who wants to share in these rewards and, by doing so, gain prestige and power within the profession cannot help being influenced by these positive and negative expectations in his concept of the social truth, of the methods by which to seek it, and of the relevant results to be expected from it.

A political science that is true to its moral commitment ought at the very least to be an unpopular undertaking. At its very best, it cannot help being a subversive and revolutionary force with regard to certain vested interests—intellectual, political, economic, social in general. For it must sit in continuous judgment upon political man and political society, measuring their truth, which is in good part a social convention, by its own. By doing so, it is not only an embarrassment to society intellectually, but it becomes also a political threat to the defenders or the opponents of the status quo or to both; for the social conventions about power, which political science cannot help subjecting to a critical—and often destructive—examination, are one of the main sources from which the claims to power, and hence power itself, derive.

It stands to reason that political science as a social institution could never hope even to approach this ideal of a completely disinterested commitment to the truth. For no social institution can completely transcend the limitations of its origin; nor can it endeavor to free itself completely from its commitments to the society of which it forms a part, without destroying itself in the attempt. Only rare individuals have achieved the Socratic distinction of unpopularity, social ostracism, and criminal penalties, which are the reward of constant dedication to the relevant truth in matters political. Yet while political science as a social institution cannot hope to approach the ideal, it must be aware of its existence; and the awareness of its moral commitment to the truth must mitigate the limitations of origin as well as the compromises between the moral commitment and social convenience and ambition, both of which no political scientist can fully escape. It is the measure of the degree to which political science in America meets the needs of society rather than its moral commitment to the truth that it is not only eminently respectable and popular, but—what is worse—that it is also widely regarded with indifference.

A political science that is mistreated and persecuted is likely to have earned that enmity because it has put its moral commitment to the truth above social convenience and ambition. It has penetrated beneath the ideological veil with which society conceals the true nature of political relations, disturbing the complacency of the powers-that-be and stirring up the conscience of society. A political science that is respected is likely to have earned that respect because it performs useful functions for society. It helps to cover political relations with the veil of ideologies which mollify the conscience of society; by justifying the existing power relations, it reassures the powers-that-be in their possession of power; it illuminates certain aspects of the existing power relations; and it contributes to the improvement of the technical operations of government. The relevance of this political science does not lie primarily in the discovery of the truth about politics but in its contribution to the stability of society.

A political science that is neither hated nor respected, but treated with indifference as an innocuous pastime, is likely to have retreated into a sphere that lies beyond the positive or negative interests of society. The retreat into the trivial, the formal, the methodological, the purely theoretical, the remotely historical—in short the politically irrelevant—is the unmistakable sign of a "non-controversial" political science which has neither friends nor enemies because it has no relevance for the great political issues in which society has a stake. History and methodology, in particular, become the protective armor which shields political science from contact with the political reality of the contemporary world. Political science, then, resembles what Tolstoi said modern history has become: "a deaf man answering questions which no one has asked him."

By being committed to a truth which is in this sense irrelevant, political science distorts the perspective under which the political world is seen. Certain eminent exceptions notwithstanding, it tends to pass in silence over such burning problems as the nature of power and of the truth about it, political ideologies, the political power of economic organizations, alternative foreign policies, the relations between government and public opinion, between tyranny and democracy, between objective truth and majority rule, as well as most of the other fundamental problems of contemporary democracy. By doing so, it makes it appear as though these problems either did not exist or were not important or were not susceptible to theoretical understanding. By its predominant concern with the irrelevant, it devaluates by implication the really important problems of politics.

Thus the political scientist, oblivious of his moral commitment, has completed his descent. The custodian of the truth and disturber of society's complacent conscience first descends to the role of the ideologue of society and mollifier of its conscience. This role still requiring a social commitment, not to the truth but to society as it is, and, hence, implying a long-term risk, the political scientist who wants to play absolutely safe must take another downward step. In this final role, concerning himself with issues in which nobody has a stake, he avoids the risk of social disapproval by foregoing the chance of social approbation. In the end, then, the concern with social convenience triumphs over social ambition. The commitment to the truth in matters political is dangerous all the time, while carrying within it the promise of ultimate triumph and spiritual perfection. The commitment to society as it is may be dangerous in the long run, carrying within it the promise of social rewards. Retreat from any commitment, to truth or to society, is free of danger, carrying within it no other reward but that freedom from danger itself.

What, then, ought a political science to be like, which does justice both to its scientific pretense and to its subject matter? The answer to this question, in so far as it concerns the scientific pretense of political science, derives from three basic propositions: the importance of political philosophy for political science, the identity of political theory and political science, the ability of political science to communicate objective and general truth about matters political.

Political science, like all science, is both in the general conception of its scope and method and in its particular concepts and operations a—largely unavowed—reflection of philosophic propositions. Even the most antiphilosophic science of politics is founded upon a philosophic understanding of the nature of man and society and of science itself. That understanding is philosophic in that its validity does not derive from its being capable of empirical verification (although it may be so verified) but rather from its logical consistency with certain general propositions which claim to present the true nature of reality. Political science needs neither to prove nor disprove the philosophic validity of these propositions but must assume the fallacy of some and the validity of others. The choice of these philosophic assumptions cannot but limit the scope, outlook, method, and purpose of political science. Political science is of necessity based upon, and permeated by, a total world view—religious, poetic as well as philosophic in nature—the validity of which it must take for granted.

During most of the history of Western political thought, the functions of political philosophy and political science were united in the same persons. The great political philosophers were also the great political scientists deriving concrete, empirically verifiable propositions from abstract philosophic ones. If the disintegration of the great political systems in the nineteenth century and the concomitant development of a separate political science to which we have referred above had led only to a division of labor between political philosophy and political science, no objection on principle would have been in order. However, the denial of the legitimacy and relevance of political philosophy for political science, prevalent in our day, is quite a different matter. For by denying that legitimacy and relevance, political science cuts itself off from the very roots to which it owes its life, which determine its growth, and which give it meaning. A political science that knows nothing but its own subject matter cannot even know that subject matter well. Contemporary political science, predominantly identified with a positivistic philosophy which is itself a denial of virtually all of the philosophic traditions of the West, has, as it were, mutilated itself by refusing itself access to the sources of insight available in the great philosophic systems of the past. Yet without that access it cannot even recognize, let alone understand, some of the perennial problems of politics which contemporary experience poses with almost unprecedented urgency.

Why is it that all men lust for power; why is it that even their noblest aspirations are tainted by that lust? Why is it that the political act, in its concern with man's power over man and the concomitant denial of the other man's freedom, carries within itself an element of immorality and puts upon the actor the stigma of guilt? Why is it, finally, that in politics good intentions do not necessarily produce good results and well-conceived plans frequently lead to failure in action, and why is it, conversely, that evil men have sometimes done great good in politics and improvident ones have frequently been successful? Here we are in the presence of the mystery, the sin, and the tragedy of politics. The problems that these questions raise are not scientific but philosophic in nature. Yet without the awareness of their legitimacy and relevance political science is precluded from even raising certain problems essential to the scientific understanding of politics.[3]

The same antiphilosophic position, prevalent in contemporary political science, is responsible for the common distinction between

[3] Cf. on this general problem the discussion on values in the social sciences in *America,* Vol. XCII (Oct. 9, 30, 1954).

political theory and political science. Theory, being by definition useless for practical purposes, was assigned that honorific but ineffectual position to which we have referred before, and main emphasis was placed upon science whose immediate usefulness for society the natural sciences seemed to have demonstrated.

Perhaps no event has had a more disastrous effect upon the development of American political science than this dichotomy between political theory and political science. For it has made political theory sterile by cutting it off from contact with the contemporary issues of politics, and it has tended to deprive political science of intellectual content by severing its ties with the Western tradition of political thought, its concerns, its accumulation of wisdom and knowledge. When American political science became sporadically aware of that impoverishment suffered by its own hands, it resorted to the remedy of adding more courses in political theory to the curriculum, or making them compulsory, or requiring knowledge of political theory in examinations. However, the remedy has been of no avail; for it derives from that very dichotomy between political theory and political science, which is at the root of the disease itself.

Of that disease, the plight of comparative government as an academic discipline provides a striking example. The comparison of different political institutions and systems requires logically a *tertium comparationis*, that is, a proposition which provides a standard for comparison. That standard, in order to be meaningful, cannot be merely empirical but must have a theoretical significance pointing to propositions of general validity. Comparative government, in order to be an academic discipline at all, then, requires a theory of politics that makes meaningful comparisons possible. In the absence of such a theory, it is not fortuitous that comparative government is hardly more than the description of, or at best a series of theories about, individual political institutions and systems without comparison.

The very distinction between political theory and political science is untenable. Historically and logically, a scientific theory is a system of empirically verifiable, general truths, sought for their own sake. This definition sets theory apart from practical knowledge, common-sense knowledge, and philosophy. Practical knowledge is interested only in truths which lend themselves to immediate practical application; common-sense knowledge is particular, fragmentary, and unsystematic; philosophic knowledge may be, but is not of necessity, empirically verifiable. What else, then, is scientific knowledge if not theory? It follows that political science cannot be made more theoretical by increasing emphasis upon the separate field of political theory but only by infusing all branches of political science susceptible of theoretical understanding with the spirit of theory.

The same philosophic position which has made political science disparage philosophy and separate itself from theory has also made it deny the existence and intelligibility of objective, general truths in matters political. That denial manifests itself in different ways on different levels of discourse. On the level of the general theory of democracy, it leads to the conclusion that the decision of the majority is the ultimate datum beyond which neither analysis nor evaluation can go. On the level of the analysis of political processes and decisions, it reduces political science to the explanation of the ways by which pressure groups operate and the decisions of government are reached. A political science thus conceived limits itself to the descriptive analysis of a complex of particular historic facts. Its denial of the existence and intelligibility of a truth about matters political that exists regardless of time and place implies a denial of the possibility of political theory both in its analytical and normative sense. What a political science of the past has discovered to be true, then, is true only in view of the peculiar and ephemeral historic circumstances of the time, carrying no lesson for us or any other period of history, or else is a mere reflection of the subjective preferences of the observer. The political science of the past is thus reduced, in so far as it seeks empirical analysis, to the description of an ephemeral historic situation and, as normative theory, becomes undistinguishable from political ideology.

This being so, contemporary political science is caught in the same relativistic dilemma and is no more able to transcend the limitations of time and place than were its predecessors. Either it will be tempted to overcome the limits of its relativist assumptions, whose nihilistic consequences it is unable to face, by taking flight in a subjective dogmatism that identifies the perspective and preferences of the observer with objective, general truth. Thus it becomes the ideology of a particular view of society, reflecting particular social interests. Or else political science will travel the relativistic road to the end and surrender the very concept of objective, general truth, concluding from the subjectivity of its own insights that there is nothing but opinion and that one opinion is as good as another, provided society does not object to it.

We cannot here enter into a detailed discussion of this fundamental problem; two observations must suffice. Political science, like any science, presupposes the existence and accessibility of objective, general truth. If nothing that is true regardless of time and place could be said about matters political, political science itself would be impossible. Yet the whole history of political thought is a living monument to that possibility. The relevance for ourselves of insights which political scientists of the past, reflecting upon matters political under the most diverse historic circumstances, considered to be true, points toward the existence of a store of objective, general truths which are as accessible to us as they were to our predecessors. If it were otherwise, how could we not only understand, but also appreciate, the political insights of a Jeremiah, a Kautilya, a Plato, a Bodin, or a Hobbes?

The content of political science is not to be determined a priori and in the abstract. A theory is a tool for understanding. Its purpose is to bring order and meaning to a mass of phenomena which without it would remain disconnected and unintelligible. There is a strong tendency in contemporary political science to force theory into a Procrustean bed by judging it by its conformity with certain pre-established methodological criteria rather than by its intrinsic contribution to knowledge and understanding. The result is an academic formalism which in its concern with methodological requirements tends to lose sight of the goal of knowledge and understanding which method must serve. One is reminded of the answer which Galileo is reported to have received when he invited some of his critics to look through a telescope at an astronomical phenomenon the existence of which they had denied; they said that there was no need for them to use this empirical instrument since according to Aristotle such a phenomenon could not exist. One is also reminded of the tendencies of the French literature of the seventeenth, the German literature of the eighteenth, and the French art of the nineteenth centuries to make the compliance with certain formal requirements the ultimate standard of literary and artistic value. And one takes heart from the impotence of such attempts to prevent for long the human mind from seeking and finding what is important in science, literature, and art.

The validity of a theory, then, does not depend upon its conformity with a priori assumptions, methodological or otherwise. It is subject to a purely pragmatic test. Does this theory broaden our knowledge and deepen our understanding of what is worth knowing? If it does, it is good, and if it does not, it is worthless, regardless of its a priori assumptions.

The content of theory, then, must be determined by the intellectual interest of the observer. What is it we want to know about politics? What concerns us most about it? What questions do we want a theory of politics to answer? The replies to these three questions determine the content of political science and the replies may well differ, not only from one period of history to another, but from one contemporaneous group of observers to another.

Hypothetically one can imagine as many theories of politics as there are legitimate intellectual perspectives from which to approach the political scene. But in a particular culture and a particular period of history, there is likely to be one perspective which for theoretical and practical reasons takes precedence over the others. At one time theoretical interest was focused upon the constitutional arrangements within which political relations take place; in view of the theoretical and practical problems to be solved, this was then a legitimate interest. At another time in the history of political science, theoretical interest was centered upon political institutions and their operations; in view of what was worth knowing and doing at that time, this theoretical interest was again legitimate. Thus political science is like a spotlight which, while trying to illuminate the whole political world, focuses in one period of history upon one aspect of politics and changes its focus in accordance with new theoretical and practical concerns.[4]

In our period of history, the justice and stability of political life is threatened, and our understanding of the political world is challenged, by the rise of totalitarianism on the domestic and international scene. The novel political phenomenon of totalitarianism

[4] Cf. the discussion of international relations below, pp. 123 ff.

puts in doubt certain assumptions about the nature of man and of society which we took for granted. It raises issues about institutions which we thought had been settled once and for all. It disrupts and overwhelms legal processes on which we had come to look as self-sufficient instruments of control. In one word, what has emerged from under the surface of legal and institutional arrangements as the distinctive, unifying element of politics is the struggle for power, elemental, undisguised, and all-pervading.[5] As recently as at the end of the Second World War, it was still held by conservatives, liberals, and Marxists alike either that the struggle for power was at worst a raucous pastime, safely regulated by law and channeled by institutions, or that it had been replaced in its dominant influence by economic competition, or that the ultimate triumph of liberal democracy or the classless society, which were expected to be close at hand, would make an end to it altogether. These assumptions and expectations have been refuted by the experience of our age. It is to the challenge of this refutation that political science must respond, as political practice must meet the challenge of that experience.

Yet while political science must thus come to terms with the problem of power, it must adapt its emphasis to the ever changing circumstances of the times. When the times tend to depreciate the element of power, it must stress its importance. When the times incline toward a monistic conception of power in the general scheme of things, it must show its limitations. When the times conceive of power primarily in military terms, it must call attention to the variety of factors which go into the power equation and, more particularly, to the subtle psychological relation of which the web of power is fashioned. When the reality of power is being lost sight of over its moral and legal limitations, it must point to that reality. When law and morality are judged as nothing, it must assign them their rightful place.

It may be pointed out in passing that all great contributions to political science, from Plato, Aristotle, and Augustine to *The Federalist* and Calhoun, have been responses to such challenges arising from political reality. They have not been self-sufficient theoretical developments pursuing theoretical concerns for their own sake.

[5] Cf. W. A. Robson, *The University Teaching of Social Sciences: Political Science* (Paris: UNESCO, 1954), pp. 17, 63.

Rather, they were confronted with a set of political experiences and problems which defied understanding with the theoretical tools at hand. Thus they had to face a new political experience, unencumbered by an intellectual tradition which might have been adequate to preceding experiences but which failed to illuminate the experience of the contemporary world. Thus they were compelled to separate in the intellectual tradition at their disposal that which is historically conditioned from that which is true regardless of time and place, to pose again the perennial problems of politics, and to reformulate the perennial truths of politics, in the light of the contemporary experience. This has been the task of political science throughout its history and this is the task of political science today.[6] There is, then, in political science what might be called a "higher practicality," which responds to practical needs not by devising practical remedies, but by broadening and deepening the understanding of the problems from which the practical needs arose.

By making power its central concept, a theory of politics does not presume that none but power relations control political action. What it must presume is the need for a central concept which allows the observer to distinguish the field of politics from other social spheres, to orient himself in the maze of empirical phenomena which make up that field, and to establish a measure of rational order within it. As economics is centered upon the concept of interest defined as wealth, its accumulation and distribution, so political science is centered upon the concept of interest defined as power, its accumulation, distribution, and control. A central concept, such as power, then provides a kind of rational outline of politics, a map of the political scene. Such a map does not provide a complete description of the political landscape as it is in a particular period of history. It rather provides the timeless features of its geography distinct from their ever changing historic setting. Such a map, then, will tell us what are the rational possibilities for travel from one spot on the map to another, and which road is most likely to be taken by certain travelers under certain conditions. Thus it imparts a measure of rational order to the observing mind and, by doing so, establishes one of the conditions for successful action.

[6] Cf. Alfred Cobban's important article, "The Decline of Political Theory," *Political Science Quarterly*, LXVIII (1953), 321–32.

A theory of politics, by the very fact of painting a rational picture of the political scene, points to the contrast between what the political scene actually is and what it tends to be, but can never completely become. The difference between the empirical reality of politics and a theory of politics is like the difference between a photograph and a painted portrait. The photograph shows everything that can be seen by the naked eye. The painted portrait does not show everything that can be seen by the naked eye, but it shows one thing that the naked eye cannot see: the human essence of the person portrayed. Thus a theory of politics must seek to depict the rational essence of its subject matter.

By doing so, a theory of politics cannot help implying that the rational elements of politics are superior in value to the contingent ones and that they are so in two respects. They are so in view of the theoretical understanding which theory seeks; for its very possibility and the extent to which it is possible depend upon the rationality of its subject matter. A theory of politics must value that rational nature of its subject matter also for practical reasons. It must assume that a rational policy is of necessity a good policy; for only such a policy minimizes risks and maximizes benefits and, hence, complies both with the moral precept of prudence and the political requirement of success. A theory of politics must want the photographic picture of the political scene to resemble as much as possible its painted portrait.

Hence, a theory of politics presents not only a guide to understanding but also an ideal for action. It presents a map of the political scene not only in order to understand what that scene is like but also in order to show the shortest and safest road to a given objective. The use of theory, then, is not limited to rational explanation and anticipation. A theory of politics also contains a normative element.

A curriculum of political science which would try to put such a theoretical understanding of politics into practice for the purposes of teaching would have to eliminate all those subjects which do not serve this theoretical understanding. It would also have to add subjects which at present are not included but which are essential to such understanding.

The process of elimination must move on two fronts. First, it must affect those subjects which have been traditionally included in the field but which have no organic connection with its subject matter or with the perspective from which contemporary political science ought to view it. In this category belong, for instance, all the legal subjects with which political science concerns itself because the law schools at one time did not. However, this practical consideration is unfounded today when law schools offer courses in jurisprudence and administrative, constitutional, and international law. Political science is not interested in any legal subject per se, yet it has indeed a vital interest in the interrelations between law and politics. It must look at law not as a self-contained system of rules of conduct, but rather as both the creation and the creator of political forces.

Second, there has been a strong tendency in political science to add to the curriculum subjects which happen to be of practical importance at a particular moment, regardless of their theoretical relevance. However, what is worth knowing for practical reasons is not necessarily worth knowing on theoretical grounds. A certain innovation in municipal administration or international organization may attract at one time wide attention by virtue of the practical results it promises, or the political developments in a certain area of the world may become a matter of topical interest for public opinion. It still remains to be shown on theoretical grounds that such topics ought to be included as independent subjects in the curriculum of political science. On a limited scale this problem raises again the issue of liberal versus vocational education.

The additions to the curriculum of political science, too, must be of two different kinds. On the one hand, the curriculum must take into account the fact that its central concept is a general social phenomenon which manifests itself most typically in the political sphere but is not limited to it. The phenomenon of power and the social configurations to which it gives rise play an important, yet largely neglected, part in all social life. A configuration, such as the balance of power, is a general social phenomenon to be found on all levels of social interaction. The theoretical understanding of specifically political phenomena and configurations requires the understanding of the extent to which these political phenomena and configurations are merely the specific instances of general social phenomena and configurations and the extent to which they grow out of their specific political environment. One of the cornerstones of the curriculum of political science, then, ought to be political sociology, which deals with the phenomenon of power and the social configurations to which it gives rise in general, with special reference, of course, to those in the political sphere.[7]

On the other hand, the contemporary political scene is characterized by the interaction between the political and economic spheres. This interaction runs counter to the liberal assumption and requirement of actual separation, which is reflected in the academic separation of the two fields. This interaction reverts to a situation which existed before political science was established as an academic discipline and which was reflected by the academic fusion of the two fields in the form of political economy. The curriculum of political science must take theoretical notice of the actual development of private governments in the form of giant corporations and labor unions. These organizations exercise power within their own organizational limits, in their relations to each other, and in their relations to the state. The state, in turn, exercises power over them. These power relations constitute a new field for theoretical understanding.[8]

Yet what political science needs above all changes in the curriculum—even though it needs them too—is the restoration of the intellectual and moral commitment to the truth about matters political for its own sake. That restoration becomes the more urgent in the measure in which the general social and the particular academic environment tends to discourage it. Society in general and that particular society of which he is a professional member pull and push the political scientist toward being useful here and now and playing it safe forever. If the political scientist cannot resist these pushes and pulls by repairing to the vision of the searcher for the political truth, which Plato brought to the world, and of the professor of the politi-

[7] Cf. the important but largely neglected monograph by Frederick Watkins, *The State as a Concept of Political Science* (New York: Harper & Bros., 1934), esp. pp. 81 ff.

[8] Morgenthau, "The New Despotism and the New Feudalism," *The Restoration of American Politics* (Vol. III of *Politics in the Twentieth Century*), chap. 10.

cal truth, which the prophets exemplified, what will become of him as a scholar, and what will become of a society which has deprived itself of the ability to measure the conflicting claims of interested parties against the truth, however dimly seen?

A society which has thus closed its eyes to the truth about itself has cut its tie with what connects it with the mainsprings of civilization. For without at least the assumption that objective, general truth in matters political exists and can be known, order and justice and truth itself become the mere by-products of ever changing power relations. In such a society the political scientist has still an important part to play: he becomes the ideologue who gives the appearance of truth and justice to power and the claim for it.

Political science, as we have tried to show before, can indeed not help performing such an ideological function. Yet it is the measure of the awareness and fulfilment of its mission as a science of politics that it is conscious of the existence of an objective, general truth behind ideological rationalizations and justifications and that it seeks the comprehension of that truth. In order to fulfil that mission the political scientist must live within the political world without being of it. He must watch it with intense interest and sympathy; yet the gaze of his mind and the impulse of his will must transcend it. He must understand it as well and better than does the politician, and yet his ambition has nothing in common with the latter's. His primary moral commitment is not to society but to the truth and, hence, to society only in so far as it lives up to the truth. Only so can he at least approach the ideal of political justice, he alone among those concerned with political matters; for in the words of Goethe: "The actor is always unjust; nobody has justice but the observer."

At such impracticality in action and ambivalence in moral commitment, the Socratic handmaids of all ages, the born servants of society, can only laugh. Of them, however clever and witty they may be, history reports nothing but laughter. Yet what they laugh at is the moral and intellectual outlook from which stems our heritage of political knowledge and wisdom.

PART **II**

UNDERSTANDING

INTERNATIONAL POLITICS

4 The Commitments of a Theory of International Politics

With these dilemmas all attempts at a theoretical understanding of politics must come to terms. The intensity of the dilemma is proportional to the political involvement of the observer and to the political relevance of the subject matter. Under present conditions, it is likely to be greater in the field of economic policy than in the field of municipal government. That intensity is greatest in the sphere of international politics, and it is compounded by the presence of a dilemma which is peculiar to that sphere.

One basic fact distinguishes international politics from all other types of politics and exerts a persuasive influence on the practice of international politics as well as upon its theoretical understanding. That fact concerns the relationship between international society and its constituent members, the nation states. The constituent members of domestic society, individuals and subnational groups, live in an integrated society, which holds supreme power and is the repository of the highest secular values and the recipient of the ultimate secular loyalties. Yet these domestic societies are the constituent members of international society which must defer to them in terms of power, values, and loyalties. What sets international society apart from other societies is the fact that its strength—political, moral, social—is concentrated in its members, its own weakness being the reflection of that strength.

A theory of international politics has the task, in applying the general principles of politics to the international sphere, to reformulate, modify, and qualify these principles in the light of that distinctive quality of international politics. A theory of international politics plays, as it were, the tune which the general theory of politics provides, but it plays it in a key and with variations which stem from the peculiarities of international society. The national interest

From W. T. R. Fox (ed.), *Theoretical Aspects of International Relations* (1959).

defined in terms of power, the precarious uncertainty of the international balance of power, the weakness of international morality, the decentralized character of international law, the deceptiveness of ideologies, the inner contradictions of international organization, the democratic control of foreign policy, the requirements of diplomacy, the problem of war—of these phenomena and problems of international politics theory must take account in terms of the general principles of politics which reveal themselves on the international scene in peculiar manifestations, owing to the peculiar character of international society.

This is obviously not the place to attempt a demonstration of the correctness of this view; for such a demonstration would require the development of a substantive theory of international politics. Since the attempt to do this has been made elsewhere and since this chapter deals with the requirements and problems of such a theory rather than with its substance, it must suffice here to point to the great and peculiar difficulties which stand in the way of the development of such a theory and to the relatively narrow limits within which it seems to be possible. Two facts deserve special attention in this context: the implicit rather than explicit character of past attempts at a theory of international politics; and the peculiar difficulties impeding theoretical understanding which arise from the relationship of power, morality, and the national interest as it reveals itself on the international scene.

That men throughout the ages have thought little of a theory of international politics is borne out by the fact that but rarely an explicit attempt to develop such a theory has been made; as rare instances of such atempts, Kautilya and Machiavelli come to mind. Men have generally dealt with international politics on one of three levels, all alien to theory: history, reform, or pragmatic manipulation. That is to say, they have endeavored to detect the facts and meaning of international politics through the knowledge of the past; or they have tried to devise a pattern of international politics more in keeping with an abstract ideal than the empirical one; or they have sought to meet the day-by-day issues of international politics by trial and error.

Yet each of these approaches presupposes, and in actuality reveals, a theoretical conception of what international politics is all about, however fragmentary, implicit, and unavowed such a theoretical conception may be. In historians with a philosophic bent, such as Thucydides and Ranke, the history of foreign policy appears as a mere demonstration of certain theoretical assumptions which are always present beneath the surface of historical events to provide the standards for their selection and to give them meaning. In such historians of international politics, theory is like the skeleton which, invisible to the naked eye, gives form and function to the body. What distinguishes such a history of international politics from a theory is not so much its substance as its form. The historian presents his theory in the form of a historical recital using the historic sequence of events as demonstration of his theory. The theoretician, dispensing with the historical recital, makes the theory explicit and uses historic facts in bits and pieces to demonstrate his theory.

What holds true of the historian of international politics applies also to the reformer. He is, as it were, a "forward-looking" theoretician. His scheme of reform provides an explicit theory of what international politics ought to be, derived from an explicit or implicit theory of what international politics actually is. What has prevented William Penn, the Abbé de St. Pierre, or contemporary World Federalists from developing a complete theory of international politics is their primary concern with practical reform rather than the absence of theoretical elements in their thinking.

This same practical concern has prevented the practitioners of international politics from developing an explicit theory of what they are doing. Even a perfunctory perusal of the speeches, state papers, and memoirs of such diverse types of statesmen as Bismarck, Wilson, Churchill, and Stalin, shows that their relationship to theory is even closer than we found that of the historian to be. For the great statesman differs from the run-of-the-mill diplomatist and politician exactly in that he is able to see the issues confronting him as special cases of general and objective—that is, theoretical— propositions. Here again it is not the substance of his thinking but the form in which it manifests itself, which distinguishes the statesman from the theoretician of international politics. Here again it is his practical concern, not his alienation from theory as such, which prevents him from becoming a theoretician. Yet it illuminates the theoretical essence of the statesman's thinking that whenever practical concerns receded into the background or seemed best served by theoretical considerations, the four great statesmen mentioned

above naturally transformed themselves from practitioners into theoreticians, making explicit in systematic or aphoristic form the theoretical foundations of their statecraft.

These observations support the case for the possibility and even
the necessity of the theoretical understanding of international politics. However, by showing the scarcity of explicit, systematic theories of international politics, they point to the difficulties which
stand in the way of the development of such a theory. The relationship of power, morality, and the national interest constitutes one of
these difficulties.

On the domestic plane, the relationship of power, morality,
and interest is so obvious as to be hardly open to controversy. In
domestic politics, individuals pursue their interests defined in terms
of power. These interests, in view of their relation to power, have
three outstanding characteristics. First, the interests to which power
attaches itself and which it serves are as varied and manifold as are
the possible social objectives of the members of a given society.
Second, these interests shift continuously from the center of political attention and emphasis to its margin until they may fade out of
the political picture altogether, only to come back again when circumstances change. Third, measured by the interests of society as a
whole, these interests are partial in nature, and their existence within
a transcendent whole both limits their nature and the manner of
their pursuit. The very nature of the interests with which the member of a domestic society may identify himself is determined by the
"common good" as society as a whole understands it, and so are the
means by which he may pursue those interests.

The relationship between interest and power is different on the
international plane. Here power is wedded to the interests of a particular nation. And while it is true, as will be pointed out in the next
chapter, that it has not always been so and it is not likely to be so
forever, the relatively constant relationship between power and the
national interest is the basic datum for purposes of both theoretical
analysis and political practice. The content of the national interest is
likewise constant over long periods of history. All the ideal and material elements which make up that content are subordinated at the
very least to those requirements—not susceptible to rapid change—
upon which the survival of the nation and the preservation of its

identity depend. Finally—and most importantly—the national interest is not a fraction of a transcendent, comprehensive social interest to which it is subordinated and by which it is limited both as to content and to the means employed for its realization. The period of history when the national interest could be said to be so subordinated and limited has been replaced by one in which the nation has become the highest secular social organization and its interest the common focus of secular social interests.

However, it is not these characteristics of the national interest which make theoretical understanding difficult. Quite to the contrary, the constancy and supremacy of the national interest, taken by themselves, favor theoretical analysis. Theoretical complications arise from the relationship which exists between morality, on the one hand, power and the national interest, on the other. Here again it is revealing to trace the different manifestations of the same theoretical structure in the domestic and international sphere.

The relationship between morality, on the one hand, power and interest, on the other, is threefold. First, morality limits the interests that power seeks and the means that power employs to that end. Certain ends cannot be pursued and certain means cannot be employed in a given society within a certain period of history by virtue of the moral opprobrium that attaches to them. Second, morality puts the stamp of its approval upon certain ends and means which thereby not only become politically feasible but also acquire a positive moral value. These moral values, then, become an intrinsic element of the very interests that power seeks. Third, morality serves interests and power as their ideological justification.

In the domestic sphere morality performs all these three functions effectively. It directs the choice of the means and ends of power away from what society considers to be harmful to its purposes and toward what it regards to be beneficial to them. What we call a civilized political community is the result of the efficiency with which morality performs these negative and positive functions. Yet civilization requires more than the negative and positive limitations of the means and ends of politics. It also requires the mitigation of the struggle for power by glossing over power interests and power relations and making them appear as something different than what they actually are.

This ideological function, which morality performs on the domestic scene together with the other two, has become its main function for international politics. On the international scene, the individual nation is by far the strongest moral force, and the limitations which a supranational morality is able to impose today upon international politics are both fewer and weaker than they were almost at any time since the end of the Thirty Years' War. The individual nation, thus having become virtually the highest moral unit on earth, has naturally been tempted to equate its own moral values with morality as such, and especially the most powerful nations have found it hard to resist that temptation. In consequence, the main function which morality performs today for international politics is ideological. It makes it appear as though the interests and policies of individual nations were the manifestations of universal moral principles. The part aspires to become the whole, and there is very little to counteract that aspiration. It is not so much morality which limits individual interests, as it is the individual interests which identify themselves with morality.

This identification of the interests and power of the nation with universal morality confronts theoretical understanding with formidable difficulties. The distinction between ideology and morality becomes blurred as does the distinction between ideology and theory. The advocate of the national crusade appears not only to promote universal moral values but also to have discovered theoretical truth. By contrast, the theoretician who seeks the truth hidden beneath these veils of ideology cannot help being in an intellectually and morally awkward position. His very probing of the moral pretenses of national interest and national power in the name of a higher truth and a higher morality makes him suspect of being indifferent to all truth and all morality. Thus to write a theory of international politics is not an easy thing. Perhaps this is why we have so many ideologies, and so few theories, of international politics.

The difficulties which stand in the way of the theoretical understanding of international politics have grown more formidable with the ever more intensive identification of national purposes and policies with absolute truth and universal morality. Yet at the same time the need for such understanding has become paramount in an age in which the nation, deeming itself intellectually and morally self-sufficient, threatens civilization and the human race itself with extinction. To look in such circumstances at one's own nation and its relations with other nations objectively, dispassionately, critically has never been more difficult, hazardous, and necessary than it is today. This task presents a theory of international politics with its supreme intellectual and moral challenge. Its performance would constitute not only an intellectual and moral but a political triumph as well. For it would indicate that at least the mind of man has succeeded in mastering that blind and potent monster which in the name of God or history is poised for universal destruction.

5 The Intellectual and Political Functions of a Theory of International Relations

In the April, 1960, issue of *International Relations*, Professor Martin Wight, then of the London School of Economics and Political Science, published a paper with the title "Why Is There No International Theory?" While I cannot, of course, subscribe to the unqualified negativism of the title for both personal and professional reasons, I find the paper a most illuminating and penetrating discussion of the problem. Its fourteen pages contain more insights into the intellectual issues posed by theoretical concern with international relations than a whole shelf of books and articles which, following the fashion of the day, spin out theories about theories of international relations and embark upon esoteric methodological studies about how to go about theorizing about theories of international relations.

Professor Wight finds elements of an international theory in writings of international lawyers, such as Grotius and Pufendorf; the so-called "irenists," seekers after a peaceful international order, such as Erasmus, Sully, Campanella, Crucé, Penn, the Abbé de St. Pierre; the Machiavellians rediscovered by Meinecke; the *parerga* of political philosophers, philosophers, and historians, such as Hume's "The Balance of Power," Rousseau's *Project of Perpetual Peace*, Mably's *Principes des Négociations;* and finally the speeches, dispatches, memoirs, and essays of statesmen and diplomatists, such as Gentz's *Fragments on the Balance of Power*[1] or Bismarck's *Memoirs*. Professor Wight concludes that "international theory is marked, not only by paucity but also by intellectual and moral poverty. For this we must look to internal reasons. The most obvious are the intellectual prejudice imposed by the sovereign State, and the belief in progress."

According to Professor Wight, the sovereign state has been the

An address given at the University of Maryland, March, 1961.

[1] Classified by Wight in the preceding category.

focus of Western political thought and experience since the Reformation. Almost all intellectual energies devoted to political studies have been absorbed by it. "It has been natural to think of international politics as the untidy fringe of domestic politics . . . and to see international theory in the manner of the political theory textbooks, as an additional chapter which can be omitted by all save the interested student." Political theory, centered upon the state and its survival within the existing state system, has prevailed over international theory, studying the state system itself as a phenomenon that owes its existence to the historic process and is destined to be superseded by it. This is what Wight calls "a small-scale field of political theory." International theorists "have not been attracted by the possibility of maximising the field of political theory through establishing a world State. Nor is it unfair to see the League and the United Nations as the expression of a belief that it may be possible to secure the benefits of a world State without the inconveniences of instituting and maintaining it." Wight finds it significant that none of the three most powerful influences on the development of the modern state system—Reformation and Counter Reformation, the French Revolution, and the totalitarian revolutions of the twentieth century—have brought forth a coherent body of international theory.

Professor Wight finds the other impediment to the development of an international theory in the fact that

the character of international politics is incompatible with progressivist theory. Thus international theory that remains true to diplomatic experience will be at a discount in an age when the belief in progress is prevalent. If Sir Thomas More or Henry IV, let us say, were to return to England and France in 1960, it is not beyond plausibility that they would admit that their countries had moved domestically towards goals and along paths which they could approve. But if they contemplated the international scene, it is more likely that they would be struck by resemblances to what they remembered. International politics is the realm of recurrence and repetition; it is the field in which political action is most regularly necessitous.

Yet when the modern mind comes face to face with this immutable character of international politics, it revolts and takes refuge in the progressivist conviction that what was true in the past cannot be true in the future; for, if it were, mankind would be in desperate

straits. This is what Wight calls "the argument from desperation."
Thus

whereas political theory generally is in unison with political activity, international theory (at least in its chief embodiment as international law) sings a kind of descant over against the movement of diplomacy . . . international law seems to follow an inverse movement to that of international politics.

This tension between international theory and international reality is already obvious in the identification of international politics with a precontractual state of nature assumed by the classical international lawyers. Yet while the state of nature among individuals leads to the social contract establishing authority over, and peace and order among, them, international theory sees no need for a similar development among states.

Wight finds it odd

that, while the acknowledged classics of political study are the political philosophers, the only counterpart in the study of international relations is Thucydides, a work of history. And that the quality of international politics, the preoccupations of diplomacy, are embodied and communicated less in works of political or international theory than in historical writings. There are out of date books like Seeley's *Growth of British Policy*, which were second-rate at best, that might be thought to convey the nature of foreign policy and the working of the State-system better than much recent literature concerned with the games theory, decision-making, politicometrics and psychological concepts.

Wight summarizes his position by pointing to

a kind of recalcitrance of international politics to being theorized about. The reason is that the theorising has to be done in the language of political theory and law. But this is the language appropriate to man's control of his social life. Political theory and law are maps of experience or systems of action within the realm of normal relationships and calculable results. They are the theory of the good life. International theory is the theory of survival. What for political theory is the extreme case (as revolution or civil war) is for international theory the regular case.

Thus in the end international theory "involves the ultimate experience of life and death, national existence and national extinction." What we call international theory, then, amounts to a kind of philosophy of history.

It hardly needs pointing out that my position coincides in large

measure with that of Professor Wight.[2] I take indeed a more san-
guine view of the possibility of international theory than he does,
finding that possibility in the very fact that "international politics
is the realm of recurrence and repetition." It is this repetitive character of international politics, i.e., the configurations of the balance
of power, that lends itself to theoretical systematization. I would
also hesitate to equate international theory with philosophy of history. Theory is implicit in all great historiography. In historians
with a philosophic bent, such as Thucydides and Ranke, the history
of foreign policy appears as a mere demonstration of certain theoretical assumptions which are always present beneath the surface of
historical events to provide the standards for their selection and to
give them meaning. In such historians of international politics, theory
is like the skeleton which, invisible to the naked eye, gives form and
function to the body. What distinguishes such a history of international politics from a theory is not so much its substance as its form.
The historian presents his theory in the form of a historical recital
using the chronological sequence of events as demonstration of his
theory. The theoretician, dispensing with the historical recital,
makes the theory explicit and uses historic facts in bits and pieces
to demonstrate his theory.

Yet both Wight's and my orientation are historic, and it is this
historic orientation that sets us apart from the presently fashionable
theorizing about international relations. This theorizing is abstract
in the extreme and totally unhistoric. It endeavors to reduce international relations to a system of abstract propositions with a predic-
tive function. Such a system transforms nations into stereotyped
"actors" engaging in equally stereotyped symmetric or asymmetric
relations. What Professor Wight has noted of international law applies with particular force to these theories: the contrast between
their abstract rationalism and the actual configurations of world
politics.[3] We are here in the presence of still another type of

---

[2] I am referring of course primarily to *Politics among Nations* and, more
particularly, to chaps. xi–xiv, xvii, xix, xxix, dealing with the balance of power,
the nation-state, and world government, respectively.

[3] See, for instance, the special issue on "The International System" of *World
Politics*, XIV, No. 1 (October, 1961), and the critique of this type of thinking
in Irving Louis Horowitz, "Arms, Policies and Games," *The American Scholar*,
XXXI, No. 1 (Winter, 1961–62), 94 ff. For criticism, see also P. M. S. Blackett,

progressivist theory. Its aim is not the legalization and organization of international relations in the interest of international order and peace, but the rational manipulation of international relations and, more particularly, of military strategy in the interest of predictable and controlled results. The ideal toward which these theories try to progress is ultimately international peace and order to be achieved through scientific precision and predictability in understanding and manipulating international affairs.

In view of their consistent neglect of the contingencies of history and of the concreteness of historic situations that all these theories have in common, they are destined to share the fate of their progressivist predecessors: they must fail both as guides for theoretical understanding and as precepts for action. However, the practical consequences of their theoretical deficiencies are likely to be more serious than those of their predecessors.

The straits in which the Western democracies found themselves at the beginning of the Second World War were in good measure the result of the reliance upon the inner force of legal pronouncements, such as the Stimson Doctrine of refusing to recognize territorial changes brought about by violence, and of legal agreements, such as the Kellogg-Briand Pact and non-aggression treaties, and of international organizations, such as the League of Nations, which were incapable of collective action. The scientist theories of our day pretend to be capable of manipulating with scientific precision a society of sovereign nations who use weapons of total destruction as instruments of their respective foreign policies. With that pretense, these theories create the illusion that a society of sovereign nations thus armed can continue the business of foreign policy and military strategy in the traditional manner without risking its destruction. They create the illusion of the viability of the nation-state in the nuclear age. If statesmen should take these theories at their pseudo-scientific word and act upon them, they would fail, as the statesmen of the interwar period failed when they acted upon the progressivist theories of their day.

"Critique of Some Contemporary Defence Thinking," *Encounter*, XVI (April, 1961), 9 ff., and Sir Solly Zuckerman, "Judgment and Control in Modern Warfare," *Foreign Affairs*, XL, No. 2 (January, 1962), 196 ff.

It is significant that until very recently no explicit theory of international relations has existed. Nobody until very recently considered even the possibility of writing a theory of international relations. This is a very significant fact which ought to give us pause. For certainly theoretically inclined, reflective people have been aware, since the beginning of the existence of international relations, of the facts of foreign policy, the fateful results of good and bad foreign policies, the significance of success or failure in foreign policy. And certainly we have not grown so much wiser in recent years or so much more acute in self-awareness that we have all of a sudden started to think in theoretical terms of one of the crucial facts of human existence, recognized as such by prophets, statesmen, historians, and political philosophers for thousands of years. There must be a profound reason why until very recently nobody has thought of writing an explicit theory of international relations. Certainly it cannot be the backwardness of Plato and Aristotle, Hobbes and Locke, which prevented them from developing such a theory.

The first reason why there has been no theory, but only history, of international relations is to be found in the philosophic outlook that prevailed until the end of the Napoleonic Wars. Until then, the relations among nations were regarded to be a fact of nature which was beyond the power of man to change. The relations among nations were regarded to be a datum of history, a state of nature, resulting from the nature of man; and nothing could be said in terms of a specific theory of international relations about their characteristics and about their manipulation. Given this outlook, the best theory could do was what political philosophy actually did, that is, to describe the state of nature and the rudimentary legal order existing, or assumed to exist, among nations.

As long as man believed that the relations among nations were beyond human control, beyond reform by the human will, there was no place in the intellectual scheme of things for a theory of international relations. International theory found itself in this respect in the same position as social theory in general. As long as people believed that poverty, for instance, was a natural state which man had to accept without being able to change it, social philosophy could do no more than affirm this natural condition. As long as this state of mind persisted, there was no possibility for the development of a social theory, a social theory of change at least. What *The Times* said in mid-nineteenth century of the misery of the unemployed: "There is no one to blame for this; it is the result of Nature's simplest laws!" people thought of international relations. Thus the intellectual possibility of a theory of international relations depended upon the recognition that the relations among nations are not something which is given to man, which has to be accepted as given, and which he must cope with as best he can, but rather that the relations among nations have been created by the will of man and therefore can be manipulated and changed and reformed by the will of man.

The second reason why theoretical concern with international relations was so late in emerging lies in the reformist orientation that characterized theoretical thinking on foreign policy in the nineteenth century and the first decades of the twentieth. The main theoretical concern during that period was not with understanding the nature of international relations, but with developing legal institutions and organizational devices which would supersede the type of international relations then existing. "Power politics" itself as a synonym for foreign policy was then a term of opprobrium, referring to something evil, not to be understood but to be abolished. To take Woodrow Wilson's position during and after the First World War as a classic and most impressive example, he was interested not in understanding the operations of the balance of power but in getting rid of it, in reforming international relations in such a way that one did not need to resort any more to the balance of power.

Secretary of State Cordell Hull echoed the Wilsonian conception when, on his return from the Moscow Conference of 1943 where the establishment of the United Nations had been agreed upon, he declared that "there will no longer be need for spheres of influence, for alliances, for balance of power, or any other of the special arrangements through which, in the unhappy past, the nations strove to safeguard their security or promote their interests." And President Franklin D. Roosevelt did the same when on March 1, 1945, in his report to Congress on the Yalta Conference, he declared:

The Crimean Conference . . . spells the end of the system of unilateral action and exclusive alliances and spheres of influence and balances of power and all other expedients which have been tried for centuries—and have failed.

We propose to substitute for all these a universal organization in which all peace-loving nations will finally have a chance to join.

As long as this negative orientation toward the very nature of international relations and foreign policy persisted, it was both intellectually and morally impossible to deal in a theoretical, that is, an objective, systematic manner with the problems of international relations.

The third and permanent factor, which does not make a theory of international relations altogether impossible, but strictly limits its development and usefulness, is to be found in the very nature of politics, domestic and international. There is a rational element in political action which makes politics susceptible to theoretical analysis, but there is also a contingent element in politics which obviates the possibility of theoretical understanding.

The material with which the theoretician of politics must deal is ambiguous. The events he must try to understand are, on the one hand, unique occurrences. They happened in this way only once and never before or since. On the other hand, they are similar, for they are manifestations of social forces. Social forces are the product of human nature in action. Therefore, under similar conditions, they will manifest themselves in a similar manner. But where is the line to be drawn between the similar and the unique? The political world appears to the theoretical mind as a highly complicated combination of numerous systems of multiple choices which in turn are strictly limited in number. The element of irrationality, insecurity, and chance lies in the necessity of choice among several possibilities multiplied by the great number of systems of multiple choice. The element of rationality, order, and regularity lies in the limited number of possible choices within each system of multiple choice. Viewed with the guidance of a rationalistic, blueprinted map, the social world is, indeed, a chaos of contingencies. Yet it is not devoid of a measure of rationality if approached with the modest expectations of a circumspect theory.

To take as an example three current situations, we can say that the situations in Laos, Cuba, and Berlin provide American foreign policy with a limited number of rational choices. For some strange reason these choices generally number three. What a theory of international relations can state is the likely consequences of choosing one alternative as over against another and the conditions under which one alternative is more likely to occur and be successful than the other. Theory can also say that under certain conditions one alternative is to be preferred over another. But all these theoretical analyses are contingent upon factors of whose occurrences we either know nothing or whose consequences we cannot foresee.

Take for instance so crucial a problem of international relations as the problem of nuclear war. It is possible to develop a theory of nuclear war, as Herman Kahn has done in his book *On Thermonuclear War*, which assumes nuclear war to be just another kind of violence, greater in magnitude but not different in kind than the types of violence with which history has acquainted us. It follows from this assumption that nuclear war is going to be much more terrible than pre-nuclear war, but not necessarily intolerable, provided we take the measures which will enable us to survive it. In other words, once you start with this theoretical assumption of the nature and the consequences of a nuclear war, you can logically arrive at Mr. Kahn's conclusion that the foreign policy of the United States does not need to limit itself to trying to avoid nuclear war, but that the United States must also prepare to survive it. And then it becomes perfectly legitimate to raise the question, provided 50 million Americans were to be killed in a nuclear war and 9/10 of the economic capacity of the United States were to be destroyed, how do we enable the surviving 130 million Americans to rebuild the United States with the remaining 1/10 of economic capacity?

The contingent element in this theory of nuclear war is its utter uncertainty, and this uncertainty is typical of all levels of theoretical analysis and prediction in the field of politics, domestic and international. Even if one were to accept all its estimates of deaths and material destruction and of the rate of material recovery, this theory would have to be uncertain about the human reaction to the kind of human and material devastation which nuclear war is likely to bring about. Obviously, if a highly complex human society could be visualized to operate like a primitive ant society, its recuperative ability could be taken for granted. If 1/3 of the ants of one ant hill have been destroyed together with 9/10 of the material of the ant hill, it is safe to conclude that the remaining ants will start all over again, building up the ant hill and reproducing until the next catastrophe will force them to start all over again.

But it is a moot question whether a human society has this type of mechanical recuperative ability. Perhaps societies have a breaking point as do individuals, and there may be a point beyond which human endurance does not carry human initiative in the face of such unprecedented massive devastation. Perhaps under the impact of such devastation civilization itself will collapse.

It is at this point that the theoretical understanding of international relations reaches its limits. It can develop different alternatives and clarify their necessary preconditions and likely consequences. It can point to the conditions which render one alternative more likely to materialize than the other. But it cannot say with any degree of certainty which of the alternatives is the correct one and will actually occur.

This is but an extreme example of the utter uncertainty of theorizing about foreign policy beyond the clarification of alternative policies, their possibilities and possible consequences. The Munich settlement of 1938 is another case in point. In retrospect, of course, we all know from practical experience that it was a great failure, and from that experience we have developed the theoretical categories which demonstrate that it was bound to be such a failure. But I remember very well the near-unanimity with which the Munich settlement was approved by theoreticians and practitioners of foreign policy and by the man in the street as well. The Munich settlement was generally regarded at the time of its conclusion as a great act of statesmanship, a concession made to a would-be conquerer for the sake of peace. E. H. Carr so regarded it then, and A. J. P. Taylor so regards it now. The flaw in that reasoning, which few people were—and perhaps could be—aware of at the time, was again the neglect of the contingencies inherent in political prediction. That which reveals itself as a simple truth in retrospect was either completely unknown in prospect or else could not be determined by anything but an uncertain hunch.

Apply the reasoning with which I have just analyzed the Munich settlement of 1938 to a hypothetical Berlin settlement of 1962. One of the alternatives for American foreign policy, which theoretical analysis can isolate, is to make certain concessions to the Soviet

Union which change the modalities of the West's presence in Berlin but leave that presence itself intact. Another alternative, also revealed by theoretical analysis, is to stand on the Western right to be in Berlin and to refuse to make any concessions because whatever concessions we make will of necessity be followed by other concessions, and so step by step our presence in West Berlin will be whittled down until it becomes untenable.

A third alternative assumes that our presence in Berlin is a priori untenable. It holds that the symbolic value of our presence in Berlin with regard to the unification of Germany has really been bypassed by history because the division of Germany has become definitive. Sooner or later, we must recognize this fact and adapt our policies to it. Especially in view of the risks involved and the odds against success, there is no point in maintaining a symbol which has no longer any active function to perform.

A theoretical argument can be made for any of those three alternatives, and nobody can say in advance with any degree of certainty which of the courses of action indicated by those three alternatives is correct in theory, sound in practice, or is likely to be chosen by actual policy. Only in retrospect, judging from the nature and the results of the action chosen, can we answer these questions. This limitation of theoretical analysis is inherent in the very subject matter of international relations, and this subject matter erects insuperable limits to the development of a rational theory of international relations. It is only within those limits that theoretical thinking on international relations is theoretically and practically fruitful. Within these limits, a theory of international relations performs the functions any theory performs, that is, to bring order and meaning into a mass of unconnected material and to increase knowledge through the logical development of certain propositions empirically established.

While this theoretical function of a theory of international relations is no different from the function any social theory performs, its practical function is peculiar to itself. The practical function of a theory of international relations has this in common with all political theory that it depends very much upon the political environment within which the theory operates. In other words, political thinking is, as German sociology puts it, "*standortgebunden*," that is to say, it is tied to a particular social situation. And we find that all great and fruitful political thought, which we still remember because of its greatness and fruitfulness, has started from a concrete political situation with which the political thinkers had to come to terms both for intellectual and practical reasons. Edmund Burke is a typical example of how great and fruitful political theory develops from concrete practical concerns. It is not being created by a professor sitting in his ivory tower and looking at a contract with his publisher, which stipulates the delivery of a manuscript on the "Theory of International Relations" by the first of January, 1962. It is developed out of the concern of a politically alive and committed mind with the concrete political problems of the day. Thus all great political theory, from Plato and Aristotle and from the biblical prophets to our day, has been practical political theory, political theory which intervenes actively in a concrete political situation with the purpose of change through action.

A theory of international relations can perform four different practical functions by approaching political reality in four different ways. I shall try to exemplify these four different ways with my own experience as a theoretician of international relations, attempting to come to terms with the issues of international relations and of American foreign policy in particular since the end of the Second World War.

I had my first experience as a theoretician of international relations under the Truman-Acheson administration of America's foreign policy. Theory then provided a theoretical justification for what the policy makers were doing, you may say, instinctively— what they were doing pragmatically, on a mere day-by-day basis.

By 1947 the new pattern of American foreign policy was set. It manifested itself in four political innovations: the Truman doctrine, containment, the Marshall Plan, and the American alliance system. These policies have in common the permanent assumption, by the United States, of responsibilities beyond the limits of the Western Hemisphere. The heart of that new policy was the policy of containment. Yet the policy of containment was never officially formulated. It grew as an almost instinctive reaction to the threat of Russian imperialism. It called a halt to the territorial expansion of Russian power beyond the line of military demarcation drawn at the end of the Second World War between the Soviet orbit and the Western world.

There was no theory in support of these new policies. It was only as an afterthought that theoreticians developed a doctrine in the form of a theoretical framework which gave rational justification to the new policies. The policy makers played it by ear; they did what they thought they needed to do under the circumstances; they embarked upon courses of action which at the time appeared to them almost inevitable in view of their knowledge of the threat and of their objectives. It was only as a kind of intellectual reassurance that a theory of American foreign policy was developed which put the stamp of rational approval upon policies already established.

The function of the theoretician of international relations under the two Eisenhower administrations, dominated by the foreign policy of John Foster Dulles, was of an entirely different nature. It was a function which has many precedents in the history of political thought. One can even go so far as to say that it is one which political theories have traditionally performed. Theory here developed a coherent system of thought which was supposed to embody the sound principles of foreign policy. The actual conduct of American foreign policy was judged by the standards of that theory and frequently found wanting. Criticism directed at that theory was similarly judged and justified or found wanting, as the case might have been, by the standards of the theory. I remember very vividly that, whenever I published an article critical of the foreign policy of Mr. Dulles, I found nowhere more enthusiastic approval of that criticism than in the Department of State. Theory here provided a rational framework for a non-orthodox, critical political position either within the government or outside it. Theory gave a rational justification to that position.

The situation in which the theoretician of international relations has found himself since January 20, 1961, when the Kennedy administration took office, is, of course, quite extraordinary. What is the function of the outside theoretician when the government itself is staffed on the command posts of foreign policy by theoreticians? It stands to reason that he has become in good measure technologically obsolete. I have, since January 20, 1961, reflected with a great deal of embarrassment upon this change of position. Hardly anybody asks my advice any more because the people in government know at least as much as I do, and probably some are convinced that they know much more—and perhaps they actually do.

What, then, is the function of the academic theoretician of international relations in a society in which foreign policy itself is determined by theoretically conscious policy makers? There is still a function to be performed. For it is in the very nature of the conduct of foreign policy in a democracy that what theoreticians regard to be the sound principles of foreign policy must be adapted to the preferences of public opinion and to the pressures of domestic politics, and thereby corrupted and distorted. I remember the statement I once heard a former secretary of state make to the effect that he had always regarded it as his function to give the President advice on the basis of what he thought the principles of a sound American foreign policy required, leaving it to the President to decide how much of those sound principles could be safely put into practice in view of the state of domestic public opinion and the pressures of domestic politics.

Thus the actual foreign policies pursued by a government staffed even by theoreticians are bound to fall short, from time to time, of the requirements of a pure theoretical understanding of what American foreign policy ought to be. It is here that the theoretician of foreign policy must perform the function of an intellectual conscience which reminds the policy makers as well as the public at large of what the sound principles of foreign policy are and in what respects and to what extent actual policies have fallen short of those principles.

There is a final task—and perhaps it is the most noble of all—which a theory of international relations can perform and which it must perform particularly in an age in which the very structure of international relations has radically changed. It is to prepare the ground for a new international order radically different from that which preceded it. Theoretical analysis, I think, can show that the principle of political organization which has dominated the modern world from the French Revolution of 1789 to this day is no longer valid. The sovereign nation-state is in the process of becoming obsolete. That is to say, the fact of nuclear power, which transcends the ability of any nation-state to control and harness it and render it both

75

innocuous and beneficial, requires a principle of political organization transcending the nation-state and commensurate with the potentialities for good or evil of nuclear power itself. Theoretical analysis can show that the availability of nuclear power as an instrument of foreign policy is the only real revolution which has occurred in the structure of international relations since the beginning of history, because it has radically changed the relationship between violence as a means of foreign policy and the ends of foreign policy.

Until the end of the Second World War, there existed a rational relationship between violence as a means of foreign policy and the ends of foreign policy; that is to say, the policy maker could rationally ask himself whether he should pursue the aims of his country by peaceful means or whether he ought to go to war. If he chose the latter alternative and if he lost the war, his nation lost in general only a bearable fraction of its human and material resources. If he won, then the risks taken were justified by the victory gained. This rational relationship between violence as a means and the ends of foreign policy has been obliterated by the availability of nuclear power. Nuclear power provides governments with a destructive force transcending all possible rational objectives of the foreign policy of any nation. For all-out nuclear war is likely to obliterate the very distinction between victor and vanquished and will certainly destroy the very objective for which such a war would be fought. It is here that a theory of international relations has a creative and vital task to perform, a task which has been performed throughout history by the political theories of domestic politics. It is at this point that the realistic and utopian approaches to politics in general and to international relations in particular merge.

It is a legitimate and vital task for a theory of politics to anticipate drastic changes in the structure of politics and in the institutions which must meet a new need. The great political utopians have based their theoretical anticipation of a new political order upon the realistic analysis of the empirical status quo in which they lived. Today political theory and, more particularly, a theory of international relations, starting from the understanding of politics and international relations as they are, must attempt to illuminate the impact which nuclear power is likely to exert upon the structure of international relations and upon the functions domestic government performs and to anticipate in a rational way the intellectual, political, and institutional changes which this unprecedented revolutionary force is likely to require.

There is another function of international theory which is not so much intellectual as psychological in nature and is of interest primarily to the sociology of knowledge. It is to provide a respectable shield which protects the academic community from contact with the living political world. That function is performed by many of the methodological activities which are carried on in academic circles with sometimes fanatical devotion to esoteric terminology and mathematical formulas, equations, and charts in order to elucidate or obscure the obvious. These activities can be explained psychologically by the fear of many academicians to come into too close contact with the political world, to become controversial in consequence, and to become contaminated in their objective scholarship by contact with political reality. By engaging in activities which can have no relevance for the political problems of the day, such as theorizing about theories, one can maintain one's reputation as a scholar without running any political risks. This kind of international theory, then, is consummated in theorizing for theorizing's sake, an innocuous intellectual pastime engaged in by academicians for the benefit of other academicians and without effect upon political reality as it is unaffected by it.

In conclusion, it may be said that the nature of a theory of international relations and the intellectual and political functions a theory of international relations performs and ought to perform are not in essence different from the nature of general political theory and the functions which such theories have performed since the beginning of history. The fact that we have only in recent years turned toward explicit theoretical reflection about international relations is in good measure due to our recognition that international relations is something not to be taken for granted, but something to be understood and to be changed and, more particularly, to be changed beyond the present limits of its political structure and organization. Here lies indeed the ultimate theoretical and practical justification of our interest in a theory of international relations. Threatened by the unsolved political problems of the day, we have come to think more and more in terms of a supranational community and a world government, a political organization and structure which transcend the nation-state. Reflecting on a theory of international relations, the politically conscious theoretician cannot help reflecting upon the political problems whose solution requires such novel structures and types of organization.

6 *The Problem of the National Interest*

We have suggested that a theory of politics, domestic or international, requires a central concept. For a general theory of politics, the concept of interest defined as power serves as the central focus, while a theory of international politics must be focused on the concept of the national interest. The controversy which has arisen since the end of the Second World War around the concept of the national interest differs from the great historical debates on American foreign policy in that it raises not necessarily a specific issue of American foreign policy but the fundamental issue of the nature of all foreign policy and of all politics as well.

The great debates of the past, such as the one over intervention versus neutrality in 1793, expansion versus the status quo before the Mexican and after the Spanish-American War, international cooperation versus isolation in the twenties, intervention versus abstention in the late thirties—all evolved around clear-cut issues of foreign policy. In 1793 you were in favor of going to war on the side of France or of remaining neutral. In the 1840's you approved of the annexation of Texas or you did not. At the turn of the century you supported overseas expansion or you were against it. In the twenties you advocated joining the League of Nations or staying out of it. In the late thirties you wanted to oppose the Axis Powers by all means short of war or you wanted to abstain from intervening. While what separates the two schools of thought, the "utopian" and the "realist," which have developed around the concept of the national interest can sometimes be expressed in terms of alternative foreign policies, more often it cannot. Frequently and typically, the very same policies can be and are being supported by both schools of thought. What sets them apart is not necessarily a matter of practical judgment but of philosophies and standards of thought.

The issue the present debate raises concerns the nature of all politics and, more particularly, of the American tradition in foreign

From the *American Political Science Review*, December, 1952.

policy. The history of modern political thought is the story of a contest between two schools which differ fundamentally in their conception of the nature of man, society, and politics. One believes that a rational and moral political order, derived from universally valid abstract principles, can be achieved here and now. It assumes the essential goodness and infinite malleability of human nature and attributes the failure of the social order to measure up to the rational standards to lack of knowledge and understanding, obsolescent social institutions, or the depravity of certain isolated individuals or groups. It trusts in education, reform, and the sporadic use of force to remedy these deficiencies.[1]

The other school believes that the world, imperfect as it is from the rational point of view, is the result of forces inherent in human nature. To improve the world one must work with those forces, not against them. This being inherently a world of opposing interests and of conflict among them, moral principles can never be fully realized, but at best approximated through the ever temporary balancing of interests and the ever precarious settlement of conflicts. This school, then, sees in a system of checks and balances a universal principle for all pluralist societies.[2] It appeals to historic precedent rather than to abstract principles and aims at achievement of the lesser evil rather than of the absolute good.

The conflict between two basic conceptions of man and politics is at the bottom of the present controversy. It provided in the sixteenth, seventeenth, and eighteenth centuries the issue for the debate on the reason of state of which Friedrich Meinecke has given the definitive account. It separated on the occasion of the neutrality proclamation of 1793 Washington and Hamilton from their opponents, and Hamilton has indeed given in the "Pacificus" and "Americanus" letters the classic American formulation of the philosophy

[1] This is the ideal type of the utopian position rather than the empirical description of any particular historic type. In actuality, and this is true particularly of the present, the utopian position in international affairs is not always consistent with its philosophic premises.

[2] It ought not to need special emphasis that a principle of social conduct, in contrast to a law of nature, allows of, and even presupposes, conduct in violation of the principle. Robert W. Tucker, in "Professor Morgenthau's Theory of Political 'Realism,'" *American Political Science Review*, XLVI (March, 1952), 214–24, has missed this and many other points in his zeal to find contradictions where there are none.

of the national interest. In general philosophic terms it found its classic expression in the polemic of Burke against the philosophy of the French Revolution.

In order to refute a theory which pretends to be scientific, it is first necessary to understand what a scientific theory is. A scientific theory, as pointed out before, is an attempt to bring order and meaning to a mass of phenomena which without it would remain disconnected and unintelligible. Anyone who disputes the scientific character of such a theory either must produce a theory superior in these scientific functions to the one attacked or must, at the very least, demonstrate that the facts as they actually are do not lend themselves to the interpretation that the theory has put upon them. When a historian tells us that the balance of power is not a universal principle of politics, domestic and international, that it was practiced in Europe only for a limited period and never by the United States, that it ruined the states that practiced it,[3] it is incumbent upon him to tell us how we can dispose by means of theory of the historic data by which, for instance, David Hume demonstrated the universality of the balance of power and Paul Scott Mowrer[4] and Alfred Vagts[5] its practice by the United States; what Kautilya was writing about in the fourth century B.C. when he summarized the theoretical and practical tradition of Indian statecraft in terms of the balance of power; what the Greek city-states, the Roman republic, and the medieval emperors and popes were doing if they did not apply the principles of the balance of power; and how the nations that either neglected these principles or applied them wrongly suffered political and military defeat and even extinction, while the nation that applied these principles most consistently and consciously, that is, Great Britain, enjoyed unrivaled power for an unparalleled length of time.

The historian who wishes to replace the balance of power as the guiding principle of American foreign policy with the "humani-

---

[3] Tannenbaum in "The Balance of Power versus the Coördinate State," *Political Science Quarterly,* LXVII (June, 1952), 173, and in "The American Tradition in Foreign Relations," *Foreign Affairs,* XXX (October, 1951), 31–50.

[4] *Our Foreign Affairs* (New York: E. P. Dutton & Co., 1924), pp. 246 ff.

[5] "The United States and the Balance of Power," *Journal of Politics,* III (November, 1941), 401–49.

[6] Tannenbaum, "The Balance of Power versus the Coördinate State," p. 173.

tarian and pacific traditions" of the "coördinate state"[6] must first of all explain how it has come about that the thirteen original states expanded into the full breadth and a good deal of the length of a continent, until today the strategic frontiers of the United States run parallel to the coastline of Asia and along the River Elbe. If such are the results of policies based upon "humanitarian and pacific traditions," never in the history of the world has virtue been more bountifully rewarded! Yet our historian must explain not only the great sweep of American expansion but also the specific foreign policies which in their historic succession make up that sweep. Is it easier to explain the successive shifts of American support from Great Britain to France and back again from the beginning of King George's War in 1744 to the War of 1812 in terms of the "coördinate state" than in terms of the balance of power? The same question might be asked about the postponement of the recognition of the independence of the Spanish colonies until 1822, when the Floridas had been acquired from Spain and Spain had thereby been deprived of the ability to challenge the United States from within the hemisphere. The same question might be asked about the Monroe Doctrine itself, about Lincoln's policies toward Great Britain and France, and about our successive policies with regard to Mexico and the Caribbean. One could go on and pick out at random any foreign policy pursued by the United States from the beginning to the First World War, and one would hardly find a policy, with the exception perhaps of the War of 1812, that could not be made intelligible by reference to the national interest defined in terms of power—political, military, and economic—rather than by reference to the principle of the "coordinate state." This inevitable outcome of such an inquiry is well summarized in these words:

Ease and prosperity have made us wish the whole world to be as happy and well to do as ourselves; and we have supposed that institutions and principles like our own were the simple prescription for making them so. And yet, when issues of our own interests arose, we have not been unselfish. We have shown ourselves kin to all the world, when it came to pushing an advantage. Our action against Spain in the Floridas, and against Mexico on the coasts of the Pacific; our attitude toward first the Spaniards, and then the French, with regard to the control of the Mississippi; the unpitying force with which we thrust the Indians to the wall wherever they stood in our way, have suited our professions of peacefulness and justice and liberality no better than the aggressions of other nations that were strong and not to be gainsaid. Even Mr. Jefferson, philanthropist and champion of peaceable and modest government though he was, exemplified this double temper of the people he ruled. "Peace is our passion," he had declared; but the passion abated when he saw the mouth of the Mississippi about to pass into the hands of France. Though he had loved France and hated England, he did not hesitate then what language to hold. "There is on the globe," he wrote to Mr. Livingston at Paris, "one single spot the possessor of which is our natural and habitual enemy. The day that France takes possession of New Orleans seals the union of two nations, who, in conjunction, can maintain exclusive possession of the sea. From that moment we must marry ourselves to the British fleet and nation." Our interests must march forward, altruists though we are; other nations must see to it that they stand off, and do not seek to stay us.

This realist appraisal of the American tradition in foreign policy was published in 1901 in the *Atlantic Monthly*. Its author was a professor of jurisprudence and political economy at Princeton by the name of Woodrow Wilson.[7]

Nothing more needs to be said to demonstrate that facts do not support a revision of American diplomatic history that tries to substitute "humanitarian and pacifist traditions" and the "coördinate state" for power politics and the balance of power as the guiding principle of American foreign policy. What, then, does support it? Three things: the way American statesmen have spoken about American foreign policy; the legal fiction of the "coördinate state"; finally, and foremost, an emotional urge to justify American foreign policy in humanitarian, pacifist terms.

It is elementary that the character of a foreign policy can be ascertained only through the examination of the political acts performed and of the foreseeable consequences of these acts. Thus we can find out what statesmen have actually done, and from the foreseeable consequences of their acts we can surmise what their objectives might have been. Yet examination of the facts is not enough. To give meaning to the factual raw material of history, we must approach historical reality with a kind of rational outline, a map which suggests to us the possible meanings of history. In other words, we put ourselves in the position of a statesman who must meet a certain problem of foreign policy under certain circumstances and ask ourselves: what are the rational alternatives from which a statesman

---

[7] "Democracy and Efficiency," *Atlantic Monthly*, LXXXVII (March, 1901), 293–94.

may choose who must meet this problem under these circumstances, presuming always that he acts in a rational manner, and which of these rational alternatives was this particular statesman, acting under these circumstances, likely to choose? It is the testing of this rational hypothesis against the actual facts and their consequences which gives meaning to the facts of history and makes the scientific writing of political history possible.

In the process of writing the history of foreign policy the interpretations by statesmen of their own acts, especially if they are made for public consumption, must needs have a strictly subsidiary place. The public self-interpretation by actors on the political scene is itself, of course, a political act which seeks to present a certain policy to its presumed supporters in terms of their moral and political folklore and to those against which it is directed in terms which intend to embarrass and deceive. Such declarations may indeed shed light upon the character and objectives of the policy pursued if they are considered in conjunction with, and in subordination to, rational hypotheses, actions, and likely consequences. Yet it is quite a different matter to interpret the American tradition of foreign policy in the light of a collection of official statements which, like most such statements, present humanitarian and pacifist justifications for the policies pursued. If anybody should be bold enough to write a history of world politics with so uncritical a method he would easily and well-nigh inevitably be driven to the conclusion that from Timur to Hitler and Stalin the foreign policies of all nations were inspired by the ideals of humanitarianism and pacifism. The absurdity of the result is commensurate with the defects of the method.

It is only from a method that accepts the declarations of statesmen as evidence of the character of the policies pursued that the principle of the "coördinate state" receives a semblance of plausibility. Statesmen and international lawyers have been wont to speak of the "equal dignity" of all states, regardless of "wealth, power, size, population or culture,"[8] which I take the principle of the "coördinate state" to mean. It is also referred to as the principle of "federalism in international relations."[9] As its prime examples are cited the relations amongst the states of the Union, the states of the American

8 Tannenbaum, "The Balance of Power versus the Coördinate State," p. 177.
9 *Ibid.*

system, the members of the Commonwealth of Nations, and the members of the Swiss Confederation. If the whole world were organized in accordance with this principle, as are already these four political entities, it is assumed that the freedom, dignity, and peace of all nations would then be assured.

There is no need to examine the theoretical and practical merits of the principle of the "coördinate state," because for none of the four political entities mentioned does the idea of the "coördinate state" provide the principle of political organization. The equality of the states as the political foundation of the United States became obsolescent when Chief Justice Marshall's Supreme Court resolved the ambiguity of the Constitution in favor of the federal government, and it became obsolete when the Civil War proved Chief Justice Marshall's point. The equality of the states survives today only in the shadow and by virtue of the federal government's political supremacy, and without the cohesive force of that supremacy there would be no union of equal states to begin with. That these powers of the federal government are limited and qualified by the principle of federalism, that is, by the constitutionally granted powers of the states, is quite a different matter; it concerns the distribution of powers between federal government and states within a general system of checks and balances, but has nothing to do with the equality of the states as the alleged political foundation of the American system of government. With the exception of the equality of senatorial representation, the principle of the equality of the states is today, as it has been for almost a century, devoid of political content. It serves only as a principle of regional organization, of administrative decentralization, and, above all, of constitutional rhetoric. What it really signifies was pointed out more than fifty years ago by W. A. Dunning when he summarized his answer to the question "Are the states equal under the Constitution?" by saying that "the theory of equal states falls to the ground."[10]

Similarly, the federalism of Switzerland is the result of a long series of civil wars, the last one fought a little more than a century ago, which established the predominance of the German-speaking cantons within the confederation. Here too, it is the existence of

[10] William Archibald Dunning, *Essays on the Civil War and Reconstruction and Related Topics* (New York: P. Smith, 1931), p. 351.

predominant power, located in one segment of the federal system, which makes federalism possible in the first place.

By the same token, the unchallengeable supremacy of the United States within the Western Hemisphere has throughout been the backbone of the system of American states. As long as this supremacy is secure, there is, on the one hand, no need for the United States to assert it in the political and military sphere, and, taking it for granted, the United States can well afford to pursue a policy of the Good Neighbor; and there is, on the other hand, no opportunity for the other members of the system to challenge that supremacy effectively. This is what the principle of the "coördinate state" amounts to in the Western Hemisphere. Consequently, whenever there was even a remote possibility that the supremacy of the United States might be challenged, generally through instigation from outside the hemisphere, the United States asserted its superior power within the hemisphere and acted as all states must act under similar conditions.

Whatever possibility for common political action there remains among the members of the Commonwealth of Nations is the result of the interests which these members may have in common. In other words, the member states may work together or each of them may work with other nations, as their interests dictate. Their membership in the Commonwealth, as the examples of India, South Africa, Australia, and New Zealand clearly show, has no influence upon this decision; that membership is but a faint remembrance of the times when Great Britain could secure co-operation among the member states on its terms by virtue of its superior power.

What, then, have these four examples of the "coördinate state" in common which would establish them as a distinct type of interstate relationship, and what conclusions can be drawn from them for the organization of the world? The only thing that these four examples seem to have really in common is the legal stipulation of the equality of the members of the respective systems, and this characteristic is not peculiar to them, but a general principle of international law applicable to all sovereign states. In the political sphere they seem to have nothing in common at all. What they tend to show, however, is the decisive importance of the distribution of political power for the operation of federal and egalitarian relations among states. The political cohesion of a federal system is the result of superior power located in some part of it. It is by virtue of its superior power that the predominant part can afford to grant the other members of the federal system a measure of equality in the non-political sphere. These observations bring us back to power politics and the balance of power to which the principle of the "coördinate state" was supposed to be the alternative.

In truth, it is not the disinterested consideration of facts which has given birth to the theory of the "coördinate state." That theory is rather the response to an emotional urge, and since this emotion is not peculiar to a particular author but typical of a popular reaction to the new role which the United States must play in world affairs, it deserves a brief analysis.

One of the great experiences of our time which have impressed themselves upon the American mind is the emergence of the United States as a nation among other nations, exposed to the same opportunities, temptations, risks, and liabilities to which other nations have been traditionally exposed. This experience becomes the more shocking if it is compared with the expectation with which we fought the Second World War. We expected from that war a reaffirmation of the secure, detached, and independent position in world affairs which we had inherited from the founding fathers and which we had been successful in preserving at least to the First World War. By avoiding what we thought had been Wilson's mistakes, we expected to emerge from that war if not more independent, certainly more secure than we were when we entered it. In fact, not even in the early days of the Republic were we more exposed to danger from abroad than we are today, and never had we less freedom of action in taking care of our interests than we have today.

It is naturally shocking to recognize that a happy chapter in the history of the nation and in one's own way of life has come to an end. There are those who reconcile themselves to the inevitable, albeit with sorrow rather than with glee, and try to apply the lessons of the past to the tasks at hand. There are others who try to escape from a disappointing and threatening reality into the realm of fantasy. Three such escapist fantasies have arisen in our midst in response to the challenge of American world leadership and power: the fantasy of needless American participation in war, the fantasy of American treason, and the fantasy of American innocence.

The first of these fantasies presumes that the present predicament is a result not of necessity but of folly, the folly of American statesmen who needlessly intervened in two world wars. The second of these fantasies attributes the present predicament to treason in high places whereby the fruits of victory were handed to the enemy. The third of these fantasies denies that the predicament is real and prefers to think of it as an intellectual fraud perpetrated upon the American people. To suport this fictional denial of the actualities of the present, it draws upon a fictional account of the past. The United States does not need to bear at present the intellectual, moral, and political burdens which go with involvement in power politics and the maintenance of the balance of power; for it has never borne them in the past, never having been thus involved. The golden age of past political innocence sheds its glow upon a but seemingly less innocent present and promises a future in which all the world will follow the example of America, forswear power politics and the balance of power, and accept the principle of the "coördinate state." Our alliances, we are told, have nothing to do with the balance of power but aim at the "organization of as much of the world as we can upon the basis of the coördinate state. . . . It may prove impossible under present conditions to build such a system without having to fight a war with Russia, but then at least we will be fighting, as we did before, for the thing we consider worth defending with our lives and treasure."[11] Thus a fictional account of the American past, begun as an act of uncalled-for patriotic piety, issues in an ideology for a third world war. Escape we must from the unfamiliar, unpleasant, and dangerous present, first into the political innocence of the past and from there into the immediate future of a third world war, beyond which the revived and universalized innocence of the more distant future will surely lie.

We have said that to present the American tradition in foreign policy as having been free from concern with power politics and the balance of power is not warranted by the facts of American history. Yet it might still be argued, and it is actually being argued, that, regardless of the evidence of history, the American people will not be reconciled to power politics and the balance of power and

[11] Tannenbaum, "The Balance of Power versus the Coördinate State," pp. 195-96.

will support only policies based upon abstract moral principles. While in the past the United States might have pursued balance-of-power policies and while it might be a good thing if it did do so again, the American people will not stand for it. Here the emotional appeal to patriotic piety is joined by calculations of political expediency. Yet the case for misrepresenting American history has nothing to gain from either.

There is a strong tendency in all historiography to glorify the national past, and in popular presentations that tendency takes on the aspects of the jingoist whitewash. Even so penetrating a mind as John Stuart Mill's could deliver itself of an essay in which he proved, no doubt to the satisfaction of many of his English readers but certainly of few others, that Great Britain had never interfered in the affairs of European nations and had interfered in those of the Indian states only for their own good.[12] Yet it is the measure of a nation's maturity to be able to recognize its past for what it actually is. Why should we not admit that American foreign policy has been generally hardheaded and practical and at times ruthless? Why should we deny Jefferson's cunning, say, in the Puget Sound affair, the cruelty with which the Indians were treated, and the faithlessness with which the treaties with the Indians were cast aside? We know that this is the way all nations are when their interests are at stake—so cruel, so faithless, so cunning. We know that the United States has refrained from seeking dominions beyond the seas not because it is more virtuous than other nations but because it had the better part of a continent to colonize.

As has been pointed out elsewhere at greater length, the man in the street, unsophisticated as he is and uninformed as he may be, has a surer grasp of the essentials of foreign policy and a more mature judgment of its basic issues than many of the intellectuals and politicians who pretend to speak for him and cater to what they imagine his prejudices to be. During the Second World War the ideologues of the Atlantic Charter, the Four Freedoms, and the United Nations were constantly complaining that the American soldier did not know what he was fighting for. Indeed, if he was fighting for

---

12 "A Few Words on Non-Intervention," *Dissertations and Discussions: Political, Philosophical, and Historical* (London: Longmans, Green, Reader and Dyer, 1875), pp. 153–78.

some utopian ideal, divorced from the concrete experiences and interests of the country, then the complaint was well grounded. However, if he was fighting for the territorial integrity of the nation and for its survival as a free country where he could live, think, and act as he pleased, then he had never any doubt about what he was fighting for. Ideological rationalizations and justifications are indeed the indispensable concomitants of all political action. Yet there is something unhealthy in a craving for ideological intoxication and in the inability to act and to see merit in action except under the stimulant of grandiose ideas and far-fetched schemes. Have our intellectuals become, like Hamlet, too much beset by doubt to act and, unlike Hamlet, compelled to still their doubts by renouncing their sense of what is real? The man in the street has no such doubts. It is true that ideologues and demagogues can sway him by appealing to his emotions. But it is also true, as American history shows in abundance, that responsible statesmen can guide him by awakening his latent understanding of the national interest.

Yet what is the national interest? How can we define it and give it the content which will make it a guide both for understanding and for action? This is one of the relevant questions to which the current debate has given rise.

It has been frequently argued against the realist conception of foreign policy that its key concept, the national interest, does not provide an acceptable standard for either thought or action. This argument is in the main based upon two grounds: the elusiveness of the concept and its susceptibility to interpretations, such as limitless imperialism and narrow nationalism, which are not in keeping with the American tradition in foreign policy. The argument has substance as far as it goes, but it does not invalidate the usefulness of the concept.

The concept of the national interest is similar in two respects to the "great generalities" of the Constitution, such as the general welfare and due process. It contains a residual meaning which is inherent in the concept itself, but beyond these minimum requirements its content can run the whole gamut of meanings that are logically compatible with it. That content is determined by the political traditions and the total cultural context within which a nation formulates its foreign policy. The concept of the national interest, then, contains two elements, one that is logically required and in that sense necessary, and one that is variable and determined by circumstances. The former is, then, of necessity relatively permanent while the latter will vary with circumstances.

The relative permanency of what one might call the hard core of the national interest stems from three factors: the nature of the interests to be protected, the political environment within which the interests operate, and the rational necessities which limit the choice of ends and means by all actors on the stage of foreign policy. Any foreign policy that operates under the standard of the national interest must obviously have some reference to the physical, political, and cultural entity which we call a nation. In a world where a number of sovereign nations compete with and oppose each other for power, the foreign policies of all nations must necessarily refer to their survival as their minimum requirement. Thus all nations do what they cannot help but do: protect their physical, political, and cultural identity against encroachments by other nations.

The nature of the threat to which the national interest is exposed remains equally constant over long periods of history. Throughout the centuries the main threat to Great Britain has come from the hegemonic aspirations of one or the other of the European nations. Russia has traditionally been threatened by a great power having access to the plains of eastern Europe. France and Germany, regardless of their changing political forms, have threatened each other throughout the ages.

The relative permanency of interest and threat is surpassed by the virtual immutability of the configurations through which the reason of man transforms the abstract concept of the national interest into foreign policy. Faced with the necessity to protect the hard core of the national interest, that is, to preserve the identity of the nation, all governments have resorted throughout history to certain basic policies, such as competitive armaments, the balance of power, alliances, and subversion, intended to make of the abstract concept of the national interest a viable political reality. Governments might have been wise or unwise in their choice of policies, successful or unsuccessful in their execution; they could not have escaped the rational necessity of selecting one of a limited number of avenues through which to bring the power of their nation to bear upon the power of other nations on behalf of the national interest.

The possibility both to reconstruct past foreign policies through the writing of history and to understand the contemporary foreign policies of one's own and other nations derives from this rational character of the national interest. If one could not assume that this rationality is identical throughout history and ubiquitous on the contemporary scene, however diminished and distorted by the irrationality of men and nations, one would be lost in a maze of unconnected data, to be explained perhaps in terms of psychology and sociology but not in terms conducive to the understanding of foreign policy. It is this assumption of the universality of the national interest in time and space which enables us to understand the foreign policies of Demosthenes and Caesar, of Kautilya and Henry VIII, of the statesmen of contemporary Russia and China. Regardless of all the differences in personality, social environment, convictions, and preferences, their thinking was predetermined and their actions could take place only within a narrow range, when they were faced with the task of protecting and promoting the rational core of the national interest. By thinking as they must have thought we can understand their thoughts, and by putting their thoughts into the context of their personalities and social environment we can understand their actions as well.

It has been suggested that this reasoning erects the national state into the last word in politics and the national interest into an absolute standard for political action. This, however, is not quite the case. The idea of interest is indeed of the essence of politics and, as such, unaffected by the circumstances of time and place. Thucydides' statement, born of the experiences of ancient Greece, that "identity of interest is the surest of bonds whether between states or individuals" was taken up in the nineteenth century by Lord Salisbury's remark that "the only bond of union that endures" among nations is "the absence of all clashing interests." The perennial issue between the realist and utopian schools of thought over the nature of politics, to which we have referred before, might well be formulated in terms of concrete interests versus abstract principles. Yet while the concern of politics with interest is perennial, the connection between interest and the national state is a product of history.

The national state itself is obviously a product of history and as such is destined to yield in time to different modes of political organization. As long as the world is politically organized into nations, the national interest is indeed the last word in international politics. When the national state has been replaced by another mode of organization, foreign policy must then protect the interest in survival of that new organization. For the benefit of those who insist upon discarding the national state and constructing supranational organizations by constitutional fiat, it must be pointed out that these new organizational forms will either come into being through conquest or else through consent based upon the mutual recognition of the national interests of the nations concerned; for no nation will forego its freedom of action if it has no reason to expect proportionate benefits in compensation for that loss. This is true of treaties concerning commerce or fisheries as it is true of the great compacts, such as the European Coal and Steel Community, through which nations try to create supranational forms of organization. Thus, by an apparent paradox, what is historically conditioned in the idea of the national interest can be overcome only through the promotion in concert of the national interest of a number of nations.

These reflections have been made particularly relevant by the atomic age. It has been said that the atomic age has rendered obsolete the idea of the national interest and the conception of foreign policy derived from it. This is too sweeping a statement to be correct. What has become obsolete is the historically conditioned connection between interest and a passing historic phenomenon, the nation state; what has not, and could not have, become obsolete is the logically required connection between interest and foreign policy. The point can indeed be made—and it will be made in greater detail in chapter 10—that the technological revolutions of our age, of which the atomic revolution is the most spectacular one, have made the political organization of the world into nation states as obsolete as the first industrial revolution did the political organization based upon the feudal state. Yet the techniques by which new and wider interest must be given a politically viable expression have not been affected by those revolutionary changes. Thus the supranational control of atomic energy is today in the national interest of all nations; for while the present bipolarity of atomic power is dangerous to all nations, the acquisition of uncontrolled atomic power by an indefinite number of nations is likely to prove fatal to civilized life on this planet. In consequence, the nations of the world are faced with, and must overcome, the dilemma that the pursuit of their interests, conceived in national terms, is incompatible with modern technology, which requires supranational political organization.

The survival of a political unit, such as a nation, in its identity is the irreducible minimum, the necessary element of its interests vis-à-vis other units. Taken in isolation, the determination of its content in a concrete situation is relatively simple; for it encompasses the integrity of the nation's territory, of its political institutions, and of its culture. Thus bipartisanship in foreign policy, especially in times of war, has been most easily achieved in the promotion of these minimum requirements of the national interest. The situation is different with respect to the variable elements of the national interest. All the crosscurrents of personalities, public opinion, sectional interests, partisan politics, and political and moral folkways are brought to bear upon their determination. In consequence, the contribution which scientific analysis can make to this field, as to all fields of policy formation, is limited. It can identify the different agencies of the government which contribute to the determination of the variable elements of the national interest and assess their relative weight. It can separate the long-range objectives of foreign policy from the short-term ones which are the means for the achievement of the former and can tentatively establish their rational relations. Finally, it can analyze the variable elements of the national interest in terms of their legitimacy and their compatibility with other national values and with the national interest of other nations. We shall address ourselves briefly to the typical problems with which this analysis must deal.

The legitimacy of the national interest must be determined in the face of possible usurpation by subnational, other-national, and supranational interests. On the subnational level we find group interests, represented particularly by ethnic and economic groups, which tend to identify themselves with the national interest. Charles A. Beard has emphasized, however one-sidedly, the extent to which the economic interests of certain groups have been presented as those of the United States.[13] Group interests exert, of course, constant pressure upon the conduct of our foreign policy, claiming their identity with the national interest. It is, however, doubtful that, with the exception of a few spectacular cases, they have been successful in determining the course of American foreign policy. It is much more likely, given the nature of American domestic politics, that American foreign policy, in so far as it is the object of pressures by sectional interests, will normally be a compromise between divergent sectional interests. The concept of the national interest, as it emerges from this contest of conflicting sectional interests as the actual guide for foreign policy, may well fall short of what would be rationally required by the over-all interests of the United States. Yet this concept of the national interest is also more than any particular sectional interest or their sum total. It is, as it were, the lowest common denominator where sectional interests and the national interest rationally conceived meet in an uneasy compromise which may leave much to be desired in view of all the interests concerned.

The national interest can be usurped by other-national interests in two typical ways. The case of treason by individuals, either out of conviction or for pay, needs only to be mentioned here; for in so far as treason is committed on behalf of a foreign government rather than a supranational principle, it is significant for psychology, sociology, and criminology but not for the theory of politics. The other case, however, is important not only for the theory of politics but also for its practice, especially in the United States.

National minorities in European countries, ethnic groups in the United States, ideological minorities anywhere may identify themselves, either spontaneously or under the direction of the agents of a foreign government, with the interests of that foreign government and may promote these interests under the guise of the national interest of the country whose citizens they happen to be. The activities of the German-American Bund in the United States in the thirties and of Communists everywhere are cases in point. Yet the issue of the national interest versus other-national interests masquer-

[13] *The Idea of National Interest: An Analytical Study in American Foreign Policy* (New York: Macmillan Co., 1934).

ading as the national interest has arisen constantly in the United States in a less clear-cut fashion.

A country that had been settled by consecutive waves of "foreigners" was bound to find it particularly difficult to identify its own national interest against alleged, seeming, or actual other-national interests represented by certain groups among its own citizens. Since virtually all citizens of the United States are, as it were, "more or less" foreign born, those who were "less" so have frequently not resisted the temptation to use this distinction as a polemic weapon against latecomers who happened to differ from them in their conception of the national interest of the United States. Frequently, this rationalization has been dispensed with, and a conception of foreign policy with which a writer happened to disagree has been attributed outright to foreign sympathy or influence or worse. British influence and interests have served as standard arguments in debates on American foreign policy. Madison, in his polemic against Hamilton on the occasion of Washington's neutrality proclamation of 1793, identified the Federalist position with that of "the foreigners and degenerate citizens among us, who hate our republican government, and the French revolution,"[14] and the accusation met with a favorable response in a majority of Congress and of public opinion. However, these traditional attempts to discredit dissenting opinion as being influenced by foreign interests should not obscure the real issue, which is the peculiar vulnerability of the national interest of the United States to usurpation by the interests of other nations.

This problem has become in our time particularly acute in the form of Communist subversion. The transference of an individual's allegiance from his own nation to another one, the Soviet Union, is here made peculiarly attractive by the identification of the interests of the Soviet Union with the interests of humanity, that is, the supranational interest par excellence. As the testimony before the royal commission investigating the Gouzenko case clearly shows, the sincere Communist identifies the interests of the Soviet Union with those of humanity and, hence, experiences his betrayal of the

---

[14] "Helvidius, in Answer to Pacificus, on President Washington's Proclamation of Neutrality," in *Letters and Other Writings of James Madison* (Philadelphia: J. B. Lippincott Co., 1867), I, 611.

interests of his own nation not as treason but rather as the establishment of the correct priority between lower and higher interests, the lower one having to yield in case of conflict to those that are superior.

The genuine usurpation of the national interest by supranational interests can derive in our time from two sources: religious bodies and international organizations. The competition between church and state for determination of certain interests and policies, domestic and international, has been an intermittent issue throughout the history of the nation state. Here, too, the legitimate defense of the national interest against usurpation has frequently, especially in the United States, degenerated into the demagogic stigmatization of dissenting views as being inspired by Rome and, hence, being incompatible with the national interest. Yet here, too, the misuse of the issue for demagogic purposes must be considered apart from the legitimacy of the issue itself.

The more acute problem arises at the present time from the importance which the public and government officials, at least in their public utterances, attribute to the values represented and the policies pursued by international organizations either as alternatives or supplements to the values and policies for which the national government stands. It is frequently asserted that the foreign policy of the United States pursues no objectives apart from those of the United Nations, that, in other words, the foreign policy of the United States is actually identical with the policy of the United Nations. This assertion cannot refer to anything real in actual politics to support it. For the constitutional structure of international organizations, such as the United Nations, and their procedural practices make it impossible for them to pursue interests apart from those of the member states which dominate their policy-forming bodies. The identity between the interests of the United Nations and the United States can only refer to the successful policies of the United States within the United Nations through which the support of the United Nations is being secured for the policies of the United States. The assertion, then, is mere polemic, different from the one discussed previously in that the identification of a certain policy with an assumed supranational interest does not seek to reflect discredit upon the former but to bestow upon it a dignity which the national interest pure and simple is supposed to lack.

The real issue in view of the problem that concerns us here is not whether the so-called interests of the United Nations, which do not exist apart from the interests of its most influential members, have superseded the national interest of the United States, but for what kind of interests the United States has secured United Nations support. While these interests cannot be United Nations interests, they do not need to be national interests either. Here we are in the presence of that modern phenomenon which has been variously described as "utopianism," "sentimentalism," "moralism," the "legalistic-moralistic approach." The common denominator of all these tendencies in modern political thought is the substitution for the national interest of an assumed supranational standard of action which is generally identified with an international organization. The national interest is here not being usurped by subnational or supranational interests which, however inferior in worth to the national interest, are nevertheless real and worthy of consideration within their proper sphere. What challenges the national interest here is a mere figment of the imagination, a product of wishful thinking, which is postulated as a valid norm for international conduct, without being valid either there or anywhere else. At this point we touch the core of the present controversy between utopianism and realism in international affairs; we shall return to it later.

The national interest as such must be defended against usurpation by non-national interests. Yet once that task is accomplished, a rational order must be established among the values which make up the national interest and among the resources to be committed to them. While the interests which a nation may pursue in its relation with other nations are of infinite variety and magnitude, the resources which are available for the pursuit of such interests are necessarily limited in quantity and kind. No nation has the resources to promote all desirable objectives with equal vigor; all nations must therefore allocate their scarce resources as rationally as possible. The indispensable precondition of such rational allocation is a clear understanding of the distinction between the necessary and variable elements of the national interest. Given the contentious manner in which in democracies the variable elements of the national interest are generally determined, the advocates of an extensive conception of the national interest will inevitably present certain variable elements of the national interest as though their attainment were necessary for the nation's survival. In other words, the necessary elements of the national interest have a tendency to swallow up the variable elements so that in the end all kinds of objectives, actual or potential, are justified in terms of national survival. Such arguments have been advanced, for instance, in support of the rearmament of West Germany and of the defense of Formosa. They must be subjected to rational scrutiny which will determine, however tentatively, their approximate place in the scale of national values.

The same problem presents itself in its extreme form when a nation pursues, or is asked to pursue, objectives that are not only unnecessary for its survival but tend to jeopardize it. Second-rate nations which dream of playing the role of great powers, such as Italy and Poland in the interwar period, illustrate this point. So do great powers which dream of remaking the world in their own image and embark upon world-wide crusades, thus straining their resources to exhaustion. Here scientific analysis has the urgent task of pruning down national objectives to the measure of available resources in order to make their pursuit compatible with national survival.

Finally, the national interest of a nation that is conscious not only of its own interests but also of that of other nations must be defined in terms compatible with the latter. In a multinational world this is a requirement of political morality; in an age of total war it is also a condition for survival.

Two mutually exclusive arguments have been brought to bear upon this problem. On the one hand, it has been argued against the theory of international politics here presented that the concept of the national interest revives the eighteenth-century concept of enlightened self-interest, presuming that the uniformly enlightened pursuit of their self-interest by all individuals, as by all nations, will of itself be conducive to a peaceful and harmonious society. On the other hand, the point has been made that the pursuit of their national interest by all nations makes war the permanent arbiter of conflicts among them. Neither argument is well taken.

The concept of the national interest presupposes neither a naturally harmonious, peaceful world nor the inevitability of war as a consequence of the pursuit by all nations of their national interest.

Quite to the contrary, it assumes continuous conflict and threat of war, to be minimized through the continuous adjustment of conflicting interests by diplomatic action. No such assumption would be warranted if all nations at all times conceived of their national interest only in terms of their survival and, in turn, defined their interest in survival in restrictive and rational terms. As it is, their conception of the national interest is subject to all the hazards of misinterpretation, usurpation, and misjudgment to which reference has been made above. To minimize these hazards is the first task of a foreign policy that seeks the defense of the national interest by peaceful means. Its second task is the defense of the national interest, restrictively and rationally defined, against the national interests of other nations which may or may not be thus defined. If they are not, it becomes the task of armed diplomacy to convince the nations concerned that their legitimate interests have nothing to fear from a restrictive and rational foreign policy and that their illegitimate interests have nothing to gain in the face of armed might rationally employed.

We have said before that the utopian and realist positions in international affairs do not necessarily differ in the policies they advocate, but that they part company over their general philosophies of politics and their way of thinking about matters political. It does not follow that the present debate is only of academic interest and without practical significance. Both camps, it is true, may support the same policy for different reasons. Yet if the reasons are unsound, the soundness of the policies supported by them is a mere coincidence, and these very same reasons may be, and inevitably are, invoked on other occasions in support of unsound policies. The nefarious consequences of false philosophies and wrong ways of thinking may for the time being be concealed by the apparent success of policies derived from them. You may go to war, justified by your nation's interests, for a moral purpose and in disregard of considerations of power; and military victory seems to satisfy both your moral aspirations and your nation's interests. Yet the manner in which you waged the war, achieved victory, and settled the peace cannot help reflecting your philosophy of politics and your way of thinking about political problems. If these are in error, you may win victory on the field of battle and still assist in the defeat of both your moral principles and the national interest of your country.

Any number of examples could illustrate the real yet subtle practical consequences which follow from the different positions taken. We have chosen two: collective security in Korea and the liberation of the nations that are captives of communism. A case for both policies can be made from both the utopian and the realist positions, but with significant differences in the emphasis and substance of the policies pursued.

Collective security as an abstract principle of utopian politics requires that all nations come to the aid of a victim of aggression by resisting the aggressor with all means necessary to frustrate his aims. Once the case of aggression is established, the duty to act is unequivocal. Its extent may be affected by concern for the nation's survival; obviously no nation will commit outright suicide in the service of collective security. But beyond that elemental limitation no consideration of interest or power, either with regard to the aggressor or his victim or the nation acting in the latter's defense, can qualify the obligation to act under the principle of collective security. Thus high officials of our government have declared that we intervened in Korea not for any narrow interest of ours but in support of the moral principle of collective security.

Collective security as a concrete principle of realist policy is the age-old maxim, "Hang together or hang separately," in modern dress. It recognizes the need for nation A under certain circumstances to defend nation B against attack by nation C. That need is determined, first, by the interest which A has in the territorial integrity of B and by the relation of that interest to all the other interests of A as well as to the resources available for the support of all those interests. Furthermore, A must take into account the power which is at the disposal of aggressor C for fighting A and B as over against the power available to A and B for fighting C. The same calculation must be carried on concerning the power of the likely allies of C as over against those of A and B. Before going to war for the defense of South Korea in the name of collective security, an American adherent of political realism would have demanded an answer to the following four questions: First, what is our interest in the preservation of the independence of South Korea;

second, what is our power to defend that independence against North Korea; third, what is our power to defend that independence against China and the Soviet Union; and fourth, what are the chances for preventing China and the Soviet Union from entering the Korean War?

In view of the principle of collective security, interpreted in utopian terms, our intervention in Korea was a foregone conclusion. The interpretation of this principle in realist terms might or might not, depending upon the concrete circumstances of interest and power, have led us to the same conclusion. In the execution of the policy of collective security the utopian had to be indifferent to the possibility of Chinese and Russian intervention, except for his resolution to apply the principle of collective security to anybody who would intervene on the side of the aggressor. The realist could not help weighing the possibility of the intervention of a great power on the side of the aggressor in terms of the interests engaged and the power available on the other side.[15]

The Truman administration could not bring itself to take resolutely the utopian or the realist position. It resolved to intervene in good measure on utopian grounds and in spite of military advice to the contrary; it allowed the military commander to advance to the Yalu River in disregard of the risk of the intervention of a great power against which collective security could be carried out only by means of a general war, and then refused to pursue the war with full effectiveness on the realist grounds of the risk of a third world war. Thus Mr. Truman in 1952 was caught in the same dilemma from which Mr. Baldwin could extricate himself in 1936 on the occasion of the League of Nations sanctions against Italy's attack upon Ethiopia only at an enormous loss to British prestige. Collective security as a defense of the status quo short of a general war can be effective only against second-rate powers. Applied against a major power, it is a contradiction in terms, for it means necessarily a major war. Of this self-defeating contradiction Mr. Baldwin

[15] The difference in these two attitudes is well illustrated by the following passage from a Moon Mullins cartoon. An elderly representative of the utopian school asks little Kayo: "Remember the golden rule. Now, supposing that boy slapped you on the right cheek, what would you do?" Whereupon Kayo replies realistically: "Jest how big a boy are you supposin'?"

was as unaware in the thirties as Mr. Truman seemed to be in 1952. Mr. Churchill put Mr. Baldwin's dilemma in these cogent terms: "First, the Prime Minister had declared that sanctions meant war; secondly, he was resolved that there must be no war; and thirdly, he decided upon sanctions. It was evidently impossible to comply with these three conditions." Similarly Mr. Truman had declared that the effective prosecution of the Korean War meant the possibility of a third world war; he resolved that there must be no third world war; and he decided upon intervention in the Korean War. Here, too, it was impossible to comply with these three conditions.

Similar contradictions are inherent in the proposals which would substitute for the policy of containment the liberation of the nations presently the captives of Russian communism. This objective can be compatible with the utopian or realist position, but the policies designed to secure it will be fundamentally different according to whether they are based upon one or the other position. A clear case for the utopian justification of such policies was made by Representative Charles J. Kersten of Wisconsin, who pointed to these four "basic defects" of the "negative policy of containment and negotiated coexistence":

It would be immoral and unchristian to negotiate a permanent agreement with forces which by every religious creed and moral precept are evil. It abandons nearly one-half of humanity and the once free nations of Poland, Czechoslovakia, Hungary, Rumania, Bulgaria, Albania, Lithuania, Latvia, Esthonia and China to enslavement of the Communist police state.

It is un-American because it violates the principle of the American Declaration of Independence, which proclaims the rights of all people to freedom and their right and duty to throw off tyranny.

It will lead to all-out World War III because it aligns all the forces of the non-Communist world in military opposition to and against all the forces of the Communist world, including the 800,000,000 peoples behind the Iron Curtain.

The policy of mere containment is uneconomic and will lead to national bankruptcy.[16]

This statement is interesting for its straightforwardness and because it combines in a rather typical fashion considerations of abstract morality and of expediency. The captive nations must be liberated not only because their captivity is immoral, unchristian,

[16] *New York Times,* August 14, 1952, p. 1.

and un-American, but also because its continuation will lead to a third world war and to national bankruptcy. To what extent, however, these considerations of expediency are invalidated by their utopian setting will become obvious from a comparison between the utopian and the realist positions.

From the utopian point of view there can be no difference between the liberation of Estonia or Czechoslovakia, of Poland or China; the captivity of any nation, large or small, close or far away, is a moral outrage which cannot be tolerated. The realist, too, seeks the liberation of all captive nations because he realizes that the presence of the Russian armies in the heart of Europe and their cooperation with the Chinese armies constitute the two main sources of the imbalance of power which threatens our security. Yet before he formulates a program of liberation, he will seek answers to a number of questions such as these: While the United States has a general interest in the liberation of all captive nations, what is the hierarchy of interests it has in the liberation, say, of China, Estonia, and Hungary? And while the Soviet Union has a general interest in keeping all captive nations in that state, what is the hierarchy of its interests in keeping, say, Poland, East Germany, and Bulgaria captive? If we assume, as we must on the historic evidence of two centuries, that Russia would at present not give up control over Poland without being compelled by force of arms, would the objective of the liberation of Poland justify the ruin of Western civilization, that of Poland included, which would be the certain result of a third world war? What resources does the United States have at its disposal for the liberation of all captive nations or some of them? What resources does the Soviet Union have at its disposal to keep in captivity all captive nations or some of them? Are we more likely to avoid national bankruptcy by embarking upon a policy of indiscriminate liberation with the concomitant certainty of war or by continuing the present policy of containment?

It might be that in a particular instance the policies suggested by the answers to these questions will coincide with Representative Kersten's proposals, but there can be no doubt that in its over-all character, substance, emphasis, and likely consequences a utopian policy of liberation differs fundamentally from a realist one.

The issue between liberation as a utopian principle of abstract morality versus the realist evaluation of the consequences which a policy of liberation would have for the survival of the nation has arisen before in American history. Abraham Lincoln was faced with a dilemma similar to that which confronts us today. Should he make the liberation of the slaves the ultimate standard of his policy even at the risk of destroying the Union, as many urged him to do, or should he subordinate the moral principle of universal freedom to considerations of the national interest? The answer Lincoln gave to Horace Greeley, a spokesman for the utopian moralists, is timeless in its eloquent wisdom. "If there be those," he wrote on August 22, 1862,

who would not save the Union unless they could at the same time save slavery, I do not agree with them. If there be those who would not save the Union unless they could at the same time destroy slavery, I do not agree with them. My paramount object in this struggle *is* to save the Union, and is *not* either to save or to destroy slavery. If I could save the Union without freeing *any* slave I would do it, and if I could save it by freeing *all* the slaves, I would do it; and if I could save it by freeing some and leaving others alone I would also do that. What I do about slavery, and the colored race, I do because I believe it helps to save the Union; and what I forbear, I forbear because I do *not* believe it would help to save the Union. I shall do *less* whenever I shall believe what I am doing hurts the cause, and I shall do *more* whenever I shall believe doing more will help the cause. I shall try to correct errors when shown to be errors; and I shall adopt new views so fast as they shall appear to be true views.

I have here stated my purpose according to my view of *official* duty; and I intend no modification of my oft-expressed *personal* wish that all men everywhere could be free.

The foregoing discussion ought to shed additional light, if this is still needed, upon the moral merits of the utopian and realist positions. This question, more than any other, seems to have agitated the critics of realism in international affairs. Disregarding the voluminous evidence, some of them have picked a few words out of their context to prove that realism in international affairs is unprincipled and contemptuous of morality. To mention but one example, one eminent critic summarizes my position, which he supposes to deny the possibility of judging the conduct of states by moral criteria, in these words: "And one spokesman finds 'a profound and neglected truth,' to use his words, in the dictum of Hobbes that 'there is neither morality nor law outside the state.' "[17] These are indeed my words, but not all of them. What I actually said was this: "There is a profound and neglected truth hidden in Hobbes's extreme dictum that the state creates morality as well as law and that there is neither morality nor law outside the state. Universal moral principles, such as justice or equality, are capable of guiding political action only to the extent that they have been given concrete content and have been related to political situations by society."[18]

It must be obvious from this passage and from all my other writings on the subject that my position is the exact opposite from what this critic makes it out to be.[19] I have always maintained that the actions of states are subject to universal moral principles, and I have been careful to differentiate my position in this respect from that of Hobbes. Five points basic to my position may need to be emphasized again.

The first point is what one might call the requirement of cosmic humility with regard to the moral evaluation of the actions of states. To know that states are subject to the moral law is one thing; to pretend to know what is morally required of states in a particular situation is quite another. The human mind tends naturally to identify the particular interests of states, as of individuals, with the moral purposes of the universe. The statesman in the defense of the nation's interests may, and at times even must, yield to that tendency; the scholar must resist it at every turn. For the lighthearted assumption that what one's own nation aims at and does is morally good and that those who oppose that nation's policies are evil is morally

[17] A. H. Feller, "In Defense of International Law and Morality," *Annals of the American Academy of Political and Social Science,* CCLXXXII (July, 1952), 80.

[18] *In Defense of the National Interest: A Critical Examination of American Foreign Policy* (New York: Alfred A. Knopf, 1951), p. 34.

[19] See, for instance, "The Machiavellian Utopia," *Ethics,* LV (January, 1945), 145–47; "Ethics and Politics," in *Approaches to Group Understanding* (Sixth Symposium of the Conference on Science, Philosophy and Religion), ed. Lyman Bryson *et al.* (New York, 1947), pp. 319–41; *Scientific Man vs. Power Politics* (Chicago: University of Chicago Press, 1946), chaps. 7, 8; "Views of Nuremberg: Further Analysis of the Trial and Its Importance," *America,* LXXVI (December 7, 1946), 266–67; "The Twilight of International Morality," *Ethics,* LVIII (January, 1948), 79–99; *Politics among Nations* (2d ed.; New York: Alfred A. Knopf, 1954), chap. 16; "National Interest and Moral Principles in Foreign Policy: The Primacy of the National Interest," *American Scholar,* XVIII (Spring, 1949), 207–12. See also below, chap. 21.

indefensible and intellectually untenable and leads in practice to that distortion of judgment, born of the blindness of crusading frenzy, which has been the curse of nations from the beginning of time.

The second point which obviously needs to be made again concerns the effectiveness of the restraints which morality imposes upon the actions of states.

A discussion of international morality must guard against the two extremes either of overrating the influence of ethics upon international politics or else of denying that statesmen and diplomats are moved by anything else but considerations of material power.

On the one hand, there is the dual error of confounding the moral rules which people actually observe with those they pretend to observe as well as with those which writers declare they ought to observe. . . .

On the other hand, there is the misconception, usually associated with the general depreciation and moral condemnation of power politics, discussed above, that international politics is so thoroughly evil that it is no use looking for ethical limitations of the aspirations for power on the international scene. Yet, if we ask ourselves what statesmen and diplomats are capable of doing to further the power objectives of their respective nations and what they actually do, we realize that they do less than they probably could and less than they actually did in other periods of history. They refuse to consider certain ends and to use certain means, either altogether or under certain conditions, not because in the light of expediency they appear impractical or unwise, but because certain moral rules interpose an absolute barrier. Moral rules do not permit certain policies to be considered at all from the point of view of expediency. Such ethical inhibitions operate in our time on different levels with different effectiveness. Their restraining function is most obvious and most effective in affirming the sacredness of human life in times of peace.[20]

In connection with this passage we gave a number of historic examples showing the influence of moral principles upon the conduct of foreign policy. An example taken from contemporary history will illustrate the same point. There can be little doubt that the Soviet Union could have achieved the objectives of its foreign policy at the end of the Second World War without antagonizing the nations of the West into that encircling coalition which has been the nightmare of Bolshevist foreign policy since 1917. It could have mitigated cunning for its own sake and the use of force with persuasion, conciliation, and a trust derived from the awareness of a partial community of interests and would thereby have minimized the dan-

[20] Morgenthau, *Politics among Nations,* pp. 210–16.

gers to itself and the rest of the world which are inherent in the objectives of its policies. Yet the Soviet Union was precluded from relying upon these traditional methods of diplomacy by its general conception of human nature, politics, and morality. In the general philosophy of Bolshevism there is no room for honest dissent, the recognition of the intrinsic worth of divergent interests, and genuine conciliation between such interests. On all levels of social interaction opposition must be destroyed by cunning and violence, since it has no right to exist, rather than be met halfway in view of its intrinsic legitimacy. This being the general conception of the political morality of Bolshevism, the foreign policy of the Soviet Union is limited to a much more narrow choice of means than the foreign policies of other nations.

The United States, for instance, has been able, in its relations with the nations of Latin America, to replace military intervention and dollar diplomacy with the policy of the Good Neighbor. That drastic change was made possible by the general conception of political morality which has been prevalent in the United States from its very inception. The United States is a pluralist society which presupposes the continuing existence and legitimacy of divergent interests. These interests are locked in a continuing struggle for supremacy to be decided by force only as a last resort but, normally, through a multitude of institutions which are so devised as to allow one or the other interest a temporary advantage but none a permanent supremacy at the price of the destruction of the others. This morality of pluralism allows the United States, once it is secure in that minimum of vital interests to which we have referred above, to transfer those principles of political morality to the international scene and to deal with divergent interests there with the same methods of genuine compromise and conciliation which are a permanent element of its domestic political life.

The third point concerns the relations between universal moral principles and political action. I have always maintained that these universal moral principles cannot be applied to the actions of states in their abstract universal formulation but that they must be, as it were, filtered through the concrete circumstances of time and place. The individual may say for himself: *Fiat justitia, pereat mundus;* the state has no right to say so in the name of those who are in its care.

Both individual and state must judge political action by universal moral principles, such as that of liberty. Yet while the individual has a moral right to sacrifice himself in defense of such a moral principle, the state has no moral right to let its moral disapprobation of the infringement of liberty get in the way of successful political action, itself inspired by the moral principle of national survival. There can be no political morality without prudence, that is, without consideration of the political consequences of seemingly moral action. Classical and medieval philosophy knew this and so did Lincoln when he said: "I do the very best I know how, the very best I can, and I mean to keep doing so until the end. If the end brings me out all right, what is said against me won't amount to anything. If the end brings me out wrong, ten angels swearing I was right would make no difference." The issue between utopianism and realism, as it bears on this point, has been put most succinctly by Edmund Burke, and what he has to say in the following passage about revolution, that is, civil war, may well be applied *mutatis mutandis* to all war.

Nothing universal can be rationally affirmed on any moral or any political subject. Pure metaphysical abstraction does not belong to these matters. The lines of morality are not like the ideal lines of mathematics. They are broad and deep as well as long. They admit of exceptions; they demand modifications. These exceptions and modifications are not made by the process of logic, but by the rules of prudence. Prudence is not only the first in rank of the virtues political and moral, but she is the director, the regulator, the standard of them all. Metaphysics cannot live without definition; but Prudence is cautious how she defines. Our courts cannot be more fearful in suffering fictitious cases to be brought before them for eliciting their determination on a point of law than prudent moralists are in putting extreme and hazardous cases of conscience upon emergencies not existing. Without attempting, therefore, to define, what never can be defined, the case of a revolution in government, this, I think, may be safely affirmed—that a sore and pressing evil is to be removed, and that a good, great in its amount and unequivocal in its nature, must be probable almost to a certainty, before the inestimable price of our own morals and the well-being of a number of our fellow-citizens is paid for a revolution. If ever we ought to be economists even to parsimony, it is in the voluntary production of evil. Every revolution contains in it something of evil.[21]

21 *The Works of The Right Honorable Edmund Burke* (4th ed.; Boston Little, Brown & Co., 1871), IV, 80–81. Cf. also Burke, "Speech on a Bill fc Shortening the Duration of Parliaments, May 8, 1780," *ibid.*, VII, 73: "I must se

Fourth, the realist recognizes that a moral decision, especially in the political sphere, does not imply a simple choice between a moral principle and a standard of action which is morally irrelevant or even outright immoral. A moral decision implies always a choice among different moral principles, one of which is given precedence over others. To say that a political action has no moral purpose is absurd; for political action can be defined as an attempt to realize moral values through the medium of politics, that is, power. The relevant moral question concerns the choice among different moral values, and it is at this point that the realist and the utopian part company again. If an American statesman must choose between the promotion of universal liberty, which is a moral good, at the risk of American security and, hence, of liberty in the United States, on the one hand, and the promotion of American security and of liberty in the United States, which is another moral good, to the detriment of the promotion of universal liberty, on the other, which choice ought he to make? The utopian will not face the issue squarely and will deceive himself into believing that he can achieve both goods at the same time. The realist will choose the national interest on both moral and pragmatic grounds; for if he does not take care of the national interest nobody else will, and if he puts American security and liberty in jeopardy the cause of liberty everywhere will be impaired.

Finally, the political realist distinguishes between his moral sympathies and the political interests which he must defend. He will distinguish with Lincoln between his *"official duty"* which is to protect the national interest and his *"personal wish"* which is to see universal moral values realized throughout the world.

The issue has been admirably put by Father Wilfred Parsons of Catholic University in defending Mr. Kennan's position:

Mr. Kennan did not say state behavior is not a fit subject for moral judgment, but only that it should not sway our realization of the realities with

---

to satisfy me, the remedies; I must see, from their operation in the cure of the old evil, and in the cure of those new evils which are inseparable from all remedies, how they balance each other, and what is the total result. The excellence of mathematics and metaphysics is, to have but one thing before you; but he forms the best judgment in all moral disquisitions who has the greatest number and variety of consideration in one view before him, and can take them in with the best possible consideration of the middle results of all."

which we have to deal. Msgr. Koenig continues: "Should we accept power realities and aspirations without feeling the obligation of moral judgment?" And he appeals to the present writer and other political scientists to say whether this doctrine agrees with Pope Pius XII's messages on peace.

I am sure that most political scientists, and also Mr. Kennan, would agree with the Monsignor that we should not accept those realities "without feeling the obligation of moral judgment." But there is a difference between *feeling* this obligation (and even expressing it) and allowing this feeling to sway our actions in concrete negotiations that deal with the national or world common good. We can still feel and yet deal.

To make my meaning clearer, I understood Mr. Kennan to hold that we went off the beam with Woodrow Wilson, when we began to make our moral disapprobation an *essential part* of our foreign relations, even sometimes at the expense of our own and the world's common good Logically, such an attitude would inhibit our dealing with Britain, France and a host of countries. Pius XI, speaking of Mussolini after the Lateran Treaty, said he would deal with the devil himself if he must. Here was moral disapprobation, but it was not "carried over into the affairs of states."

This relative position, and not the absolute one of Msgr. Koenig (with which in itself I agree), is, I think, the issue raised by Mr. Kennan, and it is worth debating on that basis.[22]

The contest between utopianism and realism is not tantamount to a contest between principle and expediency, morality and immorality, although some spokesmen for the former would like to have it that way. The contest is rather between one type of political morality and another type of political morality, one taking as its standard universal moral principles abstractly formulated, the other weighing these principles against the moral requirements of concrete political action, their relative merits to be decided by a prudent evaluation of the political consequences to which they are likely to lead.[23]

[22] *America,* LXXXVI (March 29, 1952), 700. See also Algernon Cecil, "The Foreign Office," in *The Cambridge History of British Foreign Policy, 1783–1919* (Cambridge: Cambridge University Press, 1923), III, 605, concerning Lord Salisbury: "Always, however, the motive of his policy was to be found in the political interests as opposed to the political sympathies of Great Britain; and in this way his treatment of Foreign Affairs is at the opposite policy from that of Palmerston and Gladstone." Cf. also the general remarks in Alexander H. Leighton, *Human Relations in a Changing World* (New York: E. P. Dutton & Co., 1949), pp. 155 ff.

[23] See, on this point, Shirley R. Letwin, "Rationalism, Principles, and Politics," *Review of Politics,* XIV (July, 1952), 367–93; L. Susan Stebbing, *Ideals and Illusions* (London: Watts & Co., 1951); Vernon H. Holloway, *Religious Ethics and the Politics of Power* (New York: Church Peace Union and World Alliance for International Friendship through Religion, 1951); and Dorothy Fosdick,

These points are re-emphasized by the foregoing discussion. Which attitude with regard to collective security and to the liberation of the captive nations, the utopian or the realist, is more likely to safeguard the survival of the United States in its territorial, political, and cultural identity and at the same time to contribute the most to the security and liberty of other nations? This is the ultimate test—political and moral—by which utopianism and realism must be judged.

"Ethical Standards and Political Strategies," *Political Science Quarterly,* LVII (1942), 214 ff.

7 *International Relations as an Academic Discipline*

The assumption that a central concept is necessary for the theoretical understanding of politics has been disputed implicitly through the development of theories of politics which are lacking in such a central concept and explicitly in the form of an attack upon the suggested central concept of power. The question of whether such a central concept is necessary at all and, if so, which one it ought to be has divided opinion on all levels of theory and practice. It has done so also on the level of academic curriculum and organization. The controversy about the nature and the proper place of international relations and area studies as academic disciplines is a manifestation of that division of opinion concerning the fundamental problem of understanding politics.

These two novel academic disciplines must solve the same basic problems. If one wants to put the issue in epigrammatic and, therefore, oversimplified form, one might say that the main problem, as yet unsolved, that confronts these two academic "disciplines" is that they have not been able to acquire intellectual discipline. They have no intellectually valid focus which could give unity to their intellectual endeavors, and they have no common method by which the results of their investigations could be tested. These deficiencies have been as obvious in the study of international relations as they are in area studies. They are the more obvious in the latter, since area studies have made integration their main claim for recognition as an academic discipline. Area studies are in the process of showing —and the most mature discussion of their problems shows it with particular clarity—that they stand and fall with the precise formulation of a relevant problem to which different academic disciplines are to contribute. If area studies can demonstrate in practice that success in international studies, area or otherwise, depends upon the precise definition of a common problem and the sharp focus of all relevant research upon that problem, they will indeed have made an outstanding contribution to the study of international relations.

From the *International Social Science Bulletin*, 1952, No. 4; and Bland Blanshard (ed.), *Education in the Age of Science* (1959).

When after the First World War the study of international relations gained recognition as an independent academic discipline, it had three main intellectual interests: history, international law, and political reform. It is not by accident that the first two occupants of the first chair of international politics, the one which was founded in 1919 at the University of Wales, were distinguished historians, Professors Zimmern and Webster. There can of course be no doubt that knowledge of history and, more particularly, of diplomatic history forms an indispensable element of international relations; but, as will be shown later, while the student of international relations must have a thorough knowledge of history, his intellectual interest is not identical with that of the historian.

Obviously, the intellectual interest of international relations is in the present and the future rather than in the past and, especially in the interwar years, that interest was conceived in terms of international law. International relations were considered to move on two different levels: the legal one which presented the rules by which states were supposed to act, and the empirical one which showed how they actually did act in view of the rules of international law. Thus general history, diplomatic history, and international law became three cornerstones of the study of international relations.

The fourth cornerstone of the study of international relations is less easy to identify. For it is formed by the aspirations for a better world, morally respectable in themselves but vaguely conceived and identified with whatever remedy seems to be fashionable at a particular time. Thus we find that the focus of academic interest changes continuously in accordance with the preferences of public opinion, centering on disarmament one day, the League of Nations or the United Nations another, world government or regional federation another again.

The interstices between those four cornerstones are filled in with an incoherent collection of fragmentary knowledge ranging the whole gamut of academic disciplines and having only one thing in common: that they transcend the boundaries of a particular nation. The tone is set in the letter offering in 1919 a chair of international politics to the University of Wales and describing its purposes as "the study of those related problems of law and politics, of ethics and economics, which are raised by the project of a League of Nations, and for the encouragement of a truer understanding of civilizations other than our own." Reading the voluminous proceedings of the International Institute of Intellectual Co-operation, which in the interwar years dedicated much of its work to the discussion of international relations as an academic discipline, one cannot but be struck by the amorphousness of the discussion and the vagueness of the results. One speaker seems to have well summarized the consensus of those meetings when he said:

The science of international relations has primarily a descriptive character. It is somewhat in the order of the contemporary history of nations, covering all fields: economics, trade, exchange, movement of production, of goods, of currency, as well as politics and culture. ... The factor uniting the problems which form the science of international relations is their international character, that is to say, the tie which is created among all domains of social life when that life transgresses the limits of one single nation and influences the relations among nations.[1]

The same consensus is reflected in the ironic comment, rare in its critical detachment, of another speaker who expressed himself thus:

One can without doubt call international any phenomenon because it belongs to all countries. Anything one wants to then becomes international. From this point of view, seasickness is an international fact; not only does one experience it on all oceans; but there are societies against that disease, and one can conceive of an international league whose purpose it is to do research and compare the methods with which to combat the disease. Yet the question remains outside our field of inquiry until one concerns oneself with the conclusion of an international convention obligating vessels to equip themselves with certain medicines which are recognized as necessary for the protection against seasickness.

I beg your pardon for having chosen that imaginary example. I wanted only to indicate the need for a narrow definition of international studies.[2]

The organization of academic teaching and research in international relations has largely reflected the vagueness and eclecticism of the theoretical conception of international relations as an academic discipline. There has been a general tendency to divide the field of international relations into a number of subdivisions whose common denominator is their transcendence of national boundaries either geographically or functionally. These subdivisions were selected

---

[1] Antoni Deryng, in *Coopération intellectuelle*, No. 68–69 (Paris, 1936), p. 33. Translated from the French by the author.

[2] Paul Mantoux, in *Coopération intellectuelle*, No. 57–58 (Paris, 1935), p. 490. My translation.

from the traditional academic disciplines either *in toto*, such as international law and international economics, or rearranged through the selection of individual courses taken from different disciplines. Thus all the courses which, for instance, had a reference to Russia in their title would be grouped under the area heading of Russia.

It could not have passed unnoticed that the intellectual unity of an academic field, thus established, was bound to be of a most superficial nature and that where there occurred real integration and cross-fertilization among several academic disciplines, credit was due to the creative process occurring in the minds of outstanding students rather than to the academic organization of the field. Attempts have therefore been made to give international relations the unity of an academic discipline by buttressing the eclectic organization of the field with a general or "core" course or number of courses which are supposed to present the distinctive characteristics of international relations as an academic discipline. This core generally covers the fields of international law, international organization, international politics, international economics, international geography, American and European diplomatic history, with such additions as meet the preferences of individual institutions. Most textbooks in the field reflect the eclectic character of this core. For such a core, if it has no focus other than that of the "international" character of international relations, cannot help being as eclectic and disparate as the field itself.

The problems with which area studies must cope are similar, *mutatis mutandis*, to those with which the academic discipline of international relations has dealt thus far without spectacular success. The central problem is again that of focus and method. Area studies, both historically and analytically, form a part of the field of international relations. The type of area study which is prevalent today owes its existence to the practical need to prepare members of the armed forces for service in foreign countries during the Second World War. Those who were expected to take responsible positions in foreign countries had to get acquainted as quickly as possible with the language, geography, culture, and history of those countries. Not only were these training courses successful in their immediate purpose; they also put into sharp focus a foreign area not in terms of the traditional academic disciplines but, as it were, in terms of the characteristics and problems of the area itself upon which the methods of all the relevant disciplines would be brought to bear. The process by which this objective is to be accomplished is generally called "integration"; the effect of this process upon the minds of the student goes by the name of "cross-fertilization."

Practical needs, if on a higher intellectual level, still provide one of the major arguments in favor of area studies; they are also apparrent in the selection of the areas most frequently studied. Russia and Asia vie with each other for the attention of students and the commitment of resources. It is not by accident that it is with those areas that American foreign policy is primarily concerned and that knowledge of them is fragmentary and the supply of experts available for government service falls drastically below demand. Nor is it an accident that the areas around which area studies are centered are generally defined in terms which coincide with the areas of political interest.

Aside from the training of prospective government officials, area studies are frequently motivated by the recognition of America's predominant place in world affairs, which necessitates a knowledge of the world with which the United States must deal as friend or foe. This higher level of practicality entails the desire to learn all the facts about all the regions of the world. Since the regions of prime political importance seem already to be adequately covered, late-comers among university administrations have been known to search for empty spaces on the map which they might cover with an institute for area studies. Underlying this tendency is the conviction that knowledge of unknown areas is useful in itself and that the more knowledge of this kind there is, the better will we be able to understand the world and discharge our responsibilities toward it.

The purely intellectual objectives which are connected with area studies—generally in theory and sometimes also in practice—number three. One stands on the borderline between theory and practice, one is conceived from the perspective of the social sciences, and one from that of the humanities. Area studies are aimed at conveying the experience of cultural relativity which will enable us to do justice to foreign cultures in our intellectual judgment, moral evaluation, and aesthetic appreciation and will at the same time enable us to deal effectively with foreign areas, that is, on their own terms rather than through the imposition of our culture on theirs. Furthermore, area studies are expected to contribute to the development of a universal social science which will arise from the isolation, analysis, and comparison of similar phenomena in different cultures. Finally, they are supposed to provide the intellectual and aesthetic satisfaction that comes from the understanding of any culture in all its manifestations.

These different objectives of area studies are not necessarily incompatible with one another. Yet it is obviously impossible to plan for all of them with equal emphasis at the same time. If they are all achieved at once, some of them are bound to be the by-products of those for the sake of which the studies were undertaken. There can be little doubt that in practice, as concerns the delimitation and selection of areas as well as the development of concrete research projects, practical considerations have generally prevailed over purely intellectual ones.

An interdisciplinary science of areas, in order to be theoretically valid and practically useful, must be mindful of seven principles which apply to all social sciences but which have been insufficiently heeded by area studies in particular and by international relations in general:

First, a non-directive, "objective" social science is, as we have seen, a contradiction in terms. All social sciences, in so far as they deserve the name of science at all, cannot fail to reflect both the social *Standort* and the particular intellectual interest of the observer. A social science which strives for unattainable objectivity can at best collect the raw materials of science in the form of a mass of unrelated or but superficially and irrelevantly related facts. Social science is of necessity science from a certain point of view, and that point of view is determined by the over-all outlook of the scholar as well as by the particular interest with which the scholar approaches the segment of social reality which he intends to investigate.

Second, it follows that the quantity of facts collected is not necessarily proportionate to the quantity of truth discovered. In order to understand a particular area it is not necessary, even if it were possible, to know all the facts about it. Nor is it true that our knowledge of the world around us increases necessarily with the number of areas investigated and the number of facts known about those areas.

Third, regardless of whether the immediate purpose of area research is theoretical or practical, only a theoretical approach to area research can assure useful, practical results, which are not useful merely by accident. A non-theoretical approach to area research can do no more than elaborate upon the common-sense approach which the layman uses when he must solve a practical problem. An area study, to be useful not only for the practical problems raised by yesterday's news but for a whole series of practical problems to be expected in the future, must rest on theoretical foundations which are able to support a whole series of practical solutions by virtue of their theoretical nature.

Fourth, an area for research is not necessarily identical with a geographical, political, or cultural area. The definition of the area and of the problems to be investigated within the area is a function of the intellectual interest of the scholar. Theoretically, then, one can imagine as many definitions of areas and of area problems as there are scholars interested in that particular region. In practice, of course, the number of area definitions and problem selections is limited by the number of legitimate intellectual interests with which members of a certain culture will approach other areas at a particular time. Obviously, scholarly interest in the Soviet Union today is focused in a certain way by the general intellectual interests of our culture in which all potentially interested scholars partake.

Fifth, it follows from this observation that the interdisciplinary approach to area studies that is likely to proceed by way of integration and to result in cross-fertilization must be more than the addition of a number of different disciplines concerned with the same area and the same problems within that area. The unifying element in an interdisciplinary area study is not the common concern with an area or even the common concern with certain problems within that area. It is rather the identity of focus directed toward the same problems within the same area which gives unity to an interdisciplinary area study. In other words, representatives of different disciplines stand, as it were, on the same hill looking in the same direction at the same object and try to discern the same thing about this object, be it its nature, its movements, its influence upon other objects, or the influence to which it is subjected by other objects, and the like. These onlookers differ, however, in the kind of instruments they use in order to discern the common object of thèir intellectual curiosity. This is integrated area research.

Since the different scholars use different instruments on the same object, they are bound to see different qualities in that object. By communicating to each other what they have seen, the minds of all concerned correlate the results of the researches of the others with their own. This mutual communication is what is called "cross-fertilization."

Sixth, the different disciplines that are brought to bear upon an area problem are not equal with each other. If they were, true and full integration would be impossible. We have said that integrated research means that different disciplines want to know the same thing about the same object. But who determines what that same thing is going to be? Area research may center upon the economic structure of the Siamese village, and then it is economics which determines the common object of intellectual curiosity; and the other disciplines called in for co-operation, such as anthropology, geography, political science, must subordinate their own specific interests to the interests of economics. Or we are interested in the political structure of the Siamese village, and then it is political science which sets the theme and determines the outlook of the auxiliary sciences. In one word, interdisciplinary area research requires more "discipline" than disciplinary research; for it requires the subordination of the specific interests of certain disciplines to the dominant one. Integration requires a hierarchy of interests in which one interest has the function of integrating the others.

Seventh, underlying all area research must be the awareness that all the specific manifestations of a particular culture contain an element of universality, however undiscoverable or unprovable it may be in a particular instance. Area research, then, must take into account an element that transcends the limits of any particular area. More than that, it is this transcendent element which makes area research possible in the first place. For if we could not assume that, while investigating a foreign area, we should find not only things that are strange but also things that are familiar, we would not be able even to try to understand a foreign area and would face it un-comprehendingly.

The element of universality, transcending any particular area and common to all, may be called human nature. However different its specific manifestations at different times and places, it is the same everywhere and at all times. Without assuming its identity in time and space, we could see in other cultures, past or present, nothing more than either a mass of incomprehensible facts or else a distorted image of our own culture. Thus every historian and area specialist must assume implicitly the identity of human nature in time and space in order to be able to understand at all, however loudly he may deny its existence. It is at this point that we come face to face with what is perhaps the most serious shortcoming of contemporary area studies.

Contemporary area studies assume that the key to the understanding of a foreign area lies in the investigation of the specific phenomena that make up that area. If we want to understand China we must study China; if we want to understand France we must study France. Yet might it not be said that, in order to understand China or France or any other area, it is first necessary to understand mankind, of which all areas are but particular manifestations? If I know something about human nature as such, I know something about Chinese and Frenchmen, for I know something about all men. It is true that this something I know about all men is general and liable to lead me astray if I try to explain through it the concreteness of a particular historical situation. Yet without such a conception of human nature, made articulate in a philosophy of man and society, a foreign area can be no more than a mysterious oddity, attractive or repulsive as the case may be, and at best to be understood in terms of one's own culture.

That this is not mere idle speculation everyday experience shows. Why is it that I am able to understand the Homeric heroes or Chaucer's pilgrims without having mastered the area research of ancient Troy and medieval England? Why is it that I am able to comprehend the domestic and foreign policies of contemporary Russia without being an area specialist in the Russian field? Why is it that I have a general understanding of contemporary China while I am virtually ignorant about China as an area? Why is it that the members of the British foreign service have been traditionally trained in the humanities and more particularly in the classics and then sent in succession to the four corners of the earth, showing frequently superb understanding of the areas in which they worked? The answer to these questions has already been given: if you know something about man as such you know something about all men. You know at least the contours of human nature which, when superimposed upon a concrete situation, may get blurred here and there and which always lack specific content and color. It is for area studies to provide an empirical check upon their correctness and that specific content and color. This, then, is a plea not for giving up area studies as at present executed and for reviving an exclusive humanistic approach, but rather for the recognition of the limitations of both. The future of area studies seems to lie in a combination of both approaches, with the emphasis upon one or the other according to the qualifications and preferences of the group undertaking such research.

A word might be said in passing about the lessons to be learned from the traditional classical studies which frequently have been referred to as the prototype of the area studies of our day. This they are not; for what distinguishes traditional classical studies and contemporary area studies is exactly the philosophical orientation in the former and lack of such orientation in the latter. The rationale underlying classical studies was no practical purpose or curiosity for its own sake or a special research interest, but the conviction that in the civilization of ancient Greece and Rome the nature of man in all its manifestations could be detected in its purest form, to be emulated by the generations to come. The error of that approach was its cultural absolutism which took classical civilization to be the norm by which all other civilizations were to be judged. The truth of classical studies, largely ignored by contemporary area studies, is to be found in their conviction, accepted as self-evident, that the study of any civilization requires an underlying conception of the nature of man which gives direction and form to the research to be undertaken.

Since what is wrong with area studies also handicaps international relations as an academic discipline, the remedies in both cases must be, *mutatis mutandis*, the same. We have seen that international relations has concerned itself indiscriminately with everything that is "international," that is, that transcends the boundaries of a particular nation. To establish an academic discipline with the adjective "international" as its focus is obviously no more possible than to center one on the adjective "national." Such attempts, on the national or international level, will lead either to the restoration, by dint of their own logic, of the traditional academic disciplines and consequently to the frustration of interdisciplinary integration, or else to the drowning of all discipline in a chaotic mass of unrelated data which will at best receive from the ever changing whims of public opinion a semblance of order and direction.

The need for a principle of order and a focus, narrower than the mere reference to things international and more germane to the things we want to know when we study international relations, could not have been lost on university administrations which were responsible for the organization of research and teaching in the field of international relations. The idea of the core, composed of what is considered to be the more important academic disciplines bearing upon international relations, has resulted from the recognition of that need. Yet it was a step in the wrong direction. The idea of the core fails to distinguish between the need for multidisciplinary knowledge, without which international relations cannot be understood, and the requirement of a principle of order or focus for intellectual curiosity, without which no academic discipline can exist. The idea of the core accepts the former while rejecting the latter.

An expert in international relations must of course know something about international law, international organization, international politics, international economics, international geography, diplomatic history. If he knows nothing more than that he possesses a collection of fragmentary knowledge taken from different disciplines; if he is able to integrate these fragments of knowledge into a new discipline called "international relations," as has already been pointed out, he does so by virtue of the integrative powers of his mind, not because of the training he has received. International relations, like area studies, must have a focus, and it cannot be law, politics, economics, geography, and what not at the same time. Not all that is important to know about international relations can have the same value as the integrating principle and focus of an academic discipline. International relations as an academic discipline, no less than area studies, requires a hierarchy of intellectual interests, one of which is predominant, providing the principle of integration, while the others are subsidiary, supplying the knowledge necessary for the satisfaction of the predominant interest.

What is the predominant interest of international relations as an academic discipline? Two different answers must be given to that question. The first is identical with the one we gave when we raised the same question with regard to area studies. That is to say, the possible predominant interests are as numerous as are the legitimate objects of intellectual curiosity. It is, then, as legitimate to put economics in the center of international relations as it is to put law or geography there and to subordinate other disciplines to the predominant economic, legal, or geographical interests. In this view as many "sciences" of international relations are possible as there exist predominant interests which correspond to legitimate objects of intellectual curiosity.

This answer to our question opens up three possibilities for academic organization. First, it is possible to deal with international relations, thus conceived, in the different established departments which are selected according to the predominant interest of the scholar and student. International economics would then be dealt with in the department of economics, which would request such aid from other departments as it needed. Second, special academic organizations can be established with one predominant interest as their focus. Thus one can visualize a department or institute of international economics which would group subsidiary disciplines around international economics as its center. Finally, a flexible program can be established, particularly useful for undergraduate instruction, to allow students to select within a department or committee of international relations a number of different combinations, which, however, all center upon one discipline which a student must master. It may be noted in passing that this last arrangement has been put into practice by some of the leading area institutes and schools of international relations.

The other answer to the question of what the predominant interest of international relations must be assumes that among a number of legitimate interests there is in a particular period of history one which demands special attention. The educator must ask himself which among the many foci of international relations is most important for the student's interest to center upon, and the scholar must ask himself which among the many perspectives from which one can investigate international problems is most important from the theoretical and practical point of view. Today most institutions and students have turned to the study of international relations because of their interest in world politics. The primacy of politics over all other interests, in fact as well as in thought, in so far as the relations among nations and areas are concerned, needs only to be mentioned to be recognized. The recognition of this primacy of politics cannot but lead to the suggestion that, among the legitimate predominant interests upon which international relations as an academic discipline might be focused, international politics should take precedent over all others.

For the academic organization of the discipline of international relations this answer can mean two different things. It can mean the establishment of departments, committees, or schools which focus on international politics, subordinating other disciplines to it. Or it can mean that international relations is dealt with in this same way by that traditional academic discipline whose main subject matter is supposed to be the study of politics in all its manifestations, that is, the department of political science. The advisability of this solution will depend upon whether a department of political science actually puts the study of politics in the center of its endeavors or whether—as most of them do—it merely offers a disparate collection of courses whose common denominator is a vague and general relation to the activities of the state.

While it is the task of political education to communicate the truth about matters political, it is an illusion, to which professional educators are prone, to believe that the success of the educational enterprise depends primarily upon the quality and quantity of professional education. This is not necessarily so in any field of education, and it is not even typically so in the field of political education.

It is an obvious fact of experience that professional education is only one—and not necessarily the most important—among several factors that mold the mind and character of those to be educated. Family, society, the experiences of life itself are more persistent and authoritative teachers than the schools. Education, to be effective, must be organically attuned to the totality of educational influences to which the individual is subject.

This organic relationship between professional education and the totality of educational experience is strikingly revealed in the field of political education. The measure of success that education in world affairs has had in the United States in recent years is primarily due not to the quality and quantity of its professional manifestations, but to the experiences that the American people have undergone during and after the Second World War and to their interpretation by political leaders. What is being taught today in American colleges, say, about the balance of power, to be accepted almost as a matter of course, was taught, however sporadically, thirty and twenty years ago, only to be dismissed as absurd. It is not professional education that has made political understanding in this respect possible. Rather it is political experience that has made the truth plausible. Professional education has proved the validity of political experience through historic example and analytic demonstration. Without that experience, however, political education would have remained as ineffective as it was before, while without professional education political experience would have remained unconvincing and inarticulate. What has been said of the three stages through which all truth must pass applies with particular force to political truth. First, people dismiss it as impossible; next, people dismiss it as immoral; finally, people accept it as self-evident.

This achievement of political education is the task of political leadership. Only those whom the people have elected because they have confidence in them, or those in whose judgment the people otherwise confide, can make the truth of political experience explicit. For only they have the authority to gain acceptance for a political truth which is not self-evident from the outset. What they need is the political judgment to see the truth and the political courage to tell it. Thus the most effective political educators in America have been the great presidents, senators, and commentators.

For their authority there is no substitute, either in professional education or elsewhere. Nor is there elsewhere a real substitute for the other two requirements: political judgment and political courage. Professional education may supply them in rather rare instances. But without the authority of the political leader, the voice of professional education does not carry far.

8 About Cynicism, Perfectionism, and Realism in International Affairs

In the period between the two world wars, it was fashionable to call cynics those who would disagree with the optimism of the molders of international public opinion. The cynics transformed themselves into realists when, at the end of the thirties and the beginning of the forties, it became obvious that, after all, the cynics had not always been wrong, and realism became and still is the respectable public opinion of the day. The utopianism of Geneva reappeared as the new realism of London, Moscow, and Washington. Yet, not only have the utopians of yesterday changed into the realists of today, the cynics, too, have changed. They are now called perfectionists.

All this is very bewildering. Since I have been called a cynic, realist, and perfectionist in succession or simultaneously, I have a kind of personal interest in finding out what the characteristics of a cynic, realist, and perfectionist on the international scene are.

I was called a cynic for the first time in 1929, after the signature of the Kellogg-Briand Pact in which all the nations of the world pledged themselves to forego war as an instrument of international policy. War was outlawed, and hence war had become impossible. Such was at least the consensus of the authorities. Those who then pointed to the impotence of a legal formula in the face of the formidable social forces which make for war were declared to be "lacking in imagination" or to be outright cynics. I was called a realist for the first time in 1939, after I had expressed some doubts as to the ability of the small European nations to prevent involvement in the approaching Second World War by retreating into the legal formula of neutrality. Being as doubtful today about the success of the San Francisco Charter as I was in 1928 about the promise of the Kellogg-Briand Pact and in 1938 about the chances of neutrality, I am now called a perfectionist.

Since in ordinary parlance cynicism, realism, and perfectionism

From *Critic*, Vol. XI, No. 1, November 30, 1945.

are regarded as different things, I cannot help being perturbed by the question, What am I? Have I passed, like a butterfly, through a number of metamorphoses without knowing it? Or am I afflicted with a three-way split personality?

Actually, however, neither I nor my opponents have changed, nor do we exhibit any psychological peculiarities, at least not for the reasons adduced. It is only history that has changed, and it is the historic development which has reversed our positions, transforming the utopians of yesterday into the realists of today and making the cynics of 1928 into the perfectionists of 1945.

The period between the two world wars was dominated, not only in this country but in all nations of Western civilization, by what may be called the liberal philosophy of international politics. This school of thought believed in the essential and practically complete rationality and goodness of human nature and regarded the aspirations for power, which one could not fail to notice on the international scene, as mere residues of a militaristic age which was about to leave the stage of history forever. So Herbert Spencer could proclaim that war was a concomitant of feudal society and that in the industrial age men would satisfy their greedy instincts by the peaceful means of lucrative investment and speculation. So Jeremy Bentham could find in the imperialistic struggle for colonies the main source of international friction and could consequently recommend the abolition of colonies as a means for preserving international peace. Richard Cobden pushed this philosophy to its logical conclusion by proclaiming the ideal of "no foreign policy" whatsoever. The age came to regard foreign policy and war, that is, the active participation in the struggle for power on the international scene, as a kind of atavism, a "pastime of the aristocracy" which of necessity would come to an end with the end of aristocratic rule itself. When Woodrow Wilson endeavored to stabilize international peace by destroying the autocracies of the central powers and making the world safe for democracy, he only tried to translate into political practice the prevailing philosophy of the age.

It was this same philosophy which dominated the noble experiment of Geneva. Here it developed into a legalism to which the history of the world appeared as a succession of legal cases handled most unintelligently by an unenlightened humanity. Political problems were reduced to legal ones, and the interpretation of the Covenant of the League of Nations became the principal occupation of diplomats and international lawyers. When Italy shelled the Greek island of Corfu, the question uppermost in the minds of the men of the League of Nations was not, What does this mean with regard to the distribution of power in the Mediterranean? but, Is this an act of war within the meaning of the Covenant of the League of Nations? When Germany and Italy organized the Civil War in Spain, the question was not, What does this mean for the distribution of power in Europe? but, What does this mean in terms of the international rules of neutrality?

Whoever would point to the intrinsic weaknesses of this political philosophy and of the political practices derived from it was called a cynic, a heretic who refused to believe that this was the best of all possible worlds and that legal rules, domestic and international, suspended as it were between heaven and earth, could by their own inner force transform the affairs of men. The cynics were willing to face the fact that the desire for power was more than an intellectual and moral aberration of some individuals or groups of individuals, but a perennial element of human nature itself. They could not, therefore, overlook the fact that the aspirations for power which had molded the fate of mankind up to 1919 did not disappear from the international scene because the Covenant of the League of Nations proceeded upon the assumption that they no longer existed. They still existed, but while in previous periods of history they had appeared mainly under religious or philosophic disguises or under no disguise at all, they were now hidden behind a network of legalistic concepts and formulas.

The increasing impotence of the legal instrumentalities of the League in the face of Fascist aggression made it obvious that these instrumentalities, which the Western world had taken for the essence of international affairs, were actually only the surface beneath which the age-old struggle for power went on as ever before. The struggle for power was the real thing, and the legalism of Geneva was only a new technique of diplomacy, which did not affect at all the substance of international affairs. Thus both the cynics and the utopians of 1930 became the realists of 1940.

Yet the unanimity did not last for long. While the utopians, so to speak, went to the right and took the position the cynics seemingly had held before, the cynics went to the left and are now called perfectionists, for they point out, as they have always done, that whereas international politics cannot be understood without taking into consideration the struggle for power, it cannot be understood by considerations of power alone. Man is an animal longing for power, but he is also a creature with a moral purpose, and while man cannot be governed by abstract moral principles alone, he cannot be governed by power alone either. The utopians who turned realists have remained faithful to themselves. After having overemphasized one element and neglected the other, they are now doing exactly the same thing, only in reverse. Having been late in discovering the phenomenon of power, they cannot get over the shock of recognition. In essence they are still utopians; only their utopianism is no longer of Wilsonian vintage, but has a strong Machiavellian flavor.

They now consider it perfectionism to point out that present international organization cannot succeed, based as it is upon nothing but power, and very insecure power at that, since it is carefully protected sovereign and not collective power. International politics has its rules, like any other human activity, and success depends upon the observation of those rules. If somebody tries to build a house without doors, windows, and roof and you point out to him the deficiencies of the structure, he may call you a perfectionist. If someone uses a sieve for an umbrella, he may reject your criticism as being perfectionist. So it seems that a perfectionist is a person who insists upon observance of the rules of the game and who refuses to yield to wishful thinking. If this is so, I do not mind being called a perfectionist today any more than I minded being called a cynic fifteen years ago.

PART III

THE BURDEN OF AN

OBSOLESCENT TRADITION

W‌E HAVE pointed out that all great contributions to political thought have been a response to challenges arising from political reality. Their response was necessarily conditioned by an intellectual tradition which, in turn, was a response to the political reality of another day. To what extent is our political tradition adequate to the understanding of the contemporary political world? To what extent does it reflect the perennial truths about politics, and to what extent is it but the product of a particular historic configuration, doomed to obsolescence with the disappearance of the latter? In every historic period, political thought must answer these questions anew. The answers a historic period finds set the limits within which its political thought is to fulfil its creative function, forming a new intellectual tradition fated to be superseded again.

Contemporary political thought is unable to answer these questions; it is even unable to pose them. Its relativism prevents it from raising the perennial problem of the distinction between truth and opinion. In so far as it is consistent in its relativism it cannot even distinguish among different opinions, provided they are socially acceptable. Despairing of coming to terms with contemporary political reality, it retreats, as we have seen, into a methodological dogmatism which provides a respectable shelter from the risks of political controversy.

In the absence of such consistency and by virtue of its involvement in the political situation, political thought tends to identify uncritically a particular opinion, reflecting a particular political position and interest, with truth and thereby to transform theory into ideology. It finds its tools in an intellectual tradition which has been left behind by actual political developments and, thus being removed from political controversy, provides the canons of political orthodoxy to be interposed between the observer's mind and political reality. Outmoded political ideas tend to fill the gap left by the sterility of contemporary political thought. Thus the age lives in good measure upon the intellectual capital accumulated in the past, and the uncritical acceptance of that heritage, stifling the creative awareness of the present, has become a burden which impedes the growth not only of political thought but of political institutions as well.

On the plane of domestic politics, the great new fact with which political thought must come to terms is the diminution of the individual vis-à-vis the state and the concentrations of autonomous social power in the form of giant corporations, labor unions, and mass media of communication. The present age poses anew the problem of individual freedom, and it poses it in the novel configuration of a three-cornered contest between the state, the concentrations of autonomous social power, and the individual. How can the state be made strong enough to protect the individual against these concentrations of autonomous social forces, but not so strong as to be able to subvert the freedom of the individual? In other words, the administrative state raises an issue which cannot be understood, let alone solved, by the traditional juxtaposition between the state and the individual and the ritualistic manipulation of the traditional concepts of constitutional law.

The international scene has been in our time transformed by three great revolutions. The political revolution has destroyed the modern pluralistic state system, kept in being by a flexible balance of power, and replaced it with a bipolar world. The technological revolution has created the technical means both for the total destruction and the total unification of the world. The moral revolution has split the world into two hostile camps, divided not only by political interests but also by political philosophies and ways of life. Consequently, the intellectual tools which helped us in the past to understand and master the problems of international politics all need examination and adaptation to radically new conditions. Their unexamined use, as though this were still the world of their origin, not only impedes understanding but also, as will be shown, stands in the way of successful action.

We have tried elsewhere, both systematically and on the occasion of concrete political problems, to re-examine and reformulate the basic concepts of international politics. We have selected here five concepts whose uncritical use has persistently obscured thought and impeded action: separation of powers, nationalism, naziism, neutrality and neutralism, and international law.

9 Separation of Powers[1]

In an illuminating analysis of its fundamental problems, Professor Gellhorn divides the history of administrative law into three periods, the first focusing its interest upon the constitutional divisions of power, the second searching for the appropriate boundaries of judicial review, and the third, in which we find ourselves at present, concentrating upon the procedures of administration itself.[2] Yet while addressing oneself to this latter task, one cannot but realize that the unfinished business of the preceding periods obstructs the adequate solution of the pressing problems of today.

The "pernicious abstractions" which after the Civil War superseded the great and simple truths of Marshall's Constitution are still impeding the recognition of specific problems of administrative law and their adequate solution. The delimitation of administrative powers under the rule of law is one such problem. Not only is it obscured by the philosophical and political struggle between the "planners" and the "traditionalists,"[3] but the main obstacle to its recognition and solution lies in a legal doctrine which, mistaking its legalistic abstractions for the Constitution, conceals the fundamental relations between statutory and administrative rules behind a veil of conceptualist distinctions and abstract theorems. Behind it and regardless of it, the realities of administrative and judicial practice deal with the realities of administrative problems in a realistic fashion; they may pay lip service to the theory, but they proceed as though it did not exist. It is the legal writers and the legislators who take the theory seriously and on the basis of it measure the administrative powers

From the *Iowa Law Review*, May, 1943; and the *University of Chicago Law Review*, February, 1944.

[1] Legislation and judicial decisions have been covered through 1943. More recent legal material does not affect the theoretical conclusions of this chapter.

[2] Walter Gellhorn, *Federal Administrative Proceedings* (Baltimore: Johns Hopkins Press, 1941), p. 43.

[3] Hans J. Morgenthau, book review in *Columbia Law Review*, XLII (1941), 330.

either too narrowly or too broadly but, lacking sound standards, not adequately.

We shall discuss here the theoretical problems raised by the rule-making functions of administrative agencies, in the light of both legal theory and administrative and judicial practice. We take as our point of departure the Fair Labor Standards Act, whose deficiencies, from the point of view of sound administrative theory, offer an illuminating illustration of the theoretical problems involved.

The main weakness from which the administration of the Fair Labor Standards Act suffers results from the division of functions between Congress and the administrator in regard to the coverage of the act. On the one hand, the statute in rather vague and general language circumscribes positively the coverage of the act. On the other hand, the administrator has the power to issue regulations interpreting, defining, and making definite certain general concepts determining the coverage of the statute. As a further complication, the act does not deal with these powers of the administrator in a uniform way; some derive from express delegation, others do not. According to legal doctrine, the former are considered to have the force of law while the latter are supposed to be only the private opinion of the administrator without any binding force. Primarily concerned with doing justice to the constitutional doctrine of the separation of powers, the act has failed to define clearly the boundaries between the domain of legislative enactment and the sphere of administrative rule-making. Thus it has come to pass that the administrator is, on the one hand, assuming powers which, under a sound division of functions, should be exercised by Congress, and that, on the other hand, powers that are necessary for the enforcement of the act and functionally belong to the administrator are vested neither in him nor in Congress nor anywhere else but are, in case of litigation, discharged by the courts. If there is no litigation they are actually discharged by the administrator, but, from the point of view of the theory, they are not discharged at all.

Congress, the administrator, most of the writers discussing the subject matter, and the courts pay their verbal respects to the classical doctrine that only Congress may make rules with the binding force of law, that the other departments of government are limited to applying and interpreting the legal rules created by Congress, and that, finally, Congress can delegate its rule-making powers to other branches of the government only by limiting the delegated powers to strictly defined subject matters and by subjecting them to definite standards. It follows that, on the one hand, any delegation of powers not satisfying these requirements is invalid and that, on the other hand, any rule created by non-legislative agencies without express congressional delegation is without binding effect.

The congressional deliberations preceding the enactment of the Fair Labor Standards Act took place in the shadow of the Supreme Court decisions in the Schechter[4] and Panama Refining Company[5] cases. These two decisions seemed to give new vigor to this time-honored doctrine, and hence Congress was fearful lest the Fair Labor Standards Act might suffer the fate of the National Industrial Recovery Act.[6] The attention of the members of the Senate and House committees on labor centered upon making the act safe from constitutional attack. Extreme care was therefore taken to delegate to the administrator strictly limited rule-making powers with regard to subject matter as well as standards. "This Act," stated Robert H. Jackson, then Assistant Attorney-General, in the congressional hearings, "combines everything, and is an attempt to take advantage of whatever theories may prevail on the Court at the time that the case is heard."[7]

The act, therefore, delegates comprehensive rule-making powers only in regard to the determination of minimum wages. Within this broad and comprehensive field the rule-making powers of the administrator are strictly circumscribed, apart from the general statutory standards, by the legislative determination of minimum and maximum wages as well as by the administrator's inability to change the industry committee's wage recommendation which he is permitted

---

[4] *A. L. A. Schechter Poultry Corp.* v. *United States,* 295 U.S. 495 (1935).

[5] *Panama Refining Co.* v. *Ryan,* 293 U.S. 388 (1935).

[6] The decisions seem not to have been interpreted correctly by Congress, for the issue at stake in these cases was not delegation, but alienation, of legislative powers; that is, Congress tried to confer on the President legislative powers without clear limitation of subject matter. Congress cannot divest itself of powers vested in it.

[7] *Joint Hearings before the Senate Committee on Education and Labor and the House Committee on Labor on S. 2475 and H. R. 2700,* 75th Cong., 1st sess. (1937), p. 54; 52 Stat. 1060 (1938), 29 U.S.C. § 202 (1940).

only to reject or accept *in toto*. He can accept a recommendation only under the condition that it is made in accordance with law and supported by the evidence adduced at the hearing; only in that he must determine whether the recommendation will carry out the legislative purposes does his administrative discretion enter the picture. The judicial character of the proceedings is furthermore emphasized by the provision for judicial review of the wage order. This whole quasi-judicial organization of a "sub-legislative, advisory"[8] institution of industry committees is due to the desire of Congress to meet all possible constitutional objections derived from the principles of due process and delegation of powers.

The act also delegates to the administrator the power to issue regulations and orders prescribing the reports to be made by employers subject to the act, and exempting learners, apprentices, and handicapped workers from the minimum wage provisions. In the remainder of the nineteen sections of the act, no coherent rule-making powers are delegated to the administrator. It is only in four isolated instances that the act empowers the administrator to define certain terms to be found in its provisions. Thus he may determine the reasonable cost of board, lodging, and other facilities; he may determine which industries are of a seasonal nature; he may define and delimit the terms "employed in a *bona fide* executive, administrative, professional, or local retailing capacity, or in the capacity of outside salesman"; and he may finally determine "the area of production" within the meaning of Section 13 (a) (10).

Following the popular conception of bureaucratic administration, one could have anticipated that the administrator would use to the limit the powers expressly conferred on him by Congress and take advantage of any opportunity to assume powers not expressly delegated but necessary for the administration of the act. Yet in a self-effacing fashion, which seems either to point to an administrative inferiority complex and give the lie to the popular conception of bureaucratic arrogance and tyranny or else to offer evidence of a super-Machiavellian hypocrisy, the administrator has accentuated and strengthened the legislative policy by emphasizing the narrowness of the delegated power, on the one hand, and, on the other, the

[8] The apt characterization is taken from the Attorney General's Committee on Administrative Procedure, *Administration of the Fair Labor Standards Act of 1938, Wage and Hour Division*, I, 81.

legal impotence of his opinions in the broad domain where no expressly delegated powers exist.

The regulatory activities of the administrator under the Fair Labor Standards Act reflect most faithfully the constitutional doctrine according to which the administrative rule-making powers are dependent upon express statutory delegation. In harmony with this doctrine the administrator has issued regulations claiming the force of law only with respect to those matters which the act has expressly authorized him to regulate. The act deals, however, with a number of matters which are in need of further clarification and implementation, and, as regards the power to regulate them, the act is silent. Faced with the need for regulations, on the one hand, and the apparent lack of power to issue them, on the other, the administrator has resorted to a unique makeshift in publishing interpretative bulletins, which in the language of a legal brief or a learned legal paper explain the law to the public. The administrator is careful to point out in each bulletin (with the exception of No. 4) that the binding effect of these publications is exactly what the language suggests: the private opinion of the administrator.

The distinction between regulations and interpretative bulletins in the administration of the Fair Labor Standards Act corresponds closely to the distinction, developed by legal writers, between legislative and interpretative regulations. Whereas according to this theoretical distinction legislative regulations lay down the law and have the force and effect of law, deriving from a specific delegation of power and supported by statutory sanctions, interpretative regulations only construe the statute and have no more the force and effect of law than the interpretation of a private individual. The latter add nothing to the law as laid down by the statute; they merely guide subordinate administrative officers in the administration of the statute and, furthermore, inform the public of the way in which the administrative agency plans to administer the act. While the legislative regulation, if *intra vires*, must be applied by the courts, the interpretative regulation, being "only an extrinsic aid in deciphering the meaning of an ambiguous statute," may be refused judicial recognition. The theory, however, cannot overlook the fact that frequently interpretative regulations are given great weight by the courts. This fact is reconciled with the theory by the explanation that the interpretative regulations have such weight only if they construe the statute correctly and then it is actually the statute and not the regulation which the individual must obey.

It has been pointed out by those who adhere to this doctrine that on examination of administrative regulations it is frequently doubtful whether the administrative officer intended to issue a legislative or interpretative regulation, that the examination of the statutes does not always lead to unequivocal results, and that in theory and practice the two classes of administrative regulations are frequently confounded. These practical difficulties, however, seem to point to the main objection to which this doctrine exposes itself, namely, that the significance of the distinction between legislative and interpretative regulation does not lie in the one being legally binding and the other not, but is to be found in the degree of discretion allowed by the statute to the administrative officer, which discretion tends to be greater in the former than it is in the latter.

The distinction between legislation and interpretation is, under the American form of government, a matter of degree. Under a constitutional system where the acts of the legislator must meet constitutional requirements and are with respect to them subject to judicial review, one cannot legislate without interpreting the Constitution as construed by the courts. The considerations which guided Congress in formulating the Fair Labor Standards Act are a case in point. It is true that the discretion which the Constitution gives Congress with respect to ends, means, and procedure of legislation is so broad as to make the constitutional standards with which Congress as legislative body has to comply sometimes almost invisible. This is especially so in fields where the power of Congress to legislate is generally unquestioned. The traditional interpretation of the constitutional standards which delimit and define here the legislative powers of Congress has become so ingrained into the public mind that the very existence of these standards is only noticed in case of conflicting interpretations.

If Congress cannot legislate without interpreting the Constitution, an administrative officer cannot interpret an act of Congress without legislating. The traditional theory of interpretation starts with the assumption that sometimes the legislator has been unwilling or unable to say clearly what he wanted to say, that, therefore, the statute has been made "ambiguous," and that in a scientific procedure the correct, hidden "meaning" of the law can be detected. This scientific method of detection is called interpretation. This is, how-ever, not the kind of interpretation courts and administrative agen-cies usually perform. Their interpretative function is not due to the ambiguity of the statute which is in need of clarification but to the abstractness of the statute which, being applied to a concrete factual situation, is in need of being made concrete. There exists, in other words, a gap between the abstract rule of the statute and the facts to which the rule is to be applied.

This gap judges and administrative officers are supposed to fill by creating, within the limits of the general, abstract rules of the stat-ute, concrete, individualized rules directly applicable to the facts. There is nothing ambiguous in Section 13 (a) (3) of the Fair Labor Standards Act exempting from the minimum wage and maximum hours provisions of the act "any employee employed as a seaman . . ."; nor is there in the term "seaman" a hidden meaning which the professional skill of the lawyer is able to detect in about the same fashion in which the professional skill of the fisherman may detect the pearl hidden in the oyster. The meaning of the term "seaman" on the abstract and general level of the statutory enactment is per-fectly clear. Everybody knows what a seaman is, that is to say, what the general characteristics of the abstract type "seaman" are. Yet difficulties arise when we apply the abstract definition and the gen-eral characteristics to a concrete situation. Is the ship's surgeon a sea-man? And what about the cook, the purser, and the engineer; the pilot, stevedore, and longshoreman? Do the crew of a Mississippi steamer or the skeleton crew of a ship in port come under the ex-emption? These are questions to be answered by interpretation, that is, by specific, individualized rules applicable directly to the concrete situation.

It follows also from this example that interpretation cannot be a scientific procedure which reaches with logical necessity the one correct solution. The term "seaman" with respect to the enumerated concrete situations is obviously not capable of one determination only, to the exclusion of all others. It can be determined in different ways which are all equally legitimate from the point of view of sci-ence and logic. Which way one is to choose is then a matter of per-sonal preference, not of logical necessity. This personal preference of the interpreter will be determined by pragmatic considerations of the values at stake and the interests to be protected, that is, with respect to statutory interpretation, by the policies and purposes of the act to be interpreted. The interpreter of the statute, when he makes his choice among those different logical possibilities, is therefore in search not of the one scientifically correct answer but of the answer which is best adapted to the policies and purposes of the act. Which interpretation meets this test is again a matter not of mere logical subsumption but of value judgments based upon the evaluation of those purposes and policies and of their relation to the term to be interpreted. Within the limits of those purposes and policies, on the one hand, and the abstract, general meaning of the term to be interpreted, on the other, the interpreter may choose the interpretation which in his judgment is most appropriate. How broad his discretion is depends upon the definiteness with which the act states its purposes and policies, as well as upon the strictness with which the act circumscribes the general, abstract meaning of the term.

What administrative agencies and courts do when they interpret a statutory provision such as Section 13 (a) (3) of the Fair Labor Standards Act is, therefore, not in essence but only in the degree of discretion which the interpreting official may exercise, different from what Congress is doing when it legislates under the Constitution, and from what the Supreme Court is doing when it interprets the Constitution. They all legislate by substituting specific, individualized rules for general and abstract rules[9] and by thus creating rules of law which would not exist had they not been created by them; they all interpret by remaining, while legislating, within the limits of abstract, general rules of law. He who interprets of necessity legislates, and he who legislates of necessity interprets.

With respect to the function they perform as legislators and interpreters, the only difference between the different rule-making bodies lies in the number of legislative choices which the rules to be interpreted allow them and, furthermore, in the degree of individualization and concreteness of the rules promulgated by them. At the top of the ladder, as far as broadness of discretion in rule-making and the abstractness and generality of the rules made are concerned, we find the courts interpreting the Constitution. Their discretion is lim-

9 It should be noted that the terms "general," "abstract," "specific," and "individualized" are of course relative. What is specific and individualized with respect to the general welfare clause of the Constitution may be abstract and general with respect to an administrative regulation.

ited only by the logical limits of the constitutional concepts and the policies and purposes laid down therein. To the vastness of those logical limits and the vagueness of those policies and purposes corresponds the almost limitless broadness of this discretion. Since it is constitutional legislation with which the courts are here concerned, that is, the formulation of fundamental standards with which all official acts must comply, these rules are highly abstract and general.

The discretion of Congress, as a rule-making body, is only subject to the "great generalities" of the Constitution, as formulated by the courts. Hence, Congress is able to choose from among thousands of legislative means and ends, all equally legitimate under the logic, policies, and purposes of the constitutional principles, as formulated by the courts. Since it is the constitutional function of Congress to regulate the acts of groups of people rather than of individuals as such and to deal with typical situations rather than individual ones, its rules are naturally on a high level of abstractness and generality, though being inferior in this respect to the rules of the Constitution.

The discretion of the courts and administrative agencies, with respect to their rule-making functions under the laws of Congress, is limited not only by the logic, policies, and purposes of the Constitution, as formulated by the courts, but also by the logic, policies, and purposes of the statutes. Judge and administrator will find their choice of legislative means and ends to a greater or lesser extent limited by the statutory determination of those means and ends, and under extreme conditions their discretion may be narrowed down to a few alternatives or disappear completely. The increase in the concreteness and individualization of the rules on the statutory level, as over against the constitutional one, of necessity leads to a narrowing of the rule-making discretion on the next lower level, the level of administrative and judicial determination. This, the lowest level in the hierarchy of regulatory powers, is in direct contact with individuals as such whose behavior the government wants to determine, and with individual facts which the statute wishes to regulate. The rules created on this level attain, therefore, the highest degree of individualization and partake least of the abstract and general quality of constitutional and statutory rules.[10]

[10] The idea that the relation between administrative regulation and statute is in principle identical with the one between statute and Constitution has been well stated in *Boske* v. *Comingore*, 177 U.S. 459 (1899): "In determining whether the

These are, however, differences of degree, not of essence. The administrative officer or judge interpreting the term "seaman" within the meaning of the Fair Labor Standards Act performs exactly the same intellectual function as the member of Congress or the Supreme Court judge who interprets the term "interstate commerce" within the meaning of the Constitution. Both interpret the higher rule in order to find the limits of their discretion and both legislate within the limits of this discretion.

Since there is no functional distinction between legislation and interpretation, it is obvious that the distinction between legislative and interpretative regulations cannot be maintained on functional grounds. This is readily demonstrated by a comparison between several provisions of the Fair Labor Standards Act. The administrative determination of the term "seaman" within the meaning of Section 13 (a) (3) of the act is, according to the theory we are here discussing, an interpretative regulation since the act does not expressly delegate to the administrator the power to make this determination. On the other hand, Section 13 (a) (1) of the act provides

---

regulations promulgated by him are consistent with law, we must apply the rule of decision which controls when an act of Congress is assailed as not being within the powers conferred upon it by the Constitution; that is to say, a regulation adopted under Section 161 of the Revised Statutes should not be disregarded or annulled unless, in the judgment of the court, it is plainly and palpably inconsistent with law. Those who insist that such a regulation is invalid must make its invalidity so manifest that the court has no choice except to hold that the Secretary has exceeded his authority and employed means that are not at all appropriate to the end specified in the act of Congress" (at 470); accord *Pacific States Box and Basket Co.* v. *White,* 296 U.S. 176 (1935): "Every exertion of the police power, either by the legislature or by an administrative body, is an exercise of delegated power. Where it is by a statute, the legislature has acted under power delegated to it through the Constitution. Where the regulation is by an order of an administrative body, that body acts under a delegation from the legislature. The question of law may, of course, always be raised whether the legislature had power to delegate the authority exercised. . . . But where the regulation is within the scope of authority legally delegated, the presumption of the existence of facts justifying its specific exercise attaches alike to statutes, to municipal ordinances, and to orders of administrative bodies" (at 185); *State* ex rel. *Wis. Inspection Bureau* v. *Whitman,* 196 Wis. 472, 220 N.W. 929 (1928). It should be emphasized that the statements in the text do not deny the importance of the distinction between legislation and interpretation. What we oppose is only the tendency to erect those functions into conceptualist absolutes and to derive from them legal conclusions. This is the "jurisprudence of conceptions" which belongs to another day.

that the minimum wage and maximum hours provisions "shall not apply with respect to any employee employed in a bona fide executive, administrative, professional, or local retailing capacity . . . (as such terms are defined and delimited by regulations of the administrator)." Such regulations would be legislative in nature since the act delegates the power to make them expressly to the administrator and threatens non-compliance with legal sanctions. Yet no effort is needed to show that the "legislative" function the administrator is authorized to perform in the latter case is identical with the "interpretative" one he performs in the former. The limitations to which his discretion is subject are in both cases the same and so are the functions through which his discretion asserts itself.

If no functional difference corresponds to the distinction between legislative and interpretative regulations, how, then, is the distinction to be explained? The answer will be found in a political philosophy which attributes to the statutory enactments of the legislature a particular dignity not shared by the acts of any other branch of the government.

The doctrine of separation of powers, when in the seventeenth century it was cast in its modern mold, was at once confronted with a conflict between its political intention and a political fact. Its political intention was to destroy the absolute powers of the prince by dissolving those powers into three separate compartments of government, independent from each other and co-ordinated in complete equality. Had the doctrine of separation of powers stopped here, it would, as Hobbes[11] and Kant[12] recognized clearly, of necessity have led to the dissolution of the state itself. For even under a system of separation of powers the sovereign power, that is, the highest governmental power, must reside somewhere. Whenever the doctrine was faced with the test of political performance, it had to overcome this difficulty by destroying the mechanics of its system both from without and from within. It did so by adding to the three separate powers a fourth, the sovereign power, and by elevating one of the three separate powers over the others and making it representative of the sovereign. In the monarchy this fourth power, giving unity to the separate powers and at the same time neutralizing them, is the

[11] *De Cive* (Amsterdam, 1647), pp. xii, 5.

[12] *Rechtslehre* (Königsberg: Bey Nicolovius, 1797), pp. 45, 48.

monarch; in the democracies, such as the France of 1789 and the United States, it is the people, speaking through the constitution. The branch which is thus elevated over the others is in the monarchy, with the exception of England, the executive; in the democracies it is the legislature.

The latter emphasis is most outspoken in revolutionary France, of which Duguit, the great critic of the constitutional doctrine of the French Revolution, has said: "Ils déclarent les trois pouvoirs égaux et indépendants et ils subordonnent au pouvoir législatif l'éxécutif et le judiciaire."[13] Similarly in England, modified, however, by the constitutional functions of the Crown, "[the] statute is the highest constitutional formulation of law, the means by which the supreme legislature, after the fullest deliberation, expresses its *final* will."[14] The same emphasis, even though mitigated by the institution of judicial review and the presidential veto, dominates the American legal system. Three factors have contributed to giving Congress as the legislative body a predominant position among the other powers of government.

Since the last decades of the sixteenth century it is the common possession of legal and political thought in the Western world that the statute (*Gesetz, loi, ley*), that is, the general and abstract rule of law addressed to the executive and judicial officers as such, is the successor of the *lex regia* of Roman, and of the *lex Dei* of canon law. Since the last centuries of the Roman Empire *lex* was understood as the authoritative expression of the will of the supreme power, either in the universe or in the state.[15] The general and abstract rule of law, which we call statute, even though not deriving directly from the sovereign power, is supposed to share in the dignity and the unique qualities which tradition attributes to the *lex* of Roman and canon law.[16]

Even though not a sovereign power itself, Congress, nevertheless, cannot fail to occupy in two respects a position markedly superior

[13] Léon Duguit, *La separation des pouvoirs et l'Assemblée nationale de 1789* (1893), p. 116.

[14] A. C. Allen, *Law in the Making* (Oxford: Clarendon Press, 1951), p. 489.

[15] See Ulpian, *Inst.* 12, § 6, pr. D. de const. princ. 1, 4.

[16] See Max Radin, "A Short Way with Statutes," *Harvard Law Review,* LVI (1942), 388, 391.

to the other branches of government. Congress is the only agency of the government through which the sovereign will of the people actually and directly expresses itself. In the Constitution and the institutions established directly under it, popular sovereignty manifests itself in a remote and frequently legalistic and theoretical rather than actual fashion. The popularly elected chief executive stands in a personally exalted but, with regard to concrete political action, vague and general relation to the sovereignty of the people. Only the members of Congress are the "representatives of the people," its agents sent by it to Washington in partial exercise of its sovereign powers. No branch of the government is physically closer to the seat of sovereignty.

The reputed superiority of the statutes is, however, most firmly grounded in the system of separation of powers as it functions under the constitutional form of government. Under this form the sovereign power of the people is supposed to have created the Constitution which guarantees that the co-ordinated executive, legislative, and judicial powers act only within the limits of the rule of law.[17] For the legislative branch and the judiciary, in so far as it interprets the Constitution, the rule of law is the Constitution itself; the same is true only within very narrow limits for the administrative and executive officers.[18] The great bulk of administrative, executive, and judicial acts, however, is subject to the rule of law as formulated in the statutes of Congress. In this view, it is the constitutional function of Congress and of Congress alone to make the rule of law; of the courts and of the courts alone to interpret it; of the executive and administrative branches and of them alone to apply it. Congress, by having, in seeming compliance with the doctrine of separation of powers, the monopoly of making general and abstract rules of law applicable to the great mass of public officials, appears in the eyes of the people as the lawmaker par excellence.

It is for this reason, and not only because of their closeness to the seat of the sovereign power, that the acts of Congress are considered superior to the acts of the other branches of the government. Above them there is only the Constitution, whereas theoretically beside them but actually beneath them are the judicial, executive, and

[17] See Mass. Const., Art. XXX (1780).

[18] See U.S. Const., Art. II.

administrative acts. The "will of Congress" as expressed in the statute is not, to be exact, the will of the sovereign, the people; yet it comes closer to it than the expression of any other of the constituted powers. Hence, the other branches of the government owe Congress obedience. The judges may disregard executive or administrative acts without much legalistic ado by declaring them "unreasonable," "clearly erroneous," or simply "not binding upon the courts." They may disregard their own decisions by simply stating that the former decision was wrong. Within the wide logical limits of the "great generalities" of the Constitution they may move at will. Yet they would not dare to disregard a statute because they think it is wrong, that is, because they disagree with its purpose and policies; at least they would not dare to say so. They will be most anxious to avoid the impression that they would dare to infringe upon the legislative monopoly of Congress and will invoke the voice of the sovereign power itself, that is, the Constitution, in order to justify disregard for a law of Congress.

Similarly an administrative officer may not be overanxious to prevent his acts from overlapping with the functions of other executive or administrative officers. Yet he will be careful to show due respect for the legal rules by which Congress and the courts have circumscribed the limits of his discretion. "Bureaucratic" rule-making seems to be the farthest removed from the seat of sovereignty, that is, the will of the people. It operates on the lowest level of abstractness and generality and, therefore, seems to be the outgrowth of a government of men rather than of laws. And, finally and above all, it is a novel and alien element within a system of separation of powers, which knows only three branches of government, each of them performing an exclusive governmental function. Faithful to the doctrine that the rules of law emanating from Congress possess a peculiar dignity all their own and that Congress has the constitutional monopoly to legislate, of which only Congress can deprive itself through express delegation, the administrative officer will not dare to "legislate" unless Congress has expressly told him to do so. It has been said that "There is nothing sacred in Treasury regulations or other rules," but there is something very sacred about an act of Congress.

It is in this constitutional philosophy that we must see the real roots of the distinction between legislative and interpretative regulations and the basis of the conception that only the former can have binding legal effect. In its essence this doctrine is, as it were, the homage which the vice of administrative rule-making pays to the virtue of Congress' legislative exclusiveness. It derives from, and works with, abstract legalistic concepts which, developed three hundred years ago and now petrified into conceptual absolutes, are applied to problems of government entirely different from those which the seventeenth-century writers comprehended in those concepts. Its result is not sound legal theory but constitutional philosophy falsely applied, to wit: conceptualist superstition.

This doctrine has a basis neither in the actual administrative functions performed nor in sound legal theory; nor does it find support in the practice of administrative agencies and courts. Administrative agencies and courts pay their respects to the doctrine in words but do not respect it in deed. An examination of the practice of administrative agencies and courts in this respect will show that what those agencies say they do is not exactly what they actually do.

That the denial of binding legal effect, which is stereotyped in the interpretative bulletins of the administrator under the Fair Labor Standards Act, is of a mere verbal character becomes obvious from a close examination of the exact legal significance of the formula used by the administrator. The administrator in this formula makes three statements: first, that he will be guided by the interpretation in the performance of his administrative duties; second, that the interpretation is subject to judicial review; third, that the interpretation is subject to revision by the administrator himself.

The legal significance of the first statement can only be that the administrator, as far as he is concerned, will apply the statutory rules as interpreted by him, that is, that he will consider them as legally binding. He will apply them whenever his administrative duties obligate him to do so either within the Wage and Hour Division or with regard to employers and employees affected by the provisions of the act. This is exactly what any executive or administrative officer does who interprets an act of Congress with legally binding effect. The second statement likewise refers to the obvious; being subject to judicial review is not a distinctive quality of interpretative regulations devoid of binding legal effect but is, as a matter of principle, common to all acts of government as far as questions of law are concerned. The quality referred to in the third statement interpretative regulations likewise share with all governmental acts, with the exception of certain classes of judicial decisions. Hence, the analysis of the formula pretending to demonstrate the absence of legally binding force in interpretative regulations turns out to demonstrate the exact opposite, that is, the absence of a fundamental difference between interpretative regulations and other rules of law.

The artificial character of the distinction between legislative and interpretative regulations of which only the former would have legally binding effect becomes entirely obvious from an examination of judicial decisions. The courts, fearful of the extension of administrative power and preoccupied with the constitutional aspects of the matter, have concentrated their attack upon the constitutionality of the statutes and of the administrative procedure rather than upon the legality of the administrative regulation. Once the constitutionality of the statutory delegation of power and of the procedural safeguards with respect to the due process requirements was established, the courts have viewed with rather liberal eyes the actual extent of the delegated discretion and the actual use the administrative agencies make of their discretion in promulgating substantive rules and regulations.

The courts generally make no distinction between legislative and interpretative regulations, and in the few cases where a distinction is made, it has no practical importance; that is, the same rules apply regardless of the category to which the regulations are supposed to belong. In other words, for the question whether or not an administrative regulation is legally binding the distinction is irrelevant.

The courts start with the assumption that administrative regulations are not necessarily binding. They do not always state this assumption explicitly but often lay down the conditions under which administrative regulations are held binding, whereupon it follows by implication that in the absence of those conditions the regulations lack binding effect.

What, then, are the conditions, the professed and the actual ones, under which the courts hold administrative regulations legally binding? Logically, the first condition upon which the binding effect of an administrative regulation of necessity depends is the authority of the administrative agency to issue regulations at all. In other words the regulation must not be *ultra vires*. There must also be an objective possibility for administrative regulation which is not the case where the language of the statute does not lend itself to being made more concrete by such regulation since the statutory language is clear and not ambiguous. Once the regulatory power is established the use of the administrative discretion must meet the test of reasonableness and fairness from the point of view of the purposes and policies of the statute; in other words, there must not be an abuse of discretion. The regulation must, furthermore, satisfy mechanical standards with regard to the time of promulgation and the length of time it has been followed by the administrative agency: it must be contemporaneous with the statute from which its authority derives and represent uniform administrative practice over a long period of time. Finally, when during the existence of such administrative practice the authorizing statute is re-enacted without modification of the administrative practice, the regulation from which the latter derives is considered to have become part of the statute itself.

On the face of it, it appears as if the courts require administrative regulations to comply with a number of technical rules of an exceptional character before they recognize their legally binding effect. It can, however, be shown that these apparently special rules, with the exception of the last mentioned, are identical with the general requirements upon the fulfilment of which the judicial recognition of the binding effect of all legal rules, especially statutes, depends. The apparent difference between them is one of emphasis and formulation rather than of substance. While administrative regulations are declared to be binding only when they comply with certain conditions so that there is an implied presumption that normally they are not binding,[19] the presumption with regard to statutes is exactly converse.[20] Both statements, however, say in substance exactly the

[19] There is, however, a growing tendency to assimilate administrative regulations to statutes and to hold the former valid without any special qualification, the requirement of contemporaneous and long-continued construction either being entirely omitted or applied only in additional support of the already established validity of the regulation.

[20] *United States* v. *Carolene Products Co.,* 304 U.S. 144 (1938): "We proceed upon the rule often expressed in this court that an act of Congress is to be accepted as constitutional unless on examination it clearly appears to be in conflict with provisions of the Federal Constitution."

same, namely, that the validity of administrative regulations and statutes alike is subject to judicial review.

Under a system of judicial review of questions of law, all rules of law, regardless of the source from which they emanate (with the exception, of course, of the Constitution), are subject, under certain conditions, to approval by the courts. Since the courts have the last word in interpretation, nobody else's interpretation can be absolutely binding upon them. This holds true for statutes as well as executive orders and administrative regulations. Yet while the courts with reference to administrative regulations emphasize the conditions for their binding effect, with regard to statutes they stress the conditions under which binding effect is to be denied. This difference in emphasis stems from two considerations: first, the metaphysical deference for rules of law emanating from Congress and, second, the different degrees of discretion under which Congress and administrative agencies operate.

Administrative regulations, to be respected by the courts, must comply with certain specific conditions. Statutes, to be respected, need not satisfy any specific conditions; their descent from Congress is under normal conditions sufficient legitimation. For administrative regulations to be disregarded the negative proof that certain conditions are not present is sufficient; for statutes to be disregarded positive proof that certain conditions are present is necessary. In other words, when courts declare an administrative regulation valid, they pay first their respects to Congress and then qualified respects to the administrative agency. When they declare a statute valid, they pay their respects first to Congress and then to the Constitution. When, on the other hand, courts declare a statute unconstitutional, they offer their apologies to Congress, deploring their "painful duty"[21] and "irksome"[22] task, and bow before the Constitution. When courts find an administrative regulation devoid of binding effect, they offer apologies to nobody and bow before Congress.

The difference in emphasis is, further, due to the very wide degree of discretion Congress enjoys in its lawmaking activities as compared to the limitations which statutes usually impose upon sim-

---

[21] *McCulloch* v. *Maryland,* 4 Wheat. (U.S.) 316, 423 (1819).

[22] *Trustees of Dartmouth College* v. *Woodward,* 4 Wheat. (U.S.) 518, 625 (1819).

ilar activities of administrative bodies. Where the discretion is extremely wide the lawmaking body can in the usual course of events be presumed to remain within the limits of the discretion; the validity of the rule may normally be presumed and its lack of binding force considered the exception. Where the discretion is usually strictly confined within more or less narrow limits, transgression of these limitations is more likely, and validity will not be presumed but must be proved.

That the rules regarding *ultra vires* and abuse of discretion are identically applied to both statutes and administrative regulations is obvious.[23] The same is true with respect to the requirements of contemporaneous construction and long-continued uniform practice. The rule that a clear and unambiguous term cannot be subject to construction is a general principle of interpretation which is rarely applied to the construction of the Constitution by statute since most constitutional terms do not meet the requirements of the rule. It is, however, frequently used to limit the regulatory power of administrative agencies; for the statutes, being as a matter of principle more concrete and individualized than the Constitution, will often use concepts which are self-executing and not capable of further individualization or concreteness.

The only rule which the courts apply exclusively to administrative regulations is the so-called re-enactment rule.[24] It is indeed a deviation from the uniformity with which the courts otherwise approach statutes and regulations alike. The re-enactment rule owes its existence to two factors. On the one hand, there is the age-old desire of the courts to rationalize their rule-making activity by mechanical canons of interpretation which makes the judicial decision appear to be the result of an automatic device insuring objectivity and negating the possibility of judicial lawmaking. On the other hand, the re-enactment rule is another offering upon the altar of congressional supremacy and lawmaking exclusiveness. Contempo-

[23] Both standards will generally merge into the test of the constitutionality of the statute.

[24] It should, however, be noted that the re-enactment rule in England, where it originated, is a rule of statutory interpretation, to the effect that once the courts have given a statutory term or phrase a certain meaning, all subsequent statutes are supposed to use the term or phrase with this meaning.

raneous and long-continued administrative practice entitles the administrative regulation to great, yet not absolute, respect; the dignity of a binding rule of law can only come from Congress itself. Hence re-enactment, without change, of a statute construed by an administrative agency, or silent acquiescence by Congress in the administrative construction will give a contemporaneous and long-continued administrative regulation whatever it may still lack in legislative respectability.

The theoretical unsoundness of the re-enactment rule is commensurate with the confusion to which it has led in practical application. Dean Griswold has correctly pointed to the verbal character of the rule which is used by the courts to justify a result arrived at independently from the rule and which is not used at all when the courts disapprove of the result. In so far, the rule partakes of the general criticism which has been leveled against the fictitious character of the canons of interpretation.

More specifically, the rule overshoots the mark in a double sense when it endeavors not only to derive the binding force of administrative regulations from statutory re-enactment but also through this instrumentality to elevate administrative regulations to the level of the statute itself. By doing so, it gives, on the one hand, the administrative regulation more than it deserves and, on the other, it gives it less. Whatever binding force the administrative regulation possesses it receives from the statutory delegation, and it can have no binding force outside of it. Re-enactment cannot add to, nor can its absence detract from, this binding effect. If it exists it does so regardless of re-enactment; if it does not exist re-enactment cannot create it. There is only one way in which congressional re-enactment can convey to an administrative regulation the legal quality of the statute, that is, by incorporating the administrative rule into the statute and thus revoking implicitly the delegation and destroying the binding force of the administrative regulation *qua* administrative regulation altogether. To refer to an administrative regulation as possessing the legal quality of the statute is a contradiction in terms. An administrative regulation that obtains this quality, by this very fact, loses its character as administrative regulation. It is then no longer from administrative discretion created by statutory delegation but from congressional discretion created by constitutional delegation that it receives its binding force.[25]

Since no distinction as to binding effect can be drawn between legislative and interpretative regulations, and since, furthermore, legislative regulations originate in express delegation while interpretative regulations do not, the question arises whence the latter derive their legally binding force. In the case of the administrator under the Fair Labor Standards Act the problem is aggravated by the fact that it was the indubitable intent of Congress, expressed in legislative action before and after the passage of the act, to limit the rule-making powers of the administrator strictly to those matters expressly delegated to him for this purpose.

As Congress can only exercise those powers delegated by the Constitution, so an administrative officer can only exercise the powers delegated to him by statute. Yet as Congress holds delegated powers not expressly enumerated in the Constitution, so an administrative officer may have the authority to exercise delegated powers not expressly pointed out in the statute. In other words, the doctrine of implied powers, as developed in *McCulloch* v. *Maryland*[26] for Congress and the Constitution, applies a general principle applicable whenever general powers are delegated. Hence, there are implied powers vested in administrative agencies as there are implied powers vested in Congress, the extent of those powers generally being proportionate to the extent of expressly delegated powers and therefore usually larger in Congress than in the administrative agencies.

It should be noted from the outset that the doctrine of *McCulloch* v. *Maryland* does not take its point of departure from Article I, section 8 of the Constitution[27] but from "general reasoning." Since the Fair Labor Standards Act, in contrast to most acts conveying administrative powers, does not contain a clause analogous to this provision of the Constitution—here again note should be taken of the

[25] Otherwise there would be true delegation of delegated power and a violation of the basic constitutional principle that only Congress can exercise legislative functions directly under the Constitution.

[26] 4 Wheat. (U.S.) 316 (1819).

[27] "The Congress shall have power . . . to make all laws which shall be necessary and proper for carrying into execution the foregoing powers, and all other powers vested by this Constitution in the government of the United States, or in any department or officer thereof."

structural similarity between constitutional and statutory delegation
—we are here only concerned with the propositions of this "general
reasoning," the general principle contained therein, and its application to administrative law.

Chief Justice Marshall's argument sets forth the general proposition that the government of the United States is a government of
enumerated powers and, hence, can exercise only the powers granted
to it, and that with respect to the extent of these powers, the Constitution of the United States does not limit the powers of the federal government to those expressly granted; in other words, it does
not require "that everything granted shall be expressly and minutely
described;"[28] it does not exclude incidental or implied powers. Indeed, it cannot exclude them since, as a Constitution, it cannot "contain an accurate detail of all subdivisions of which its great powers
will admit, and of all the means by which they may be carried into
execution. . . . Its nature, therefore, requires that only its great outlines should be marked, its important objects designated, and the
minor ingredients which compose those objects be deduced from
the nature of the objects themselves. . . . In considering this question, then, we must never forget, that it is a constitution we are
expounding."[29]

The general reasoning which led Chief Justice Marshall to these
propositions grows out of the natural and necessary relationship between delegating and delegated authority which exists wherever
powers are delegated within the framework of a system of legal
rules. As far as the end of rule-making is concerned, the holder of
delegated powers can have only the powers expressly delegated to
him. With regard to the means appropriate to the end, he must have
the power to put into effect the measures necessary for achieving the
end, regardless of whether or not the delegating rule expressly in-
trusts him with such power; in so far, he has implied powers. Among
the means at his disposal he may choose the one he deems most appropriate to achieving the end; in so far he has discretion. His im-

[28] *McCulloch* v. *Maryland*, 4 Wheat. (U.S.) 316, 406 (1819).

[29] *Ibid.*, at 407. Chief Justice Marshall continued by saying that a government
which has the right to act "must according to the dictates of reason be allowed to
select the means" and that a construction which would impede the exercise of
expressly delegated powers by withholding a choice of means may only be
adopted when "the words imperiously require it" (*ibid.*, at 408–9).

plied powers are delegated powers; for they are only an incident of the expressly enumerated powers which they serve as means to an end. Since the delegating authority must have intended the recipient of the delegation to perform the delegated functions effectively, it must have given him the means through which alone those functions can thus be discharged. The delegating authority, then, says in substance this: "I want you to achieve these ends (enumerated powers); you may do all that is necessary to achieve these ends (implied powers); among the means thus put at your disposal you may choose the one you deem most appropriate to the end (discretion)."

The implied powers being an incident of the enumerated ones and subordinated to them as means to an end, the extent of the former is to a high degree concomitant with the latter. The larger the powers conferred with regard to the ends, the larger the powers regularly to be implied as to means.[30] This correlation will be lessened or be entirely absent when the delegating rule, while conferring large enumerated powers, determines not only the end to be pursued but also the means to be employed and thus leaves little to implication. The same will be true when the nature of the end, though far-reaching, is such as to lend itself to easy realization, so that the power to be employed to this end need not be great.[31]

It was Chief Justice Marshall himself who in *Osborn v. The Bank of the United States*[32] recognized the general importance, beyond the relationship between Constitution and Congress, of the general reasoning of *McCulloch v. Maryland*. Whereas in the latter decision the Court discovered implied powers bestowed by the Constitution upon Congress, in *Osborn v. The Bank of the United States* the Court went one step further. Here the question arose whether a bank created by Congress, which performs some public functions as an agency of the federal government, whose principal business is, however, of a private nature, consisting of the usual banking operations, can be taxed by a state. The Court answered in the negative

---

[30] "It has been found, indeed, in the practical administration of the government, that a very large part, if not the largest part, of its functions have been performed in the exercise of powers thus implied." *Hepburn v. Griswold,* 8 Wall. (U.S.) 603, 613 (1869).

[31] The same distinction which is made in the text with regard to power applies to discretion.

[32] 9 Wheat. (U.S.) 738 (1824).

since the ordinary banking operations are a necessary means for the performance of the public function. The Court does here no longer deal directly with the relationship between the constitutionally determined ends and the means for achieving those ends, as left by constitutional implication to the determination of Congress (primary means). The performance of normal banking operations does not serve directly the constitutional end, but only indirectly by enabling the bank, the primary means, to function properly. In other words, the performance of normal banking operations is a means (secondary means) for a statutory end which, in turn, serves as a means (primary means) for the constitutional end. It is to the power of Congress to legislate with regard to these secondary means, subordinate to statutory ends, that the Supreme Court in the Osborn case and in the cases following it applies the doctrine of implied powers.

It is true that in these cases the powers with respect to secondary means were expressly conferred on the banking agencies by the statute. The question then arises whether those agencies would possess the same powers in the absence of express congressional delegation. Since without those powers the agencies were unable to perform the functions for which they were created by Congress, it seems to follow from the general premises of the doctrine of implied powers that they would enjoy those powers even in the absence of express congressional delegation.

It is in this sense that the Supreme Court answered the question in *Edward's Lessee* v. *Darby*.[33] Here the question arose whether commissioners under a North Carolina statute had the authority to have surveys made of certain reservations, located around salt licks and springs and not subject to the provisions of the act establishing land grants for soldiers. The statute authorized the commissioners to appoint surveyors for the more speedy and effective laying-off and surveying of the lands subject to such grants. With respect to the power of the commissioners to cause surveys of the reservations, the Court said:

> We admit the statute does not give the authority to survey the reservations, in express terms, but do not admit that the authority may not, and does not, result by necessary implication from the duties they were ex-

[33] 12 Wheat. (U.S.) 206 (1827).

pressly required to perform, and from the general provisions of the statute. They were not expressly required by the statute to detemine what licks and springs were proper objects for reservation, and came within the provisions of the statute; but they were required to lay off and cause to be surveyed the lands granted to the officers and soldiers, subject to and so as not to interfere with these reservations. . . . It seems to result necessarily from these provisions, that the commissioners must first determine what were the proper subjects of reservation, and having determined that a given salt lick or spring came within the provisions of the law, the power and duty of laying off by survey the 640 acres reserved, and to be avoided, around the lick, seems necessarily and irresistibly to result to the commissioners, in all cases where they might deem it necessary to do so, in order to enable them to lay off the lands for the officers and soldiers, so as to avoid these reservations. . . . But more especially it was indispensable wherever the commissioners were about to lay off lands for the officers and soldiers, adjacent to a salt lick or spring, to have a survey made of the reservation, to give it figure and fixed locality; otherwise, the reservation being of quantity only, without boundary, one of two consequences must have resulted, namely, that it might lawfully be encroached upon on one side, and if on one, on any other side; or that, practically its uncertainty must have excluded a much larger quantity than was intended by law to be be reserved from the satisfaction of the claims of the officers and soldiers.[34]

The doctrine of implied powers with regard to executive departments was recognized by the Supreme Court in most sweeping terms in *United States* v. *Macdaniel.* Here the power of the Secretary of the Navy to pay a clerk of the department for services not authorized by law was in controversy. The Court said:

A practical knowledge of the action of any one of the great departments of the government, must convince every person that the head of a department, in the distribution of its duties and responsibilities, is often compelled to exercise his discretion. He is limited in the exercise of his powers by the law; but it does not follow that he must show a statutory provision for every thing he does. No government could be administered on such principles. To attempt to regulate by law the minute movements of every part of the complicated machinery of government, would evince a most unpardonable ignorance of the subject. Whilst the great outlines of its movements may be marked out, and limitations imposed on the exercise of its powers, there are numberless things which must be done, that can neither be anticipated nor defined, and which are essential to the proper action of the government. Hence, of necessity, usages have been established in every department of the government, which have become a kind of

[34] *Ibid.,* at 209.

common law, and regulate the rights and duties of those who act within their respective limits.[35]

The Supreme Court has thus far decided only a few cases in which the question as to the applicability of the doctrine of implied powers to administrative agencies was clearly put. In Mr. Justice Stone's dissenting opinion in *Arrow-Hart & Hegeman Electric Co. v. Federal Trade Commission,* the doctrine of implied powers is unmistakably applied to administrative agencies:

No more here, than there, should it be said that the purpose of the statute must be defeated because the law-makers did not attempt to provide with a meticulous precision how the Commission should proceed in every contingency that might arise. The dominating purpose of the statute is to restore to its original state the competition suppressed by the acquisition of the stock, and, just as we rejected a rigid literalism there in order to effect that purpose, and upheld an order which was but incidental, though necessary, to the effective exercise of the power specifically granted, so we should reject it now. . . . In this, as in most schemes for regulation by administrative bodies, there must be a balance between the general and the particular. When the courts are faced with interpretation of the particular, administration breaks down and the manifest purpose of the legislature is defeated unless it is recognized that, surrounding granted powers, there must be a penumbra which will give scope for practical operation. In carrying such schemes into operation the function of courts is constructive, not destructive, to make them, wherever reasonably possible, effective agencies for law enforcement and not to destroy them.[36]

The Supreme Court has come closest to applying the doctrine of *McCulloch* v. *Maryland* to administrative rule-making in *Phelps Dodge Corp.* v. *National Labor Relations Board.*[37] Section 10 (c) of the Nation Labor Relations Act authorizes the National Labor Relations Board "to take such affirmative action as will effectuate the policies of this Act." The Court proposes through Mr. Justice Frankfurter to pursue "the central clue to the Board's powers—effectuation of the policies of the act. . . ." By doing so the Court sets forth certain general standards by which the powers of administrative agencies are to be determined.

A statute expressive of such large public policy as that on which the National Labor Relations Board is based must be broadly phrased and necessarily carries with it the task of administrative application. There is an

[35] *United States* v. *Macdaniel,* 7 Pet. (U.S.) 1, 14 (1833).
[36] 291 U.S. 484, 606 (1934).   [37] 313 U.S. 177, 191 (1941).

area plainly covered by the language of the Act and an area no less plainly without it. But in the nature of things Congress could not catalogue all the devices and stratagems for circumventing the policies of the Act. Nor could it define the whole gamut of remedies to effectuate these policies in an infinite variety of specific situations. Congress met these difficulties by leaving the adaptations of means to end to the empiric process of administration. The exercise of the process was committed to the Board, subject to limited judicial review. Because the relation of remedy to policy is peculiarly a matter for administrative competence, courts must not enter the allowable area of the Board's discretion and must guard against the danger of sliding unconsciously from the narrow confines of law into the more spacious domain of policy. On the other hand, the power with which Congress invested the Board implies responsibility—the responsibility of exercising its judgment in employing the statutory powers. . . . All we are entitled to ask is that the statute speak through the Board where the statute does not speak for itself.[38]

Even though this reasoning proceeds technically in interpretation of Section 10 (c) of the National Labor Relations Act, its substance is of a general nature and capable of general application independently from the statutory provision which it purports to interpret. The standards by which the powers of the National Labor Relations Board under Section 10 (c) are to be defined, are the standards by which the powers of any administrative agency under any congressional enactment must be defined.

The issue came clearly into the open in *Cudahy Packing Co.* v. *Holland*. Here the administrator under the Fair Labor Standards Act claimed the authority to delegate his subpoena power to regional directors. This claim was founded upon express provisions of the act as well as upon the argument that the said authority was to be implied from the structure of the act and the nature of the duties imposed by the act upon the administrator. The Supreme Court, through Chief Justice Stone, refused to follow this argument for three reasons: first, the authority thus claimed would be without limitation with regard both to the addressees and the subject matter of the delegation; in other words, the administrator could delegate the subpoena power to any subordinate, and he could do so with regard to any other power he possesses; second, "unlimited authority of an administrative officer to delegate the exercise of the subpoena power is not lightly to be inferred. It is a power capable of

[38] *Ibid.*, at 194.

oppressive use, especially when it may be indiscriminately delegated and the subpoena is not returnable before a judicial officer;"[39] and third, the intent of Congress as revealed by the express grant of authority to delegate the subpoena power in other acts, and by the legislative history of the Fair Labor Standards Act itself, supports the view of the majority.

Nor can we assume, as the Government argues, that Congress is wholly without design in withholding the power in this case and granting it in others, or even if it had been that it is any part of the judicial function to restore to the Act what Congress has taken out of it. Even though Congress has under-estimated the burden which it has placed upon the Administrator, which is by no means clear, we think that the legislative record establishes that Congress has withheld from him authority to delegate the exercise of the subpoena power, and that this precludes our restoring it by construction.[40]

In a dissenting opinion, four justices, through Mr. Justice Douglas, pushed the doctrine of implied powers beyond the limits within which it had been recognized by *McCulloch* v. *Maryland, Osborn* v. *The Bank of the United States, Edward's Lessee* v. *Darby*, and *United States* v. *Macdaniel. McCulloch* v. *Maryland* recognized the authority of the Constitution to delegate by implication to Congress powers incidental to those expressly delegated. *Osborn* v. *The Bank of the United States, Edward's Lessee* v. *Darby*, and *United States* v. *Macdaniel* recognized the authority of Congress to delegate by implication to an administrative agency powers incidental to those expressly delegated. The dissenting opinion in *Cudahy Packing Co.* v. *Holland* recognizes the authority of Congress to delegate by implication to an administrative officer the power to subdelegate powers expressly delegated to him. The dissent establishes between the administrator and Congress a relation similar to the one which Chief Justice Marshall's opinions created between Congress and the Constitution; that is to say, the dissent accepts fully the doctrine of implied powers for administrative law. The parallelism between both opinions is not limited to the results; it reveals itself in the very line of reasoning by which Chief Justice Marshall's and Mr. Justice Doug-

[39] *Cudahy Packing Co.* v. *Holland,* 315 U.S. 357, 363 (1942).
[40] *Ibid.,* at 367.

las' opinions arrive at their conclusions.[41] Here and there, the importance of the functions expressly delegated is the basis of the argument. Next comes the assertion that without the implied powers
claimed those functions cannot be effectively exercised. Finally, the
argument derived from legislative practice and history is disposed
of.[42]

The attempt to define the administrator's regulatory powers with
regard to the coverage of the Fair Labor Standards Act by the doctrine of implied powers is marked by two problems peculiar to this
act and not to be found in any of the decided cases.

In all cited cases, with the exception perhaps of *Edward's Lessee*
v. *Darby*, the implied power was conceived as an incident of the expressly delegated power in terms of a means to an end. So in *McCulloch* v. *Maryland* the power of creating a corporation was considered
a means for the effective carrying-out of the enumerated constitutional ends. In *Osborn* v. *The Bank of the United States* private
banking operations were regarded as a means for carrying into effect the public functions of the bank. In *Phelps Dodge Corp.* v.
National Labor Relations Board the powers of the board under consideration are clearly subordinate to the effectuation of the purposes
of the act. The same holds true for the dissent in *Arrow-Hart and
Hegeman Electric Co.* v. *Federal Trade Commission*. In *Cudahy
Packing Corp.* v. *Holland*, finally, the authority to subdelegate the
subpoena power is conceived as a means to put the law-enforcing
functions of the administrator into effect.

The interpretation of the statutory terms limiting the coverage of
the Fair Labor Standards Act cannot be conceived as a means for
the accomplishing of the statutory ends as laid down in the minimum wage and maximum hour provisions. It is not so that the
administrator has his choice among several means of which the determination of the coverage by interpretation of statutory terms is
one. The relation between this interpretative activity and the legis-

---

[41] It must be noted that in Mr. Justice Douglas' opinion the argument concerning the existence of the administrator's implied powers is not separated from the
argument dealing with the kind of power delegated to him by implication, that is,
the power of subdelegation.

[42] Cf. *McCulloch* v. *Maryland,* 4 Wheat. (U.S.) 316, 422, 423, 427, 428, 430
(1819) (opinion of Marshall, C.J.) with *Cudahy Packing Co.* v. *Holland,* 315
U.S. 357, 368, 372, 373 (1942) (opinion of Douglas, J.).

lative purposes is one not of functional or teleological but of logical subordination. That is to say, it is logically impossible for the administrator to effectuate the policies and purposes of the act without limiting the coverage of the act by interpretation of the statutory terms. He may choose one among several interpretations, all equally remaining within the logical confines of the statutory term, but interpret he must. He has no choice between interpreting the statute or refraining from doing so. Interpretation is necessary for the effective discharge of the administrator's duties, not as a means to an end, but as a logical incident of the duties themselves.

This is so in a dual sense. The determination of minimum wages itself is to a certain extent dependent upon the coverage of the wage order; coverage is one of several factors which the administrator must take into consideration as a logically indispensable determinant of the rule-making process. Furthermore, the wage order as an enforcible rule, a command addressed to employer, employees, and public officials, is logically incomplete without making clear to whom it is addressed and to whom not. It is for those reasons that, regardless of the absence of express statutory delegation, the administrator could not help but issue interpretative bulletins determining the coverage of the act and that the courts have either accepted these interpretations as a matter of course or, when they have rejected them, they have done so for reasons which would invalidate any interpretation, whether or not issued under express delegation.

The conception of interpretative powers as the logical incident of the powers expressly conferred is also capable of meeting the problem of legislative practice and history. In this regard, too, the situation is different from the one in which the same problem presented itself in *Phelps Dodge Corp.* v. *Holland.* According to Chief Justice Marshall and Mr. Justice Douglas, the express grant of a certain power in one instance and the lack of such a grant in another is not, in the absence of a clear manifestation of the legislative intent, conclusive proof for the intention to withhold the power in the latter case. The legislative history of the Fair Labor Standards Act, however, shows clearly that the all-inclusive rule-making powers of the administrator, which the original bill envisaged, were finally limited to wage orders and the interpretation of a few scattered statutory terms and that Congress intended with this limitation to meet the constitutional objections which had led to the invalidation of the National Industrial Recovery Act. Neither were subsequent legislative attempts at giving the administrator general rule-making powers approved by Congress.

When, as in the case of the Fair Labor Standards Act, the legislative history shows unmistakably that the legislator did not expressly grant certain powers because he did not want to delegate them, the doctrine of implied powers is confronted with a serious obstacle. Powers which the legislator intends to withhold by refusing to grant them expressly, cannot be implied. When the silence of the statute cannot be interpreted as implied delegation but must be taken to mean refusal to delegate, considerations of rule-making convenience will not justify judicial and administrative officers in adding to the powers expressly granted. There seems to be nothing left but the appeal to the legislature.

Yet this conclusion is justified only when the withholding of powers limits the choice of means, making the performance of rule-making functions more difficult and, hence, is exclusively a matter of rule-making convenience. The conclusion has actually been drawn only with respect to such cases. When, however, the powers withheld are an essential element of the powers conferred so that without them these powers cannot be intelligently executed at all, the problem is no longer of legislative or administrative convenience with respect to rule-making but of the very existence of the expressly delegated regulatory powers. In such a case the presumption that it was the intent of Congress to grant effective regulatory powers must prevail over the legislative history which shows the congressional intent to withhold unconstitutional powers, this intent being mistakenly applied to incidental powers of doubtless constitutionality. Congress, when empowering the administrator to issue wage orders, cannot be presumed to have intentionally withheld powers without which the administrator cannot issue wage orders, that is to say, without which he cannot do what Congress wants him to do.

Once certain powers have been expressly delegated, the delegation of all incidental powers, essential for the execution of the former, must be presumed to have been intended, too. Congress may withhold powers for certain means, necessary for executing the expressly delegated powers, but not for all means or for essentials of the expressly delegated powers themselves. Congress cannot be presumed to have intended to confer no effective powers at all and thus to defeat its own legislative purpose.

What Congress actually intended to do was to grant those powers without which the purposes and policies of the act cannot be attained and to withhold those powers the delegation of which the Supreme Court was likely to consider unconstitutional. It is in the light of this intent that the act must be construed. The unconstitutionality of the delegation of powers essential from the point of view of the policies and purposes of the act would make the act itself unconstitutional. The mistaken congressional belief, however, about what is constitutional and what is not, is not able to defeat the policies and purposes of the act. Congress cannot by implication delegate unconstitutional powers which are of the essence of expressly delegated constitutional powers; here the unconstitutionality of the former is fatal to the constitutionality of the whole. Yet neither can Congress, mistakenly believing them to be unconstitutional, withhold powers, otherwise to be implied, which are of the essence of expressly delegated constitutional powers. As Lord Hobhouse said in *Salmon* v. *Duncombe:* "It is a very serious matter to hold that when the main object of a statute is clear it should be reduced to a nullity, by the draftsman's unskillfulness or ignorance of law."[43] In this case, the application by courts and administrative agencies of the presumption referred to above will protect the legislative purposes of Congress from being frustrated by the errors of its constitutional doctrine. By obliterating in actual performance the distinction between expressly delegated and not delegated but essential powers the administrator and the courts have done exactly that.

This is, however, not the last word. "For the question respecting the extent of the powers actually granted is perpetually arising, and will probably continue to arise as long as our system shall exist."[44]

43 *Salmon* v. *Duncombe,* 11 App. Cas. 627, 634 (1886).

44 *McCulloch* v. *Maryland,* 4 Wheat. 316, 405 (1819). *United States* v. *Bailey,* 9 Pet. (U.S.) 238 (1835), and *Caha* v. *United States,* 152 U.S. 211, 218 (1894) may also be quoted. The idea that the power to interpret is implied in the power to administer is also clearly expressed in *United States* ex rel. *Hall* v. *Payne,* 254 U.S. 343 (1920): "He [the Secretary of Labor] could not administer or apply the Act

Whenever there is an implied grant of power, there must be also an implied limitation of the power granted.

Looking at administrative law through the distorting lenses of a conceptualist theory of the Constitution, one has difficulty in admitting that the administrative function has developed into a co-ordinate fourth branch of the government which must be controlled directly by the Constitution and not by the "sterile refinements unrelated to affairs,"[45] by which the courts have connected verbally the exercise of the executive, judicial, and legislative functions with the constitutional text. It is only through such a direct confrontation of the problems of administrative law with the language and spirit of the Constitution that the administrative agencies can be made subject to the constitutional limitations upon which our system of government is founded, without losing the ability to fulfil their regulatory functions.[46] It is only through such an approach that administrative needs and constitutional abstractions can be built into a synthesis of concepts and principles, which will do for administrative law what the great decisions of Chief Justice Marshall's Supreme Court have done for the three traditional branches of the government.

We have endeavored to find in the administrative function itself a positive standard for determining the content of the powers of administrative agencies. Following the same approach, we will now search for a negative standard by which the scope of regulatory powers can be delimited.

Here again, the discrepancy between political philosophy and legal theory, on the one hand, and the actual solution of concrete

---

without construing it, and its construction involved the exercise of judgment and discretion"; cf. also *Marbury* v. *Madison,* 1 Cranch (U.S.) 137, 177 (1803): "Those who apply the rule to particular cases, must of necessity expound and interpret that rule."

[45] Mr. Justice Frankfurter, concurring in *Graves* v. *New York* ex rel. *O'Keefe,* 306 U.S. 466, 488 (1939). Cf. also what Lord Bryce, *The American Commonwealth* (New York: Macmillan Co., 1912), p. 375, has to say about the same problem.

[46] For the general aspects of this problem see Charles Howard McIlwain, "The Fundamental Law behind the Constitution of the United States," in *Constitutionalism and the Changing World* (New York: Macmillan Co., 1939), pp. 244 ff.; with respect to administrative law see A. A. Berle, "The Expansion of American Administrative Law," *Harvard Law Review,* XXX (1917), 430.

problems by the courts, on the other, is characteristic of the traditional point of view. We have seen how the traditional doctrine, unwilling to admit that an administrative agency may have powers not expressly delegated but implied, can nevertheless not fail to realize that administrative agencies actually perform functions of this kind, and tries to reconcile theory and facts by a series of legalistic distinctions and conceptualist doctrines.

With respect to the problem of implied limitations on regulatory powers the situation is somewhat similar. On the constitutional level, the reasoning takes as its point of departure the doctrine of the separation of powers and the principle that delegated powers cannot be delegated, and arrives at the conclusion that the legislature cannot delegate rule-making powers to administrative agencies. In the face of the obvious fact that such powers are actually delegated with the approval of the courts, the principle is interpreted so as to refer only to delegation unlimited as to subject matter and regulatory policy. Since, however, the absence of a defined subject matter would amount to a blanket delegation, nothing short of the surrender of the lawmaking function altogether could be considered unconstitutional. The practical importance of this requirement is, therefore, extremely limited; it was found lacking only once, in *Schechter* v. *United States*.[47] The requirement of a defined policy in the form of a legislative standard has become practically obsolete since standards of extreme vagueness have been considered to meet the constitutional requirement. Hence, Elihu Root's much quoted statement of 1916 holds even more true today: "Before these agencies the old doctrine prohibiting the delegation of legislative power has virtually retired from the field and given up the fight."[48]

Another and seemingly more effective method of limiting the regulatory powers of administrative agencies is the extension of judicial review under the due process clause. Yet judicial review, conceived as trial *de novo*, does not solve the problem of limiting the administrative function but rather eliminates it by doing away with the coordinate function altogether. It contributes nothing to the solution of the problem with which we are here concerned but rather attempts to destroy the very conditions under which the problem could arise at all.

47 295 U.S. 495 (1935), especially at 551.
48 *Report of the American Bar Association*, XLI (1916), 368.

On the statutory level, the traditional canons of interpretation are applied to the language of the statute in order to ascertain whether the administrative agency has remained within the limits of the statutory standards or else has acted *ultra vires*. The courts have, however, not failed to recognize that there are cases of administrative rule-making which, even though remaining within the verbal limits of the statute, are nevertheless *ultra vires*. The courts have justified the invalidation of administrative rules of this kind by either straining the words of the statute as well as the canons of interpretation or by declaring the regulation arbitrary and unreasonable.

It is with the latter category of administrative regulations that we propose to deal. The test of reasonableness, where the term does not refer to standards well defined and clearly understood, is obviously less a standard by which the scope of administrative rule-making power can be delimited than the admission that such a standard cannot be found. The analysis of the cases invalidating administrative regulations which are not clearly in violation of the words of the statute will show that underlying these decisions is the inarticulate awareness of implied limitations which administrative regulations are not allowed to overstep. These limitations follow from the very nature of the administrative function and its relation to the legislative branch. It will furthermore be shown that these implied limitations upon regulatory powers in administrative law have their counterpart in the three traditional branches of the government.[49]

We take as our point of departure the Fair Labor Standards Act. This act, as pointed out before, constitutes a most serious and elaborate attempt to meet all possible constitutional requirements with

[49] The doctrine, preoccupied with the pseudo-problems of constitutional theology, has paid scant attention to the problem of implied powers and limitations in administrative law. Ernst Freund was, however, already aware of the existence of the problem and the unsatisfactory state of its solution; in *Standards of American Legislation* (Chicago: University of Chicago Press, 1917), p. 302, he stated: "The precise line of demarcation between matter to be determined by statute and matter to be left to regulation has not yet been satisfactorily settled"; see also Freund, "The Substitution of Rule for Discretion in Public Law," *American Political Science Review*, IX (1915), 666 and especially 676. See also James Hart, "The Exercise of Rule-Making Power," in *Studies on Administrative Management in the Government of the United States* (Washington, D.C.: Government Printing Office, 1937), p. 34: "Possibly the policy or standard need not be expressed in the delegation of rule-making power, if it may be implied with sufficient certainty and clarity."

respect to the scope of delegated regulatory powers and administrative procedure. Despite those unusual precautions, the act in practical operation has not avoided some of the difficulties which have befallen other administrative agencies. On the one hand, the act has refrained from delegating expressly to the administrator interpretative powers, believed to have been thus withheld, which are actually inherent in the administrative function. On the other hand, the act has delegated to the administrator apparently well-defined rule-making powers, the exercise of which has posed the problem of the scope of regulatory powers in administrative law.

One of the characteristic features of the regulations under the act is the tendency to circumscribe the categories of employees exempt from the operation of the act by rigid, mathematical formulas. It is with respect to the numerical standards of these regulations that the reported cases show an as yet uncertain and inarticulate awareness of implied limitations on regulatory powers. The courts do not limit to regulations under the Fair Labor Standards Act their opposition against abstract, rigid standards of a numerical nature. There is rather a general tendency to invalidate such standards whenever the statutory terms to be defined do not lend themselves to definitions of this kind but need for the adequate limitation of their content to be confronted with the facts of the individual case.

The courts have shown reluctance to follow the administrator in limiting the coverage of the statute by mathematical formulas and especially percentage rules, where the act itself uses terms such as "greater part," "substantial," "area," and the like. Technically, the argument of these decisions follows the familiar lines of statutory interpretation. The courts declare that it would be "unreasonable," "arbitrary," or "impossible" to define the statutory terms by rigid, mathematical formulas.

From the point of view of statutory interpretation it might, however, be argued that it is not outright impossible to define terms such as "area of production," "local retailing," "bona fide executive," and the like numerically and by percentages. If, for instance, Congress should have defined the constitutional term "interstate commerce" on the same percentage basis as the administrator under the Fair Labor Standards Act defines the identical statutory term, the courts would undoubtedly have approved of the statutory definition of the constitutional term. Why, then, are the courts hostile to similar definitions on the administrative level? The answer lies in the particular relationship between administrative regulation and congressional enactment. The clarification of this relationship, in turn, depends upon the answer to two questions: (1) What was the legislative policy under which the rule-making powers under consideration were delegated to the administrator? and (2) What function do the mathematical standards of these administrative regulations fulfil from the point of view of this legislative policy?

The delegation of regulatory powers to administrative agencies stems from "the inability of the legislature to formulate standards sufficiently definite for private guidance. This inability in turn may be due either to the inherent inapplicability of uniform standards to varying individual cases or to the temporary failure to discover such principles."[50] The outstanding example of the latter alternative is the delegation of rate-making powers to administrative agencies. In this case, administrative agencies, on the basis of technical and scientific knowledge that Congress does not possess, develop gradually, through the trial-and-error method not accessible to Congress, a definite or even rigid formula which will ultimately take the place of the legislative enactment and according to which future cases will uniformly be decided.

The specific rule-making powers[51] of the administrator under the Fair Labor Standards Act are obviously not of this kind. If Congress did not feel able to determine in the statute itself concepts such as "area of production," "bona fide executive," or "local retailing capacity," it was not because it did not possess the expert knowledge and experience which would be at the command of the administrator. No such knowledge and experience is needed for the understanding of the terms under consideration, and when Congress left the definition of these concepts to the administrator, it did not do so with the expectation that the particular technical competency of the administrator would enable him to do what Congress was unable to do.

[50] Ernst Freund, *Administrative Powers over Persons and Property* (Chicago: University of Chicago Press, 1928), p. 29.

[51] In contradistinction to the general powers relative to the determination of minimum wages.

The implied inability of Congress to define these terms is rather the result of the very nature of the terms which in the majority of cases are applicable to individual situations without further definition but which in a number of marginal cases are inherently incapable of abstract, uniform determination. In these marginal cases the determination must be made "upon all the facts shown in the record," "upon the facts in each particular case." Since, on the one hand, the nature of the terms to be defined makes abstract, uniform determination impossible and since, on the other hand, Congress is unable to give the individualized determination, on the basis of the particular case, which those terms require, Congress has delegated to the administrator the power to define these terms. For the administrative regulation, in contrast to the legislative enactment, is capable of flexibility in the light of changing circumstances and adaptable to the individual case, thus doing justice to these terms.

The administrator, when defining these terms in regulations of mathematical rigidity, has acted counter to the legislative policy under which he received these regulatory powers. If Congress had thought that formulas of mathematical precision could solve the problem of defining the terms under consideration, Congress could have written such formulas into the statute. For legislation in abstract, general, rigid terms is the province of congressional rule-making, while legislation in flexible, concrete terms is the proper field of administrative rule-making. By doing what Congress could have done but did not want to do, that is, to make abstract, general, inflexible regulations in mathematical terms, the administrator has neglected the implicit congressional mandate and overstepped the implied limitations to which the division of functions between Congress and administrative agencies subjects his regulatory powers. It is to this discrepancy between congressional intent and administrative regulation, between the proper delimitation of the spheres of congressional and administrative legislation and the actual extension of the latter, that the courts refer, when they declare regulations of this kind invalid as being "unreasonable" or "arbitrary."

This evaluation of the administrator's regulations is supported by the analysis of the functions which these mathematical standards are intended to fulfil according to the statements of the administrator himself. They lie exclusively in the realm of administrative convenience.

The foregoing discussion has led to four conclusions: (1) that administrative regulations of mathematical rigidity meet with wide disapproval by the courts; (2) that the functional relationship between statutory delegation and administrative regulation may require, in the latter, flexibility and adaptability to the particularities of the individual case; (3) that regulations of the rigid, general type owe their existence to considerations of administrative convenience; and (4) that there is a judicial trend against letting considerations of administrative convenience prevail over limitations which the statute, expressly or by implication, has placed upon administrative discretion.

These conclusions point toward the existence of implied limitations on regulatory powers in administrative law. These implied limitations have their roots in the same element to which the implied regulatory powers owe their existence, that is, the administrative function itself. In the same way in which the power to interpret is the logical by-product of the power to administer, the power to administer under an act of Congress precludes implicitly the power to do what Congress could have done but did not want to do. The administrative agency is, then, under a duty, the positive counterpart of this limitation, to execute the mandate of Congress whose explicit command must be read in the literal text of the statute and whose implicit injunctions must be sought in the particular purpose which Congress wishes to achieve through the delegation of regulatory powers. The administrative agency, in other words, must perform the particular administrative function, the performance of which is the implicit purpose of the delegation of regulatory powers.

How can this purpose be ascertained? The traditional answer, that it is the administrative function to "fill in the details"[52] of incomplete congressional legislation, has impeded rather than furthered the recognition of the problem and of its solution. This answer was correct when it was given, that is, when the traditional three branches of the government performed all governmental functions in relative separation and when, therefore, the assistance which the executive gave to the legislative branch in the performance of the latter's

[52] *Wayman v. Southard,* 10 Wheat. (U.S.) 1, 43 (1825).

functions could be explained correctly in the traditional terms of the separation of powers.

The problem today, in constitutional terms, lies in the development of a fourth branch of the government which, far from filling in mere details, has become quantitatively as well as qualitatively a co-ordinate partner of the three traditional branches. Quantitatively, administrative legislation exceeds by far enactments by Congress. Qualitatively, administrative regulations are genuine legislation, in many instances no more limited by statutory standards than congressional legislation is by constitutional standards. The attempt at limiting administrative regulative powers must therefore start with the recognition that a co-ordinate administrative function exists.

The second step toward a solution of our problem is the recognition of the source from which this co-ordinate administrative function derives. This source is congressional delegation, at the basis of which there may be one of two possible purposes. It is either that Congress does not wish to legislate even though it could and so for whatever reason, such as time-saving, political caution, and the like, delegates legislative powers to an administrative agency, or that Congress did not legislate because it could not have legislated without putting in jeopardy the very purposes for which the law was enacted and therefore delegated regulatory powers to administrative authorities. In the former type of delegation the administrative powers are limited only by the words of the statute, and expressed and implied limitations coincide. Hence, no particular problem with respect to implied limitations can arise. It is therefore with the latter category alone that we are concerned.

Here Congress may delegate regulatory powers for three kinds of reasons. It may do so in order to have the facts determined upon which the application of the law depends in an individual case. This is what is meant by "execution of the laws" in the traditional meaning of the term and is part of the traditional executive function. Second, Congress may delegate regulatory powers for the purpose of determining certain legislative standards, a determination which requires experimentation on the basis of scientific knowledge and technical skill; such trial-and-error method is beyond the reach of congressional action. Third, the purpose of congressional delegation may be to create flexible standards adaptable to the particular conditions of the individual case. Here again, Congress is incapable of discharging this particular function.

Under these three types of delegation the regulatory powers of the administrative agency are implicitly limited by the kind of administrative function it has to perform. One type of delegation allows only the exercise of regulatory powers of the executive type; the other, only the exercise of regulatory powers of an experimental nature; the third, only flexible administrative regulations. Consequently, under the executive type the administrative agency could not substitute its own standards for the statutory ones (which it would be allowed to do under the experimental and flexible types) without violating the implicit limitations which the statute prescribes. When only powers to regulate by trial and error are delegated, a regulation laying down at once a ready-made, definite standard which was at the disposal of Congress, without experimentation or the use of technical skill or scientific expertness, would again overstep the implied limits which the statute has marked out. Finally, under the flexible type a regulation which replaces the rigid standard of the statute by another rigid one, would, as we have seen, find itself outside the implied limitations imposed by the statute.

These three types of administrative regulation, violative of statutory standards, have this in common that they do what Congress could have done but did not want to do. The test according to which a doubtful case of violation must be determined is to be found in the administrative function which the regulations are supposed to fulfil in each particular case.[53] The nature of this function is revealed by the source of administrative power, that is, the statutory delegation.

We arrived at this conclusion by an empirical examination of a particular situation arising under the Fair Labor Standards Act and of the court decisions dealing with this situation and the problems underlying it. It can, however, be shown that these conclusions are only the special manifestation of a general principle of our constitutional system. In other words, the doctrine of implied limitations on

[53] Cf. Freund, *Administrative Powers over Persons and Property*, p. 91: "Delegated discretion is subject to unexpressed limitations which follow partly from the supremacy of the statute over its instrumentalities, and partly from the presumptive reservation of certain considerations for exclusive legislative control."

regulatory powers in administrative law is only the special application of a general doctrine of implied limitations in constitutional law. In the same implicit way in which administrative powers are limited by the functions which the statute delegates, the respective powers of the federal and the state governments as well as the powers of the legislative, executive, and judicial branches of the federal government in relation to each other are limited by the functions which the federal constitution delegates to the federal government and its three traditional branches. "Every positive direction contains an implication against anything contrary to it, or which would frustrate or disappoint the purpose of that provision. The frame of the government; the grant of legislative power itself; the organization of the executive authority; the erection of the principal courts of justice, create implied limitations . . . as strong as though a negative was expressed in each instance."[54] According to Judge Cooley, "There is no difficulty in saying that any such act, which under pretext of exercising such power is usurping another, is opposed to the constitution and void."[55]

It follows by implication from the nature of the federal system which protects the federal government as well as the several state governments in their existence and in the proper discharge of their functions, that neither government may tax agencies of the other.[56]

[54] *People v. Draper,* 15 N.Y. 532, 544 (1857).

[55] Thomas McIntyre Cooley, *A Treatise on the Constitutional Limitations* (8th ed.; Boston: Little, Brown & Co., 1927), pp. 357–58; cf. *ibid.,* p. 355. See also Judge Cooley in *People v. Salem,* 20 Mich. 452, 473 (1870): "It is conceded . . . that there are certain limitations upon this power, not prescribed in express terms by any constitutional provision, but inherent in the subject itself, which attend its exercise under all circumstances and which are as inflexible and absolute in their restraints as if directly imposed in the most positive of words." See Chief Justice Marshall in *McCulloch v. Maryland,* 4 Wheat. (U.S.) 316, 407 (1819). It was the intention of the Constitution that "the minor ingredients which compose those objects [of our political life] be deduced from the nature of the objects themselves." Cf. also *Knox v. Lee,* 12 Wall. (U.S.) 457 (1871); Thomas McIntyre Cooley, *The General Principles of Constitutional Law in the United States of America* (Boston: Little, Brown & Co., 1891), p. 100; Robert Kenneth Carr, *The Supreme Court and Judicial Review* (New York: Farrar and Rinehart, Inc., 1942), p. 96.

[56] W. W. Willoughby, *The Constitutional Law of the United States* (New York: Baker, Voorhis & Co., 1910); Walter Farleigh Dodd, "Implied Powers and Implied Limitations in Constitutional Law," *Yale Law Journal,* XXIX (1919), 140, 147.

It has even been suggested that the express limitations which the federal constitution imposes upon the states are relatively less important than the limitations derived from implication.[57] The constitutional principle of the supremacy of the federal government together with a grant of power to the federal government may impose an implied limitation upon the power of the states with regard to the matter delegated for regulation to the federal government. Whether such an implied limitation exists depends upon the nature of the power concerned. If the power granted to the federal government can be exercised only by one government within the same territory, such a limitation must be implied. As Chief Justice Marshall put it in *Sturges* v. *Crowninshield:* "Whenever . . . the nature of the power requires that it should be exercised exclusively by Congress, the subject is as completely taken from the state legislature as if they had been expressly forbidden to act on it."[58]

Turning from the relations between federal and state governments to the relations among the three traditional branches of the government, we find that the very principle of the separation of powers is an implied limitation upon the powers of the three branches in relation to each other. This limitation follows from the establishment by the Constitution of three branches of the government, each exercising a particular function of its own. It is from the nature of these functions that derive by implication the particular limitations by which the powers of the legislative, judicial, and executive branches of the government are circumscribed in their relation to each other.

The constitutional doctrine of implied limitations, manifesting itself as the doctrine of the "higher law" and in other natural law doctrines, was originally developed for the purpose of preventing a legislative absolutism which, unchecked, would encroach upon the liberties of the individual. Thus Judge Cooley wrote in the Preface to the second edition of his *Constitutional Limitations:* "In this sympathy and faith, he had written of jury trials and the other safeguards to personal liberty, of liberty of the press, and of vested rights; and he had also endeavored to point out that there are on all sides definite limitations which circumscribe the legislative authority,

---

[57] Dodd, *op. cit.*, pp. 138, 160.   [58] 4 Wheat. (U.S.) 122 (1819).

independent of the specific restrictions which the people impose by their State constitutions."[59]

Yet besides these implied limitations upon the legislative power, upon which attention has mainly been focused, there exist less spectacular ones, which, growing out of the legislative function itself, are similar in nature to, and fulfil a similar function as, implied limitations in administrative law. In the same way in which an act of Congress delegates administrative powers to an administrative agency, the Constitution delegates legislative powers to Congress; and in the same way in which, consequently, the administrative agency can perform no other but administrative functions, the legislative department can exercise no other but legislative authority. When Congress has only delegated the power to make flexible, concrete regulations, the administrative agency cannot make abstract, rigid ones which under the circumstances would be administrative regulations in form only but not in substance and would actually encroach upon the powers of Congress. Likewise, Congress cannot, in the form of a statute, make rules which are alien to the legislative function and belong actually to the judiciary. "The assumption of judicial power by the legislature in such a case is unconstitutional, because, though not expressly forbidden, it is nevertheless inconsistent with the provisions which have conferred upon another department the power the legislature is seeking to exercise."[60]

In *Schneiderman* v. *United States*,[61] for instance, the Supreme Court recognized the plenary powers of Congress over the jurisdiction of the federal courts. Once the power of the courts is established by act of Congress, the latter has, however, no power to "decree in the same breath that the judgment rendered shall have no conclusive effect. Limits it may place. But that is another matter from making an adjudication under Article III merely an advisory opinion or prima facie evidence of the fact or all the facts determined." This limitation upon the powers of Congress is implied from the very nature of the legislative and judicial functions and their relation to each other. On the same grounds, Congress could not, even if the Due Process Clause were omitted from the Consti-

[59] P. vii.   [60] *Ibid.*, p. 356.

[61] 63 S.Ct. 1355, 1357 (1943); cf. also *Gordon* v. *United States,* 117 U.S. 697 (1864); *In re Sanborn,* 148 U.S. 222 (1893).

tution, pass the property of·one citizen over to somebody else on the assumption that the latter was entitled to the property according to law.

Implied limitations, protecting the executive from encroachments by the legislative branch, are less obvious. This is so because the relation between the legislative and executive functions, with the latter charged with the execution of the acts of the former, makes for the subordination of the latter to the former. The inability of Congress to interfere with the removal power of the President offers, however, an example of implied limitations on the legislative power in its relations with the chief executive. In *Myers* v. *United States*[62] the Supreme Court declared the Tenure of Office Act of 1867 unconstitutional as interfering with a presidential power which by its nature is executive and not legislative. In other words, the investment of the chief executive with the general executive functions, with the power to execute the laws, and with the power to remove as an incident of the power to appoint, limits by implication the power of Congress in this matter.

Conversely, the executive branch is limited in its relations with Congress by the constitutional distribution of functions. Since the legislature makes the laws and the executive branch executes them, the latter's discretion is limited by the words and policies of congressional enactments. In applying the acts of Congress to concrete cases, the executive branch must interpret the terms of the statute and in so far may even be allowed to legislate. As noted before, express and implied limitations coincide here.

As regards implied limitations on the executive branch in its relations with the judiciary, one can quote decisions where the Supreme Court has refused to entertain appeals against decisions of a district judge, the execution of which depended upon the discretion of the Secretary of the Treasury.[63] Such decisions, not being the autonomous and, in the absence of appeal, final disposition of the issue, are not recognized as judicial ones against which an apeal to the Supreme Court would lie. The encroachment of the executive upon the judicial process deprives the latter of its judicial character.

[62] 272 U.S. 52 (1926), especially at 117, 161, 164.

[63] *United States* v. *Ferreira,* 13 How. (U.S.) 40 (1851); *Hayburn's Case,* 2 Dall. (U.S.) 408 (1792).

Finally, implied limitations upon the judiciary with regard to both the executive and legislative branches are at the foundation of the principle that the exercise of the discretionary powers of these two departments is not subject to judicial review. With regard to the executive branch, this principle was first laid down in *Marbury* v. *Madison*[64] relative to so-called political questions, and in *United States* v. *Eliason*[65] relative to executive rules and regulations. With respect to the legislative branch the principle is generally expressed in form of the requirement of judicial self-restraint or the prohibition of judicial legislation.

The investigation of implied regulatory powers and implied limitations on regulatory powers in administrative law has led to three conclusions whose importance reaches beyond the immediate purpose of this investigation:

1. The recognition of the administrative function as a co-ordinate fourth branch of the government is indispensable for a solution of the problems with which the spread of administrative law confronts our legal system, if we want this solution to do justice both to the need of administrative agencies for clearly defined and effective powers and to the necessity of keeping these powers within constitutional limits and under legal controls.

2. The traditional constitutional concepts and principles must be marshaled to this task by freeing their creative potentialities, dormant in the original meaning and functions, from the legalistic adulterations and conceptualist refinements by which a stagnant constitutional doctrine has endeavored to make them permanently subservient to a particular political philosophy.

3. From an examination of the court decisions relative to administrative law in the light of the original constitutional principles and concepts, certain general principles of administrative law, fulfilling the functions under 1, can be developed. Thus the decisions reveal clearly that the power to administer carries implicitly the power to interpret or, in other words, that administrative and interpretative powers are coextensive. That he who administers must interpret can be considered a recognized principle of administrative

64 1 Cranch (U.S.) 137 (1803).
65 16 Pet. (U.S.) 291 (1842).

law. The principle that the administrative power is implicitly limited by the delegated administrative function and that consequently administrative agencies cannot do what Congress could have done but did not want to do, is less clearly recognizable in the court decisions, but follows from the distribution of governmental powers on a functional basis, which is characteristic of the structure of American government.

10 *Nationalism*

The Western world faces in the universal triumph of nationalism some extraordinary paradoxes, pregnant with tragic irony. These paradoxes test its political imagination; they challenge its moral judgment; they put in jeopardy not only its own existence but the survival of civilized life on this planet. Yet it was not the enemy of the West and of civilization that gave the idea of nationalism to the world. That idea, together with Marxism, is the last great original contribution the West has made to the political thought and practice of the world. What has become a threat to civilization, the West has claimed as a condition of civilized life. What has become a source of political anarchy and oppression, the West has offered as the principle of political order and freedom. With what has become a mockery of political morality, the West set out to establish political justice throughout the world.

The idea of nationalism, both in its historic origins and in the political functions it has performed, is intimately connected with the idea of freedom and shares the latter's ambiguity. Nationalism as a political phenomenon must be understood as the aspiration for two freedoms, one collective, the other individual: the freedom of a nation from domination by another nation and the freedom of the individual to join the nation of his choice.

As the aspiration of a collectivity to be free, nationalism originated in the sixteenth and seventeenth centuries from the struggles of the territorial state against its two enemies, one—the feudal order—resisting it, as it were, from below; the other—the imperial power—from above. Both, defeated in the dynastic and religious wars of the age, proved to be incapable of exerting the functions of government in the territories claimed by the territorial princes who, in turn, were able to impose their rule upon the feudal lords and free themselves from the rule of the emperor. Thus the territorial state emerged in the political form of dynastic sovereignty, the monarch being the highest secular authority within his territory.

From the *Yale Review*, June, 1957.

Dynastic sovereignty found its philosophic justification in its ability to defend the territory under its control against enemies from without and disorder from within. Bodin in the sixteenth century and Leibniz in the eighteenth justified the absolute monarchy in these terms. It remained unchallenged both in theory and practice as long as it met this test in actual performance. Yet when in 1791 the king of France appeared to be plotting with foreign monarchs against his country, the absolute monarchy failed the test as defender of the nation and its territory. First in practice and then in theory, the nation itself was called upon to defend its freedom. Thus nationalism as the collective expression of a nation's political identity was born.

That birth coincided with, and was really an integral part of, the triumph of individual liberty within France. The absolute monarchy was destroyed because it had betrayed the nation abroad and oppressed the individual at home. It left the stage of history as a defeated enemy of both individual and collective freedom. Individual freedom was taken as a precondition of national freedom, and the latter, in turn, was regarded as a mere extension of the former to the international scene. The political and legal principles, originally formulated to support and guarantee the freedom of the individual, were applied to the nation. The nation came to be regarded as a kind of collective personality with peculiar characteristics and inalienable rights of its own; and the typically liberal antithesis between individual freedom and feudalistic oppression was transferred to the nation where it was duplicated in the hostility between the national aspirations and the feudal state. The nation should be free from oppression, both from within and from without. Free nations had only one enemy, and he was common to all of them: the dynastic oppressor of their freedom, individual and collective. Political evil was, as it were, localized in the enemies of freedom.

Given these assumptions, there could be no enmity among free nations who were united in a solidarity of individual and collective self-interest against the enemies of anybody's freedom. The popular will should decide how and by whom the people were to be governed, and the determination of the state to which a people was to belong was part of this decision. Thus the principle of national self-determination fulfils the postulates of both democracy and nationalism.

The practical political consequences of this new philosophy of nationalism, merging the ideas of individual and collective liberty, were immediate and striking. The Decree of Armed Propaganda of November 12, 1792, proclaimed: "The National Convention declares in the name of the French nation that it shall accord fraternity and aid to all peoples who want to recover their liberty, and charges the executive power with giving to the generals the orders necessary to bring aid to those peoples and to defend the citizens who are or might be persecuted for the cause of liberty." Napoleon conquered Europe in the name of this principle, destroying in the process more than two hundred dynastic sovereignties which were incapable of effective defense and disqualified from ruling in the name of their subjects.

In the struggle, dominating the better part of the nineteenth century, for the national unification of Germany and Italy and the national liberation of the Balkan nations from Turkish rule, the causes of national unity and freedom from oppression merged, for the liberal champions of nationalism as well as for their dynastic enemies. While the German liberals cried, "Through unity to liberty," Mazzini's flag of 1831 bore on one side the words "Unity and Independence," on the other "Liberty, Equality, Humanity." Metternich's policies, on the other hand, were opposed to the national movements as a manifestation of democratic tendencies. The foreign policy of Napoleon III, who favored the national movements because he saw, according to his foreign minister, "a real equilibrium only in the satisfied wishes of the nations of Europe," was ironically called "the diplomacy of universal suffrage."

The First World War seemed to confirm, rather than deny, the assumptions and expectations of nationalism; for was it not caused by the unfulfilled aspirations of the nationalities of the Austro-Hungarian Empire? Thus the Western alliance fought the war in the name of national self-determination, and Germany turned the same weapon against Russia. The result was a peace settlement that reflected to a very high degree the principle of national self-determination. Austria-Hungary and western Russia were dissolved into their national components, and the new frontiers of Germany followed in good measure the will of the populations concerned, which was either obvious, as in Alsace-Lorraine, or was determined by internationally supervised plebiscites, as in Silesia.

Yet that triumph of the principles of nationalism did not bring a viable order to central and eastern Europe. Nor did it bring justice to the populations concerned; it rather made the oppressors and oppressed exchange their roles. Thus what appeared at the time as the consummation of the expectations of nineteenth-century nation-alism—peace, order, and justice built on the satisfaction of national aspirations—turned into its first great moral and political crisis. That crisis revealed the insufficient, self-contradictory, and self-defeating nature of nationalism as the exclusive principle of international order and justice and its inevitable subordination in fact, and requisite subordination in theory, to an overriding political system.

Nationalism, taken by itself, is both in logic and experience a principle of disintegration and fragmentation, which is prevented from issuing in anarchy not by its own logic but by the political power which either puts a halt to its realization at a certain point, as did the peace settlement of 1919, or else uses it for its purposes up to a certain point, as did the unifiers of Germany and Italy in the nineteenth century. There are no inherent limits to the appli-cation of the principles of nationalism. If the peoples of Bulgaria, Greece, and Serbia could invoke these principles against Turkey, why could not the people of Macedonia invoke them against Bul-garia, Greece, and Serbia? If it was right for the Czechs and Slovaks to free themselves in the name of nationalism from Austrian rule, it could not be wrong for the Slovaks and Sudeten Germans to free themselves from Czech rule in the name of the selfsame principle. Poland, the very moment she had recovered her national identity from Austrian, German, and Russian rule, felt she had to defend it against the German, Ukrainian, and White Russian minorities within her borders, comprising one-third of her total population. Thus yesterday's oppressed cannot help becoming the oppressors of today because they are afraid lest they be again oppressed tomorrow. Hence, the process of national liberation must stop at some point, and that point is determined not by the logic of nationalism but by the configurations of interest and power between the rulers and the ruled and between competing nations.

This paradox of B invoking the principles of nationalism against A and denying them to C—both for the sake of his own survival—is accentuated by the practical impossibility of applying these principles consistently to mixed populations. The individual's rights to his property and pursuit of happiness become incompatible with his right to choose his government according to his national preferences when he is a member of a minority which is inextricably intermingled with the majority controlling the government. Not being able to enjoy both rights simultaneously, he must sacrifice one or the other. The treaties for the protection of minorities, to which Bulgaria, Montenegro, Romania, and Serbia were subjected in 1878 and Czechoslovakia, Poland, and Romania in 1919, tried to mitigate the dilemma by protecting certain minorities in the enjoyment of a free national life at least in certain fields, such as language, schools, religion.

However, such attempts were largely frustrated by the fact, which constitutes the second manifestation of the crisis of nationalism in the interwar period, that the conflicts between the new national states and their minorities were more intimately interwoven than ever before with the international conflicts among the new nation states and the great powers. This had always been the case within certain limits; Russia, for instance, had always supported the Balkan nations against Turkey and the Czechs and Serbs against Austria-Hungary. Yet as in the interwar period the new nation states competed with each other for power and were at the same time the pawns of the great powers in their struggle for hegemony, the national minorities became to an ever increasing extent, as it were, sub-pawns whose aspirations and grievances the contestants used to strengthen themselves and their friends and weaken their enemies.

All of central and eastern Europe from the Baltic to the Mediterranean became the stage for continuous interconnected and overlapping rivalries and conflicts: Poland versus Lithuania, Czechoslovakia versus Poland, Hungary versus Romania, Bulgaria versus Greece, Italy versus Yugoslavia, Germany versus Poland, and, overshadowing them all, the decline of France, the rise of Germany, the indecision of Britain, and the ever present threat of the Soviet Union. The instability which from 1878 to 1914 had been confined to the

Balkans, always threatening and in the end destroying the peace of Europe, now extended to all of central and eastern Europe, for the same causes and with the same results. As the fragmentation of the European part of the Turkish Empire into its national components brought forth the "Balkanization" of the Balkans, so did the fragmentation of the Austro-Hungarian and the western part of the Russian Empires lead to the Balkanization of that part of Europe. And while the First World War arose from the threat of Serb nationalism to Austria-Hungary, the Second World War became inevitable when Germany succeeded in using the German minority to destroy Czechoslovakia and was started on the pretext that the German minority needed protection against the government of Poland.

Nationalism, far from creating a juster and more viable international order, became the great disruptive and anarchical force of the interwar period. Into the severed members of the empires it shattered, nationalism poured the same passions which, first, as lust for power had created these empires and, then, as aspiration for freedom had destroyed them. The endemic disorder thus created cried out for a "new order," which only the strong could make and maintain. Germany and Russia, the new empire builders, saw their opportunity, and in a series of swift and effective strokes, starting in 1938 and ending in 1941, they seized the new nation states of central and eastern Europe, endeavoring to melt them down into new structures of empire.

It is another of the paradoxes of nationalism that its defeat on the eve of the Second World War was achieved in the name of the same principle which brought it victory in the aftermath of the First: national self-determination. Germany justified her use of the German minorities of Czechoslovakia and Poland for the destruction of these nation states with the same principle of national self-determination with which before the Czech, Slovak, and Polish nationalities had justified their attack upon, and destruction of, the Austro-Hungarian Empire. Yet while the words were the same, the passions behind them and the philosophy which roused and justified them were different not only in degree but in kind. The nationalism with which Nazi Germany and the Soviet Union set out to conquer the world has only the name in common with the nationalism of the nineteenth century and the first three decades of the twentieth.

The libertarian goals of the older nationalism were the rightful possession of all nations who wanted to be free; the world had room for as many nationalisms as there were nations that wanted to establish or preserve a state of their own. The international conflicts growing out of this nationalism were of two kinds: conflicts between a nationality and an alien master and conflicts between different nations over the delimitation of their respective boundaries. The issue at stake was either the application of the principles of nationalism or else their interpretation.

The new nationalism has only one thing in common with the old: the nation is the ultimate point of reference for political loyalties and actions. But here the similarity ends. For the old nationalism, the nation is the ultimate goal of political action, the end point of the political development beyond which there are other nationalisms with similar and equally justifiable goals. For the new nationalism, the nation is but the starting point of a universal mission whose ultimate goal reaches to the confines of the political world. While the old nationalism seeks one nation in one state and nothing else, the new one claims for one nation and one state the right to impose its own values and standards of action upon all the other nations.

The new nationalism is in truth a political religion, a nationalistic universalism which identifies the standards and goals of a particular nation with the principles that govern the universe. The few remaining nations of the first rank no longer oppose each other within a framework of shared beliefs and common values which impose effective limitations upon the means and ends of their policies. Rather they oppose each other now as the standard-bearers of moral systems, each of them of national origin and each of them claiming to provide universal moral standards which all the other nations ought to accept. The moral code of one nation flings the challenge of its universal claim into the face of another, which reciprocates in kind.

This transformation of nationalism was foreshadowed by the Napoleonic Wars and the First World War. The Napoleonic Wars were fought in the name of particular principles claiming universal validity: here the principles of the French Revolution, there the principle of legitimacy. For the West, the First World War transformed itself with the intervention of the United States into a crusade "to make the world safe for democracy." "It is our inestimable privilege," said Woodrow Wilson in his Fourth of July speech of 1918, "to concert with men out of every nation who shall make not only the liberties of America secure but the liberties of every other people as well." A few months after the democratic crusade had got under way, in October, 1917, the foundations were laid in Russia for another moral and political structure that, while accepted by only a fraction of humanity, also claimed to provide the common roof under which all humankind would eventually live together in justice and in peace.

This well-nigh universal commitment to the principles of nationalism revealed a profound difference between the attitude of the Western democracies and that of their totalitarian enemies. That difference was to have far-reaching moral and political consequences. The West had come to see in the principles of nationalism the revelation of universal truth to be lived up to regardless of political consequences. Totalitarianism looked at those principles as political tools to be used if their use promised results, to be discarded otherwise. Hitler did not hesitate to sacrifice the Germans of northern Italy for the friendship of Mussolini by transferring the majority of them to Germany. The nationalities policy of the Soviet Union, while committed in theory to national autonomy, has been at the service of the political and economic interests of the central government which, as the instrument of "democratic centralism," has manipulated, controlled, and destroyed their national life without regard to principles of any kind.

Yet when totalitarianism turned the principles of nationalism against the West, the West stood morally and intellectually disarmed. The totalitarian arguments being its own, it could not answer them. The West had welcomed the victory of national self-determination in the aftermath of the First World War on moral and political grounds, and it found itself now incapable, when Hitler used the German minority for the destruction of Czechoslovakia, of defending its interests against its principles. It even lent a helping hand to its defeat and congratulated itself upon its moral consistency. "Self-determination, the professed principle of the Treaty of Versailles, has been invoked by Herr Hitler against its written text, and his appeal has been allowed," wrote the London *Times* on September 28, 1938, commenting upon the Munich settlement.

The Second World War and the Cold War following it have both qualitatively and quantitatively magnified the paradoxes of nationalism which the interwar period had brought to the fore, and they have added a new one which has made nationalism altogether obsolete as a principle of political organization. The new fact that has created that new paradox is the feasibility of all-out atomic war.

The justification of the nation state, as of all political organization, is its ability to perform the functions for the sake of which political organization exists. The most elementary of these functions is the common defense of the life of the citizens and of the values of the civilization in which they live. A political organization which is no longer able to defend these values and even puts them in jeopardy must yield, either through peaceful transformation or violent destruction, to one capable of that defense. Thus, under the impact of the invention of gunpowder and of the first industrial revolution, the feudal order had to yield to the dynastic and the nation state. Under the technological conditions of the pre-atomic age, the stronger nation states could, as it were, erect a wall behind which their citizens could live secure and the weak nation states were similarly protected by the operation of the balance of power which added the resources of the strong to those of the weak. Thus under normal conditions no nation state was able to make more than marginal inroads upon the life and civilization of its neighbors.

The feasibility of all-out atomic war has completely destroyed this protective function of the nation state. No nation state is capable of protecting its citizens and its civilization against an all-out atomic attack. It safety rests solely in preventing such an attack from taking place. While in the pre-atomic age a nation state could count upon its physical ability to defend itself, in the atomic age it must rely upon its psychological ability to deter those who are physically able to destroy it. The prospective enemy must be induced to refrain from attacking; once he attacks, the victim is doomed.

This psychological mechanism of deterrence operates only on the condition that the prospective atomic aggressor is clearly identified beforehand, that is, that no more than two nations are capable of waging all-out atomic war; for it is only on this condition that deterrence operates with automatic certainty. Today, the Soviet Union knows that if it should attack the United States with atomic weapons, the United States would destroy it, and vice versa; that certainty deters both. Yet the time is close at hand when other nations will have the weapons with which to wage all-out atomic war. When that time has come, nations will have lost even the preventive capacity of psychological deterrence, which they still possess today. For the United States, if then attacked with atomic weapons, will no longer be able to identify the aggressor with certainty and, hence, deter the prospective aggressor with the certainty of retaliation. When this historic moment comes—as it surely must if the present trend is not reversed—the nation state will connote not life and civilization but anarchy and universal destruction.

It is in the shadow of this grim reality and grimmer prospect that the inherent paradoxes of nationalism have taken on a novel urgency, threatening to overwhelm the remnants of international order. Balkanization, demoralization, and barbarization on a world-wide scale are the result.

The age which has seen the nation state become obsolete witnesses the emergence of a multitude of new states fashioned from the fragments of the colonial empires. The number of sovereign states has approximately doubled since the First World War. Many of these new states would not have been viable political, military, and economic entities even in the heyday of the nation state, deficient as they are in the essential prerequisites of nationhood. They could not have fed, administered, and defended themselves then, nor can they now. The disorder and threats to peace which the dissolution, first, of the Turkish and, then, of the Austro-Hungarian and western part of the Russian Empires brought in its wake is being spread, in the name of nationalism, to ever wider areas of Africa and Asia. In our age, even the infinitely stronger nation states of Europe are no longer viable political, military, and economic entities, but must submit either to the support or the conquest of the two remaining nations of the first rank, which are significantly not nation states in the traditional sense but continental states. The tragedy of Hungary and the collapse of the British and French intervention in Egypt in November, 1956, have demonstrated in different ways both the continuing emotional strength of national aspirations and the political and military weakness of the nation state. Is it then reasonable to expect that these new nations, some of them so artificial as to be even lacking the ethnic and historic foundations of nationhood, will be able to create a viable order among themselves and with their more powerful neighbors?

Only two alternatives appear to be in store for them, perhaps one following the other: Balkanization and a new colonialism. The rivalries which have beset the successor states to the European empires have already appeared among them. Some of the former colonies would like to have colonies of their own. The natural resources of some continue to make them attractive as colonies for stronger nations who need these resources. Their weakness, necessitating continuous support from stronger nations, predestines them as pawns in the power struggles of the latter. Their attractiveness, coupled with weakness, is thus a standing invitation to conquest, conquest by one or the other of them or else from the outside. In any event, the disorder which is taking the place of the old order of empire is likely to call forth, as it did before in Europe, a new order which will be again an order of empire.

It is ironic—and perhaps inevitable—that the great nations of the West should actively promote and support this Balkanization of much of the world, and it is equally ironic—and certainly not inevitable—that they should applaud it. For while they may have no choice but to give up their empires, they cannot afford to look with indifference, let alone with satisfaction, upon the prospect that disorder and violence, exploited by communism, will spread over ever wider areas of the globe. Here we encounter on a world-wide scale and in the form of anticolonialism that moral perversion which made Great Britain congratulate herself upon having helped Hitler to destroy Czechoslovakia in the name of nationalism.

There was a time when the Western world looked upon empire as a respectable and even a noble thing. The libertarian standards and aspirations of the West itself gave empire a bad name. It was Jeremy Bentham who as far back as 1793 wrote a pamphlet with the title, "Emancipate Your Colonies." And the United States, ever mindful of its colonial origins, has throughout its history felt an emotional attachment to national and anticolonial movements, even though, if there were logic in such historic analogies, its sympathies ought to be today not with the Algerians but with the French *colons*, with the British planters and not with the Malayans.

With characteristic philosophic consistency and lack of political judgment, the West has applied the democratic principles of freedom and equality to the international scene, transforming them in the process from concrete political goals into abstract moral postulates. Yet wherever democracy has succeeded within the nation state, it was imbedded in a structured social order from which it received its vital strength and to which, in turn, it imparted form and direction.

It is this Western dedication to national freedom, not as a concrete political goal but as an eternal verity, which has made the West morally and politically helpless in the face of the anticolonial onslaught of the age. When Japan swept through Asia, carrying the banner of anticolonialism before her, the new colonialism supplanted the old with such immediacy and undisguised exploitation and oppression as to provide a ready target for the West's anticolonial indignation. The anticolonialism of the Soviet Union, Communist China, and the indigenous peoples of Africa and Asia is different and has had a different effect upon the moral consciousness of the West.

While it is for all of them a tool at the service of concrete political goals, used and discarded especially by the Soviet Union and Communist China as the occasion requires, its immediate goal appears to be national liberation and nothing more. What disorders will follow liberation and what new colonialism will follow the disorders is a matter for long-term concern, not for immediate political calculation. Furthermore, the colonialism which the Soviet Union has practiced in Europe since the end of the Second World War is geographically far removed from Africa and Asia, protected from immediate recognition by the "salt-water fallacy" which requires that a colony, to be recognized as such, be separated from the colonial power by some ocean. Finally, in Africa and Asia, as in the European resistance during the Second World War, communism fights in the forefront of nationalism, making for the time being little of the fact that its nationalism serves the interests of China or the Soviet Union. Thus in a strange and disquieting transformation, nationalism, the moral principle of the West, becomes the most potent weapon in the arsenal of its enemies; and disarmed before the triumph of its own ideal, the West applauds its own destruction.

This confrontation of nationalism as an absolute moral principle with nationalism as a tool of political power is novel only in its worldwide dimensions and world-shaking results. The contrast itself, and the moral and political dilemma it presents, is as old as nationalism itself. The ideologues of the French Revolution, the Frankfort Parliament of 1848, Mazzini, and Wilson provided the ideas and the moral fervor; Napoleon, Cavour, Bismarck, and Clemenceau fashioned the political and military tools of victory, harnessing the libertarian impulses of nationalism to the purposes of power, leaving the ideologues behind approving or disillusioned but in any event in impotence. Yet nationalism, from the French Revolution to the peace settlement of 1919—however bent to, and distorted by, the purposes of power—never completely lost sight of the individual and his freedom of choice. When, in violation of this principle, Bismarck expelled in 1885 thirty thousand Poles who were not German citizens, the principle still had sufficient strength to induce the Reichstag to register its protest. During that period, nationalism retained its essential democratic orientation. The ideal of "one nation, one state" was implemented by the principle of national self-determination which postulated the primacy of individual choice over the political interests of governments. As a matter of principle, frontiers were to be determined by the will of the people not by considerations of political and military expediency.

This order of priority has been reversed since the Second World War. Not only do the interests of the state now take precedence over the will of the people, but the people themselves—their life, liberty, and pursuit of happiness—count for nothing if they appear to stand in the way of the interests of the state. No longer are national minorities to be protected against the state; it is now the state which must be protected against the minorities. The gulf that separates international treaties for the protection of national minorities from the deportation and extermination of national minorities and whole nations also separates the old libertarian nationalism from the totalitarian nationalism of the age. By whatever causes one may explain this transformation—the political and military use which great powers made of small nations and national minorities in the interwar period and during the Second World War; nationalistic universalism taking the place of the pluralistic nationalism of the nineteenth century—its barbarous consequences deny all that nationalism once stood for.

How different that world is from the world our fathers thought they lived in! Nationalism, they thought, meant of necessity freedom, civilization, and justice; we know now that it can also mean slavery, barbarism, and death. Nationalism, they thought, would bring of necessity peace and order to the relations among nations; we know now that it has brought us disorder and war and threatens us with universal destruction. When the experiences from which that knowledge derives had still to be made, a very wise liberal voiced his disillusionment and implied the remedy. "It may be said," wrote John Morley in 1874,

that the very fate of these aspirations has had a blighting effect on public enthusiasm and the capacity of feeling it. Not only have most of them now been fulfilled, and so passed from aspiration to actuality, but the results of their fulfilment have been so disappointing as to make us wonder whether it is really worth while to pray, when to have our prayers granted carries the world so very slight a way forward. The Austrian is no longer in Italy; the Pope has ceased to be master in Rome; the patriots of Hungary are now in possession of their rights, and have become friends of their old oppressors; the negro slave has been transformed into an American citizen. At home, again, the gods have listened to our vows. Parliament has been reformed, and the long-desired mechanical security provided for the voter's freedom. We no longer aspire after all these things, you may say because our hopes have been realised and our dreams have come true. It is possible that the comparatively prosaic results before our eyes at the end of all have thrown a chill over our political imagination.

"Political imagination" is indeed the key word. If the West cannot think of something better than nationalism, it may well lose the opportunity to think at all. It has been its moral virtue and besetting political sin to look at nationalism as though it were a self-sufficient political principle and could bring freedom, justice, order, and peace simply by being consistently applied. In truth, no political principle carries within itself such a force for good. What good and what evil it will work depends not only upon its own nature but also upon the configurations of interest and power in which and for the sake of which it is called upon to act.

The West has consistently tended to misunderstand the subtle and complex relationships between these configurations and political principles. Thereby, it has blunted its political will, its political judgment, and its political imagination. It has failed to see that political principles, such as nationalism, must direct, rechannel, even transform these configurations but that they cannot replace them. Yet when their work is done, they must themselves be replaced.

Nationalism has had its day. It was the political principle appropriate to the post-feudal and pre-atomic age. For the technology of the steam engine, it was indeed in good measure a force for progress. In the atomic age, it must make way for a political principle of larger dimensions, in tune with the world-wide configurations of interest and power of the age.

11 *National Minorities*[1]

Of the obsolescence of nineteenth-century political philosophy and, more particularly, of its conception of foreign affairs, the fate of the nation-state offers a striking example. In its heyday Hegel saluted it, in its Prussian form at least, as the ultimate embodiment of the World Spirit. For the nineteenth century the aspiration for national unity and liberation was but the echo of the aspiration for individual liberty. Nationalism was the great liberating and pacifying force which would destroy autocratic government and unite those who belonged together by nature. For Woodrow Wilson it had become the magic formula which, by removing the main cause of modern wars, would assure permanent peace.

Yet the nineteenth-century liberals did not see, as Aristotle had already intimated, that the aspiration for liberty and equality is only the first phase of a struggle for power in which those who are oppressed want first to be equal with their oppressors and, once they have achieved this equality, want to oppress their equals. So it has come about that freedom for the nationalities of Central and Eastern Europe meant first of all freedom from foreign rule but, once this freedom was achieved, also freedom to dominate those who had formerly dominated them. The latter would in turn raise the cry of national unity and liberation on their own behalf, and the ideologues, firm in principles but weak in political insight, would support the claims of nationalism regardless of the political interests involved. Thus, as quoted before, the London *Times* could write on September 28, 1938, immediately after the Czechoslovakian crisis: "Self-determination, the professed principle of the Treaty of Versailles, has been invoked by Herr Hitler against its written text, and his appeal has been allowed." The Treaty of Versailles was inspired by the Wilsonian ideal of national self-determination and was

From the *Harvard Law Review*, Vol. LIX, No. 2, December, 1945.

[1] Review of Oskar I. Janowsky, *Nationalities and National Minorities* (New York: Macmillan Co., 1945).

more just from the national point of view than any preceding European peace settlement. Yet it did not bring peace and stability to Europe; for politically the territorial organization of Europe on primarily national lines resulted in the atomization of Central and Eastern Europe, destroyed the equilibrium which had maintained general peace during the better part of the nineteenth and the beginning of the twentieth centuries and, in the absence of an effective system of alliances, made the resurgence of Germany as the dominant power on the European continent inevitable.

Finally, Hitler proposed to terminate the vicious circle by transforming nationalism into racial imperialism and solve the problem of nationalities by doing away with those who by their very existence had created it. In the recent past the consistent application of the idea of the national state in Central and Eastern Europe has reduced national minorities to the status of cattle, to be shipped away or to be slaughtered like cattle. And the world of the Four Freedoms, which our victory was supposed to usher in, witnesses the expulsion and persecution of national minorities in the name of the national state. Thus the vicious circle which Hitler hoped to stop once and for all still swings around, making yesterday's hounded the hunters of today and sweeping today's masters into the ashcan of history. The national principle, the great liberating force of the nineteenth century, becomes in the third and fourth decades of the twentieth the great source of instability, anarchy, and war, and issues in the fifth in the barbarization of international politics on a gigantic scale.

This development has given pause to the more thoughtful observers of the international scene who in recent years have re-examined the history, philosophic assumptions, and political manifestations of nationalism. In the field of history, the books by Hans Kohn[2] and Friedrich Hertz,[3] and in the philosophic-political field the books by E. H. Carr,[4] Alfred Cobban,[5] and W. Friedmann[6] have contributed

[2] The Idea of Nationalism (1944).

[3] Nationality in History and Politics (1944).

[4] Nationalism and After (1945).

[5] National Self-determination (1945).

[6] The Crisis of the National State (1943).

to the clarification of the problem. Professor Janowsky's volume belongs to the latter group.

The author is well aware of the inner contradictions which have beset the consistent application of the national principle. He is also well aware of the failure of the remedies of the past to show a way out of the impasse. Mere changes in boundaries will only create a new problem where an old one appears to have been solved. The international protection of minorities, which was put into effect in the period between the two world wars, has proved to be only a very limited success. For the loyalties of the majority government and of the minority population had different national centers, and thus the international obligations were interpreted by both parties in the light of the loyalty involved. The governments would interpret their obligations under the minorities treaties restrictively, since they saw in those obligations an impairment of their sovereign rights and a threat to the coherence of their state. Some of the minorities, on the other hand, gave support by their own acts to the suspicion that an appeal to an international organization against their own government by virtue of a provision of a minorities treaty was really an act of treason carried out on behalf of a foreign government to which the minority was bound by national ties.

The author rejects also the forced assimilation and transfer of minorities on humanitarian grounds. Yet it is significant for the rapidity of the decay of the political order in Europe that, at this point, this book, finished in the spring of 1945, has already become obsolete. When Dr. Janowsky wrote, he was still able to interpret in a restrictive and humanitarian sense the statements which President Beneš and Dr. Osusky, both prominent Czechoslovakian statesmen, had made with regard to the forced transfer of minorities. While political developments have made the author's prognosis in this regard invalid, his evaluation of this policy seems to have retained all of its validity.

So ruthless a policy can solve the minorities problem only in a Nazi "new order" which is insensible to human suffering. Democratic states and statesmen must regard the compulsory transfer of minorities as a "surgical operation," to be performed only when every other remedy has been tried and found wanting.[7]

[7] P. 141.

Instead, the author suggests a new remedy, which he calls "national federalism." "In essence this means that minorities are not to be endowed with special privileges, that their status is not to be an exceptional one involving toleration, but that they be organically incorporated in the structure of the multi-national state."[8] The model of such a multinational state in which all nationalities with regard to language and culture enjoy equal rights is to be found in the Union of South Africa, Switzerland, and particularly in the Soviet Union. It is especially the example of the multinational character of the Soviet Union which encourages the author in his hope that similar constitutional arrangements might solve the problem of the European nationalities.

It must, however, be pointed out that the solution of the nationalities problem by the Soviet Union, in order to be understood, must be put into the political framework of the proletarian state. It was Stalin himself who, as commissar for nationalities, said as early as 1918:

The national question is not something self-contained and fixed for all time. Being only part of the general question of the transformation of the existing order, the national question is wholly determined by the conditions of the social environment, the character of the power in the country, and by the whole course of social development generally.[9]

This social development took the form of the "democratic centralism" of the dictatorship of the proletariat. In other words, it is the totalitarian character of the Communist state which provides the cohesive force which in Eastern and Central Europe had been furnished by the dominant nationality and which in Russia enables different nationalities to live peacefully together without any single one dominating others. The solution of the problem of nationalities by the Soviet Union is therefore but the by-product of the overriding power of the proletarian state. It is only under the assumption that a substitute can be found for a dominant nationality in another, at least equally dominant, factor, proletarian or otherwise, that the Russian solution of the problem of nationalities can be used as the model of the solution of the problem of nationalities as such.

Dr. Janowsky falls into the error of so many well-meaning liber-

[8] P. 145.

[9] *Stalin, Marxism and the National and Colonial Question* (1936), p. 68.

als of taking the solution of a political problem out of its political context, abstracting from its concrete political aspects, and erecting its technical characteristics into absolutes, applicable everywhere and at all times. Yet the destruction of the Austro-Hungarian Empire has removed the politically dominant power which could hold the different nationalities of Central and Eastern Europe together. In the absence of such a dominant power, it is vain to hope that the nationalities of Central and Eastern Europe suddenly will be able to forget their history of rivalry and bloodshed and combine freely in a multinational commonwealth with no nationality dominating any other.

12 _Why Nations Decline_

Let me say, first of all, in contrast to what some philosophers of history have proclaimed, that there is no iron law according to which nations must decline. Much has been written in the last 100 years or so about the biological analogy between the development of societies and the development of living organisms. As a living organism grows, reaches maturity, declines and dies, so, it is said, societies, nations, civilizations grow, reach a period of flowering, decline, and disappear. It is certainly true that most nations which once were prominent in the affairs of the world have either declined or disappeared altogether. But not all of them have. Think of Japan and China, to mention only two outstanding examples of nations who have maintained themselves as great powers over thousands of years, while all around them, and more particularly in Europe, nations declined and faded away continuously. So, it seems to me, it is important to realize, first of all, that any analogy with biological or other natural-science data is very much misleading. There is no iron law according to which a nation must decline after a certain period of greatness. However, it is an unequivocal fact that most nations actually have declined and disappeared.

The second point I would like to make is that there is a kind of mystery about the rise and fall of nations, as there is a kind of mystery about the rise and fall of individuals, a mystery which some might try to explain in the fashionable terms of the day, particularly in psychological, psychoanalytical, or behaviorist terms. In actuality we are really confronted with a mystery. Take, for instance, the example of Spain.

Why was it that in the sixteenth century what is called the _siglo del oro_, the golden century of Spain, started with an enormous flowering in the fields of literature, art, statesmanship, and all other human endeavors? And why was it that after a hundred years or so

Lecture given at the National War College, April 10, 1959.

this flowering suddenly stopped, and from then on to this day Spain has lived in a kind of somnolescent stupor, never being able even to approach the greatness which it had reached for a short span of time?

Why is it, for instance, that the Low Countries for a considerable period of history were prominent not only in warfare and foreign policy but also in art, science, and other endeavors, and all of a sudden this development stopped? Why is it that the empires of the Huns and the Mongols fell and left no trace after them?

All those are questions which many have tried to answer but to which there is really no satisfactory rational answer. I would suggest that, when we approach so great a topic, we ought to approach it with a considerable degree of humility, with an awareness of our ignorance. We are here surrounded by developments which transcend our understanding.

The third point I want to make is the enormous extent to which the rise and fall of nations is a result of circumstances over which the nations have no control. The rise of a great man may bring about the rise of a nation and his disappearance may bring about its downfall. Take the short flowering of Macedon under Alexander. When he died after a very short reign, the Macedonian Empire disintegrated. Nobody can say what would have happened if Alexander had died of the measles as a child. In all probability there never would have been a Macedonian Empire. And nobody can say what would have happened had Alexander not died as a young man without heirs but had reached a ripe old age, being able to consolidate his empire.

Take, in more recent history, the rise of France under Napoleon, the rise of bolshevism under Lenin, the rise of fascism in Italy under Mussolini, and the rise of naziism under Hitler. If those men had not existed, certainly history would have been different. And it is a good bet that the temporary rise of some of those nations and the permanent rise of others would not have occurred without the presence and activities of those outstanding men.

The factors over which nations have no control and which determine their fate are not only and primarily of a personal nature; they are to a very great extent of a technological and geographic nature.

Take, for instance, the example, which has been correctly mentioned in your "Syllabus," the decline of the power of Great Britain, and the question asked in your "Syllabus" whether different policies pursued by British governments could have prevented that decline of British power. Now, let me ask: In what did British power consist? What brought about the greatness of Great Britain as a world power from Henry VIII at the beginning of the sixteenth century to, say, Sir Edward Grey at the outbreak of the First World War? It was in essence the concatenation of two circumstances, the insular position of Great Britain in close proximity of the European continent and the decisive importance of sea power for world politics, together, of course (and this is the third factor which one should not forget) with the effective exploitation of those factors by British statesmanship.

With sea power having been replaced as the decisive factor in world politics, especially for an insular nation, and with the insular position in the proximity of the European continent having been transformed from a factor of safety into a factor of extreme exposure to danger, the power of Great Britain was bound to decline. While fifty years ago Britannia still ruled the waves, today intermediate ballistic missiles placed anywhere on the European continent rule Great Britain. While experts differ on how many H-bombs are necessary to reduce the British Isles to a heap of radioactive rubble, there is no doubt that a few are sufficient within a couple of minutes to wipe out the very physical existence of the British Isles.

This drastic change in the objective conditions of British existence, no British statesman, no British foreign policy could have altered. Perhaps under certain favorable circumstances, the consequences of these conditions might have been postponed; their effects even today might be mitigated by wise statemanship. But essentially the indefensibility of the British Isles under modern technological conditions of warfare is a fundamental fact which no British statesman could have changed and over which no British foreign policy could have had any control. This impossibility for foreign policy to change the fundamental conditions of a nation's existence became obvious in that famous episode of 1938, which has gone into history as the surrender at Munich.

We all realize today, of course, the fateful consequences of Mr.

Chamberlain's surrender of Czechoslovakia to Germany. But we are less aware today than, as I can readily remember, the contemporaries were in 1938 of the inescapable dilemma that confronted Mr. Chamberlain. It is easy to say today that Mr. Chamberlain was wrong. But what was the alternative? Mr. Chamberlain realized that the objective conditions of British existence had changed to such an extent that any kind of war, even a war from which Great Britain would emerge victorious, would mean the end of Great Britain as a first-rate power. And this prognosis was, of course, proved correct by the results of the Second World War. So Mr. Chamberlain was confronted with an inescapable dilemma which no British foreign policy could have eliminated. It is a matter of judgment as to which horn of the dilemma Mr. Chamberlain should have chosen. I myself believe that he chose the wrong horn. But, even if he had chosen the other one, he could not have escaped the final decline of British power, a decline which was a result not of deficient British statesmanship but of the inescapable objective conditions of British existence.

Take another example closer to home which again exemplifies the enormous weight which the objective conditions of their existence have for the fate of nations. The unique and privileged position which the United States occupied during the first century and a half of its history was the result primarily of the objective geographic and military conditions under which the United States lived, those conditions again being exploited by wise statesmanship, especially at the very beginning of American history. It is the actual fact of isolation from the great conflicts in which other nations were continuously involved which determined the foreign policy and the advantageous consequences of that foreign policy for the United States.

The contrary fact, the disappearance of that privileged position, the disappearance of isolation, the involvement of the United States into the affairs of the world is not the result, as some have thought it to be, of an act of will on the part of American statesmen, but it is again the result of the objective conditions of the world over which no American statesman had any control. American statesmen after the First World War could recognize the end of isolation or they could refuse to recognize it; they could base their foreign policies upon the assumption that the United States was still isolated or they could base their foreign policies on the contrary assumption that the United States was no longer isolated, but the objective fact of isolation or non-isolation was beyond the control of American statesmen. Thus, when we deal with the topic of this lecture, the reasons for the decline of nations, we must be aware of the enormous importance which objective factors have upon the decline of nations, factors over which nations themselves have no control.

Look at the American situation from still a different point of view. The rise of the United States to the position of a colonial power in consequence of the Spanish-American War was of nobody's making. Once the United States became involved in the Spanish-American War and won it, it fell almost naturally heir to the Asian and American fragments of the Spanish empire. President McKinley, in his famous account of how he reached the decision to annex the Philippines, made exactly this point when he said that we could not give them back to the Spaniards; we could not turn them over to a rival power; we could not leave them to the natives—"there was nothing left for us to do but take them all. . . ." Here you have the implicit recognition of the power which objective factors have upon foreign policy and their consequences.

Take the rise of the United States, in consequence of the Second World War, to world power, to the position of the other great power in the world. No American statesman planned it that way. It was again the concatenation of objective conditions which brought about, very much against the intentions and against the preferences of American statesmen and of American people, this rise to power, responsibility, and liability.

Once one has said all this—leaving in the dark, as it were, that broad arena over which statesmen have no control, where, in other words, fate reigns over nations—we must consider that area which is subject to human control. Within those predetermined limits, what are the factors through which human action typically contributes to the decline of nations?

Here the greatest single factor which throughout history has brought about or has contributed to the decline of nations has been the lack of the correct evaluation of the power of one's own nation as over against the power of other nations.

Nations, when they devise their foreign policies, must, of course, evaluate their own power as over against the power of other nations; and it is in good measure upon the correctness of that evaluation that success and failure of foreign policy depends. Frequently and typically, nations have fallen because they had an erroneous conception of their own power in comparison with the power of other nations. Here three typical mistakes must be considered. First, nations tend to believe in the absolute character of power—that is to say, a nation which has proven to be powerful in one period of history is tempted to believe that this superiority of power is a kind of natural quality that exists irrespective of the power of other nations.

Power in actuality is a relative thing, of course, as you all know. The United States can be said to be powerful compared with the power of other nations. You can say the power of the United States is unchallengeable in the Western Hemisphere—which means, compare the power of the United States with that of the nations of Latin America, either singly or collectively, and you arrive at the conclusion that the power of the United States is superior to that of the nations of Latin America.

There is a tendency in all nations to look at the power of one's own nation as a kind of absolute, to take it for granted, and not to realize that it is the result of comparison. Let me give you two examples from military history.

When the army of Prussia met the army of Napoleon in 1806 in the battle of Jena and Auerstädt, the Prussian generals were confident that the power of their army was superior to that of Napoleon. On what was that erroneous evaluation of their power based? Upon the fact that the Prussian army of 1806 was as good as the army of Frederick the Great had been thirty or forty years earlier. The military might of Prussia, taken by itself, had not only not declined, it might even have increased. What the Prussian generals should have done was to compare the power of the Prussian army of 1806 not with the power of the Prussian army of 1760 or 1770 but with the power of the French army of 1806.

A very similar situation arose from the estimates of French military power immediately preceding the Second World War and during the period of the so-called "phony" war. The French army was then regarded to be the most powerful instrument of land power existing in 1940. I remember very vividly hearing Mr. Churchill say in Paris in 1937 that nothing stands between barbarism and civilization but the French army.

The events of 1940 showed very clearly how completely mistaken this estimate of French power was. On what was it based? It was based upon the same erroneous mental operation which had led in 1806 to the miscalculation of Prussian as over against Napoleonic power. That is to say, we compared the power of the French army of 1940 with the power of the French army, say, of 1920; and we found the results of the comparison extremely satisfactory. Conversely, we had still the mental picture of a German army in 1940 which somehow resembled the insufficient German army of ten years earlier. In other words, we regarded the military weakness of Germany as an absolute, as we regarded the French military superiority as an absolute; and, in consequence, we miscalculated completely the distribution of military power between the two nations.

The second typical error which is frequently made in evaluating the power of a nation lies not so much in believing in its absolute character but in believing in its permanency. Here we refuse to make a projection in time, and we regard the power of a nation in a particular period of history as a permanent attribute which is not subject to change in itself. Remember, for instance, the shock which we all experienced when the Russian Sputniks went up. In what did this shock actually exist? It existed in the sudden awareness that the technological superiority of the United States which we had taken for granted, which we had taken to be a permanent attribute, as it were, of America, like the Rocky Mountains, something which nobody could take away from us, was only a temporary advantage which could be taken away from us by a more determined competitor.

Take as another example Great Britain's reliance at the beginning of the war against Japan upon traditional sea power unprotected by air power and the catastrophe which befell the Pacific fleet of Great Britain at the beginning of that war, some of her best ships being sunk by Japanese air power in a matter of minutes. This catastrophe was the result of the same mistake of believing that since British sea power had proven to be the unchallengeable main element of British power in the past, it was bound to be so forever. Especially in a period of rapid technological change, in a period of not one revolution in the technology of warfare but a continuous succession of such revolutions, there is very great danger in fixing one's gaze upon one particular period and projecting the distribution of power of that period into the future. The survival of a nation and the continuation of its greatness may well depend upon its ability to project correctly, or at least without making disastrous mistakes, the distribution of power of today into the future, five or ten years hence.

The third typical mistake which nations make in the evaluation of their power and which in the past has frequently led to their decline is the error of the single factor. That is to say, nations have a tendency, as do individuals as well, to put their bets upon one factor which is particularly advantageous to them and to forget about all the other factors which are not so advantageous to them. Take, for instance, the isolation of the United States which as a concept, as a myth, as an idea determining American foreign policy survived for a considerable stretch of time the actual isolation of the United States.

What we call "militarism" is a particular manifestation of this error, the idea that a particular type of weapon or a particular military service or military preparedness itself is the only and the most decisive element in a nation's power, although military power is certainly the indispensable foundation of national power. But anybody, especially in the Free World, who would overlook the vital importance of diplomacy and of what is called "the struggle for the minds of men" through propaganda, foreign aid, and all the other factors which go into that struggle would certainly misunderstand the power of one's own nation and the requirements, in terms of power, of the foreign policy of one's own nation. Nations who try to determine their power in comparison with other nations in terms of the number of their divisions or of their airplanes make a fundamental mistake when they equate the totality of their power with material military might.

Another manifestation of this fallacy of the single factor lies in the field of what has been called "geopolitics"—that is to say, the belief that the power of the nation is predetermined by its geography. The American isolationism of the twenties and thirties comes of course again to mind. As you know, there has been a whole school of thought, particularly in England and Germany, which has tried to develop a theory of foreign policy on the basis of the geographic factor. Nobody will doubt that geography is the most fundamental and the most permanent of all the factors which go into the making of national power; but it is by no means the only one. Certain nations have been greatly favored by the geographic factor, and the geographic factor has by no means prevented their decline. Others have not been favored at all and have risen to heights of greatness because of the intangible factors which go into the making of a nation's greatness. So here in the metaphysics of geography you have another fallacy against which one has to be on guard.

Finally, there is the fallacy of another single factor, and that is nationalism, conceived as chauvinism, which attributes all the good qualities to one's own nation and deprives all other nations, especially the enemy, of all good qualities—which bestows all bad qualities, in other words, upon the enemy. This psychological tendency has proven to be a disaster for nations which surrendered to it without reservations and qualifications. The downfall of Germany in recent history resulted in good measure from this chauvinistic overestimation of one's own nation's qualities and the underestimation of the qualities of other nations.

Take, for instance, the consistent underestimation and, in certain periods, overestimation of Russian power. Certainly this fallacy has done great harm either way, by either overestimation or underestimation, to the interests of the nations which have indulged in this kind of error. There is great need for a nation, if it wants to preserve its standing in the world and increase its greatness, its power, and whatever else goes into its greatness, to look at itself and at its competitors in the world with a certain detachment, with a certain critical faculty, the absence of which will lead to errors which in turn will be detrimental to a nation's greatness. Throughout history, many nations have fallen because they believed too strongly in their superiority.

I think nobody has phrased this problem better than the great

British political philosopher Edmund Burke who said in 1793, when Great Britain was engaged in the War of the First Coalition against Napoleon: "Among precautions against ambition, it may not be amiss to take one precaution against our own. I must fairly say I dread our own power and our own ambition. I dread our being too much dreaded. It is ridiculous to say that we are not men and that as men we shall never wish to aggrandize ourselves in some way or another. Can we say that even at this very hour we are not invidiously aggrandized? We are already in possession of almost all the commerce of the world. Our empire in India is an awful thing. If we should come to be in a condition not only to have all this ascendant in commerce, but to be absolutely able, without the least control, to hold the commerce of all other nations totally dependent upon our good pleasure, we may say that we shall not abuse this astonishing and hitherto unheard-of power. But every other nation will think we shall abuse it. It is impossible but that, sooner or later, this state of things must produce a combination against us which may end in our ruin."

This is a very wise observation, one that is borne out by historic experience. Nations which have acquired enormous power—too great a power, as it were, for their own good—have frequently declined at the very moment they reached such heights of power. Again a certain humility, here in terms of judging how far one wants to go in aggrandizing one's self, is, it seems to me, in order.

Let me say finally that there is another area which is important for the preservation of a nation's greatness, and the absence of certain qualities here has frequently led to a nation's decline. That area is in the field of domestic government. Nations, especially in our age, are continuously confronted with new tasks, new challenges. In order to meet them they must use institutions, ideas, concepts, policies which had been framed for different tasks and different challenges. So there is always a gap between the experiences of a nation and the institutions and ideas and policies which have been formed by the experiences of the past, on the one hand, and the tasks of the present, on the other.

The continuing greatness of a nation depends in good measure upon its ability to readjust its institutions, to redevise its policies, to reformulate its ideas in the light of new tasks, new conditions, new challenges. The pages of history are full of great empires which became ossified, which because they had solved the problems of the past with institutions, ideas, and policies of the past, thought that they could apply the same institutions, the same ideas, the same policies to the new tasks of the present and of the future. And when those tasks became too great to be dealt with successfully by those institutions, ideas, and policies, those nations declined and diasappeared. There is, I think, an analogy between those ossified empires who were unable to move, as it were, with the times and the dinosaur whose biological structure was perfectly adapted to one kind of environment, and, since he could not adapt it to another kind of environment, he had to perish.

In view of the tasks before us, I must say, if I may come to the present and close to home, I cannot look with equanimity at the procedures of our government, especially of our executive branch, of what I have recently called "government by committee." This system, I think, is totally inadequate to the tasks of the present and of the foreseeable future. Our government has been divided into what you might call "a multitude of security councils of the United Nations," where each member has a veto and can forestall action. I have been told that the State Department is a member of about 700 interdepartmental committees which deal with different problems of defense and foreign policy, and this does not include, of course, the committees within the State Department itself. This cumbersome, almost monstrous establishment of the executive branch, this slow-moving, if moving at all, establishment constitutes great danger to the greatness of the United States in an age which requires swift, audacious, and radically new decisions.

I do not know whether I have answered the question which was posed in the topic. I am quite sure I have not answered it, but I hope I have made a small contribution to showing how difficult and how essentially unanswerable a question it is.

13 *Grandeur and Decadence of Spanish Civilization*

The modern history of Spanish civilization is determined, to a much greater extent than any other European civilization of the same period, by politics. The relationship between Spanish civilization and the political powers, however, is of a peculiar kind in so far as the Spanish civilization of the last centuries has developed in the shadow of a decaying state. The political history of Spain since the last years of the reign of Philip II is the history of an almost uninterrupted decline from the power of a world-wide empire to the impotence of a political phenomenon that in world politics is reckoned with only because of its strategic situation and the value of its raw materials; object of international politics, it is no longer a center of political power of its own.

The political power of other states came to a sudden end through one unfortunate war or was gradually exhausted in the changing fortunes of victory and defeat. Spain's political greatness withers away in a continuous process which during three centuries slowly but irresistibly approaches its seemingly predestined goal. In the history of other dynasties, greatness follows meanness, virtue vice—thus establishing in the long run a kind of balance between the positive and the negative. In the deeds of the Spanish monarchs the negative is predominant. The reign of each of the Hapsburgs succeeding Philip II, and of the Spanish Bourbons—with the sole exception of Charles III—meant a new loss of political and cultural values and a new variety of princely incompetence and degeneration. These princes and their nobles spent money for women and horses, for the church and for war, for senseless luxuries and doubtful pleasures, but not for the spirit and its achievements. But since they were interested in having their likenesses transmitted to posterity, they happened occasionally to support the arts, when the painter was by chance Velasquez or Goya. Institutional patronage of arts and letters—this principal contribution of the absolute monarchy

From the *University* (of Kansas City) *Review*, October, 1939.

to European civilization—has never existed in Spain, with the sole exception again of the reign of Charles III. Whatever values the Spanish civilization has created in the last three centuries, the state has been hostile or at best indifferent to them; when the state did not attempt to destroy the manifestations of the national spirit, it at any rate refused to further them.

It is from the background of this political decadence that the tragic struggle of Spanish civilization wins meaning and weight. Have the national character and the spiritual vitality of the Spanish people, the permanent elements which in a positive way determine the growth of civilizations, been able to survive this atmosphere of political decay? To this question, put in a general way, no other than Bismarck has given an answer. Asked by William I which European people seemed to him the most excellent, he replied that there were no more excellent people in Europe than the Spaniards; for, although their masters for three centuries had been busy trying to destroy them, the Spanish people managed to keep intact their vital force and their good qualities. The hero of the history of Spanish civilization in the period of its decadence is not an outstanding man or a particular intellectual or artistic movement, but the people—that people which, as a great Spaniard has put it, "keep silent, pray, and pay the bill." Spain's political power disappears; her cultural life, once incomparably rich and influential, declines; but the national character and mental vitality of her people miraculously survive.

The history of Spanish civilization in the last centuries is the story of a political and cultural sickness against which the patient stands up in an admirable manner. The sickness proceeds in different fields with different intensity and speed. In the political sphere it begins, still under the reign of Philip II, with the destruction of the Spanish Armada by England in 1588 and leads under the last Hapsburgs abruptly downward. The cultural decline proceeds at a much slower pace and culminates in a real catastrophe only at the end of the seventeenth century.

From now on Spanish civilization is nothing but mere mental vitality, aimlessly moving in the dark. No longer able to manifest itself in cultural creations of its own, Spanish civilization lives chiefly on three substances: on the sentimental and self-complacent worship of the glorious past; on a not less sterile scholasticism which exploits the audacious innovators Vitoria and Suarez for educational purposes; and finally on a limitless eclecticism which grasps with real passion the creations of alien civilizations and thus produces one of the most eclectic and encyclopedic literatures Europe has ever known (it is not an accident that the Spanish Encyclopedia is the richest of all). When, however, the Spanish people succeed in expressing themselves in the cultural sphere, as in the second half of the eighteenth century under Charles III, the political, spiritual, and social forces ruling Spain do their best to discredit this period of Spanish "Enlightenment" as "un-Spanish," to exclude its representatives as "afrancesados" from the community of Spanish tradition, and to extirpate whatever vestiges it may have left in the institutions of the country. After such fruitless effort, Spain falls back into the slumber of centuries. "Under a paralyzing atmosphere," says Unamuno in "The Marasmus of Spain" (the last of the essays combined under the title *En torno al casticismo*) "expands an intellectual desert of terrifying poverty. There is nothing fresh, nothing spontaneous: there is no youth." Such was the intellectual landscape of Spain when the military catastrophe of 1898 originated that intellectual movement which is known in history as the Generation of 1898.

The unlucky end of the Spanish-American War was for the history of this movement scarcely more than a catastrophic incident. It made obvious a condition which had long before been in existence and had been known or suspected by many, and gave the forces of regeneration—which had been waiting for the great moment ever since the end of the eighteenth century—a common experience and a common starting point. It was not so much the fact of the lost war and its consequences in terms of power politics which stirred up the intellectual leaders of the nation. The loss of the last remainders of the colonial empire was certainly sad enough; but since it threw the Spaniards back upon themselves, could it not become a necessary condition of national regeneration? What moved the Spaniards so deeply and drove them into despair of their destiny was the manner in which this war was begun, carried on, and lost. The history of this war seemed, with the force of a symbol, to condense and at the same time to outdo all the experiences and sufferings which governmental incompetence had accumulated in 300 years. When the

Duke of Medina Sidonia, completely inexperienced in maritime warfare and exposed to seasickness, implored Philip II not to send him as head of the Armada against the English navy, the King could justify his unreasonable choice with the trust in God, who was the true admiral of the Spanish fleet. When in 1898 the Spanish fleet, at the moment of the decisive battle, came to realize that its ammunition did not fit into its guns, there was no longer a metaphysical justification for that. The more the people became acquainted with the unprecedented irresponsibility of their leaders, the deeper grew their conviction that a people who had to suffer such things, without any chance for resistance or remedy, were definitely done for. The "Pessimismo Español" developed into a mass movement which threatened to wipe out the forerunners of intellectual and political regeneration and the very vitality of the nation as well.

It was at this historical moment that a few young men, most of them university professors, raised their voices in behalf of the Spanish future. These men set themselves against the wave of fatalism and endeavored to restore to the Spanish people the consciousness of their value and the faith in their mission. In the very year of 1898, Rafael Altamira gave in the University of Oviedo his inaugural address on the subject *Patriotism and the Universities,* and Joaquín Costa published his book on agrarian collectivism, which became instrumental in the foundation of a national league for agrarian reform. Already in 1891 Macías Picavea's *The National Problem,* and in 1897 Angel Ganivet's *Idearium español,* had been published, works which tried to interpret the history and destiny of the Spanish people in philosophical terms and made a profound impression upon their contemporaries. In 1899 Altamira submitted to the public his translation of Fichte's *Addresses to the German Nation.* Finally, to the immediate impression of the catastrophe of 1898 two volumes owe their existence, both of which endeavor to restore the Spanish people's consciousness of themselves, of their place and task in the world: Altamira's *Psychology of the Spanish People,* and Unamuno's *En torno al casticismo.*

Sometimes the Generation of 1898 is associated with the next generation, composed of very gifted historical and political essayists who in the decisive year of 1898 still were going to school. But neither from the chronological nor from the historical standpoint can this association be justified. Ortega's sociological analyses and Madariaga's political essays—to mention only the two most impressive of those writers—may surpass the manifestations of the authentic Generation of 1898, as far as literary influence goes; they do not attain the latter's pathos and exemplary moral virtue, nor do they even try to fulfil the mission with which the men of 1898 had charged themselves.

When we ask what has been the lasting contribution which Spanish civilization owes to that magnificent effort of the Generation of 1898, the answer cannot be but definite in at least one respect: the Generation of 1898 has not reached its goal, the regeneration of Spanish national life. The reasons for this failure lie in its own limitations. Against the immobility of that sterile intellectual life, which state and church support with the full weight of their social influence, the Generation of 1898 had not much more to maintain than two abstractions: "Spirit" and "Education."

It inherited the idealistic belief in the redeeming power of the pure spirit from the "Krausismo," that pathetically inadequate philosophical movement which revered in Krause, third-rate disciple of German idealism, its master. In the thirties of the nineteenth century Sanz del Rio, one of the foremost Spanish philosophers of that century, made one of those intellectual pilgrimages to Germany which have since become traditional with a great majority of Spanish intellectual youth. There he became acquainted with the writings of Krause, whom Schelling had declared unworthy of a professorate at the University of Munich, who had invented, after the misunderstood model of the great idealistic system builders, an abstruse "All-in-God-Philosophy," presented in a queer philosophical language of his own, and who had devised a "Bund" of all mankind, the other planets and remaining celestial bodies included. This philosophy was to become for the Spanish intellectuals a kind of pseudo-religious revelation and for almost a century, through being translated, annotated, interpreted, developed, applied, it has dominated Spanish philosophical thought.

The belief in the reforming power of education came to the Generation of 1898 from a much purer source. It was the teachings and the example of an incomparably great man, as great a personality as perhaps only Spain can produce—Francisco Giner de los Ríos. This man, whom the ancient Stoa would have recognized as one of its authentic members as to modes of thought as well as to style of life, realized that one cannot revive an old civilization and remake a political system with illiterates. Hampered and persecuted by state and church, relying solely upon the moral force of a great soul and the enthusiasm of a group of patriotic youths, Giner founded in the last decades of the nineteenth century a private university and model schools in Madrid, equipped ambulant libraries, and sent his disciples to the villages. This grandiose educational enterprise, together with the idealism of the "Krausistas," was still the only intellectual force not hostile or indifferent to reform, when the Generation of 1898 entered the scene.

"Spirit" and "Education" remain empty abstractions which can mean everything and nothing, as long as they are not understood within the context of the intellectual, political, social, and economic situation which they are appealed to work upon. It was the historic mission of the Generation of 1898 to give these abstractions a meaning commensurate to the exigencies of the Spanish problem and thus to make them a sure guidance for resurrection and reform. In this, the Generation of 1898 has failed. It did not come to know by what kind of spirit and what kind of education Spain should be saved, nor did it make clear for what kind of Spain it wanted to educate and evoke the spirit. What the Generation of 1898 lacked was a universally accepted idea of man, a system of first principles, and a realm of values, which alone elevate cultural efforts above the futility of the subjective and give them objective meaning. The Generation of 1898 produced great historians and literary men but no philosopher. When it turned from the sphere of pure reasoning to the solution of social problems—as in the instance of Joaquín Costa—its abstract idealism had no chance in the face of the hostile immobility of social conditions, economic interests, and political power relations; the same abstract idealism, nourished by the same intellectual sources, in our day has led Azaña's republic of scholars and writers in the struggle against the same forces and into defeat. When the Generation of 1898 remained within the limit of the intellectual sphere, however, it exhausted its energies in literary controversies, like that in which the partisans of Spain's "Europization" and "Hispanization" were involved. The Generation of 1898 remained "literature"; that is, if we apply the highest standard, it was an uncreative movement. From this viewpoint it is not accidental that the most significant accomplishment of the Generation of 1898 lay in the realm of history; and the activity of the historian is in its very nature reproductive.

When finally Unamuno, the philosopher of the movement, left behind him the doubtful depths of his paradoxes and entered the domain of original philosophical creation, his philosophy became the very expression of the negative side of the Spanish character which has so greatly contributed to the decline of Spanish civilization: an anarchic intellectualism which neither in the political nor in the intellectual sphere recognizes any rule, an irrationalism which originates in the inability to think and live rationally, and finally a fanatically anachronistic and subjective spiritualism which considers flight from reality a philosophical virtue. Unamuno's philosophy was instrumental in bringing the decline of Spanish civilization into philosophical consciousness rather than in contributing to the latter's resurrection. In the subjective isolation of its own nihilism it revealed the philosophical vacuum in which this civilization, nourished only by the memory of past grandeur, had managed to live on. Whatever moral impression this philosophy may make upon the reader is to be attributed less to its philosophical substance than to the tragic struggle of its author, to which the work testifies; the reaction to it which the reader is likely to feel is biographical sympathy rather than philosophical participation. And how could the Spanish people expect the interpretation of their destiny and the rule of their actions from a philosopher whose spiritualism led him to call civil war the cleanest kind of war—a war less easily infected by material and egotistic motives and generally embarked upon for spiritual reasons. So far had the "Pure Spirit" finally gone!

The Generation of 1898 had no philosophy which could give guidance to its actions, and hence it was unable to create a civilization and to lay the foundations for political and social reform. This failure in the political and social field it possessed in common with its admired model, the German idealistic philosophy which—although incomparably more creative in the philosophical and artistic fields—started with a similarly remote and abstract notion of the Spirit moving in serene solitude above the turmoil of political and social life. Both pay the price for their seclusion in the ivory tower by being for the history of their peoples what, after Nietzsche's prophetic, though exaggerated, judgment, Goethe has been for German civilization—"an incident without consequences."

The signal contribution which the Generation of 1898 has made to Spanish civilization, beside Altamira's imposing historical writings, is in the final analysis something in which, since the end of the great epoch of Spanish civilization, the creative force of the Spanish people has almost exclusively been concentrated—great characters. The astounding vitality of the Spanish people has outlasted the centuries of decline; but it has lost the capability of objectifying itself in authentic cultural manifestations. The greatness of the Spanish people lives on as pure force. Of their sufferings, their heroism, their dignity in misery, their wisdom and goodness of heart, no epic, no monument, no philosophical system tells. Silenced human greatness—that is perhaps the ultimate answer to the question of what the Spanish civilization in the period of its decadence has been. Spain's greatness is not in books nor in formed matters; it is in the very men themselves, and in them alone. That it perishes with them is the ever renewed tragical failure of Spanish civilization. As Somerset Maugham has said of the Spaniards:

Their preëminence was great. It was a preëminence of character. In this I think they have been surpassed by none and equalled only by the ancient Romans. It looks as though all the energy, all the originality of this vigorous race has been disposed to one end and one end only, the creation of men.

14 *The Political Philosophy of Prussianism*

Every people has talked back to other peoples at various times. It is the way in which a nation becomes aware of its own individuality, as well as of the individuality of others. The Russia of Dostoevski and Tolstoi, no less than that of Lenin, Trotsky, and Stalin, has talked back continuously to the West. England in all periods of her history has talked back to the Continent. The Spaniards have been talking back to the rest of Europe, and especially to the French, ever since Philip II. So have the Italians and the French, especially when the Germans were on the receiving end. The Americans have done a lot of back-talking to Europe, and the Chinese have been so sure of their own superiority that during most of their history they have refused to talk back at all and have dismissed non-Chinese as barbarians.

Thus it ought not to surprise us that the German talks back. It will surprise only those who still hold the blind and naïve prejudice of the Victorians that all the right people everywhere conform to one pattern, their own, and that it is their duty to carry the blessings of middle-class normality to the rest of the globe. We know, or ought to know from our own national experience, how self-defeating such an attitude toward other peoples is, for we have tried to make the world safe for democracy by assuming that all peoples would think and act like Americans once the fetters of autocratic government were removed and democratic institutions established. When the German nationalists talked back in the twenties we refused to listen. When Hitler, Mussolini, and Hirohito talked back, ever louder and ever more menacing, we heard only what we wanted to hear—the hurt voices of some misunderstood gentlemen whose grievances might even be just.

The German who talks back to us in the following pages [Heinrich Hauser in *The German Talks Back*] can help us to understand better the one nation on whose account we have twice gone to war

Introduction to Heinrich Hauser's *The German Talks Back* (1945).

in one generation. He can also help us to understand ourselves better. But we shall understand what he is talking about, and why he and we must talk with different voices, only when we recognize the basic difference between the philosophy of this German and our own.

Mr. Hauser does not speak for himself alone; if he did, we could learn nothing from him about the political thinking of Germany. Nor does he speak for the German people as a whole; if he did, we need say only, "This is Germany," and no introduction would be necessary. But, though he does not speak for all of Germany, he certainly speaks for the politically active intellectual elite who have been endeavoring to express in civilized language what millions of Nazi and non-Nazi Germans have felt and thought at least since the beginning of the thirties.

The group to which Mr. Hauser belongs has much in common with the disillusioned generation of the twenties in America; only its disillusionment started a few decades earlier and has much deeper roots. It was nourished by two great experiences which impressed themselves upon the German mind at the turn of the century. One of them was the decadence of the German classical tradition, and the other was the emptiness of the substitute which the Germany of William II offered for that tradition. It was Nietzsche who told his compatriots that "Goethe, not only a good and great man but a whole civilization, was in the history of the Germans an incident without consequences." And the same philosopher, who hid his morbidity and despair behind a mask of affected brutality, pointed up not only the vulgarity and sham of William's imperial splendor, but also the inherent spiritual and political weakness of Bismarck's political construction.

The worship of the humanitarian and esthetic ideals of the classical period by "the people of poets and thinkers" had indeed become a mere literary ritual, a kind of intellectual folklore, the practice of which lent charm and enjoyment to the hours of leisure, but which had no relation to the world of political action. The separation of the German intellectual tradition from political life was the consequence both of the failure of the revolution of 1848 and of Bismarck's success as founder of the Reich. The impotent philistinism in which the revolution of 1848 ingloriously ended seemed to offer experimental proof of the fact that the "poets and thinkers" who had led the revolution might be all right in the studio or the class-room but would better keep their fingers out of politics. This was Bismarck's opinion, at least, and—by realizing in action what the others could only dream and talk about—he demonstrated to the German people the superiority of Potsdam, seat of Prussianism, over Weimar, fountain of classical tradition. The schism between the in-tellectual and the political life, which is a disquieting problem in our country as elsewhere, was made unbridgeable in Germany. Two Germanies lived side by side, not only in the nation as a whole but also within many of its citizens: the Germany of Frederick the Great and Bismarck, and the Germany of Beethoven and Goethe.

The intoxication of the First World War, welcomed by many as deliverance from insecurity and doubt, brought about a temporary and apparent rather than a real union between the two Germanies. It was this war that seemed to prove the doubters wrong—to reaffirm the vitality of the spirit of Potsdam as well as that of Weimar. The breakdown in 1918 shattered all these hopes and demonstrated dra-matically the hollowness of William's empire and of the classical tra-dition as well. What force, material and spiritual, remained to hold the German nation together? On what power of the spirit and of the sword could one rely when the spirit of Weimar was dead and the sword of William II was broken? The leaders of the German Re-public themselves gave the answer. They called back, or left in power, the representatives of that force which, since the days of the Great Elector, if not of the Teutonic Knights, had developed a spe-cial philosophy of life and of the state: Prussia. While the Socialists and liberals of 1918–19 could think of nothing better than to make the existence of the Republic dependent upon its deadly enemies, the Prussian bureaucracy and army, the disillusioned intellectual youth turned to the spiritual roots of this bureaucracy and this army, the Prussian spirit. Here it seemed to find what it had searched for in vain in the classical tradition and in William's empire—that is, a com-bination of genuine ideals with successful political action.

The worship of the Prussian spirit became a religion not only with the particular group to which Mr. Hauser belonged, but with the intellectual avant-garde of all political groups. The Nazis identified themselves most openly with the Prussian tradition, which presuma-bly had been founded by the Teutonic Knights. So Alfred Rosenberg, the official philosopher of national socialism, could declare that naziism was "the continuation of the traditions of the Order of the German Knights of Prussia." East Prussia was renamed by the Nazis "Order State Prussia," and the historic seat of the order, the Marienburg, became a model after which a number of order schools for the education of the Nazi elite were founded in different parts of Germany. Yet before the Nazis had become intellectually respectable, conservative writers such as Moeller van den Bruck and Oswald Spengler, democratic poets such as Fritz von Unruh, nationalists such as Ernst Jünger, and leading Socialists such as August Winnig had been the apostles of the new cult.

If one searches for a fundamental principle that gives the tenets of a political philosophy unity and distinction, one finds always a particular conception of the nature of man. It is so with the philosophy of Prussianism. Its essence has been called militarism, imperialism, autocracy; and it is all this, but also more than this. At its base is the idea that the common man can transcend his animal nature only by coercion from the outside, can learn only from authority what he ought to know, can do only by fear of force what he ought to do. In this philosophy, man is in truth born a soldier who obeys without question, who reacts without thought, and who must be made into an efficient cog in the military machine through his fear of authority. If obviously no man comes into this world in uniform, he might at least be imagined as leaving it in one. When King Frederick William I was dying, his favorite hymn was read in his presence. When the reader came to the lines "Naked I came to the world, and naked I will leave it," the dying monarch exclaimed, "No, no—I shall have my uniform!"

In such a scheme of things, independence of thought, of conscience, and of action is a handicap rather than an asset, a source of weakness rather than of strength. Obedience, belief in authority, and self-denial are the conditions of individual as well as collective success. That any government, or any army, can function without these qualities is either flatly denied or marveled at without any suspicion that there may be resources in human nature that do not yield to force. Frederick William I, after a visit to King George I at Hanover, wrote with great admiration of the high military qualities of the Hanoverian troops and added: "What in my opinion is wanting is subordination; they do their duty because they delight in it, not from a sense of subordination, for scarcely a blow can be dealt any man among them under pain of the King's displeasure. Every private soldier knows this, and yet the army is in good order; which greatly surprises me." There have been similar surprises since, the most memorable ones in 1918 and in 1945; but they have hardened rather than weakened the Prussian opposition to the democratic way of life.

Democracy easily lays itself open to the Prussian attack, for it is of necessity vulnerable at a point at which Prussianism is perfectly safe: at the cleavage between democratic pretensions and democratic reality. This cleavage is inevitable, for the democratic claims of human equality and freedom can never be fully translated into political reality but only approximated at best. It is of the very essence of political life that there shall always be an element of political domination preventing the full realization of equality and freedom. Prussianism is exposed to no such danger. The tragic tension between freedom and power, which makes the democratic conscience so ill at ease, never appears in Prussia because freedom itself—nay, the very idea of freedom—never appears: power is all that counts. The Prussian virtues of obedience, discipline, submission to authority, and self-denial are but the reflection in the subject of the power of the superior. The individual has significance only as the subject of authority, military or otherwise, to be used as a means to an end, but never as an end in itself. The Prussian is right in saying that democracy does not give the individual all that it promises him. Yet Prussianism promises the individual nothing at all, for it does not even know that inside the individual called "subject" there is something that has a claim to be heard in its own right.

It is for this reason that the attempt to identify Prussianism with socialism and the "church militant" is doomed to failure. Whatever the theories and practices of socialism and the church may have been in different periods of history, respect and concern for the individual, recognition of his unique worth, has been common to all of them. The political organization—that is, the state, the church, or the religious order—exists for the sake of the individual, for his economic, political, or spiritual salvation. External similarities in organization and social techniques cannot obscure the fundamental philosophic difference between Prussianism, which knows only one end—

the state—and is not even aware of the existence of individuals as such, and socialism and religion, for which political organization is only a means to the end of the individual good.

The attempt to explain Prussian militarism, which is indeed an apology in disguise, by Prussia's poverty and her lack of *Lebensraum* (living space) must also fail. Poverty was actually a result, not the cause, of Prussian militarism. In order to have a big army, Frederick William I spent from a revenue of seven million thalers five million for military purposes, and for this reason Prussia was poor. In our own day Hermann Göring chose guns for the Germans instead of butter, and consequently the German standard of living was low. More living space is no cure for this voluntarily contracted disease but only an excuse for its perpetuation. The simile of the need for living space—that is, of people suffocating in too small a room—is as plausible on its surface as it is unfounded in its essence. There may be primitive tribes that must either find new grazing and hunting grounds or perish. No civilized people has even been confronted with such a choice. More particularly, modern economic conditions are so varied and so susceptible to manipulation that the ingenuity of the economist and the statesman rather than of the conqueror is called for in order to solve the problem of living space.

Yet it is significant that Prussianism, confronted with the economic problems of our age, has no other realistic remedy to offer but a war of conquest. The final test of a political philosophy is the way in which it deals with the problems of contemporary life. For these problems, the spokesman of the Prussian spirit suggests two solutions, one realistic, the other romantic: the solution of nihilism in the form of war, veiled either by the *Lebensraum* argument or by association with Russia, or the escapist solution, which would have us turn our backs on the technological age and return to the fictitious idyl of the countryside. When Prussianism thus comes face to face with the problems of our age, its whole spiritual and moral emptiness, born of ignorance of man and contempt for him as a human person, becomes obvious. It can only think either of war—that is, the destruction of man and of the world created by him—or of the negation of modern man and his technological world, which takes the form of romantic flight into a rural Eden that has never existed.

The spiritual and moral emptiness of the Prussian spirit also explains why the Prussians have always been so formidable in war and so weak in political construction, why they could win so many battles in 1914 and 1940 and still fail in the end. If it is true that one can do anything with a bayonet except sit on it, it is no less true that with the military machines of Frederick the Great, William II, and Hitler, one can destroy empires but cannot build them; one can win battles but cannot win the peace; one can enslave but one cannot free —for in order to free, one must believe in at least a modicum of goodness and rationality in man, one must trust in certain spontaneous resources in human nature which enable man to co-operate freely in a common enterprise. Of all this, Prussianism knows nothing. With ever renewed surprise it watches, as Frederick William I did in Hanover, the strange spectacle of free men working freely together and even "delighting in it." Under various ideological disguises, it revives the Spartan ideal of the military life in a military state—the latter being a machine for the production of armies, and man being a machine within a machine for the production of victories. If this is all Prussianism is able to offer us, we indeed owe no apologies to the memory of Thomas Jefferson.

15 Naziism

If a political philosophy is a coherent system of thought intent upon justifying before ethics and reason a certain political program and certain political institutions, naziism has not developed a political philosophy. What passes as the political philosophy of naziism is a conglomeration of fragments of ideas, often inconsistent with each other, always vague and capable of contradictory interpretations, and hence adaptable to the exigencies of changing political conditions. Its intellectual quality is low, and its literary style is crude. Its appeal is to emotions rather than to reason.

It is not by accident that these are the general characteristics of the political philosophy of naziism. On the one hand, they grow out of the particular political conditions under which the doctrine of naziism originated. On the other hand, they bear the mark of disdain for reason which characterizes the Nazi movement.

Political philosophies, such as liberalism or communism, which appeal to one clearly defined social group, the middle classes or the proletariat, can afford to develop a coherent doctrine which reflects faithfully the conditions, interests, and aspirations of this particular group. Naziism does not appeal to any social group in particular, but to certain elements in all groups. Since the conditions, interests, and aspirations of these groups are largely contradictory, a political doctrine, which intends to appeal to all of them at the same time, cannot fail to be itself incoherent and contradictory. While, however, pre-Nazi political philosophy would have regarded such inconsistency a serious weakness, naziism, in so far consistent with its general philosophic assumptions, sees in it an actual virtue.[1]

For the tradition of Western civilization, man is a rational being. It is upon this rationality, which is the common possession of all men, that the possibility of universal truth, binding upon all men, is

From Joseph S. Roucek (ed.), *Twentieth Century Political Thought* (1946).

[1] *Mein Kampf* (New York: Reynal and Hitchcock, 1940), I, 283 *et seq.*; Vol. II, chaps. v, vi, vii, xi.

founded. Naziism is essentially anti-intellectualist and irrationalist. Naziism has a low opinion of the common man. The masses are by their very nature stupid, sullen, ignorant, irresolute, swayed by emotions. It is for the elite and their leader to impose their will upon the masses and to give directions to their blind instincts. If such is the nature of the common man, a political philosophy, instead of being a rational system appealing to reason, becomes an instrument, cleverly and unscrupulously managed by the elite, for molding mind and will of the masses. Ideas become truly weapons, that is, weapons of propaganda, and the standard to which they must comply is no longer truth but effectiveness. It, then, is quite irrelevant whether a political idea is true, precise, and consistent with others. A lie is to be preferred if only it is capable of bringing about the desired political result.[2]

It follows from the same anti-intellectualist premises that naziism has no use for elucidation and development of its political doctrine by discussion. Since political doctrine is an instrument for the domination of the masses, it must ask unquestioned acceptance. If it would allow the masses to debate its merits and to improve upon it, it would put into jeopardy the very objectives for which it is used.

In sum, naziism is less a political philosophy than a political religion. It has in Hitler its savior, in S.A., S.S., and party its sacred orders, in *Mein Kampf* its bible, in the immutable twenty-five points of the party program its catechism, in the racial community its mystical body. It has its miracles and rituals, its apostles, martyrs, and saints.[3] With genuine religion it has in common that it derives its claim to acceptance not from the truthfulness of its suppositions, which is verifiable by experience, but from authority, and, furthermore, that its claim to acceptance is absolute and not subject to critical doubt. It differs from genuine religion in that its manipulators are not supposed to believe in it, that it constantly changes according to the exigencies of the political situation, and, finally and most important, that its avowed objective is not to establish relationships between the individual and supernatural forces, but to establish and

[2] *Mein Kampf*, I, 230 *et seq.*, 313; *The Speeches of Adolf Hitler* (London: Oxford University Press, 1942), pp. 62, 863.

[3] *The Speeches of Adolf Hitler*, pp. 137, 138, 158, 159, 405 *et seq.*, 1458, 1543, 1559, and innumerable other passages. Cf. also *Mein Kampf*, I, 573 *et seq.*

perpetuate the political power of a self-appointed elite over the masses of humanity.

According to democratic tradition, all men are born equal. It is the most fundamental tenet of the political philosophy of naziism that men are not born equal.[4] By equality is of course meant not actual equality in ability and achievement, but equality in individual worth and, hence, legal status. It is the latter that naziism denies. It asserts the value of personality against the supremacy of mere numbers, which is regarded as the constitutive principle of democracy. Individuals, as well as groups of individuals, such as nations, differ not only in their intellectual and psychological traits, which may be important for their social and economic position, but also in those qualities which determine their political and legal status. Naziism sees each nation divided into two groups: those who are born to rule, and those who are born to be ruled. The same distinction is made on a world-wide scale: there are nations whose destiny it is to rule, and there are others who are preordained to serve. This political status is determined by one's blood or race.

The racial doctrine of naziism has little, if any, connection with the findings of biology and anthropology. "Blood," in the Nazi doctrine, is essentially a mystical entity, a substance which creates life in all its biological, psychological, and cultural manifestations, and it is the kind of blood flowing in one's veins which will determine the kind of life one is to lead. Nothing can escape the determining influence of "blood." Physical appearance and character no less than political convictions and attitudes are determined by race. Religion, art, science are functions of "blood." Race and "blood" become synonymous with soul and vital energy. In the concepts, materialistic and mystical at the same time, of race, blood, and soil, the concepts of "nature" and of the "folk spirit" of the German Romantic school find their resurrection.[5]

[4] *Mein Kampf*, Vol. I, chap. xi; Vol. II, chaps. ii, iv.

[5] A popular school of thought sees in the political philosophy of naziism only the logical consummation of the age-old tradition of German political thought. It is indeed obvious that with respect to many of its tenets, such as the emphasis upon will and emotions as over against reason, the glorification of the state and the disdain for the individual as such, the worship of power pure and simple, the political philosophy of naziism builds upon foundations laid by the German tradition. Yet one looks in vain in the pre-Nazi tradition of German political

This race concept of naziism has three distinctive characteristics. First, it advances a biological interpretation of history, culture, and politics. Hegel had found the determining element in the spirit, Marx had found it in economic conditions, others had found it in religion, in the nation, or in ideas in general. For naziism, biological characteristics are both the source and the outer manifestations of morality, culture, and personal worth. Tell me what your, your parents', and your grandparents' biological characteristics are, and I will tell you what kind of a man you are. Race, then, becomes the yardstick by which the worth of the individual is measured. Race explains his personality, and whatever he is, sees, and does, is explained in the light of his membership in a certain race.

It is a further belief of the race doctrine of naziism that racial characteristics are constant. They are today what they were two thousand years ago. Race seems to be a kind of primordial biological fact which is completely impervious to the influences of physical and social environment. What holds true for the race as such is also true for the individual member of the race. For him race is a kind of fate into which he is born and from which he cannot escape. Education may be able to make him race-conscious, that is, proudly aware of the race to which he belongs and contemptuous of the others. Yet it cannot alter the biological fact of race, from which all individual qualities stem.

It can, however, impress upon the members of the race the importance of racial purity. The belief in it is the third distinctive characteristic of the racial doctrine of naziism, and it is difficult to overemphasize its bearing upon Nazi theory and practice. When a higher and a lower race mix, it is, according to the Nazi doctrine, strangely enough the contribution of the inferior race which dominates the mixture. Consequently, the superior race decays. Since racial characteristics as such remain constant, race mixture becomes the deadly danger against which the higher race must guard.

The race, which throughout history has proved itself to be superior to all others, is the Aryan or Nordic race. Whatever is val-

---

thought for the intellectual crudeness, the moral nihilism, and the pseudoreligious fervor which characterize Nazi political thought. In other words, naziism brutalizes and vulgarizes certain traits which are part of the tradition of German political thought.

uable in ancient and modern culture was created by members of the Nordic race. Whatever good there is in the creations of an inferior race, such as Christianity or Marxism, is due to the contribution made by members of the Nordic race. All history is envisaged as a struggle between the Nordic and inferior races. Thus the decadence of France, for instance, is attributed, on the one hand, to the destruction of the Nordic element, as represented in the nobility, through the religious wars and the Revolution, and, on the other hand, to the infiltration of Negro blood into the body of metropolitan France. Similarly, the struggle between Germans and Slavs is explained as a struggle between the master race of the Nordics and the half-barbaric peoples of the East.

The race doctrine fulfilled for the political practice of naziism a fourfold function. First, it integrated the German people into a new community transcending the traditional cleavages into political, social, and religious groupings. Second, it set up within the traditional German community itself a zone of racial contamination, comprehending minorities and individual dissenters of all kinds, in the destruction of which the newly discovered racial community could experience its own superiority. Furthermore, it established the claim to world-wide conquest as a mission to be fulfilled by the master race. Finally, it created and justified in the totalitarian state the political organization through which this triple function of integration, elimination, and conquest was to be accomplished.

The dominant principle of political integration from the middle of the nineteenth century to the advent of the Nazi movement had been nationalism. Germany and Italy became unified nations under the guidance of this principle. The independence movements of the Finns, the Poles, the Czechs, the Hungarians, and the Balkan peoples drew inspiration and justification from the same source. The principle of national self-determination was made the basis for what was believed to be an enduring peace by the peace settlements of Versailles and Saint-Germain.

Yet the triumph of the national principle in 1919 made obvious its limitations as a principle of political integration. Its consistent application gave rise to economic difficulties, such as the division of economic units (Silesia) and the creation of political units without economic foundation (Austria). It gave rise also to political and military difficulties, such as the atomization of the Danube Valley and the separation of East Prussia from the bulk of Germany through the Polish Corridor. Finally, political and military considerations prevented the national principle from being applied to all cases where its logic would have required its application. Thus, Austria was artificially maintained as an independent state and prevented from uniting with Germany, and the Sudetenland, predominantly settled by Germans, was made part of Czechoslovakia.

These weaknesses and inconsistencies gave the Nazis the opportunity of using the national principle as a weapon with which to destroy the territorial order which was based upon this selfsame principle of nationality. In order to be able to do this, the Nazis transformed the national principle by interpreting the concept of nation in terms of race.

Throughout the nineteenth century nationalism was intimately connected with the liberal movement. In a sense the principle of national self-determination was simply the principle of individual self-determination, that is, of individual liberty, transferred to a group of individuals who have certain characteristics in common. The cry for national self-determination is but the collective echo of the cry for individual liberty. The political goal of the individual was essentially identical with the goal of the national group, that is, freedom from oppression by autocratic government. Consequently, membership in a nation was a matter of individual choice; the nation, in the words of Renan, is "a daily plebiscite." This goal of individual and collective freedom was furthermore in harmony with the economic interests of the middle classes which were the main supporters and beneficiaries of liberal nationalism.

The postwar conditions which determined the growth of naziism altered completely the political, social, and economic implications of nationalism. To the Nazis, at least, liberal nationalism no longer seemed to have sufficient strength, in the face of powerful disintegrating influences, to integrate Germany into a working political community. Versailles turned the national principle against Germany, whose territorial losses were justified by it. More especially, the Weimar Republic, which identified itself with the idea of liberal nationalism, was also identified with the German defeat of 1918 and the Treaty of Versailles growing out of it, as well as with the political and economic disappointments of the postwar period. For all these reasons, the value of the traditional national principle as a political weapon became doubtful in the eyes of the German nationalists. Furthermore, the lower strata of the middle classes were economically proletarized under the impact of inflation and unemployment. Because of this, they could no longer derive satisfaction from their separate existences as individual shopkeepers or employees. Nor could they find compensation, as in former times, in the idea of the national state, as it was represented by the Weimar Republic. They gave up the individualistic aspirations of liberalism for the realization of which the economic and social realities offered no opportunity, and gave the libertarian aspirations of nationalism a collectivist turn against the destructive forces inside and outside Germany and in favor of the suffering true Germans. They were able to do this by making nationalism identical with racism. Thus it became possible to transform the struggle for national liberation at the same time into a revolutionary struggle inside Germany and into a struggle for conquest on a world-wide scale.

The constitutive principle of the nation was then no longer the free choice of the individual on the basis of cultural preferences but certain biological characteristics which once and forever divided each nation into two hostile camps. The pseudoreligious energies engendered by liberal nationalism could thus be directed against any objective within or without the political frontiers, which was stigmatized as racially inferior or at least hostile to the master race.

Whereas in liberal political philosophy tne individual is the center around whose worth and aspirations the political system revolves, the racial community now takes this central place. Life, liberty, and happiness of the individual amount to nothing as compared with the existence, safety, and greatness of the community. "Germany will live even if we must die" and "The common good comes before individual advancement" become the slogans of the new collectivist creed. By merging his individuality with the mystical body of the racial community, the individual would regain the awareness of his worth, which he had lost in the turmoil of national humiliation, social disintegration, and economic insecurity. The dissensions between capital and labor, city and farm, government and parliament, the Right and the Left, seemed to disappear once it was discovered that the members of all these warring groups were united in the greater community of the race. This community would solve the political, economic, and social problems with which these groups had struggled in vain, by leading its members back to the source of all strength and wisdom, the mainspring of the race itself: "blood and soil." The mystical communion with "blood and soil," whose processes escape rational analysis, becomes thus the key to the solution of all the problems which the Weimar Republic had not been able to solve.

The racist interpretation of history, its fusion with the nationalist tradition, and the emergence of a new racially determined collectivism provided naziism with a number of political and propagandistic weapons which, ingeniously used, decided the struggle for domestic power in favor of the Nazis and brought them very close to victory over their foreign enemies as well.

Naziism has never developed a consistent or even intelligible economic program; its intellectual deficiencies are nowhere more glaring than here. While it opposed the socialist parties, the labor unions, and the republican program of social reform, it appealed to the proletarized members of the middle classes and to the unemployed members of the laboring class in the name of socialism. While it proclaimed the principle of social revolution, it applied for and received the moral and financial support of those who sought through this support to buy protection against social revolution and even social reform. National Socialist collectivism showed a way out of these dilemmas. Since the traditional social, economic, and political conflicts, to which terms such as socialism, capitalism, class struggle, and the like refer, have been superseded by the struggle between races, the traditional conflicts are interpreted in the light of this struggle. Thus naziism is opposed to capital, but not to the racially good, that is, Germanic, capital, which is creative and benevolent, but to the racially evil, that is, Jewish and international, capital, which is parasitic and destructive. Thus naziism is in favor of socialism, but of the racially good, that is, German, variety, which manifests itself in service for the racial community and finds its noblest expression in the Prussian army and the state of Frederick the Great. On the other hand, naziism is hostile to Marxian, that is, Jewish socialist, values which place allegiance to an international class higher than loyalty to the racial community. Thus naziism can be against and in favor of socialism and against and in favor of capitalism at the same time, and by the same formula placate, and through common opposition to the same enemy unite, antagonistic groups.

Similarly naziism is able at once to oppose and defend Christianity. It opposes the racially contaminated type of Christianity which is internationalist, unheroic, and pacifist. Yet it defends and promotes German Christendom which glorifies the manly virtues, cultivates the combative instincts, and expresses the deepest aspirations of the racial soul.

Furthermore, the reduction of all domestic conflicts to racial ones makes it possible strictly and definitely to localize the conflicting principles and interests in biologically determined and therefore easily identifiable groups. Hence, whenever a conflict arises, the German race is on the side of the angels, and the Jews and other "racial degenerates" are on the side of the devil; and once the problem is posed in such terms, the solution presents no intellectual or physical difficulties. When the Nazis call the Jewish question the key to the solution of all the problems of the age, they show, beyond the immediate propagandistic purpose, a clear awareness of the decisive function which National Socialist collectivism fulfils for their political theory and practice.

The idea of racial community not only destroys the concept of the national state as the main instrumentality of political integration in the domestic field; it also has a revolutionary effect upon the relations between states. From the collapse of the Holy Alliance to the advent of naziism, the principle of non-intervention determined the attitude of a government with regard to the domestic affairs of other governments. Naziism replaces this principle by the idea of intervention on a dual basis. Since the biological fact of race supersedes the free choice of nationality as the principle of political integration, the members of the German race, wherever they live and whatever their nationality, are the racial comrades of the members of the German race living within the German boundaries. They owe allegiance to the German government, in which the racial community finds its political manifestation, and confronted with a conflict between loyalty to the nation of their choice and allegiance to the racial community, they must give precedence to the latter.

It is furthermore the mission of the master race to bring racial salvation to the peoples of the earth by freeing them from the domination of racially inferior groups and establishing the dominance of the master race. Hence, disruptive interference, on the basis of racial distinctions, in the domestic affairs of other nations, corresponds as a technique of political conquest to the substitution of the struggle between races for the traditional conflicts on the domestic scene. Ultimately, the distinction between domestic and international affairs tends to be obliterated, and social and political conflicts everywhere appear as phases of a gigantic struggle between races for supremacy.

It follows from the postulate of the racial inequality of men and from its particular manifestation in the National Socialist community that within a certain territory only the members of the superior race can enjoy political rights. Yet the political hierarchy, based upon racial excellence, does not end there. Within the superior race, a fundamental triple distinction must be made between the masses, which have no inborn racial consciousness or political judgment of their own and are therefore the mere raw material for political leadership; the relatively small group of the elite, a political aristocracy and sacred order in one, which, because of its racial qualities, is predestined to lead the masses, to imbue them with racial consciousness, to show them the political goals, and to use them for the realization of these goals; finally, the leader, the incarnation of the racial spirit itself, statesman and savior in one, who, drawing strength and wisdom from the mystical sources of blood and soil, guides with unfailing instinct the destinies of the racial community.[6]

While according to democratic political thought the ultimate power rests with the people to whom the political leaders and public officials are responsible, naziism reverses the distribution of power and responsibility between people and government. Naziism conceives of the relationship between government and people essentially in military terms, and Hitler himself has referred to the army as the model of political organization.[7] Consequently, the fullness of politi-

[6] *Mein Kampf*, Vol. II, chaps. ii, iv, viii, ix, xi.

[7] *Mein Kampf*, I, 384 *et seq.*, 620; *The Speeches of Adolf Hitler*, pp. 442, 556, 789.

cal power is vested in the political leader, who delegates part of it to his "political soldiers," that is, the members of the political oligarchy, the Nazi party. The leader is politically responsible to nobody and morally responsible only to his racial conscience, the Germanic god, or the German people as the embodiment of the racial spirit. The members of the party are politically responsible to the leader from whom they derive their political power. The people as such, while providing at times ideological justification for the exercise of political power by the elite, have disappeared as the seat of autonomous political power and the receptacle of political responsibility. Under such premises, the popular election of public officials and the determination of policies by majority vote become absurd relics of a bygone age which believed in the rational nature and the individual worth of the common man.

It also follows from these premises that the traditional dichotomy between state and society, that is, the spheres of government action and of individual freedom, becomes obsolete. In pre-Nazi political philosophy, even in the doctrine of the absolute monarchy at least as a matter of principle, the government has only as much power as the constitution and the laws of the land permit it to have. As for the rest, the people are free to do as they please. In Nazi doctrine the concept of law loses its character as an objective rule of conduct to which government and people alike are subject. Legal rules now are mere instrumentalities of political domination which assure to the party dictatorship the element of order without which no organization can function, and which, furthermore, are used as a means of coercion by which recalcitrant members of the community are brought into line. Law is used and interpreted according to the political exigencies of the hour; beyond this usefulness as a political instrumentality, it has no objective, rational value at all. "Law is what benefits the German people," and what benefits the German people is determined by the supreme decision of the leader.

The supreme will of the leader, far from being restrained by an objective rule of law, is the absolute source and measure of governmental power. He determines how far the power of the party shall extend, what spheres of individual endeavor it shall control, and by what means. This absence of legal restraint makes the power of the state potentially limitless, that is, total. The very nature of the leadership principle makes it actually so.

The doctrine of democracy starts with the assumption that all citizens are potentially capable of arriving at the right political decision and that, consequently, nobody has a monopoly of political wisdom to which, at least potentially, the others would not have access. It follows from this premise that all citizens have an equal right to hold and express their own opinion on any matter political or otherwise and to propagandize for it with the final aim of making it the dominant one. "The best test of truth is the power of the thought to get itself accepted in the competition of the market." Philosophic relativism, political pluralism, the protection of minorities of all kinds and with respect to all kinds of activities, are therefore the earmarks of democratic theory and practice.

Naziism, on the contrary, recognizes only one truth, political and otherwise, that is, the truth which emanates from the leader's supernatural insight and wisdom. Consequently, non-conformism is more than mere dissension but a sacrilegious revolt against the "voice of the blood," through which the genius of the race makes itself known. Since "Hitler is always right," he has not only the right but the obligation to impose what he has found to be right upon the passive and confused mind of the masses and to destroy the heretic who dares to dissent in thought, word, or action. Totalitarianism is therefore not by accident the distinguishing characteristic of the Nazi state. The power of the state, as represented in the leader, is total since no legal restraint puts limits to the exercise of governmental power. In its actual exercise, the power of the state regulates, controls, and circumscribes all activities of the individual, be they political, religious, artistic, educational, economic, or of the most intimate personal nature. Government, society, and the individual merge into one gigantic political organization which, as the totalitarian state, forms the political counterpart to what the racial community is in the biological and spiritual spheres.[8]

[8] Much has been made by some writers of the apparent subordination in Nazi philosophy of the state to the race (see, for instance, *Mein Kampf*, I, 592 *et seq.*), and of the apparent opposition, especially emphasized by the official Nazi philosopher Rosenberg, of naziism to the state worship of Hegel. Closer analysis, however, shows that this element in Nazi political thought fulfilled a useful political function while the Nazi movement stood in revolutionary opposition to the legitimate government representing the state and needed a legitimation superior to the legality of the established order. As soon as the Nazi movement

The principle of organization through which the totalitarian state molds the racial community for its purposes is coercion, intellectual and physical, and the traditional agencies of the state are transformed into instruments of coercion. The party, which in pre-Nazi doctrine was an instrumentality in the competitive struggle for political power, now becomes the monopolistic keeper and dispenser of the political gospel, an army of "political soldiers" who have to see to it that the political decision of the leader is transformed into the political action of the "racial comrades." The universities are no longer busy discovering new truths but fulfil the public function of imbuing the public with the political truths already discovered by the leader. They become, like primary and secondary education, press, radio, and official religion, agencies of governmental propaganda and, since the state keeps them under monopolistic control, of intellectual coercion.

These instrumentalities of intellectual coercion are, however, implemented by an instrumentality of physical coercion, that is, the political police. Its functions illuminate another distinctive element of Nazi political thought, that is, the estimation of organized physical violence not as a necessary evil but as a positive good. Pre-Nazi political thought considers physical violence, especially in its organized form, an evil the elimination of which is one of the main tasks of civilized governments. Hence, pre-Nazi political thought is pacifist with respect to foreign affairs and upholds the ideal of government by discussion and law in domestic affairs.

This abhorrence of the use of force, concomitant with the ascendancy of the commercial spirit, is for naziism an unmistakable sign of weakness, of intellectual and physical decadence. The racially healthy man, the blond hero, finds enjoyment in the demonstration of his physical superiority. The soldier is the ideal man, warfare the ideal occupation. The history of nations as well as of individuals is the story of an unending struggle for power, which,

---

had conquered the state and state and race had become identical, the subordination of state to race lost all political meaning in domestic affairs. It was, however, still useful for the ideological justification of state action and as a means of undermining the authority of foreign governments and of dissolving the national coherence of foreign states. As a check upon the total power of the state, it has never had any importance.

sometimes fought with non-physical means, is always ready to transform itself into the use of individual and organized violence. In this clash of hostile forces the stronger reveals himself as such and establishes his claim to rule. Domestic strife and international war are the selective principles through which the hierarchy of the strong over the weak is created and put to the ever renewed test of actual combat. Since, as we have seen, this hierarchy is of the very essence of the social and political order, as conceived by Nazi philosophy, the hidden will of nature and of racial destiny becomes manifest in combat and war. War, then, is not only inevitable but even desirable. Far from shunning it, the master race, which as such claims the right to rule the world, must concentrate the national effort upon preparation for it in order to be able to prove the justice of its claim. In the same way in which the totalitarian state of naziism finds its ultimate aim in the victorious war, the political philosophy of naziism culminates in the glorification of war.[9]

[9] *Mein Kampf,* I, 221 *et seq.,* 728 *et seq.;* Vol. II, chap. ix; *The Speeches of Adolf Hitler,* pp. 185, 196, 197.

16 *National Socialist Doctrine of World Organization*

I am in a somewhat embarrassing position in having to discuss a subject which, strictly speaking, does not exist, at least not within the traditional meaning of the term, and to have to rationalize upon something which, by its very nature, defies rationalization.

If a doctrine of world organization is a system of thought coherent within itself and with reality, a National Socialist doctrine of world organization does not exist. National socialism takes a predominantly negative and critical attitude toward world organization. It regards doctrines of world organization as manifestations of the decadence of liberalism and rationalism, and not worthy of imitation. Its positive contribution is limited to fragmentary statements which change not only from person to person but also with each new political development.

We find that previous to 1936 a doctrine was advanced which had as its basis the natural-law idea of fundamental rights of nations. We find between 1936 and 1939 an entirely different theory, based upon the idea of racially satisfied nations, and we find since 1939 another complete change of attitude. Now the ideas of the new order and of living space come to the forefront.

It is not by accident that this is so, because those three periods in the history of National Socialist doctrines of world organization correspond closely to three different phases in National Socialist foreign policy. Until 1936 it was the chief aim of National Socialist foreign policy to shake off the disabilities which the Treaty of Versailles had imposed upon Germany, and for this reason it was convenient to advance a theory of fundamental rights, especially of equality of rights, based upon natural law. After that equality had been achieved, the Austrian and Czechoslovakian questions were the center of German political interest; the idea that world organiza-

From the *Proceedings of the Seventh Conference of Teachers of International Law and Related Subjects* (1941).

tion should be based upon racially homogeneous nations was advanced in support of those political aims. Since 1939 Germany has won the domination of Europe, opening new political vistas, and now new concepts have replaced the preceding ideologies.

This complete dependence of German political thought upon the ever changing political situation is neither an accident nor, from the German standpoint, a deficiency, but a deliberate application of the new concept of science which national socialism has developed. It is the mark of all political ideology to be the product of political events, political interests, and political aims; and in so far as political ideology reflects the state of mind of the writer rather than the political reality, it cannot fail to falsify the latter. Western political thought is no exception to this rule. We have only to think of the doctrine of collective security, which to a certain extent at least was simply the rationalization of the French desire for security, that is, the rationalization of French foreign policy in a certain period of history. Yet, inherent in Western political thought from the times of the Greeks, there has been the idea of objective universal truth, which even if it should never be completely realized remains forever the guiding principle and ultimate ideal to which all scientific thought aspires. National Socialist thought has expressly discarded the ideal of objective universal truth and has replaced it with the concept of an exclusively German science whose value depends upon its usefulness for German needs. The absence of a coherent National Socialist doctrine of world organization in the traditional meaning of the term is thus the outgrowth of the National Socialist concept of science in general.

Furthermore, only such a fragmentary, incoherent conception of world organization, ever dependent in its contents upon actual political developments, corresponds to the character of National Socialist foreign policy. Since this foreign policy has no definite goal but is aimed at power for its own sake and without rational limits, a coherent, elaborate doctrine of world organization in the Western tradition would be either too narrow or too broad to correspond to the particular phase of the foreign policy it is supposed to interpret and to rationalize. It would either fall short of the aims and possibilities of the foreign policy, or it would advance too much beyond those aims and possibilities, at a given moment of history. Where there is limitless aspiration for power, ever shifting, dynamic and irrational, there cannot be a coherent system of rational thought corresponding to it. Hence, national socialism has no more developed, and is no more in need of, a coherent doctrine of world organization than were Xerxes, Alexander, Cesare Borgia, or Napoleon.

Nevertheless, there are certain permanent elements, inherent in the general philosophy of national socialism, which, in different degrees of explicitness, underlie National Socialist doctrines of world organization. The nature of those elements, despite all their vagueness, will become clear when we contrast them with the permanent elements of Western thought on world organization and thus ask what they are not rather than what they are.

Western thought on world organization has been dominated throughout the centuries by three main ideas: humanity, law, progress. The idea of humanity implies two fundamental concepts: the equality of all men and their intrinsic rational nature. It is because of this unity of all mankind in reason that there could develop the idea of a system of law binding upon all men, that is, the idea of natural law. The rule of law, through its rationality and objectivity, would thus guarantee to man that equal status which is inherent in the idea of humanity. The idea of progress, strictly speaking, is a product of the eighteenth and nineteenth centuries. But long before, in Greek philosophy and early Christian thought, we find the idea of progress in the broader meaning of the faculty of man to ameliorate his lot and to ascend to a better life either by an act of grace or by individual effort. This eternal hope of mankind has been crystallized since the eighteenth and nineteenth centuries in the idea of progress.

The denial of those three main ideas of Western thought characterizes both general National Socialist philosophy and the National Socialist doctrines of world organization. To the idea of humanity national socialism opposes the idea of race; to the idea of law it opposes the concept of technical rules of domination; to the idea of progress it opposes the concept of the unending struggle for power. From those main concepts the theory and practice of National Socialist foreign policy derive.

Instead of the concept of a community of nations which are essentially equal, we have in National Socialist thought the idea of a hierarchy of races which are essentially unequal, and of one race which is qualified to dominate the others; and this is not only a question of qualification, not only a question of right in National Socialist thought—and I think this is very important—but it is also a question of obligation. According to National Socialist thought, the German race has not only the right to dominate other peoples, it has also the holy mission because of its higher qualities to redistribute and to reorganize the world upon the foundations of National Socialist justice and to convert all other nations to the National Socialist philosophy of government and social life.

At the service of this conception there are no longer the instrumentalities of a rational and objective law before which all subjects are equal. Objectivity and equality are replaced by the superior value and interests of the master race to which the inferior races owe tribute. Four specific techniques have been developed in order to establish the National Socialist domination over the world and to secure its stability.

Deriving directly from the idea of the hierarchy of races, the relationship between the National Socialist state and the other nations is conceived as one between master state and vassal states. The vassals would have the approximate status of protectorates without army, economy, or policy of their own. National Socialist writers compare this new relationship to a solar system, the sun being the National Socialist state and the planets its dependencies.

The concrete relations between the master state and the vassal nations are conceived in terms of colonial exploitation, which for the first time in modern history is thus introduced into the relations between European nations themselves. Yet the traditional concept of colonial exploitation, like many other traditional concepts of politics and law, acquires in National Socialist practice a novel meaning. Whereas the classical colonial policy of the nineteenth century at its best aimed positively at the welfare of the native populations or at least was indifferent to their lot and accepted their self-development as a by-product of the colonial regime, national socialism aims positively at the permanent subjugation of conquered peoples through planned depopulation and organized destruction of national and economic life.

In the third place, national socialism discards the principle of non-intervention and makes it not only the right but the duty of all Germans and descendants of Germans to intervene in the affairs of the nations where they live. Thus national socialism no longer recognizes the national state as the ultimate achievement of modern political development but tries to dissolve national geographical units from within by combining the antagonism of classes and races with the traditional opposition of states. The traditional principles of non-intervention and independence thus become obsolete, the distinction between domestic and international affairs disappears, and diplomatic immunities become a means for warfare in peace times.

Finally, national socialism has developed the technique of domination, that is, the planned use of modern technology for the domination of wide geographical areas. The National Socialists have not been the first to recognize the possibilities of modern technology in this respect. Ironically enough, it was the pacifists of the nineteenth century—William Ellery Channing in this country, for instance, Victor Hugo in France—who realized first the possibilities for international unification implicit in modern technology. "Every railroad, connecting distant regions," said Channing, "may be regarded as accomplishing a ministry of peace," and Victor Hugo saluted the airship as an "instrument of universal peace." Whereas the liberals of the nineteenth century believed in the necessarily pacifying results of modern technology, national socialism has stripped the liberal assertion of its pacifist and optimistic connotations, appropriated whatever truth it may contain, and thus created the technical foundations for world domination.

Those four new techniques as well as the concept of the master race are not at the service of any positive ideal that is capable of rational formulation. The driving force which has created this concept as well as those techniques, and which determines the goals for which they are used, is the lust for power which knows no limits nor values beside or above it. Here again I want to make clear that the aspiration for power is, of course, no monopoly of national socialism. The aspiration for power is a permanent social phenomenon which I think cannot be abolished by legal reform. But since the Renaissance in Western Europe, those aspirations for power have generally been held within certain bounds by a few moral principles to which the law of nations as well as Western civilization as a whole owe their existence. By discarding those moral principles and by elevating political power to the top of the hierarchy of values, national socialism has abandoned the Western tradition and has revived the concept of world organization which Xerxes, Alexander, Napoleon, and the Italian Renaissance tried to put into practice: aspiration for power for its own sake and without moral limitations or rational justification. If you compare, let us, say, the foreign policy of Bismarck with the foreign policy of Hitler, you will realize the difference between aspiration for power within the framework of Western tradition and the aspiration for power which tends to destroy this framework; and I feel that in this moral backwardness or moral indifference of national socialism, on the one hand, and in its realization of the technical possibilities of our age for domination, on the other hand, there lies the challenge of the National Socialist doctrines of world organization to Western thought.

17 *The Tragedy of German-Jewish Liberalism*

The disaster which befell the Jews of Germany under the Nazi regime was not only a disaster of the kind which Jews have suffered throughout their history. It was a tragedy in a triple sense. For, first of all, all previous persecutions and all previous decimations suffered by Jews were intimately connected with the Jewish religion. That is to say, Jews were persecuted because they embraced a religion different from that of the persecutors, and out of this connection between persecution and religion persecution itself received its meaning and, in a sense, its justification.

I cannot do better, not only in view of the auspices under which this lecture is held but also in view of the subject matter itself, than to quote from an article which Leo Baeck wrote in September, 1930, in which he made this point: "The migrations which characterize the history of the Jews have been virtually always migrations for the sake of faith. The Jew could have stayed if he had departed from his religion, but he departed because he was determined to stay with his religion." To the persecutions of recent times this statement does not apply. For not only were those persecutions not justified in terms of religion, but the abandonment of their religion would not have saved, and in the few cases in which it actually occurred did not save, the Jews. In other words, for the first time, persecution of the Jews, seeking their total destruction, was based upon something different from religion, and so persecution became inescapable and it lost its meaning in the eyes of its victims.

The second tragic aspect of the disaster which has befallen German Jewry has to do with the political philosophy which the main bulk of German Jewry embraced, and with the political institutions which were intended to protect the rights of the Jews vis-à-vis their enemies, that is, the philosophy and the institutions of liberalism. For it is obvious that the emancipation of the Jews in the nineteenth century, especially as the result of the French Revolution, is inti-

The Leo Baeck Memorial Lecture, 1961.

mately connected with the rise of liberalism. Liberalism assumes that all men are created equal and that all men have certain inalienable rights, regardless of their natural and social diversities upon which the feudal system of society and government based social and political distinctions. In consequence, the new liberal age would treat all men as equals within the limits of equal situations.

The liberation of the Jew was a by-product, and in a sense an inevitable by-product, of the rise of liberalism, and the rights of Jews in the Western world stand and fall with the belief in, and the practice of, liberal principles. For, once you assume that men are not endowed with inalienable rights which require that with regard to their social and political positions they be treated as equals, you have already left behind the basic principle upon which the rights of Jews depend. If you can assume that any particular minority, however defined, does not have a claim on the enjoyment of equal rights, you have already destroyed the very moral and philosophical basis upon which the rights of Jews depend as well.

However, it so happens that the philosophy and the institutions of liberalism are not the expression of eternal verities. That philosophy and those institutions arose under certain historic conditions and, hence, were bound to disappear under different historic conditions. It is not by accident that the rise of liberal philosophy and of liberal institutions is intimately connected with the rise of the middle classes. The liberal philosophy is the philosophy par excellence which expresses the interests of the middle classes, and the liberal institutions are the bulwarks safeguarding their position in society.

It is not by accident either that, at least in Germany, the great bulk of the Jews belonged to the middle classes. Many of them were at the same time eminent and typical representatives of the middle classes and of German Jewry. When the middle classes suffered political and economic defeat in the aftermath of the First World War and economically became in a large measure proletarized in consequence of a succession of economic crises, the position of the Jews radically changed. Here we are at the beginning of the development of naziism.

For this change, German Jewry was not prepared. Three factors account in the main for this lack of preparedness. First of all German

Jewry, being predominantly middle class in social composition and liberal in political and philosophic outlook, shared to the full the optimistic mood of the liberal middle classes. The world, as it existed before the First World War, was perhaps not the best of all possible worlds, but it was certainly a good world for the middle classes, and it was bound to get better and better as time went on. German Jewry appeared to have a particular reason for partaking in this general optimism; for it had progressed further and faster and against much greater odds than the general middle-class population. Within less than a century, a tiny minority, despised, disenfranchised, and confined to the ghetto, had made a creative contribution of the first order to the intellectual, moral, and economic life of Europe, and this in the face of continuing disabilities and discrimination. Why should it not look to the future with optimistic anticipation? When, before the First World War, a rabbi raised the question of the possible destruction of German Jewry, the president of the Jewish community of Berlin could say at a banquet of the *"Verband der deutschen Juden"*:

And when in this hour I raise the same question: Is German Jewry going to perish? I do not hesitate for a moment as a layman to answer that question unqualifiedly in the negative. I answer this question with a triple forceful no when I allow my gaze to wander over these rows of tables and find with admiration, joy, pride, and satisfaction that hundreds of men in the most respected and prominent professional and social positions, luminaries of scholarship, leading artists, tycoons of commerce, pathfinders of industry, pioneers of technology, are here united as the authentic representatives of the German Jews and their interests.

In the second place, from this general optimistic outlook grew the assumption that the emancipation of German Jewry through the application of liberal principles was tantamount to the permanent solution of the Jewish problem in Germany. German Jews were Germans who happened to have a different religion from the majority of their fellow Germans; they were *"Deutsche Staatsbürger Jüdischen Glaubens."* What was still missing in that solution of the Jewish problem in the form of disabilities and discrimination was regarded as nothing more than minor deficiencies to be remedied by the application of liberal principles to situations which still resisted them. The persistence of such situations was attributed to "prejudice," a preliberal and, hence, backward and unenlightened state of mind, bound to be erased by the continuing progress of mankind.

Finally, the very success of Jewish emancipation and assimilation, however temporary it should prove to be, created within German Jewry a psychological predisposition against contemplating any alternative to the favorable and seemingly promising situation which German Jews enjoyed. The very conception of German Jews as Germans of a minority religion and of the Jewish religion as one religion among many made it impossible for German Jewry to recognize the precariousness of their position and the possibility of a catastrophic separation from Germany. If they were just Germans like any other Germans and if Judaism was just a religion like any other religion, why should a Gentile German, except a small minority of prejudiced bigots, treat them as anything else? Yet these assumptions, upon which the very existence of German Jewry rested, were denied by the anti-Semites and by the great mass of the German people when the Nazis came to power.

The rise of naziism to power is obviously connected with the economic, social, and moral decline of the German middle classes. It is no exaggeration to say that the main body of the supporters of naziism was recruited from the proletarized middle classes and that the very impetus which moved naziism forward was the result of an inner contradiction within these proletarized middle classes.

According to Marx, the members of these proletarized middle classes should have all become Marxist socialists, that is to say, their political philosophy should have corresponded to their actual economic position. But the exact opposite occurred. This is one of the great disavowals of Marxist philosophy. A proletarized middle class revolts in its own consciousness against that proletarization and as a movement of protest creates and supports and brings to victory a Fascist movement.

In this situation, the Jews remain as the only important, conspicuous, and seemingly potent fraction of the middle classes. They retain their economic position and cling to their political rights. And so for the proletarized middle classes with a Fascist psychology and a Fascist philosophy, the Jews became the main enemy, a reminder of what they once were and of what they might have been but could no longer be.

The third and most important element in the tragedy of German-Jewish liberalism is the fact that the rise of the Jews in Germany and in Western and Central Europe in general goes hand in hand with the rise of nationalism. For nationalism is in a sense the application of the liberal principles to the collectivities which we call nations. As the individual, according to liberal philosophy, is assumed to have inalienable rights and the right to determine for himself by what kind of government he shall be governed, so the nation, composed as it is of individuals, is assumed to be endowed with the right to determine for itself what kind of government it should have. "One nation in one state" is the postulate of nineteenth-century nationalism. Thus the nationalism of the Jewish middle classes is a mere reflection of the common origin of both nationalism and liberalism from the same source: the postulates of freedom and equality, the right of self-determination for individuals as well as for the collectivities called nations.

It is at this point that a great change took place which was not recognized by Jewry at large; nor was it recognized by most other contemporary observers. That is the fact that the nature of nationalism radically changed in the course of the twentieth century. Twentieth-century nationalism is fundamentally different from nineteenth-century nationalism. Twentieth-century nationalism is fundamentally illiberal. It is essentially a political religion. Nineteenth-century liberal nationalism believed that conflict among nations would disappear once the national question was solved according to the principles of liberalism guaranteeing self-determination to all nations and protection to all national minorities. Once all nations had chosen their own state, once national minorities had been protected in their rights, nations had really no longer anything to fight about. This was the philosophy underlying Woodrow Wilson's foreign policy. The principle of national self-determination was taken to be the remedy for all the political ills from which nations suffer. This was an equalitarian conception of nationalism, applying the principle of liberal equalitarianism to the relations among nations. One can paraphrase Ranke's famous statement that all epochs of history are equally close to God by saying, in the true spirit of the liberal nationalism of the nineteenth century, that all nations are equally close to God, that there is no master nation, that no nation is superior to another nation, and that no nation has the right or the mission to subject other nations to its rule.

The nationalism of the twentieth century—and this is as true of Fascist and Nazi nationalism as it is of Marxist nationalism—believes in the concept of a chosen nation. That is to say, there is one nation which stands out among all other nations and which has the sacred mission of bringing salvation to the other nations of the world. This nationalism is in truth a nationalistic universalism which seeks to transform all other nations in the image of the one chosen nation. It makes for our purposes no difference whether you define that one chosen nation in terms of the master race or the fatherland of socialism. In both cases, the claim of one nation to superiority replaces the acceptance of all nations in the spirit of equality. Once the claim to superiority has been established, it becomes not only a right but a duty, a sacred mission, for the master race or the fatherland of socialism to bring salvation to the rest of the world, if necessary by fire and sword.

It is the fate of the Jews, and this is as true of the Jews of the Soviet Union as it was of those of Nazi Germany, that they constitute, as it were, an implicit denial of competition to this claim of the master nation. For the Jews, however identified they are with the nations of which they are members, somehow have ties, however defined, which transcend the boundaries of the nations of which they are members. And whether you define these ties in terms of religion or in any other term, if it is not obvious to Jews, it is obvious to the Gentiles that somehow the Jews owe allegiance to a God which transcends national boundaries.

This Jewish situation can be interpreted in religious terms and explained through the concept of the Chosen People. This concept shows clearly the competitive aspect of the relationship between the remnants of the Jewish people, on the one hand, and the master nations, on the other. Between them an inevitable, existential conflict exists; for the claim of a master nation to supremacy is incompatible with the Jewish claim to a special relationship to God.

The Jews, by their very existence, deny the validity of the master nation's claim. The German Jews performed, however, for the Nazi regime another peculiar function which they did not perform anywhere else. That function, too, resulted from the lack of their complete identification with Germany's claims to superiority. The impossibility of complete Jewish identification could be used by Nazi anti-Semitism for the purpose of reintegrating German society through the exploitation of the peculiar position of the Jewish minority.

In order to explain this particular function which the Jews performed for German anti-Semitism, one has to consider the social and philosophical situation from which naziism arose. Naziism arose essentially, as did Italian fascism as well, as a reaction to Marxism. Marxism is the most elaborate, most sophisticated of the great modern political religions. All political religions stand and fall with the experimental proof of their truth. In contrast, other worldly religions are based on faith. Nobody has come back from the other world and told us whether the biblical description of heaven corresponds to reality. But a political religion, which pretends to bring salvation to men in this world and which, like Marxism, pretends that salvation is just around the corner, stands and falls with the experimental proof of the correctness of its prophecies. It is of decisive significance for the development of naziism that Marxism suffered, at the beginning and end of the First World War, two great denials. That is to say, two of the fundamental prophecies of Marxism were denied by experience.

One denial occurred at the beginning of August, 1914. According to Marxism, the proletarian has no fatherland. The international solidarity of the proletariat has replaced national allegiance, and so it was unthinkable in Marxist terms that any proletarian would fight for his country. And it was generally expected in the summer of 1914 that, if for no other reason, war would be impossible because no proletarian would fight for his country. We know that the exact opposite happened and that the overwhelming majority of the proletarians of all belligerent nations fought for their respective countries. Yet this strength of national loyalty, shattering one of the cornerstones of Marxist philosophy, came as a great shock to a small minority of activist Marxists, who in consequence became either Communists or Fascists. One needs only to glance at the history of Mussolini, who was a militant Marxist in those days, in order to see how profound was the shock of this great denial of the truth of Marxism.

The second great denial occurred at the end of the First World

War when the world revolution which Marxism had promised did not take place. Instead there was anarchy, weakness in government, and indecisiveness and seeking after parochial advantages among the Marxist proletariat. The Marxists were capable neither of governing effectively nor of making a successful revolution. This was the second denial of a basic tenet of Marxism. The disillusionment which arose from it gave fascism in Italy and naziism in Germany their chance. It is not by accident that both fascism and naziism referred to themselves as "worker's movements" and that the Nazis in particular added "socialist." In this connection between the defeat of Marxism by experience and the Nazi claim to be able to succeed where Marxism had failed, that is, to make a revolution and to govern effectively, we find one of the origins of naziism.

Naziism, faced with the disintegration of society into warring classes and with economic crises and their moral and economic devastation, had to find a principle upon which it could reintegrate German society. It found this principle in the conception of the master race. In order to make this principle effective, it had to have a counterfoil to the master race, a group which, by dint of its very existence, was a denial of that concept, and it found that group in the Jews. So it came about that the continuing existence of the Jews either in Germany or elsewhere was a necessity for the continued regeneration of Germany on the basis of the Nazi principle of integration.

This principle was effective because the members of the master race could prove to themselves every day that they were actually superior to their chosen opposition, the Jews, by humiliating and abusing them. Furthermore, they could experience that superiority at no risk whatsoever. Thus every Aryan, even the lowliest one, could feel himself as an aristocrat compared with a Jew. Nazi philosophers could prove, to their own satisfaction at least, that the Aryans were superior to the Slavs and to the Negroes and to all the other so-called lower races. But this superiority could only be experienced intellectually. By contrast, the man in the street, by experiencing his superiority vis-à-vis a Jew by actual deeds, could prove to himself as a matter of fact that he was actually superior.

In this relationship between the Nazi and the Jew, terror is an intrinsic element and plays an indispensable role. It is not only, nor primarily, the result of the sadistic instincts of certain individuals or of excesses due to a particularly difficult situation. It is organically connected with the very nature of naziism as a social system.

It is the peculiar characteristic of this terror that it does not make any difference whether the one who is hit by the terror is guilty in terms of the prevailing standards of right and wrong. Anybody can be hit by it. Anybody can become his victim, anyone, defined as a non-Ayran, regardless of his religion, regardless of his conviction. The very fact that he is there, susceptible to be terrorized, makes him a prospective victim of the terror. The religious faith of German Jewry was irrelevant to this situation. This strange use of a minority for the hostile purposes of the nation among which it lived and of which it thought itself to be a part is a reflection, not only upon the character of naziism, but also upon the character and the needs of modern Jewry. For if a Jew is persecuted and killed, not because he professes a different religion or belongs to a different class, but simply because he is a Jew and by his very existence denies the universalistic aims and philosophies of the country in which he lives, then he needs a justification of his own which gives meaning to his existence and to his suffering.

This is a problem obviously not for the Gentiles but for the Jews. This is a problem with which, to the best of my knowledge, Jewry has not been confronted before. For the optimistic outlook of the nineteenth and the beginning of the twentieth centuries anticipated that with the abatement of religious fanaticism and the concomitant religious tolerance there would be no longer any reason for anybody, in the long run at least, to despise and maltreat and persecute and kill Jews. But it so happens that in an age which is essentially a secular age and in which people do no longer persecute and kill each other for the sake of religion, they still persecute and kill each other for other, primarily political reasons.

This persistence of anti-Semitism poses a problem not only in terms of the survival of Jewry but also and more particularly of giving meaning to Jewish existence. For while it is tolerable, and it may even be ennobling, to suffer and die for a cause which one has voluntarily embraced, it is degrading to suffer for a purpose which is not one's own, especially if it is for the purpose of providing a continuous scapegoat for a society by which one has been rejected.

Thus Jewry must find a new meaning—it is perhaps a very old meaning—in order not only to guarantee its survival but also in critical situations which it may face again to find a meaning which will sustain it and which will give dignity to its suffering.

There is then, as in all true tragedy, a positive element in the tragedy of German-Jewish liberalism. German Jewry took what was an ephemeral historic configuration, that is, its emancipation and assimilation, as a permanent possession which was liable to be increased in the future but not to be diminished, let alone destroyed. For it did not see the intimate and organic connection between its emancipation and assimilation, on the one hand, and the ascendancy of a liberal middle class on the other hand. Nor did it see that its very existence as a separate community, regardless of its religious commitment, was tolerable to the Gentile majority only during the ascendancy of liberal nationalism. Naziism destroyed these illusions and, through its very excesses, laid bare the truth of the Jewish condition. By doing so, it paved the way for restoring to the Jewish existence its meaning and cosmic significance. This is, as it were, the redeeming element in the tragedy of German-Jewish liberalism.

18 *Neutrality and Neutralism*

President Eisenhower, at his press conference of June 6, 1956, had this to say about neutrality and neutralism:

If you are waging peace, you can't be too particular sometimes about the special attitudes that different countries take. We were a young country once, and our whole policy for the first hundred years was, or more, 150, we were neutral. We constantly asserted we were neutral in the wars of the world and wars in Europe and antagonisms.

Now, today there are certain nations that say they are neutral. This doesn't necessarily mean what it is so often interpreted to mean, neutral as between right and wrong or decency and indecency.

They are using the term "neutral" with respect to attachment to military alliances. And may I point out that I cannot see that that is always to the disadvantage of such a country as ours....

So let us not translate this meaning of the word "neutral" as between contending military forces, even though the conflict is latent, and neutral as between right and wrong.[1]

On June 7 the White House issued the following official statement, intended to clarify the President's remarks:

Questions have been presented to the White House concerning the exact meaning of expressions in the President's press conference yesterday defending the right of certain nations to a neutral position. He particularly referred to neutrality as a refusal to take sides in any military line-up of world powers.

It is obvious that in some countries of the world there are certain ideological, geographical or other reasons making military alliances impractical. Such nations may declare themselves to be neutral, hoping thus to secure the support of world opinion against attack from any quarter. Neutrality does not mean either disarmament or immunity from attack. We have had historical examples of this kind of neutrality for many decades.

The President believes in the principle of collective security whereby the nations associate themselves together for each other's protection. This is the modern and enlightened way of obtaining security.... The President does believe that there are special conditions which justify political neutrality but that no nation has the right to be indifferent to the fate of an-

From the *Year Book of World Affairs*, 1957.
[1] *New York Times*, June 7, 1956, p. 10.

other, or, as he put it, to be "neutral as between right and wrong or decency and indecency."[2]

The very same day on which the President of the United States sought to clarify the American attitude toward neutrality and neutralism, the Foreign Minister of France shed light upon the Russian position:

When we insisted on the importance of reunification as the symbol of European balance, Monsieur Khrushchev declared that he preferred 20,-000,000 Germans with him to 70,000,000 against him, even neutralized. That does not mean he is against a neutral Germany but that he is against a Germany neutralized against him.[3]

On June 9, 1956, the Secretary of State of the United States, in the address which the President had heralded as "a definite attempt to bring this thing down to its realities, to its specifics, so we can all understand it," defined neutrality as the pretense "that a nation can best gain safety for itself by being indifferent to the fate of others. This has increasingly become an obsolete conception and, except under very exceptional circumstances, it is an immoral and short-sighted conception."[4] Queried at his press conference of June 12, 1956, about the relationship between his statement and that of the President, the Secretary of State affirmed three times "that there is no difference whatever between the President and myself on this subject." Asked about the "very exceptional circumstances" which would not render neutrality obsolete, he replied: "Well, the outstanding example of neutrality is, of course, Switzerland. Switzerland has declined to join the United Nations because it recognizes that the United Nations Charter is incompatible with strict neutrality."[5]

On July 4, 1956, Vice-President Richard Nixon gave an address at Manila, which is reported to have been prepared at the White House for use by the President who could not present it in person by reason of illness. In this address the Vice-President made the following statement about neutralism:

2 *New York Times,* June 8, 1956, p. 2.

3 *Christian Science Monitor* (Boston), June 9, 1956, p. 2.

4 *New York Times,* June 10, 1956, p. 24.

5 *Ibid.,* June 13, 1956, p. 4.

We have heard recently a great deal of discussion of the attitude that goes by the name of neutralism. Let us see how it bears on the problem of independence. I would feel that generally a nation that rejects the principles of collective security because it feels its independence will be compromised by association with other powers is not reading rightly the trends of modern history. It has far more to gain by standing together with free nations than by remaining aloof.

But there may be other reasons for neutralism. Many nations have the same principles which we share in common, and they are prepared to defend them. Yet they feel that their own internal problems compel them to abstain, at least for the moment, from mutual-security pacts and associations. They wish to devote all their energies to building their own political and economic systems. Or they may feel that they are too geographically exposed to risk provoking Communist colonial imperialism.

We in the United States can understand the attitudes of such powers. For over a century we tried to avoid being identified with any of the warring powers *blocs* of Europe. But we learned from hard experience that policies which worked well in the nineteenth century were completely inadequate in the twentieth. In 1917, we were forced to enter a terrific world war. Again in 1941, we were plunged into the blood bath of the Second World War.

Finally we learned our lesson. Together with most of the other nations of the world, we joined in a world organization designed to promote justice and insure peace. In addition, we joined regional alliances permitted under the charter of the United Nations. We found that the world is too small today for effective isolation. . . .

But there is still another brand of neutralism that makes no moral distinction between the Communist world and the free world. With this viewpoint, we have no sympathy. How can we feel toward those who treat alike nations that believe in God and honor, religion and morality, and nations that boast of atheism and the rule of force and terror alone?

How can anyone treat as equals those who believe in the dignity of man and the basic rights of all men, and those who treat their subjects as mere machines? Is democracy to be equated with dictatorship? Is freedom the same as tyranny? . . .

I know there are those who feel that friendly neutrality toward the Kremlin and Peiping may spare them. But you know the proverb: He who sups with the devil, must have a long spoon. The Communists have been ruthless toward the people of the nations that they have engulfed. They have no memory of former favors, no kindness toward those who tried to be friendly. They are cold and calculating masters. Those who feel that they can outmaneuver them are taking a fearful risk.[6]

[6] *Ibid.*, July 4, 1956, p. 2.

The Prime Minister of India took exception to Messrs. Nixon's and Dulles' statements at his press conference of July 7, 1956.

"I submit for consideration that Mr. Nixon and Mr. Dulles are saying something that is opposed to the democratic way of life," Mr. Nehru declared. "The very basis of democracy," he said, "is tolerance for differing points of view. . . ." He made clear his dislike of the term "neutralism" which, he said, connoted war and which in peacetime had no real validity.

"India's policy could better be explained as one of non-involvement in either the Soviet or Western bloc, of eschewing war and seeking peaceful settlements to all international problems and of concentrating mainly on internal Indian development," he said.[7]

The Prime Minister of Laos went one better by declaring: "Our country has no intention of joining any *bloc*, even the neutralist *bloc*. . . . Neutrality is more neutral than neutralism."[8]

Confronted with these contradictory statements which are but recent examples of a veritable Babel of tongues, the layman will be forgiven when he is confused. Yet the professional observer of foreign policy must search for the reasons which are responsible for these contradictions, and he will find them in certain legal and political trends which have come to dominate the international scene since the end of the First World War. Three such trends are relevant for our investigation: the legal commitment to collective security, the helplessness of an ever increasing number of nations faced with the threat of all-out war within a bipolar system of world politics, and the identification of international conflicts with irreconcilable philosophic and moral positions.

In order to understand the changes brought about by these factors, it is first necessary to visualize the legal and political situation which existed before these factors appeared on the international scene. That legal situation is encompassed by the status of neutrality as defined by international law. The political situation is determined by the desire of certain nations, for reasons of expediency, to keep out of certain wars.

Neutrality as a status of international law results from the desire of a nation not to be involved in a war waged by other nations. Therefore, neutrality is essentially a negative status depending upon

[7] *Ibid.*, July 7, 1956, p. 1.

[8] *Economist* (London), CLXXX (Sept. 22, 1956), p. 968.

the existence of definite relations between two nations, which the law calls war. Where there is no war in the legal sense of the term there can be no neutrality. Hence, the development of neutrality as a legal status depends upon the possibility of differentiating clearly between peace and war as two distinct situations defined by international law.

But neutrality is also a negative status in that the complex of rights and obligations which constitute the legal status of neutrality is determined less by the neutral, who desires to keep out of war and thereby retain the greatest possible freedom of action, than by the belligerents, who want to prevent the neutral from joining the other side and assure themselves of his support. In the struggle between war and neutrality for the delimitation of their respective spheres, war is the stronger contestant.

Neutrality and war are complementary concepts; the more there is of the one, the less there is of the other. The rights and obligations flowing from the status of neutrality are the result of a balance between the interests of the belligerents and the interests of the neutrals. The former seek to win the war by maximizing their advantages and minimizing those of the enemy. The latter seek to keep out of the war without renouncing those activities which they consider essential for the pursuit of their national interests. As long as these antagonistic interests are held in balance, international law safeguards the legal status of the neutrals.

Neutrality implies two fundamental obligations on the part of the neutral: abstention from interference with the military activities of the belligerents and impartiality toward them in their position as belligerents. The particular duties these two fundamental obligations impose on the neutral cannot be deduced from the abstract concepts of "abstention" and "impartiality." They depend exclusively upon the kind of warfare being waged. For the extent to which the neutral has to abstain from interference is determined by the extent of the military activities of the belligerents. If the scope of warfare is limited, the domain into which the neutral may extend his activities without risking involvement in the war will be vast. For example, because wars were conducted mainly by hired soldiers with the bulk of the population not actively participating in them, it was not regarded until the end of the eighteenth century as a violation of the duties of neutrality to assist belligerents with man-power. When, however, the whole population capable of bearing arms participated actively in the war, that is, with the introduction of universal military service, such assistance became incompatible with the legal status of neutrality.

The same interrelationship between the development of warfare and the rules of neutrality applies to the implements of war the neutral is allowed to supply to the belligerents. As long as but a small fraction of the economic resources of the belligerents was used for military purposes, the neutrals were free to give the belligerents all possible material aid. With the mobilization of the total material resources of the belligerents, the rules of neutrality were bound to change again. Material aid by non-belligerents now became as de-cisive an intervention in war as the assistance with manpower had been since the beginning of the nineteenth century, and therefore became incompatible with the status of a neutral.

Not only the content of the rules of neutrality but also the very possibility of remaining neutral depends upon the military-political situation in which the neutral finds himself. The neutral pursues a double aim: to keep out of war and to pursue his national interests with regard to the belligerents and other nations. The interest of the belligerents, on the other hand, is only one: to win the war. In the pursuit of his interests, the neutral may be faced with a dual dilem-ma: his aim to keep out of war may conflict either with his other aim to pursue his national interests vis-à-vis other nations or with the belligerents' aim to win the war.

The dilemma of the belligerents presents itself in much simpler terms. The belligerents look at the existence, the interests, and the "rights" of neutrals only from one angle: in what way are they likely to influence the outcome of the war? The position and in-terests of the neutrals may be respected as far as the belligerents believe this respect not to affect their mutual position in the war. But should a belligerent come to believe that the violation of the position or interests of the neutral would be detrimental to the enemy or advantageous to himself, he will not hesitate to violate them. He will only refrain from doing so if the disadvantages result-ing from such violation are likely to outweigh the advantages. In other words, neutrals owe their status as neutrals to considerations of political expediency on the part of the belligerents, not to the latter's respect for legal principles. And the desire of a nation to remain neutral counts for considerably less than objective conditions over which it has no control and, more particularly, the interests of the belligerents.

Hence, geographic isolation which puts the neutral's territory beyond the reach of military operations has always been—as the history of Great Britain, the Scandinavian countries, and the United States shows—the most reliable protection of neutral status. In the absence of such protection, a nation can eliminate a motive from the belligerents for violating its neutrality by pursuing, with regard to their conflicts, a policy of abstention and impartiality and by making it at the same time too costly for them to gain advantages at the expense of its neutral status. To that end, the neutral must make his armed forces a serious factor in the military calculations of the belligerents. He must secure the support of other powerful neutrals or of one of the belligerents or of both of them in defense of his neutrality against violation by either. There exists, then, an intimate relationship between the politico-legal status of neutrality and the balance of power.

The period between the Treaty of Westphalia and the First World War was the classical period of the balance of power in Europe. To the relative stability of the state system—the period of the Napoleonic Wars is the main exception—corresponded the relative security of the status of the neutrals. Wars were localized; the economic rights of neutrals were violated only in minor instances, their political status remained by and large intact. The First World War marks, as general wars have always done, the wholesale violation of the economic rights of all neutrals and the destruction of the political status of two of them, Belgium and Greece. The other nations which succeeded in remaining neutral owed the preservation of their neutrality either to the geographic factor—as did the non-European and Scandinavian countries as well as Spain—or to military-political considerations of expediency—as did the Netherlands and Switzerland.[9]

[9] On this point and those immediately following see Hans J. Morgenthau, "The Resurrection of Neutrality," *American Political Science Review,* XXXIII (1939), 473 ff.

THE BURDEN OF AN OBSOLESCENT TRADITION

With the end of the First World War began a new chapter in the history of neutrality. Collective security challenged neutrality as a legal status. The radical transformation which the state system underwent weakened the political foundations of neutrality.

Neutrality as a legal concept assumes the legality of war as an instrument of national policy as well as the right of any nation to intervene or not to intervene in a war on one side or the other as it sees fit. Collective security, on the contrary, derives logically from the distinction between lawful and unlawful war and stipulates the legal duty for all nations to join the nation waging lawful war. Collective security requires partiality leading to intervention; neutrality requires impartiality and abstention. Under collective security, the need for assistance of a victim of aggression determines action; under neutrality, action is determined by the interests of the individual nations.

It is obvious, then, that neutrality and collective security are mutually exclusive. Collective security, implying the universalization of war by virtue of an abstract legal principle, and neutrality, seeking the localization of war for reasons of expediency, cannot coexist. As it is with war, so it is with collective security in relation to neutrality: the more there is of the one, the less there is bound to be of the other. Had the Covenant of the League of Nations and the Charter of the United Nations established a full-fledged, working system of collective security, neutrality would indeed, as has been claimed, have been outlawed and become politically inoperative. In point of fact, neither the Covenant nor the Charter went so far. They embraced the ideal of collective security and left gaping holes in its legal fabric. Conversely, they did not kill neutrality but rather sentenced it to die, staying indefinitely the execution of the sentence.

The loophole through which both legal instruments have allowed neutrality to escape from execution by collective security is the non-automatic nature of enforcement measures. For in so far as a nation has the legal right to decide for itself whether and to what degree it shall participate in measures of collective security, it has also the legal right to substitute for the principle of collective security any other guide for action more consonant with its national interest, such as the principle of neutrality.

First of all, Articles 12 and 15 of the Covenant of the League of Nations, by allowing explicitly resort to war under certain circumstances, recognized by implication also the right to remain neutral with regard to such a war. Furthermore, the Covenant explicitly recognized the right to neutrality with regard to collective military measures, Article 16, paragraph 2, making such measures dependent upon a mere recommendation by the Council of the League. This discretionary nature of military measures, explicit in the text of the Covenant, was extended to all collective security measures to be taken under the Covenant through the interpretative resolutions passed by the Assembly of the League in 1921. These interpretative resolutions shifted the locus of decision from the Council to the individual member states and reduced the Council to a co-ordinating agency for the measures taken by the member states through the exercise of their own discretion.

Chapter VII of the Charter of the United Nations, comprising Articles 39 to 51, is the counterpart of Article 16 of the Covenant. These provisions take a decisive step beyond the Covenant in that they establish the complete authority of the Security Council over measures of collective security. Nothing in this system of collective security seems to be left to the discretion of the member states. And there appears to be no loophole through which the member states could escape from collective security into neutrality. Yet while indeed the Charter of the United Nations leaves no room for neutrality on condition that its system of collective security operates as intended, its very operation is contingent upon two conditions which restore the discretion of the member states and, through it, neutrality as a legal status.

One of these conditions is laid down in Article 43 of the Charter which makes collective military action dependent upon agreements to be concluded between the member states and the Security Council concerning "the numbers and types of forces, their degree of readiness and general location, and the nature of the facilities and assistance to be provided." While Article 43 provides that these agreements "shall be negotiated as soon as possible on the initiative of the Security Council," none has been negotiated. In the absence of such agreements, the provisions of the Charter concerning collective military measures remain a dead letter and the member states remain free to decide for themselves whether and to what extent they are to participate in such measures. Their discretion in this respect encompasses their right to remain neutral. This discretion is implicitly recognized by Article 106 of the Charter which provides that in the absence of the special agreements envisaged by Article 43 the great powers shall consult with one another and with other member states about collective military measures to be taken.

The other condition which goes to the very heart of the collective security system of the Charter is Article 27, paragraph 3, stipulating that "decisions of the Security Council . . . shall be made by an affirmative vote of seven members including the concurring votes of the permanent members." This provision for a great power veto eliminates from the outset any possibility of applying the collective security measures of the Charter against a permanent member of the Security Council. With the great powers thus beyond the reach of such measures, it remains for the individual nations to decide on the basis of expediency whether and to what extent they want to take measures against a great power. In other words, they have the right to remain neutral.

The Security Council is then capable of applying collective security measures only against nations of the second or third rank, that is, those which are not among its permanent members. This, however, is not likely to happen as long as the great powers are pitted against each other in fierce, interconnected, and world-encompassing competitions for power. Under such circumstances, collective security measures executed against any nation of the second or third rank are bound to affect the respective power positions of some or all of the great powers, and those who stand to lose through the application of such measures will use their discretion to interpose a veto against them. The result for the member states is again freedom of action, which includes neutrality.

This interpretation of the Charter is borne out by the legal situation which arose when the United Nations instituted in 1950 collective security measures against North Korea and Communist China. The Security Council was able to discharge its functions only so long as the Soviet Union, because of its temporary absence, was unable to veto the collective security measures the other members had agreed upon. With the return of the Soviet Union to the Security Council, the General Assembly was called upon to carry the burden of organizing the collective action of the United Nations. The functions of the General Assembly with regard to measures of collective security are limited by Articles 10 and 18 of the Charter to making recommendations to the member states by a two-thirds majority. Thus again the freedom of action of the member states and, with it, the right to remain neutral are preserved. This legal situation has not been affected by the "Uniting for Peace" resolution of November, 1950, seeking to strengthen the General Assembly as the principal agency for the co-ordination of collective measures.

This legal compatibility of neutrality with collective security, as conceived by the Covenant and the Charter, was demonstrated by the manner in which the legal provisions were put to the test of actual performance in terms of military measures. The attack of North Korea against South Korea on June 25, 1950, joined by Communist China in November of the same year, was a clear-cut case of aggression. Collective security would have required that all members of the United Nations come to the aid of South Korea as the victim of that aggression. In view of the nature and the military consequences of the aggression, this aid, to be effective, could only have taken the form of the dispatch of armed forces to the battle-front. Yet of the sixty members of the United Nations, only sixteen sent armed forces of any kind. The others—among them nations with military capabilities, such as Argentina, Brazil, Czechoslovakia, India, Mexico, Poland—remained neutral in that they abstained from active participation in the war on either side.

The survival of neutrality under the aegis of collective security is also attested to by the fact that by no means all wars which have occurred during that period became general wars, as they should have if no nation had remained neutral with regard to it. The very incidence of local wars, such as the Chaco War, the Italo-Ethiopian War, the Sino-Japanese War, the Russo-Finnish War, the Israeli-Arab War, demonstrate the incidence of neutrality. In the autumn of 1956 the government of the United States declared that it did not intend to participate in a war which might break out between some users of the Suez Canal and Egypt, that is, it intended to remain neutral. And even during so general a war as the Second World

War, some nations remained neutral, and their neutrality was universally respected.[10]

What has made neutrality problematical in the contemporary world is not so much the new international law of collective security as a novel political and military situation. The rationale of neutrality has always been the desire to keep out of war without having to forsake one's national interests. The realization of this dual objective has always depended upon the operations of the balance of power. A nation of the second or third rank has a chance to preserve its neutrality vis-à-vis the great powers only if an approximately equal distribution of power among the latter deters all of them from violating it. The history of Belgian and Swiss neutrality bears out this relationship between neutrality and the balance of power. Switzerland, in particular, owed the preservation of her neutrality in the two world wars to the fortuitous conditions of the military balance of power, effectively supported, it is true, by the consistent Swiss policy of abstention.[11]

Neutrality, being a function of the balance of power, partakes of the latter's precarious and unstable nature. Thus when the Covenant of the League seemed to offer an automatic and, hence, reliable alternative to the balance of power, the small nations were among the most fervent supporters of collective security. Yet this support involved them in an insoluble contradiction. Collective security, if it could be made to work, provides the best hope for the avoidance of war. Yet it could not be made to work without the active support of all nations, big and small; in order to make collective security a success, those nations whose survival depends upon remaining neutral in case of war must cease being neutral in order to avoid war. Yet if collective security should fail to deter a prospective aggressor, the commitment to collective security would expose the nations of the second and third rank to the very risks which their support of collective security was intended to avoid.

The small nations tried to reconcile these two positions by maxi-

[10] Cf. also Hans J. Morgenthau, *Politics among Nations* (2d ed.; New York: Alfred A. Knopf, 1954), pp. 274 ff., 388 ff.

[11] On Swiss neutrality see Hans J. Morgenthau, "The End of Switzerland's Differential Neutrality," *American Journal of International Law,* XXXII (1938), 558 ff.

mizing the protective effects of collective security for themselves and at the same time minimizing their own commitments to it. Thus in 1920 and 1921, the Scandinavian countries suggested that certain nations which, by fully participating in the measures provided for by Article 16 of the Covenant, would be exposed to grave dangers on account of their geographic and economic situation, be exempted from the rigorous application of this article. The same countries were in 1935–36 among the strongest supporters of League of Nations sanctions against Italy, the main burden of which, for military and geographic reasons, would have had to be borne by others.

The failure of these sanctions ended the League experiment in collective security. The collective security of the League was the institutional manifestation of Anglo-French military and political supremacy in Europe. It was under the umbrella of that supremacy that the small European nations sought, and believed to have found, protection. The overwhelming military power with which Great Britain and France emerged from the First World War signified the end of the European balance of power on which the neutrality of the small European nations had rested. Its heritage was taken over by the collective security of the League of Nations. Membership in the League seemed to guarantee those nations military protection superior to that which the balance of power would have afforded them. When Italy succeeded in defying the collective security of the League, she also demonstrated at the very least the unreliability, if not the disappearance, of Anglo-French supremacy in Europe. The small nations found themselves again face to face with a number of great powers of comparable strength, competing for power and openly following the counsels of expediency. The restoration of the balance of power called forth the traditional reaction of the small nations: neutrality.

After withdrawal from the League had been seriously discussed in some of the small European nations, Belgium, Denmark, Finland, Norway, Sweden, the Netherlands, Spain, and Switzerland, in a number of joint and several declarations, canceled for all practical purposes the obligations under Article 16 of the Covenant. While the League of Nations took formal cognizance of the restoration of the neutrality of Switzerland only, there can be no doubt that what the so-called traditional European neutrals had declared for themselves held equally true, regardless of legal theories and pretenses, for all nations, big and small: they would act in the face of war according to their interests as they saw them, to intervene or to remain neutral as they saw fit.

Thus the small European nations fell back upon the traditional safeguards of neutrality: rearmament and isolation. They tried to buttress the latter by regional understandings, such as the Scandinavian Rules of Neutrality of May 27, 1938, and the Convention of the Baltic States of November 18, 1938. They debated, but did not act upon, the idea of a "Third Europe," an organization of all nations who wanted to stay out of the approaching Second World War. This idea called for collective action on the part of the members of the organization for the purpose of preventing the outbreak of such a war and, if it should break out, of protecting their neutrality. The feasibility of this proposal depended upon two nonexistent conditions: a community of interests transcending the mere negative desire to stay out of the next general war and a concentration of power comparable to that which might threaten the neutrality of a member nation.

The members of the League, thus returning from the world of collective security to that of the balance of power, did not return to the same world they had left in 1919. The distribution of power that existed on the eve of the Second World War was not identical with the one that existed at the end of the First. It showed three tendencies which decisively impaired the protection which neutrality used to afford.

While in 1919 the distribution of power favored Great Britain and France, inducing the small European nations to seek their protection within a system of collective security, on the eve of the Second World War military and political power had almost as decisively shifted to the Axis powers. They had come to occupy a quasi-hegemonic position in central Europe. Furthermore, the fate of Austria and Czechoslovakia had shown that Great Britain and France could no longer be counted upon, even if they were still able, to take military risks in defense of the neutral status of small nations. Thus each of the three courses of action available to the traditional neutrals appeared equally unsatisfactory. They could follow the shift of power and join the Axis, thereby not only giving up their neutrality but also risking the loss of their national identity; they could join Great Britain and France, thereby running mortal risks without gaining additional protection; they could retreat in the impartial and abstemious isolation befitting a neutral, thereby running the same mortal risks but with the outside chance of being spared destruction and conquest.

Second, the technology of warfare had progressed to a point at which the protection of geographic location was largely eliminated. Furthermore, these technological developments greatly widened the gap separating the powers of the first rank from the others. Lacking the industrial basis for a modern war machine, the traditional neutrals had lost the military means with which to deter aggression by great powers.

Finally, the rise of totalitarian imperialism, already foreshadowed in the international policies of the Soviet Union in the twenties, added a new dimension to international politics, hostile to neutrality. To nations that consider themselves the repositories of universal truths which it is their historic mission to bring to the rest of humanity, the impartial aloofness of the neutrals becomes intolerable indifference, if not treason. In the contest between truth and falsehood, good and evil, neutrality appears to the crusading nations tantamount to passive hostility to be fought by all means fair or foul. What point can there be in the traditional impartiality and abstention of the neutral when subversion becomes one of the foremost weapons in the arsenal of nations, when races, classes, and parties fight on the domestic political plane the battle of nations?

The political and military developments following the Second World War have accentuated these tendencies, destructive of neutrality. The disparity of strength between the great powers and the other nations has developed into a bipolar political system in which there are only two nations of the first rank, separated by a gulf of unprecedented dimensions from all the other nations. The increase in the destructiveness of modern weapons needs but to be mentioned in order to show the utter impossibility for any nation not possessing them to deter another nation from their use.

These developments have been aggravated by the political context within which they have occurred: the Cold War. The political relationship called the Cold War signifies the absence of peace between the two blocs in that there has been no moral and legal agreement upon their relationships and, more particularly, upon the boundaries between them. Rather these political relationships are the result of the provisional *de facto* settlement established at the end of the Second World War primarily on military grounds. It is characteristic of the Cold War that both sides refuse to consider this settlement as either permanent or legitimate and try to change it in their favor by all means short of war. Thus psychological warfare, intervening directly in the domestic affairs of other nations through subversion, propaganda, and foreign aid, has become a major undertaking of the active contenders.

The effects of these developments upon neutrality as a viable legal and political status are of course beyond doubt. General war is bound to wipe out the distinction between belligerents and neutrals. Before the atomic fall-out and bacteriological contamination all men and nations, big and small, neutrals and belligerents, are equal. The Cold War has made many nations of the second and third rank the main bone of contention. Under these conditions they have no chance to remain neutral either in a "cold" or "hot" war since it is their fate, decided by others, to belong to one or the other bloc.

However, the effects of these developments in terms of policy have been both contradictory and ambivalent. Two periods have followed each other, not dissimilar to those that followed the First World War: one characterized by the virtual disappearance of neutrality as the objective of policy; the other, by attempts at its revival. Yet during the first period some nations gave the appearance of holding both positions at the same time, wanting simultaneously to be neutral and not to be neutral, to reap the benefits both of neutrality and of association with a great power. While both objectives cannot be attained simultaneously, the former is not attainable at all. Out of this conflict between desire and reality rises the first type of neutralism: the impotent striving for neutrality.

This period covers roughly the first decade following the Second World War. It was characterized by the tendency of the bipolar system to transform itself into a two-bloc system. That is to say, the two centers of first-rate power remaining in the world exerted an irresistible attraction upon most of the other nations to the point of complete identification with one or the other of these superpowers. The result was what might be called "bipolar collective security." Most nations of the world, instead of banding all together for mutual protection as the ideal of collective security would have required, huddled around one or the other of the superpowers, expecting and receiving their protection. Only a few nations, of which India is the outstanding example, were able during that period to resist that attraction of the two superpowers and to decline alignment with either side.

This development resulted from the drastic decline in the viability of all nations except the two superpowers in consequence of the Second World War. During that period, none of the European nations found within itself the political, military, and economic resources for survival. Thus the nations of western Europe had to lean for support upon the United States, while the eastern European nations fell victim to Russian conquest.

To this general factor must be added a specific one which applies, in varying degrees, only to the nations outside the Soviet orbit. These nations found in the atomic monopoly of the United States the main protection against the threat of Soviet imperialism. The intensity of this type of identification with the United States varied with the intensity with which the Soviet threat was experienced by different nations at different times. It reached its peak in the period between the coup d'état in Czechoslovakia and the end of the Korean War, having its main impact in western Europe.

Those were the objective conditions under which most nations had to exist, and their policy of identifying themselves with one or the other of the superpowers followed inevitably from them. Yet these conditions and policies were not accepted enthusiastically or even willingly by most of these nations. Nations who but recently had either been great powers or had at least been able to choose their allies could hardly welcome the force of circumstances which left them no choice. Thus, while they had to accept for the time being the dire necessity of identifying themselves with one or the other superpower, they hoped to be again able to pursue an independent foreign policy.

That hope had to remain inarticulate in the members of the Soviet bloc. In the West it was articulated in different rationalizations whose uniform aim was to conceal the fact of dependence and to make it appear as though the nation concerned still had freedom of choice. Thus a nation might insist upon enjoying the prestige of a great power in terms of participation in international conferences, a position of eminence in international organizations, and the like. Or a nation, might engage in a public debate about alternative foreign policies, asserting its ability and, if need be, resolution to choose one of them. Or a nation might indulge in Anglophobia, Francophobia, or anti-Americanism, thus proving to itself and to others—primarily, however, to itself—its continuing independence.

These manifestations of escapism were politically irrelevant as long as the objective conditions of world politics made it impracticable to follow them up with actual policies. As such, they called for sympathy and understanding rather than for moral condemnation. They are of immediate political concern only in so far as they find opportunities for political action. For they reveal a state of mind longing for such an opportunity.

It is the characteristic of the second period in which we find ourselves at present that new developments have made it possible at least for some nations to translate into actual policy this desire to escape identification with one or the other of the two superpowers. In other words, neutrality is no longer a daydream expressing itself in neurotic symptoms but has again become the possible objective of rational policy. Consequently, neutralism has taken on a new significance as a foreign policy seeking avoidance of a consistent alignment with either bloc. The trend of the bipolar system to transform itself into a two-bloc system has been arrested and reversed. Centrifugal tendencies counteract the magnetic attraction which the two major power centers exerted during the first decade following the Second World War. Nations of the second and third rank tend to move toward the outer confines of the two spheres of influence dominated by the superpowers and not only look longingly beyond these confines but also have started to pursue policies without regard to the preferences of the superpowers. Four factors are in the main responsible for this new trend.

First, many of the nations who had to join one of the superpowers for sheer sake of survival have regained much of their economic strength and political stability. For them to remain within the orbit of one of these powers has again become in good measure a matter of expediency, of choice rather than of necessity. This is true in particular of West Germany and Japan. Only in the Soviet bloc, as the experience of Poland and Hungary has shown, necessity still reigns.

Second, the distribution of military power in the world has been drastically altered by the emergence of the Soviet Union as an atomic power comparable to the United States. The American monopoly of atomic weapons has been replaced by an atomic balance of power which amounts to an atomic stalemate. With the American and Russian stockpiles canceling each other out, American atomic power has lost its protective function for the allies of the United States. While there is today, as has been pointed out above, no safety from atomic destruction for any nation, the risk is increased almost to the point of certainty for nations which are closely allied with one or the other of the superpowers. Or, to put it the other way around, there may be a somewhat better chance for a nation not so allied to escape atomic destruction than for one that is.

Third, the need for American military protection appears to be further diminished by the "new look" of Russian foreign policy. The Soviet Union, minimizing the expansionist tendencies of communism and stressing instead the mutual benefits to be derived from cultural, economic, and technological exchanges as well as from disarmament, creates an additional incentive for the allies of the United States to minimize their military and political commitments.

Fourth, such commitments may well appear as a positive handicap in view of the Russian promise of such benefits. For in so far as the United States and the Soviet Union are willing to compete in terms of economic assistance, a nation may well expect to maximize such assistance by placing itself uncommitted between the two competitors. What more can such a nation hope for than to have the best of both worlds without belonging to either?

This type of neutralism which, as a matter of policy, seeks, at the very least, to minimize a nation's identification with either bloc and may aim at an uncommitted position between both, is in its economic aspects nothing but a matter of calculated self-interest. Its success will depend both upon the bargaining strength of the neutralist nations and the policies of the superpowers. Burma, Egypt, Finland, India, Indonesia, and Yugoslavia have followed this course with different degrees of success; others are likely to follow their example, their success again depending upon the distribution of power and the quality of the policies pursued.

This type of neutralism is similar in its political purpose to the attempt to revive neutrality on the eve of the Second World War. It is born of the recognition that to keep out of war is for all nations no longer merely a question of expediency but of survival. It is impossible not to be skeptical about its chances of success. Iceland might have increased her chances to escape atomic destruction by embarking upon a neutralist policy. But how many other nations are in a similarly favorable geographic position? And it may well be argued that salvation for all nations, big and small, lies in the prevention of an atomic war, not in staying neutral once it has broken out.

The prevention of such a war, however, depends upon the continuation of the atomic stalemate which, in turn, requires a maximum of military strength on either side. To the extent that a nation shifting from an allied into a neutral position decreases the military strength of one side, without a compensating decrease on the other, the atomic balance of power is altered to the advantage of the latter and the chance for the outbreak of an atomic war is thereby increased. By pursuing such a course, a nation may well in the short run increase its security, while it contributes to the destruction of the very foundations upon which its security ultimately rests.

This argument may not be good for all nations in all circumstances, as Ireland, Sweden, Spain, and Switzerland proved in the Second World War. Yet, as a matter of principle, the futility of neutrality under the conditions of modern warfare seems to be borne out by the fate which befell the small European nations which tried to stay out of the Second World War by pursuing a neutralist policy. Thus the paradox seems to be inescapable that under contemporary conditions a nation serves the purpose of neutrality, which is to stay out of war, by giving up neutrality in order to prevent war from breaking out.

These doubts about the political wisdom of a policy of neutrality apply also to what may be called the grand design of both the escapist and the political type of neutralism: the idea of a "third force." Such a third force, composed of all or some European nations or members of the so-called Asian-African bloc, has been visualized as being poised in independence between the two superpowers and forming a bridge between them, taking Britain's place as the "balancer" in the world balance of power, thereby mitigating international conflict and contributing to the preservation of peace. It was first forcibly and brilliantly expressed in 1946 by General de Gaulle. It has since then been broached time and again by spokesmen for both kinds of neutralism. It partakes, however, of their fatal weakness: it is incapable of realization in the contemporary world.

For such a third force to be an effective instrument of restraint in the world balance of power, its members must, first of all, have permanent vital interests in common which enable them to act in unison on the political scene. Yet there is nothing but anticolonialism which unites the members of the so-called Asian-African bloc, and the nations of western Europe are united by their common opposition to Soviet imperialism only. Some of these nations have been able to act in unison with regard to a specific political problem. They have proved incapable of common political action on a permanent basis. Cases in point are the political impotence and military disintegration of NATO, the failure of all attempts at the political unification of Europe, the political emptiness of the Declaration of Bandung of April, 1955, and the political inconclusiveness of the meeting of Nasser, Nehru, and Tito in July, 1956. Yet even if such permanent common interests existed, they could not be supported by the power necessary to transform them into common policies.[12]

The third typical manifestation of neutralism is of an entirely different kind. It is not primarily concerned with the political and military struggle between East and West, but rather with the identification of that struggle with irreconcilably hostile philosophic and moral positions. It refuses to see the East-West struggle in terms of a struggle between right and wrong, good and evil and, hence, to be drawn into a "crusade" to extirpate evil on either side. In other words, when it comes to passing moral judgments upon either of the hostile political philosophies, social systems, and the policies pursued by them, a nation which is neutralist in this sense at the very

---

[12] The best analysis of this and the following type of neutralism is R. A. Scalapino, "Neutralism in Asia," *American Political Science Review,* XLVIII (1954), 49 ff.

least refuses to let its moral judgment influence its political attitudes and decisions.

This type of neutralism can, but does not need to, coincide with the desire, characteristic of the other two types, to keep out of, or leave, a military bloc. While a nation which espouses the latter types is likely also to be in sympathy with the former—India is a case in point—the reverse is not necessarily true. Quite to the contrary, the refusal to identify political and military judgments with moral ones, to subordinate the former to the latter, and to transform the political and military struggle into a world-wide crusade is indeed the prevailing governmental and popular attitude on this side of the Iron Curtain, even among the staunchest allies of the United States. This important fact is being obscured only by the vociferous and prominent criticism to which moral neutralism is from time to time exposed.

This criticism revives on the level of practical politics the controversy between utopianism and realism which has been one of the great issues of Western political philosophy since Machiavelli and which some of us thought had been settled once and for all, at least on that level of practical politics. This criticism takes the utopian side in assuming that the actions of nations toward each other must be judged by abstract moral principles, while realism sees in the national interest the standard by which such action must be judged. In the former view, a nation whose foreign policy does not reflect the ideal of international solidarity in terms of collective security is subject to moral reprobation, and so is a nation from whose foreign policy implacable hostility to the Communist philosophy and way of life is absent.

This criticism is untenable both on moral and political grounds. We have dealt with the philosophic merits of this position elsewhere[13] and limit ourselves here to four observations specifically relevant to the issue under discussion.

First, nations like to invoke abstract moral principles in justification of their position and in condemnation of those of their adversaries, but they act, as they must, in view of their interests as they see them. No nation has risked its existence or even its interests for the ideal of collective security, but all nations have, as has been

[13] Cf. Morgenthau, *Politics among Nations*, pp. 3 ff., and pp. 100 ff. above.

shown above, been guided in their support of measures of collective security by their respective interests. Some nations have at times talked as though they were willing to risk everything for the sake of wiping communism off the face of the earth, but during four decades of Communist rule there has been no nation actually willing to take such a risk for its moral convictions.

The invocation of abstract moral principles in foreign policy, then, performs the typical function of a political ideology, masking with the veil of morality the true nature of the interests and policies pursued. What this criticism of neutralism conceals is an immature approach to foreign policy which some of us hoped we had out-grown. We are impatient and disappointed with other nations who dare look at the world from the vantage point of their interests and not ours. Yet since we like to think that what we stand for is what all good men must stand for and that what we are doing is what the moral law requires of all men, we are shocked and morally outraged at the spectacle of nations who stand for different ideals and act in different ways. In a mature, realistic view of foreign policy which assumes the paramountcy of the national interest, this is as it must be. Given their different positions in the world and their different interests, there is nothing surprising in, say, India's not speaking and acting like the United States. It would indeed be surprising if it were otherwise.

Second, this criticism of moral neutralism is also politically imma-ture in its assumption that a nation is necessarily the stronger and the more successful in foreign policy the more nations support it without qualification. This assumption may or may not be correct. It had at least the appearance of correctness as long as the bipolar system of world politics seemed to move inextricably toward a two-bloc system. A case could then have been made for a policy of max-imizing membership in one's own bloc and minimizing that of the other. However, a case could even then have been made, and must now be made emphatically when the trend toward a two-bloc sys-tem is being reversed, in favor of the proposition that uncommitted nations, by virtue of their being uncommitted, are able to perform a vital function for the individual nations as well as for the community of nations as channels of communication, sources of information, and mediators.

Third, the critical approach to moral neutralism is morally and politically unconvincing when it makes foreign policy the test of anticommunism. How does this test account for the following facts: Communist Yugoslavia has been both neutralist internationally and anti-Stalinist domestically; pro-Russian Egypt and neutralist India have suppressed their Communist parties with unsurpassed fierceness; non-neutralist France and Italy harbor powerful and unmolested Communist parties? Is India to be condemned on moral grounds for combining a neutralist foreign policy with an anti-Communist domestic policy, and is France worthy of moral praise for combining a non-neutralist foreign policy with toleration of domestic communism? And how is one to fashion a sensible foreign policy guided by such moral judgments? Must one treat all these nations as equally unreliable partners and prospective enemies, since none of them is consistently anti-Communist in its policies? And must one overlook the fact that to be anti-Communist means in terms of foreign policy to be anti-Russian and anti-Chinese, an attitude which, in view of their respective interests, some nations can afford to take without limitation, others only up to a certain point, and others not at all? Must we condemn a nation of the latter type for not being able to do what we think it ought to do, thus doing our part in making sure that if such a nation should take sides it will not take ours? There must be something essentially wrong with a moral philosophy which finds itself caught in such absurdities.

What is essentially wrong with it—and this is the fourth observation we wish to offer—is the confusion between the sphere of private moral judgment and the realm of public action. Every man has the right and the duty to judge others, as he must himself, by a moral yardstick. Yet for him to act toward others as he judges them would be intellectually impertinent, morally repugnant, and impractical; for such action would leave out of account the limitations of moral judgment, the moral imperfection of human action, and the consequences, liable to be destructive of moral values, of action guided by nothing but an abstract moral judgment.

What is true of individuals applies by the same token to nations. There is something intellectually, morally, and politically preposterous in a nation's meting out with divine assurance moral praise and blame among the nations of the world. Such a nation is oblivious of the corruption to which moral judgment on matters political is particularly prone. It is also oblivious of the narrow limits within which nations, by virtue of the conditions under which they must live, are able to comply with abstract moral standards. Finally, and most importantly, it is oblivious of the responsibility for its own interests and survival, a responsibility which nobody else will discharge if it does not. The moral commitment to anticommunism as the standard by which to judge the foreign policy of nations is likely to have supremely immoral consequences. For the anti-Communist crusade as an instrument of foreign policy is likely to destroy all nations, Communist and anti-Communist alike.

19 *International Law*

If an event in the physical world contradicts scientific forecasts and thus challenges the assumptions on which the forecasts have been based, it is the natural reaction of scientific inquiry to re-examine the assumptions and attempt to reconcile scientific theory and empirical facts. The social sciences do not always react in that way. They have an inveterate tendency to stick to their assumptions and to suffer constant defeat from experience rather than to change their assumptions in the light of contradicting facts. This resistance to change is uppermost in the history of international law. None of the schemes and devices by which great humanitarians and shrewd politicians endeavored to reorganize the relations between states on the basis of law has stood the trial of history. Instead of asking whether the devices were adequate to the problems which they were supposed to solve, it was the general attitude of the internationalists to take the appropriateness of the devices for granted and to blame the facts for the failure. When the facts behave otherwise than we have predicted, they seem to say, too bad for the facts. Not unlike the sorcerers of primitive ages, they attempt to exorcise social evils by the indefatigable repetition of magic formulas. As the League of Nations was a failure, let us have another League. As the first and second peace conferences of the Hague did not succeed, let us have a third one. As arbitration never settled a political conflict which otherwise would have led to war, let us have more arbitration for the prevention of war. As the last disarmament conference was a waste of intellect and time, why not convoke another disarmament conference?

It is a strange paradox that the lay public has observed a much more skeptical and realistic, therefore scientific, attitude toward international law than the science of international law itself. The laymen were much quicker to recognize the gap between the rules of international law as represented by science, and the rules of international law as they exist in actual experience. The collapse, on the eve of the Second World War, of the hopes which the interwar period had placed on international law altogether destroyed public confi-

From the *American Journal of International Law*, April, 1940.

dence in a science which, unmoved by what experience may show, invariably follows its preconceived pattern.[1] This breakdown implied the practical refutation of the ideas which had determined the development of international law since the last decades of the nineteenth century. Hence, the science of international law has since been confronted with the alternative of maintaining the traditional pattern of assumptions, concepts, and devices in spite of the teachings of history, or of revising this pattern and trying to reconcile the science of international law and its subject matter, that is, the rules of international law as they are actually applied. It ought to be obvious that only the latter way leads to theoretically correct and practically useful results. Yet that re-examination and revision has to overcome the methodological assumptions with which the traditional science of international law starts. These assumptions are embodied in the positivist doctrine of law.

Positivist philosophy restricts the object of scientific knowledge to matters than can be verified by observation and thus excludes from its domain all matters of an a priori, metaphysical nature. Legal positivism transfers this delimitation into the legal sphere. The legal positivist delimits the subject matter of his research in a dual way. On the one hand, he proposes to deal exclusively with matters legal, and for this purpose strictly separates the legal sphere from ethics and mores as well as psychology and sociology. Hence, his legalism. On the other hand, he restricts his attention within the legal sphere to the legal rules enacted by the state and excludes all law whose existence cannot be traced to the statute books or the decisions of the courts. Hence, his statist monism. This "positive" law the positivist accepts as it is, without passing judgment upon its ethical value or questioning its practical appropriateness. Hence, his agnosticism. The positivist cherishes the belief that the "positive" law is a logically coherent system which virtually contains, and through a mere process of logical deduction will actually produce, all rules necessary for the decision of all possible cases. Hence, his system worship and dogmatic conceptualism.

[1] Professor Quincy Wright could report in 1930 (*Research in International Law since the War* [Washington, D.C.: Carnegie Endowment for International Peace, 1930], p. 25): "Of the twenty jurists with whom the writer has corresponded, only two betrayed a note of pessimism at the prospects, and that in both cases was qualified."

The historic importance of the positivist school of jurisprudence for the science of law was fourfold. First, positivism accepted the breakdown of the great metaphysical systems of the eighteenth and the early nineteenth centuries and the resulting decadence of metaphysical jurisprudence as an established fact. It endeavored to save the scientific character of jurisprudence by eliminating from it all metaphysical elements, thus separating it from the discredited doctrines of natural law. In the second place, positivism recognized that the subject matter of jurisprudence was the law and nothing but the law, and that neither non-legal subjects nor non-legal considerations could have any place in it. Furthermore, legal positivism learned from the positivist movement in philosophy and the natural sciences that scientific objectivity is dependent upon an object intelligible in experience, and a method aimed at knowledge, not at evaluation. Finally, the great legal codifications of the European continental countries and the Anglo-American statutory law found in positivism a technique of interpretation and presentation. This technique fulfilled its purpose satisfactorily as long as the social and political philosophy of the statutes, either directly expressed by them or indirectly derived from them by way of logical deduction, was sufficient to meet the economic and social needs as well as the political demands and ethical requirements of a given society at a given historical moment.

To be sure, this correspondence between the statutes and the standards of society has never existed completely; even under static conditions there will always be a marginal sphere where the mere logical subsumption of a given case under statutory law would violate the standards of society. In order to satisfy the positivist assumptions of the logical completeness of the legal order and at the same time meet the standards of society, these standards had first to be read into the statutes from which they then appeared to have been derived by a mere logical process. Through the back door of pseudo-logical interpretation the outlawed company of natural law and extra-legal value judgments re-entered the legal system. This kind of pseudo-logical legerdemain became the predominant interpretative technique of legal positivism in the period of its decadence. In the last decades of the nineteenth century the standards of society departed farther and farther from the economic, social, political, and ethical assumptions from which the systems of statutory law had started.[2] Hence, the positivists were compelled to resort to a series of pseudo-logical makeshifts in order to maintain the fiction of legal self-sufficiency, on which positivist jurisprudence had founded its theoretical system.

From three sides this fiction was, and still is, under attack. From one side, sociological and realist jurisprudence, inspired partly and indirectly by the original sociological positivism of Comte, does away with the artificial barriers by which positivism has separated the legal sphere from the whole domain of the social sciences to which it actually belongs. Thus it destroys the positivist assumptions together with the positivist conclusions. From another side, the neo-positivism of Kelsen's pure theory of law maintains the basic assumptions of positivism but undertakes to achieve the positivist ends by purifying the legal science from all material, non-legal elements, thus eliminating the subject matter of positivist crypto-metaphysics.

Several schools of revived natural law, as well as the politico-ideological power of totalitarianism, joined in this dual scientific attack. Totalitarianism ostracized positivist jurisprudence as a manifestation of liberal decadence in Germany and Italy, where the domination of legal thought by positivism has been at times almost undisputed and where positivism has exerted its most far-reaching and fertile influence on the development of the legal science. Deprived of its traditional strongholds by political suppression and undermined by scientific criticism, positivism lost its dominant influence in modern legal thought.

In international law, unlike the other branches of legal science, positivism is still a determining influence. Ever since the turn of the century, internationalists have started with positivist assumptions, have followed the positivist method, and have professed adherence to the principles of positivism. Neither the opposition of natural law, nor Kelsen's neopositivist criticism, nor, finally, the rather implicit criticism of legal sociologists has been able to affect the predominance of positivist thought over the science of international law.[3] The

[2] An excellent analysis of this development is to be found in Julien Bonnecase's history of the French "École de l'Exégèse," *La pensée juridique française de 1804 à l'heure présente* (Bordeaux: Delmas, 1933), Vol. I.

[3] H. Lauterpacht, in *Private Law Sources and Analogies of International Law* (London: Longmans, Green & Co., 1927), p. 27, n. 5, and p. 58, n. 7; L. Oppen-

International Court of Justice still follows the time-honored pseudo-logical method of traditional positivism which prevailed in the domestic courts at the turn of the century. The annals of this highest international tribunal record no instance of a lawyer, like Brandeis in *Muller v. Oregon*,[4] daring to break through the network of positivist formulas, nor of any majority opinion which would not have clung, on a very high level of technical perfection, to the traditional pattern of positivist argumentation. When Judge Hudson looks for a realistic decision with respect to international law, he has to turn to the Court of Appeals of the State of New York.[5] Compared to municipal law, international law is in a retarded stage of scientific development.

The collapse of the international law of Geneva, when for the first time its fictions were confronted with the stark reality, meant of necessity the breakdown of the science which had been its ideological reflection. The post–World War I science of international law shared the short-lived and delusive splendor of its political master, and then shared with him the final detection of their common sham existence as well as the resulting disrepute. The helplessness of the science of international law in the face of those dangers, its very unawareness of them, its sincere self-deception as to its scientific character, are perhaps the gravest indictments which can be brought against the scientific value of the positivist doctrine of international

---

heim and H. Lauterpacht, *International Law* (8th ed.; London: Longmans, Green & Co., 1955), I, 106 ff., defends the opinion that positivism no longer dominates the science of international law but has been replaced by a new doctrine of moderate natural law. It is difficult to share this opinion. Natural law and the science of international law have in common only that they overstep the limits of experience. However, one would do injustice to the great metaphysical systems of natural law by identifying them with the science of international law. Whereas Suárez and Grotius were fully aware of the aprioristic, metaphysical character of their propositions and had good philosophical reasons for adhering to them, the positivist science of international law helplessly confuses reality and imagination, wish and fact, because it does no longer possess the scientific means of distinguishing between them.

[4] 208 U.S. 412 (1908). An excellent appraisal of the theoretical importance of this case is to be found in Felix Frankfurter, "Hours of Labor and Realism in Constitutional Law," *Harvard Law Review*, XXIX (1916), 353.

[5] See the reference to Cardozo's opinion in *Techt v. Hughes*, 229 N.Y. 222, 241 (1920) in Manley O. Hudson, "International Law in the Twentieth Century," *Cornell Law Quarterly*, X (1925), 435, n. 75.

law. The failure of the post–World War I science of international law is not due to accidental circumstances; it grows out of the very assumptions and methods which have led legal positivism to defeat in the domestic field. Yet, in the international field the disastrous consequences of the genuine weakness of the positivist doctrine are magnified by the absence of the conditions which in the domestic domain made legal positivism at least a temporary and apparent success.

Legal positivism starts with the assumption that its subject matter is to be found exclusively in the written law of the state. Only the rules of law, and all the rules of law which statutes and court decisions present as such, are the material with which the positivist doctrine has to deal. The criterion of the existence, that is, the validity of a legal rule, is, then, its incorporation into the written law of the state. This criterion for the validity of legal rules means, if transferred to the international field, that the only valid rules of international law are those that are revealed by the decisions of courts and international treaties duly ratified and not formally revoked. Yet this concept is at once confronted with two problems for which the positivist doctrine of international law has no solution. On the one hand, all rules embodied in written documents are not valid international law, and, on the other hand, there are valid rules of international law other than the rules embodied in written documents. The positivist formula as applied to international law is at once too narrow and too broad.

The science of international law has not developed a criterion to distinguish, in an objective way, between *seemingly* and *actually* valid rules of international law. "One can assert that nine-tenths of the traditional doctrines of international law are not actual international law," said Professor Georg Jellinek as far back as 1905.[6] Declared Professor Oppenheim a few years later:

It is also indispensable that the science should free itself from the tyranny of phrases. As things are, there is scarcely a doctrine of the law of nations which is wholly free from the tyranny of phrases. . . . Any one who is in touch with the application of international law in diplomatic practice hears from statesmen every day the complaint that books put forth fanciful doctrines instead of the actual rules of law. Now it is often not difficult to push the irrelevant to one side and to extract what is legally essential from

[6] *System der subjektiven öffentlichen Rechte* (Tübingen, 1905), p. 321.

the waste of phrase-ridden discourse. But there are entire areas in which the tyranny of phrases so turns the head that rules which absolutely never were rules of law are represented as such.[7]

"On no subject of human interest, except theology," said John Chipman Gray at about the same time, "has there been so much loose writing and nebulous speculations as on international law."[8]

If these statements were true in the first decade of the century, the development of the post–World War I science of international law only added to their significance. The Covenant of the League of Nations, for instance, was a duly ratified document which was never repealed. But was it ever valid international law as a whole? If not, which provisions never had the quality of valid legal rules and which ones lost this quality in the course of the gradual collapse of the institution of Geneva? No treatise of the law of nations offers any general criterion to answer these questions, nor do the concrete answers given with reference to the actual validity of Article 16 of the Covenant reveal any such underlying objective criterion. The absolute denial of any validity, the assertion of a so-called *de facto* revision, and the defense of full validity, are advanced side by side. Similar problems arose with respect to the Briand-Kellogg Pact and the peace treaties of 1919, as well as to other political treaties, such as the Pact of the Little Entente, alliance treaties, the concepts of aggression, independence, intervention, government, and so forth. These provisions are embodied in written documents which were duly ratified and never invalidated. Have they ever been valid law from the beginning, and what has become of them in the years of their violation? Are they still valid? If they are not, what destroyed their validity? These are questions which the interpreter of domestic statutes, subject to a rational process of validation and invalidation, is not likely to be asked, and hence the positivist doctrine of international law, following the pattern of domestic positivism, has nothing with which to answer them.[9]

[7] L. Oppenheim, *The Future of International Law* (Oxford: Clarendon Press, 1921; first in German, 1911), pp. 58, 59; see also L. Oppenheim, "The Science of International Law," *American Journal of International Law,* II (1908), 315, 334.

[8] *The Nature and Sources of the Law* (New York: Macmillan Co., 1921; 1st ed., 1909), p. 127.

[9] This absence of any scientific test for the validity of the rules of international law is responsible for the perplexity into which some of the foremost representa-

The basic assumption of legal positivism that its exclusive subject matter is the written law of the state leads legal science not only to the inclusion of alleged legal rules which no longer have or never have had legal validity, but also to the exclusion of undoubtedly valid rules of law. Positivist jurisprudence, starting with the axiom of legal self-sufficiency, separates the law from the other normative spheres, that is, ethics and mores, on the one hand, and from the social sphere, comprehending the psychological, political, and economic fields, on the other hand. By doing so, positivism severs the actual relations between the law and the other branches of the normative and social sphere. It proceeds on the assumption that the law, as it really is, can be understood without the normative and social context in which it actually stands. From the application of this assumption to international law there results a threefold delimitation of legal research, contrary to the exigencies of reality, and hence a threefold misconception of what international law really is.

1. The normative sphere, comprehending the totality of rules governing a given society, is one whole with regard to the basic precepts it contains. Although there may be in a given society particular legal rules which contradict particular ethical rules or mores, and vice versa, the main bulk of basic ideals to be realized, of ends to be achieved, and of interests to be protected, is generally the same in the different branches of a given normative order. Law, ethics, and

---

tives of the international law of Geneva fell in the interwar period. Professor Georges Scelle, who had founded a whole system of "positive" international law upon "international solidarity," "international federalism," and like "social facts," in 1937 arrived at the conclusion that there is no such thing as international law at all. "Il n'y a plus en Europe de droit des gens," he wrote in the *Journal des nations,* No. 1665 (Feb. 28 and Mar. 1, 1937). "Il n'y a plus des traités." "The conclusion seems unescapable," said Professor Alfred Zimmern ("The Decline of International Standards," *International Affairs,* XVII [1938], 12), "that positive international law, so called, has no claim to the name of law." (See also Alfred Zimmern, *The League of Nations and the Rule of Law, 1918–1935* [London: Macmillan & Co., 1936], p. 94.) These scholars, who never cared for such "abstract" problems as criteria of the validity of a rule of law, fell from one error into the other. First, they accepted the assumed validity of post–World War I international law without question; then, since it had become obvious that the main bulk of this so-called international law never was valid law at all, they identified this product of their imagination with the main bulk of pre–World War I international law, which today is as valid as it has ever been, and declared that international law simply does not exist.

mores support each other in the pursuit of these aims. Legal rules refer to ethics and mores for the determination of their meaning and vice versa. The guiding influence, however, as to the ideals, ends, and interests to be pursued by the norms under which a given society lives, emanates from the ethical sphere. From it law and mores receive the fundamental distinctions between the good and the bad, the ends to be advanced and the ends to be opposed, the interests to be protected and the interests to be repudiated. At the foundation of any legal system there lies a body of principles which incorporate the guiding ideas of justice and order to be expounded by the rules of law. The intelligibility of any legal system depends upon the recognition of such a set of fundamental principles which constitute the ethical substance of the legal system and shed their illuminating light upon each particular rule of law.

This recognition is relatively easy in the domestic field where the constitution codifies the main bulk of those fundamental principles and a highly integrated public opinion provides supplementary moral guidance. The task is much more difficult with respect to international law. Here no such integrated body of principles exists separate from the rules of law. Some of those principles may be only partly expressed in these rules; others may not be expressed at all and hence have to be detected, in a dangerously uncertain procedure, in the general moral ideas underlying the international law of a certain time, a certain civilization, or even a certain nation. Yet the successful search for these principles is as essential for the scientific understanding of international law as for the understanding of any legal system.

Legal positivism is unable to grant this recognition; for at its basis there is the hostility to all matters metaphysical, that is, those which cannot be ascertained by actual observation. Since non-legal rules have generally entered the horizon of the positivist jurist as metaphysical rules of natural law, the positivist is inclined to identify natural law and ethics as such and to repudiate both as metaphysics. However, to exclude a priori a certain subject matter from scientific research by calling it metaphysical, instead of examining actual experience, is to blind one's self to a preconceived idea originating not in experience but in mere reasoning and thus to do violence to the facts. Hence, the positivist concept of the normative sphere itself reveals a metaphysical attitude, a kind of negative metaphysics which plainly contradicts the very assumptions of a positive science.

Yet positivism has never been quite able to live up to its legalistic and antimetaphysical assumptions. The very nature of its subject matter has compelled it time and again to violate its own assumptions and make use of fundamental principles not revealed by "positive" law. In order to give at least apparent satisfaction to these assumptions, positivism dares to make use of such principles only under the disguise of positivist concepts, and therefore develops a fictitious method which tries by pseudo-logical arguments to derive from "positive," that is, written rules of international law something that those rules do not contain. The interminable and quite sterile discussions on the foundation of the binding force of international law are evidence of this word-juggling, since this is a problem which, as defined in the positivist terms of mutual consent and the like, is contradictory in itself, and hence insoluble within the framework of positivism. The foundation of the binding force of "positive" law can logically be found, not in this "positive" law itself, but only outside it. Another example is the problem of sovereignty as defined and solved by positivism. Here again a fundamental principle which, by its very nature, cannot be derived from "positive" law, but from which "positive" law itself rather derives its meaning, is to be dealt with as if it were a rule of "positive" international law. It is because of these helpless attempts to reconcile its legalistic assumptions with actual legal experience that the positivist doctrine of international law is bound to misrepresent the reality of international law and fail to do justice to its actual content.

2. The rules of international law need to be interpreted not only in the light of the ideals and ethico-legal principles on which they are based but also within the sociological context of economic interests, social tensions, and aspirations for power, which are the motivating forces in the international field and which give rise to the factual situations to be regulated by international law. The correctness of this postulate for the interpretation of municipal law is today self-evident. Nobody would try to interpret social legislation without reference to the conflicting social interests to be evaluated and the social relations to be settled. Nobody would endeavor to grasp the

legal meaning of economic legislation without making economic interests and conflicts part of the reasoning. Even where the reference to the underlying economic and social forces and relations is not always explicit, as in the field of contracts, the sociological context is nevertheless always referred to by implication. It is only because of the highly typical and familiar character of the factual situations and their social and economic significance, which are completely and adequately expressed in the legal rules, that the mere reference to those legal rules implies the consideration of the social and economic factors basic to them.

It was, historically, the most disastrous error of positivism to misunderstand completely this implicit reference to the sociological context which every legal rule contains. This error can be traced to the tradition of the pandectists, who had in the Roman law the classical model of a highly typified legal system which expressed with perfect appropriateness the fundamental interests and relationships arising from the social activities of men. So perfectly was this sociological context represented in the abstractions of the Roman law that the pandectists were only too prone to forget its very existence and to deal with those abstractions as though they were independent logical entities. So did the positivists, both in the municipal and international fields.

This methodological error was of minor importance when the legal concepts were true abstractions from the interests and relations which they were supposed to regulate. When, however, those legal rules were applied to interests and relations to which some of them referred only partly, others not at all, that methodological error was bound to have a disastrous influence upon the scientific value of positivist jurisprudence. In the domestic field, it became instrumental in distorting legal reality and creating that positivist conceptualism with which a decadent legal science attempted to adapt the old legal rules to new economic and social needs while, at the same time, maintaining the fictitious assumption that the written law already contained logically all the rules necessary for the solution of those new problems. Thus juridical pseudo-logic became the artificial makeshift by which a static law could be reconciled with a dynamic social reality.

In the international field, the methodological error of neglecting the sociological context of international law led to even worse consequences. In the domestic field, the correspondence between legal concepts and sociological context was at least a temporary fact, and within this limit the neglect of the sociological context and the assumption of the self-sufficiency of the written law could be justified. In the most important branches of international law this correspondence has never, and could never have, existed. The sociological relationships underlying those branches of international law are characterized by their individual, atypical nature. A political situation in the international field is not likely to repeat itself exactly since the variety of factors of which it is composed makes for an indefinite number of possible combinations. Hence, only a strictly individualized rule of law will be adequate to it. International law provides partly for such individualized rules by restricting the application of a rule to one individual case and leaving the regulation of similar future cases to new legislative efforts. Peace treaties are instances of such individualized rules of international law.

In part, however, international law does maintain the form of the general, typical rule of law and depends on the interpretation of the rule to provide the flexible meaning which the ever changing sociological context requires. All political treaties which are intent upon establishing permanent rights and duties between the contracting parties are of this kind. The same generally and typically worded text may imply quite different rules, according to the political function which it is supposed to fulfil. Thus one is able, for instance, to distinguish three different periods in the history of the treaties of Locarno. Those three periods are characterized by three significant changes in the normative content of the rules, resulting from changes in the political context, although the wording of the rules remained unchanged. The Covenant of the League of Nations as a whole as well as particular provisions, for instance Article 16, were subjected to similar modifications as a result of factual sociological developments and not of legislative changes.

The same phenomenon occurs not only in temporary succession but also under contemporaneous yet different sociological conditions. The identical text of an arbitration treaty or non-aggression pact may have quite different legal meanings, according to the political situation existing between different contracting parties. Even one and the same legal rule, as, for instance, Article 16 of the Covenant, lends itself to different interpretations with respect to nations living under different political conditions.

The positivist doctrine of international law has ignored this particular relationship between the rules of international law and their sociological context. Positivism transplanted schematically the highly refined positivist method of formalist and conceptualist interpretation of municipal law into the domain of international law. This method developed under, and was justified by, the specific domestic conditions of a temporarily stabilized society where there was little tension between law and sociological context but almost complete rationalization and representation of the sociological context within the concepts of positive law. Schematically applied to a law and a society of a distinctly different nature, this method was bound to produce entirely inadequate results. Where the experience of international law showed that an individual situation required an individual interpretation of the legal rule, the positivist method could not fail to disregard all individual aspects of the factual situation and concentrate upon the general wording of the legal rule which, by virtue of its logical self-sufficiency, was supposed to contain all elements necessary for its understanding; and to this the sociological context could contribute nothing. An arbitration treaty which submitted all conflicts between the contracting parties to international tribunals was a legal document that revealed its legal significance through its text, i.e., another step toward the establishment of an international order based upon respect for law. Whether the treaty was concluded between Switzerland and Uruguay, or Denmark, Sweden, and Norway, or Great Britain and France, or Germany and Poland in 1925, 1935, or 1939—these were "political" considerations, irrelevant and lying beyond the scope of positivist interpretation.

3. The positivist doctrine, by recognizing as international law only the rules enforced by states, excludes from the domain of international law all rules whose validity cannot be traced to written official documents. On the other hand, the positivist doctrine cannot deny that such rules, such as many rules of general international law, actually exist. Confronted with the embarrassing dilemma of violating its own statist assumptions or of disregarding an obvious

part of legal experience, the positivist doctrine has taken refuge in a concept which has become a veritable panacea for its theoretical troubles. We are referring to the concept of customary law, which has served for the traditional doctrine of international law as a kind of collective designation for all the rules of international law the origin of which cannot directly be traced to written sources. I have pointed to the insurmountable theoretical difficulties of explaining the existence of a so-called customary law elsewhere,[10] and this is not the place to resume the discussion. It is sufficient to state that the reconciliation which the positivist doctrine is able to establish between its monist, legalistic assumptions and the existence of a so-called customary law is merely apparent. In order to save these assumptions as well as those facts, it resorts to a series of fictions, like tacit consent, recognition, judicial admission, and so forth, which indirectly endeavor to attribute the existence of the so-called customary rules of international law to the legislative will of states.

The fundamental weakness of the positivist doctrine of international law lies in its inadequacy to understand international law as it really is. Unfaithful to its own assumptions, it contains at the same time more and less than the actual rules of international law, which it furthermore submits to subjective evaluation in the light of ethical and political principles of assumedly universal, yet doubtful, validity. A truly scientific theory of international law must avoid these mistakes in order to come closer to reality. It seems to be a logical choice to call such a theory by the name of realist. There are, however, two objections to this choice. On the one hand, the increasing disrepute of the traditional doctrine of international law has led many practitioners of this doctrine to demonstrate their closeness to the reality of international law by calling themselves "realists."[11] This misuse has deprived the term of its distinctive character. On the other hand, realism has become a collective designation for several

---

[10] *La réalité des normes* (Paris: Alcan, 1934), p. 89.

[11] See, for instance, Erich Kaufmann, *Recueil des Cours de l'Académie de la Haye,* LIV (1935), 319, 320; Georges Scelle, *ibid.,* XLVI (1933), 691; Alfred Verdross, *ibid.,* XXX (1929), 277; Louis Le Fur, in *Revue de Droit International,* XVII (1936), 7—authors who have certainly not very much in common besides the claim of being "realists." Cf. also Roscoe Pound, *An Introduction to the Philosophy of Law* (New Haven: Yale University Press, 1937), p. 145, according to whom A. V. Lundstedt calls Pound, Kelsen, and Duguit "realists"!

tendencies in modern jurisprudence, all aiming at replacing, by different means, the fictitious legalism of traditional jurisprudence with a conception nearer to the realities of the law. All these tendencies have this in common: they do not regard the legal rules as definitely determined by their legislative or judicial formulation but search for the psychological, social, political, and economic forces which determine the actual content and operation of legal rules and which, in turn, are determined by them. In other words, their scientific goal is to formulate uniform functional relationships between those forces and the legal rules. Hence, "realist" jurisprudence is, in truth, "functional" jurisprudence.

The legacy which positivism has left to the science of international law consists in the task of comprehending the international law of a given time as standing in a dual functional relationship with the social forces of this time. On the one hand, international law is the function of the civilization in which it originates, that is, of the regulative ideas laid down in the ethics and mores of this civilization, of the political, economic, and general social forces prevailing in it, and, finally, of the specific psychological factors manifesting themselves in the individuals determining it. On the other hand, international law is a social mechanism working toward certain ends within this same civilization which, in turn, becomes a function of this same international law. By systematizing the rules of a given international law in terms of this dual functional relationship between rules and social forces, the functional theory will achieve a real scientific understanding of the legal rules which positivism even at its best was able to describe and systematize only according to superficial legalistic criteria.

Six important consequences for a functional theory of international law can be drawn from this recognition of the functional relationship between social forces and international law.

I. A functional theory of international law must start with the recognition of the particularly intimate nature of this relationship. In the domestic field, legal rules can be imposed by the group which holds the monopoly of organized physical force, that is, the officials of the state. The international sphere is characterized by the absence of such a group. International law owes its existence to identical or complementary interests of nations, backed by power as a last resort or, where such identical interests do not exist, to a balance of power which prevents a nation from breaking these rules of international law. Where there is neither community of interests nor balance of power, there is no international law. Whereas domestic law may originate in the arbitrary will of the lawmaking agencies of the state, international law is usually the result of objective social forces. When, in the international field, an arbitrary lawmaking power tries to impose rules supported neither by common interests nor by a balance of power, these rules never become valid law or gain only ephemeral existence and scant efficacy; the history of some of the rules embodied in the Treaty of Versailles and the Covenant of the League of Nations provides a striking example.

It is also due to this intimate relationship between social forces and legal rules that in the international field fundamental changes of the social forces and, hence, of the legal rules follow each other at frequent intervals and in an abrupt, often violent manner. In the domestic field the regulative social force dominating all others is the state. It has developed not only an overwhelming power apparatus but also highly refined mechanisms of legislative and judicial readjustment, which lead the social forces into certain channels without disrupting the legal and social continuity. The state selects in authoritative decisions the social forces to be recognized by the law. It decides to what extent the existing legal rules shall yield to changing conditions, to what extent they shall resist them, and in what ways they shall try to transform them. In the international field the authoritative decision is replaced by the free interplay of political and military forces. This makes a gradual readjustment of the law to changing social conditions extremely difficult. Any fundamental change of the social forces underlying a system of international law of necessity creates in the prospective beneficiaries of the change the desire to bring about a corresponding change of the legal rules, whereas the beneficiaries of the legal status quo will resist any change of the old order. Here a competitive contest for power will determine the victorious social forces, and the change of the existing legal order will be decided, not through a legal procedure provided for by this same legal order, but through a conflagration of conflicting social forces which challenge the legal order as a whole.

Where such a conflict between social forces and the rules of law exists, the character and function of the whole legal order undergo a transformation. We have proposed to call this relationship by the name of "tension" and have dealt with its legal consequences elsewhere.[12]

II. This recognition of the peculiar relationship between social forces and rules of international law provides the clue for restating, in functional terms, the criteria for the validity of international law. A rule of international law does not, as positivism was prone to believe, receive its validity from its enactment into a legal instrument, such as an international treaty. There are rules of international law which are valid although not enacted in such legal instruments, and there are rules of international law which are not valid although enacted in such instruments. Enactment, therefore, is no objective criterion for the alleged validity of a rule of international law. A rule, be it legal, moral, or conventional, is valid when its violation is likely to be followed by an unfavorable reaction, that is, a sanction against its violator. An alleged rule, the violation of which is not followed by such a sanction, is a mere idea, a wish, a suggestion, but not a valid rule. An alleged rule of international law against the violation of which no state reacts, or is likely to react, is proved, by this very absence of probable reaction, not to be a valid rule of international law. The gradual invalidation of the territorial provisions of the Treaty of Versailles and of most articles of the Covenant of the League of Nations, by violation and non-intervention of sanctions against these violations, provides experimental proof of the correctness of this concept of validity.

How, then, are we to know beforehand when such sanctions are likely to intervene on behalf of a violated norm and when not, and, hence, how can the science of international law determine which norms are valid and which are not? The consideration of the functional factor will give the answer.

1. The commonest and simplest test for the validity of an alleged rule of international law is this: nation A has, in the past, requested

---

[12] On the theory of international "tensions" see Hans J. Morgenthau, *La notion du "politique" et la théorie des différends internationaux* (Paris: Sirey, 1933), pp. 37 ff. This theory has been discussed in detail by Jean Ray, in *Annales sociologiques,* Ser. C, No. 1 (1935), pp. 163 ff. Cf. also Hans J. Morgenthau, *Politics among Nations* (2d ed.; New York: Alfred A. Knopf, 1954), pp. 404 ff.

nation B to perform certain actions corresponding to the rule, and nation B, in turn, has requested nation A to perform certain actions corresponding to the same or another rule. Where these identical or complementary interests in the mutual observance of these rules did not suffice to guarantee the actual observance, both nations were willing to enforce compliance with the rule by protest, reprisal, or military action. Where there was, in the past, a recognized identical or complementary interest in a certain action on the part of two or more nations, together with the willingness to enforce this action, there exists the likelihood that the same sanctions for the sake of the same interests will also be performed in the future. Respect for the status of diplomatic representatives has been, in the past, an interest recognized and guaranteed with sanctions by all nations; therefore, the forecast is justified that nations will follow the same course of action in the future.

The enactment of rules corresponding to such interests in international treaties may indicate the permanent nature of those interests, but this is an assumption which needs support from the facts and which can be disproved by them. Another indication of the permanence of such interests is their sublimation into moral principles, which pretend universal validity and endeavor to give certain interests of exceptional importance a justification superior to that which they could derive from the law.

2. The situation, however, is not always so simple. Three possible situations present themselves for examination.

a) Identical or complementary interests survive the willingness to enforce the actions corresponding to them. The provisions of the treaties of Locarno were the function of identical and complementary interests of the contracting parties. When Germany violated these treaties by remilitarizing the Rhineland, the interests of the signatories in the demilitarization survived their willingness to enforce an attitude corresponding to their interests, and thus the respective rules of international law lost their validity.

b) The willingness to enforce certain actions corresponding to identical or complementary interests survives the interests themselves. From the outset the provisions of the Treaty of Versailles establishing the German-Polish frontier did not correspond to the interests of either nation. These provisions were observed for a period of twenty years because there existed a balance of power between both nations and their respective allies, which prevented either of them from violating the law.

c) The interests and the willingness to enforce the actions corresponding to them disappear altogether. In this category belong the Franco-Russian alliance, the Pact of the Little Entente, the political provisions of the Covenant of the League of Nations, and numerous provisions of the peace treaties of 1919.

What does the analysis of these cases show with regard to the validity of international law? In the cases (*a*) and (*c*) the rules of international law become invalid according to the functional concept of validity because no longer does there exist a likelihood of sanctions being performed, should those rules be violated. In case (*b*) the validity of the rules depends upon a balance of power, which may be stable for a certain time and then suddenly become unstable. All cases have this in common: they make forecasts as to the likelihood of sanctions extremely uncertain. The enactment of the rules in international treaties is here of no avail and, as our examples have shown, is rather misleading. Their conformity with moral principles is scarcely more illuminating because of the difficulty mentioned above of ascertaining the exact content of such principles.

Where the functional relationship between social forces and international law is in a state of transition from (1) to one of the situations under (2) the development may stop at an intermediate point between (1), on the one hand, and (2*a*) and (*c*), on the other; proceed to (2*b*); or, finally, come to an end at (2*a*) or (*c*). Here, the validity of the respective rules of international law is, so to speak, in suspense and may be either maintained or destroyed. With respect to such rules the science of international law becomes a system of guesses, enjoying a greater or lesser chance of being proved true according to the factual development of the functional relationship between the social forces and the rules of international law.

III. It follows from this analysis that there exist two obviously different types of international law, one founded upon permanent and stable interests, the other based upon the temporary and fluctuating interests of nations. This differentiation is not only of fundamental importance for the understanding of the validity of international law; it leads to still more far-reaching consequences as to the subject matter, the methods, and the scientific character of the science of international law. One might even say that it leads to the recognition of two different sciences of international law which deal with different subject matters and require different methods of research and systematization.

The main bulk of the concepts and principles of international law has been derived from municipal civil law. These concepts and principles have been developed within a legal system characterized by the extraordinary stability of the interests underlying it. Hence, its application is, of necessity, restricted to legal systems based upon equally stable interests. In the international field such stable interests exist, for instance, with respect to diplomatic privileges, territorial jurisdiction, extradition, wide fields of maritime law, arbitral procedure, and so forth. This is the classical field of traditional international law as it has gradually developed in the practice of nations since the sixteenth century. We propose to call these rules non-political international law, originating in the permanent interests of nations to put their normal relations upon a stable basis by providing for predictable and enforcible conduct with respect to these relations.

But there is another type of international law which expresses, in terms of rights and duties, temporary interests ever given to change. In this category belong political agreements, especially treaties of alliance and their modern substitutes, which, under the legalistic disguise of treaties of general arbitration, consultation, or friendship, frequently pursue aims at least preparatory to close political ties. The traditional science of international law treats both types of international law alike, applying to both the concepts and methods developed in municipal civil law. By doing so, it cannot but draw a completely distorted picture of those rules which belong in the category of political international law. Under such treatment, their validity appears to be firmly established, whereas it is actually always precarious; the interests which they are supposed to serve appear to be permanent and definite, whereas they are actually exposed to continuous change and tend to be uncertain; and consequently, the rights and duties established by them appear to be clearly determined, whereas they are actually subject to the most contradictory interpretations.

This writer knows of only one monograph dealing with political international law as an independent subject matter requiring concepts and methods of its own: Rafael Erich's *Alliances and Alliance Treaties*.[13] He is aware of only one systematic treatise clearly stating the functional relationship between the political rules of international law and the underlying social factors: Charles de Visscher's *Theory and Practice in Public International Law*.[14] Only one judicial opinion clearly points to the practical consequences of this relationship: Judge Anzilotti's dissenting opinion in the Austro-German Customs Union case.[15] It remains for a functional theory of international law to develop systematically concepts and methods capable of conveying the legal characteristics, as well as the functional dependence on political factors, of political international law.

IV. As we have seen, there exist functional relationships not only between the law and the non-normative social forces, but also between the law and the other branches of the normative sphere, that is, ethics and mores. The latter are threefold with regard to the validity and the content of the rules of law.

As has been shown elsewhere,[16] the validity of any legal system reposes upon a fundamental norm which itself cannot be of a legal nature but belongs of necessity to the domain of ethics and mores. Thus, the validity of the legal system of the United States reposes, on the one hand, upon an ethical rule enjoining the President, the members of Congress and of the Supreme Court to obey the Constitution, and, on the other hand, upon the mores keeping alive among the citizens the respect for the Constitution. When one or the other of these ethical foundations is lacking, the validity of the Constitution and of the legal system founded upon it is in a precari-

[13] In German, Helsingfors, 1907.

[14] Princeton: Princeton University Press, 1957.

[15] As to the defectiveness of the majority decision from the functional standpoint, see Hudson, "The World Court and the Austro-German Customs Régime," *American Bar Association Journal*, XVII (1931), 793: "In our national courts, a refusal to take account of the social and political conditions to which law must be applied, has produced some of the sharpest criticism of our legal systems. . . . An international court might similarly build a law in disregard of the political factors which condition its application, but it would almost certainly lack both the appearance and the substance of reality."

[16] *La réalité des normes,* pp. 76 ff., 174 ff., 216 ff.

ous state. When both are lacking, the Constitution, and with it the whole legal system, have ceased to exist as a living legal order even though they may not have been formally invalidated.

Not only does the validity of the legal system as a whole repose upon ethics and mores, but the validity of individual legal rules also stands frequently in a particular functional relationship with ethics and mores. The validity of one and the same precept, for instance, "Thou shall not kill," may repose upon the likelihood that against its violation there will intervene sanctions pertaining to the domains of ethics and mores as well as of law. Many provisions of the Constitution, of civil and criminal law, belong to this category and, therefore, are at the same time legal rules, ethical rules, and rules of the mores. It is obvious that this double or triple guaranty has an important bearing upon the observance and validity of a given precept. When such a multiple guaranty exists, that is, when ethics, mores, and law co-operate to realize a certain order of things, there is a much greater likelihood that this order will be realized than when the law alone seeks it.

It has already been pointed out that legal rules receive their precepts partly from ethics and mores. The meaning of these precepts requires explanation in the light of these other rules from which it is derived. The Constitution itself, for instance, does not reveal what "due process of law" or "freedom of contract" is; it is only by reference to the ethics and mores of a certain period of constitutional history that the meaning of these constitutional concepts can be determined. The moral order gives the law the standards on the basis of which its agents and subjects can distinguish between right and wrong. Implicit in any legal order is a system of moral standards according to which the law distinguishes between actions which it approves, actions which it disapproves, and actions with regard to which it is indifferent. These moral standards guide the judicial and executive agents of the law in interpreting and applying it. They relate the legal order directly to the moral convictions of the individual. It is from the conformity of those moral standards with these moral convictions that the particular legal rules receive their concrete meaning for the individual and their normative function for society.

The recognition, for international law, of these three fundamental relationships, calls for the discussion of a series of problems which the traditional science of international law does not even care to pose. What is, for instance, the empirical nature of the dual relationship between international law, on the one hand, and ethics and mores on the other? Are there ethics and mores of a truly international nature, or do we call by the name of "international" ethics and mores the precepts of which have been developed under the determining influence of the individual nations and are applied to international affairs in the interest of these nations? Which rules of international law belong at the same time to ethics and mores and so have a greater chance of being observed? The content of which rules of international law can be determined only by reference to ethics and mores, and to what kind of ethics and mores do these rules refer?

V. It follows from the preceding discussion that no branch of the traditional science of international law is more in need of reform than the doctrine of interpretation. The traditional doctrine has limited its efforts to transferring schematically the time-honored common and Roman law principles of interpretation to the international field. It has discussed the problem whether the wording of a treaty or the intentions of the parties shall be the main source of interpretation; it has gone deeply into the question whether preparatory materials may be used for purposes of interpretation; and it has advanced a great variety of so-called rules of construction. Yet it has completely overlooked the fact that, because of the peculiar relationship between social forces and rules of international law, the problem of interpretation in the international field shows unique aspects for which the traditional civil law technique of interpretation is utterly inadequate.

When in the domestic field the meaning of a contract is ascertained by the usual means of interpretation, the interpretative job is done. It is generally not too difficult to perform the same task with regard to an international treaty; but then the real problem of interpretation just begins. A contract of civil law generally uses standardized language whose legal meaning is definite or at least can be ascertained according to objective, universally recognized standards. On the other hand, the real meaning of an international treaty may be disguised with diplomatic language so that its wording is indicative only of what it does not mean. Under such circumstances, it is only from the social context that this treaty will receive its meaning. The political situation of the parties and their intentions with respect to this situation have to be ascertained in view of the subject matter of the treaty, for the time of the conclusion of the treaty as well as for the time of interpretation; for, as we have seen, the legal meaning of an international treaty is ever subject to change. From this analysis one may then conclude, in a laborious and always highly uncertain manner, what might be the probable objective of the treaty and the legal meaning of the particular stipulations serving this purpose.

What, for instance, does the term "independence" in an international treaty mean? Its meaning may coincide with the accepted meaning of the term, it may be somewhat different, it may be the exact opposite, or it may have no legal meaning at all. The rules of construction will not answer that question. It is only from the background of the social context and of the function the treaty is supposed to fulfil within it that a scientific interpretation can hope, at least within certain limits, to receive a satisfactory answer. The answer will, for instance, vary according to whether the nation to which the term applies is a colonial, semicolonial, or non-colonial country; whether the treaty is concluded between two nations of equal or different political power; whether or not, in the last case, the more powerful nation has imperialistic intentions with respect to the other party; whether the treaty is of a bilateral nature, pursuing a specific political aim, or is supported by the consensus of a great number of nations for the sake of a general purpose common to all of them.

VI. To fulfil its task, a functional theory of international law must take another step beyond positivism. Positivism assumed that it was more scientific than any previous attempt at understanding. Positivist science was supposed to be free from all metaphysical elements, not asking how things ought to be and what their "real" essence might be, but seeking only uniform relations between things verifiable in experience. "Je ne propose rien, je ne suppose rien, j'expose," was Comte's credo. But just as Comte ended in the metaphysics of his "religion of humanity," so legal positivism was not satisfied with knowing what the law actually was and how it worked. It was only too eager to remodel the world of the law after idealistic assumptions whose universal validity the respective authors took for granted. This tend-

305

ency, variously strong in the different branches of municipal law, is uppermost in the positivist doctrine of international law. The science of international law, completely absorbed by practical problems of what the rules of international law should be, paid almost no attention to the psychological and sociological laws governing the actions of men in the international sphere or to the possible legal rules growing out of such actions. Whoever would dare embark upon such research would be called "impractical," and the results of his studies, if ever mentioned at all, would be qualified as "worthless." Grandiose legalistic schemes purporting to solve the ills of the world replaced the less spectacular, painstaking search for the actual laws and the facts underlying them. This presumptuous enterprise has contributed nothing to the improvement of international relations, let alone the knowledge of what these international relations actually are. It has only shown the utter futility of all attempts to reform human conditions on the basis of idealistic assumptions without knowing the laws under which these conditions stand. As William Graham Sumner put it:

In this view, the worst vice in political discussions is that dogmatism which takes its stand on "great principles" or assumptions, instead of standing on an exact examination of things as they are and human nature as it is. . . . The social sciences are, as yet, the stronghold of all this pernicious dogmatism; and nowhere does it do more harm than in politics. The whole method of abstract speculation on political topics is vicious. It is popular because it is easy; it is easier to imagine a new world than to learn to know this one; it is easier to embark on speculations based on a few broad assumptions than it is to study the history of states and institutions; it is easier to catch up a popular dogma than it is to analyze it to see whether it is true or not. All this leads to confusion, to the admission of phrases and platitudes, to much disputing but little gain in the prosperity of nations.[17]

"The eagerness for premature practical application," to express the same thought in the words of Vilfredo Pareto, ". . . is ever obstructing the progress of science, along with a mania for preaching to people as to what they ought to do—an exceedingly bootless occupation—instead of finding out what they actually do."[18]

[17] *The Challenge of Facts and Other Essays* (New Haven: Yale University Press, 1914), pp. 245–46.

[18] *The Mind and Society* (New York: Harcourt, Brace & Co., 1935), II, 185.

Why, then, is it that the field within which the social sciences are able to work successfully is much narrower than the corresponding field of the natural sciences? It is again Sumner who knows the answer to this question. "The reason is because the elements of any sort of problem which we do not know so far surpass in number and importance those which we do know that our solutions have far greater chance to be wrong than to be right."[19] Thus the problem which the science of international law has to solve is clearly posed. The natural sciences had to discover the laws governing nature before they could hope to dominate the forces of nature, to prevent the dangers emanating from them, and to use them for human goals. In the same way, the social sciences cannot hope to master the forces of society unless they know the laws which govern the social relations of men. In the natural sciences, the discovery of the infinitesimal calculus by Newton and Leibniz was bound to precede modern technical inventions. The millennial attempts at constructing the airplane could not succeed as long as Carnot had not established his purely theoretical propositions on thermodynamics. Were it not for the theoretical efforts of Faraday, who himself did not invent anything of practical value, there would not be today any of the multiple uses of electricity for practical purposes. Had not Maxwell and Hertz, without any practical objective, carried out certain "abstruse and remote" calculations in the field of magnetism and electricity, Marconi could never have invented the radio.

The science of international law and the social sciences in general are still awaiting their Newton, their Leibniz, their Faraday, their Carnot, their Maxwell, and their Hertz. In all likelihood, they are waiting in vain.[20] In any event, to expect the contemporary lawyer to be an "engineer" or "technician" of the law means to expect Edison before Faraday, Wright before Carnot, Marconi before Maxwell and Hertz. And this is certainly a futile expectation.

[19] *Op. cit.,* p. 219.

[20] For the reasons, see *Scientific Man vs. Power Politics* (Chicago: University of Chicago Press, 1946).

PART IV

THE AUTONOMY

OF POLITICAL

ACTION

Political action is beset by three dilemmas. One threatens its autonomy by substituting for its own proper rules those appropriate to other spheres of action. The other threatens its integrity by corrupting its rules in the service of alien ends. The third dilemma threatens failure through the mistaken choice of means and ends. The first dilemma, one might say, is intellectual in nature, while the second is a moral one; the third dilemma raises the issue of practical statecraft. In view of the theoretical compass of this book, we shall concern ourselves here only with the first two of these dilemmas.

The first dilemma, which raises the issue of the autonomy of the political sphere, grows from a general quality of our culture: the tendency to escape from the facts of political life, which bear the indelible and ubiquitous mark of the aspirations and the struggle for power. The escapist from politics seeks refuge in a realm of thought and action that allows him to think and act as though the facts of political life either did not exist at all or, at the very least, could be discarded by an act of will. The escapist from politics lacks respect for the existential qualities of political life. He refuses to acknowledge that the facts of politics are the children of necessity, not the bastards of some psychological or sociological aberration.

Yet the facts of politics are no more misconstrued and disregarded with impunity than are the facts of physics. Both take vengeance on their violators. The vengeance of the facts of physics is stark, swift, and unequivocal; but that of the facts of politics is often circuitous and ambiguous and may be recognized only by reflective hindsight. Violate the law of gravity, and the consequences will be clear for all to see. Violate the rules of the balance of power, and the consequences are likely to be obscure, at least to the contemporaries. The observance of the laws of nature is vouchsafed by man's instinct for self-preservation. The violation of the rules of politics does not as simply call forth their observance because the human mind does not as instinctively connect the untoward consequences with the violation of the rules.

The mind of Western man, in particular, doubts the very existence of those rules and their ineluctability. In consequence, confronted with a crisis in his political affairs, he tends to search not for the principles of right political action but for non-political substitutes. He tends to think about politics in non-political, e.g., moralistic, legalistic, militaristic, or economic, terms. He finds himself ever more deeply involved in the self-created dilemma between the requirements of right political action and his non-political preconceptions of what politics is all about, and, as long as these preconceptions persist, each political failure calls forth yet another non-political remedy only to join its predecessors in failure.

20 *The Escape from Power*

The refusal of our civilization to recognize the facts of political life is nowhere more strikingly formulated than in the first sentence of the first chapter of Rousseau's *Social Contract:* "Man is born free, but everywhere he is in chains." This statement expresses a persistent conviction of Western political thought, and its correctness has not often been questioned. It is, however, one of the most erroneous and distorting statements one can make about the facts of political life. The historian Émile Faguet has very well pointed to the logical weakness of this statement by explaining through the same kind of argument the nature of cows. "All cows," he said, "are born carnivorous, and everywhere they live on herbs." The absurdity of the statement as applied to cows is obvious. The absurdity of the same type of reasoning as applied to humans is less obvious, but not less real; for it is impossible to distinguish empirically between the status in which a man is born and the status in which he lives.

Yet this erroneous statement has had very important consequences for the understanding of the realities of political life; for it has made it appear that the normal and natural state of man is freedom and that his living in chains, his living in political servitude, is only an accident, something that can be remedied and abolished by a political mechanism or a legislative device or a social reform or an economic artifact.

Any realistic conception of politics must start with an assumption which is the exact opposite of Rousseau's. It must assume that man is born and lives in chains. He is the object of political domination, and the fact that points to his freedom is not an empirical fact, is not a condition of his existence, but is a condition of his moral life. In other words, freedom is a condition not of his empirical existence but of his moral existence. Man lives in chains, but everywhere he wants to be free. He revolts against the empirical fact of political domination, and he wants to escape those chains which bind him in servitude.

This is, however, not the whole story; for man living in chains not

From Lyman Bryson *et al.* (eds.), *Conflicts of Power in Modern Culture* (1947).

only wants to be free but also wants to be master. In other words, man's aspiration for power is not an accident of history; it is not a temporary deviation from a normal state of freedom; it is an all-permeating fact which is of the very essence of human existence. So we find, when we look at the facts of political life as they really are, that man lives in chains, but everywhere he wants to be a master.

This conception of man as a political being differs indeed fundamentally from the optimistic and superficial philosophy by which, in imitation of Rousseau and others, the nineteenth and twentieth centuries have conceived political life. They tried to escape the recognition of political domination and of the aspiration for power as ubiquitous facts by four fundamental devices: scientism, the dual moral standard, perfectionism, and totalitarianism. Most, if not all, of these devices are children of the nineteenth century. One of them, perfectionism, has an older history, but the other three have their roots, if not their flowering, in the intellectual movements of the nineteenth century.

What is scientism? It is the belief that the problems of social life are in essence similar to the problems of physical nature and that, in the same way in which one can understand the laws of nature and, by using this knowledge, dominate nature and harness it to one's own ends, one can understand the facts of society and, through this knowledge, create a gigantic social mechanism which is at the command of the scientific master.

However, three basic distinctions between the social and the physical world defeat this scientist conception of society. First of all, in the natural world we deal primarily with typical situations and typical phenomena as such. In the social world we deal primarily with individual events and individual phenomena as such. Furthermore, the social scientist is not a detached observer of social events as the natural scientist is a detached observer of the phenomena of nature. A physicist or chemist who investigates the qualities of uranium does so regardless of the religious, moral, political, social, or economic stake he may have in the result of his investigations. The political scientist or economist who investigates, say, a labor problem is of necessity determined in his outlook and in his methods and in the results at which he arrives by his personal involvement in the problem. Finally, the natural sciences deal with lifeless matter, and even where they deal with human beings or living matter they deal with them as some sort of mechanism. They do not deal with man as a rational being or a moral person. On the other hand, the social scientist deals with human beings as such, with the particularly human quality of human beings which is their rational and moral character. It is for these three reasons that the analogy between the natural and the social sciences falls to the ground.

Furthermore, scientism holds to the belief that political conflicts and political problems can be solved scientifically in the same way in which the problems of nature can be solved scientifically. The existence of political problems, of political conflict, of war, and of revolution, is assumed to be primarily the result of lack of knowledge, of lack of skill in the handling of social and political situations. Here, we are again in the presence of the idea, which we found underlying the first sentence of the first chapter of Rousseau's *Social Contract*, that the political phenomenon is a kind of accident, a kind of temporary deviation from the rule of reason which ought to dominate the life of man.

Actually, political problems grow out of certain conflicts of interests, certain basic antagonisms which no amount of knowledge can eliminate as such. Knowledge and political skill may solve these problems peacefully, but there is no scientific device that can solve the problems of war, of labor, of freedom, of authority in the same way in which the problem of, say, the air-cooled engine has been solved.

The problem of the air-cooled engine was solved when the scientists dealing with it found the formula by virtue of which the air-cooled engine could be constructed, and, once the formula was found, the natural scientists could, as it were, forget about the problem of the air-cooled engine and direct their attention to other problems. Political problems are not of this kind; they cannot be solved by the invention of a mechanical formula which will allow mankind to forget about them and turn its attention toward a not-yet-solved political problem. Being projections of human nature into society, they cannot be solved at all. They can only be restated, manipulated, and transformed, and each epoch has to come to terms with them anew.

The ideal of scientism as applied to politics is the disappearance of politics altogether. Scientism assumes that the abolition of politics can and will usher in an ideal state of society. The political philosophy of Marxism, for instance, is inspired by the belief, typical of scientism, that political domination and war are the outgrowth of a single cause, in this case of a particular economic system, and that with the disappearance of that system war and political domination will of themselves disappear. The main idea of scientism is clearly recognizable here: one needs only to use the right formula, to apply the right mechanical device, and the political domination of man by man and the violent clashes of human collectivities will disappear as temporary aberrations from the rule of co-operation and of reason.

The second attempt at escaping from the facts of political life we find in the idea of the dual standard of morality. This idea assumes that politics cannot perhaps be eliminated completely from human life but that it can be, as it were, quarantined. It can be relegated to a certain corner where certain bad principles of ethics apply, whereas the great majority of mankind will continue to live according to the good rules of ethics. In other words, there exists a dual standard of morality, one applicable to the political sphere and to the politicians, and another applicable to the rest of mankind. It is this dual standard of morality that was strikingly formulated by the greatest Italian statesman of modern times, Cavour, when he said: "If we had done for ourselves what we have done for Italy, what scoundrels we would have been."

But political domination and the lust for power cannot be limited to a particular segment of humanity which, because of its profession, is unable to comply with the generally applicable, respectable rules of ethics. This lust for power and this fact of political domination are universal experiences of mankind. In politics, it is true, they find their most extreme, violent, and brutal manifestations, but they are to be found wherever men live together in social groups, and that is everywhere. They are everywhere, hidden behind ideologies, disguised by the conventions of the good society. Hence, the idea of the dual standard of morality is another form of escapism from the brutal facts of political life and the ubiquitous lust for power.

The third type of escapism from these facts is perfectionism. Perfectionism recognizes the facts of political life as they exist. The perfectionist, however, believes that, by a sheer act of will on the part of the individual either through social reform or education or moral exhortation, man can be changed and can be made to abandon the evils of politics and the lust for power out of which those evils grow. The political philosophy of Woodrow Wilson provides the classical example of perfectionist escapism. Political domination and power politics with all the liabilities they impose on man, with all the evils they create, are the outgrowth of certain wicked political systems, such as autocracy or monarchy. Once democracy, brought to all countries of the earth either by force of arms or preferably by education and exhortation, has been universally accepted, the evils of politics will have been made an end to, and reason will rule over domestic and international society.

The contemporary advocacy of world government contains an element of perfectionist escapism. Actually, even if it were possible to establish world government tomorrow, the facts of political life would still be with us. The same problems growing out of the lust for power, the same conflicts resulting from the competition for power, the same mastery of one man over the other, and the revolt of the others against the mastery of one, the same basic fact that man is born in chains and everywhere wants to be master—these would still remain the elemental experiences of political life, even if world government were established.

The technological conditions and potentialities of the age have indeed made world government a rational necessity, but they have not made it a panacea for the evils and liabilities of politics. World government as such cannot resolve, for instance, the conflict between the Soviet Union and the United States by peaceful means. Regardless of constitutional changes on the international scene, this problem will continue to exist as it exists today, and, hence, the question of war or peace will continue to demand an answer. The answer to this question, under present world conditions, does not lie in world government but in facing squarely concrete problems which, if they are not solved peacefully, could lead to war—concrete problems such as American security as against Russian security, the unification of Germany, peace in the Middle East.

These problems are not to be solved by world government, any more than the problem of slavery was solved by the establishment of the government of the United States. A civil war, which after all is also a war, against the established government had to be fought in order to solve at least superficially the problem of slavery. Since the political problem was not solved when the government was established, it continued to pose itself, demanding a solution, and the lack of a solution led to the same disastrous results it would have led to if the government had not existed. The same would be true of world government. If the political problems separating the Soviet Union from the United States cannot be solved peacefully on their own terms, that is, by political means, world government would not save the world from the next war. The next war would, then, be a civil instead of a world war, and it would be only a matter of terminology whether Western civilization would perish in the course of the one instead of the other.

Western civilization has resorted during the past one hundred and fifty years to many other perfectionist devices in order to escape the facts of political life. For instance, men like Proudhon, Cobden, and Bright saw in free trade the one mechanism, the one political and economic reform, that would enable man to escape the fate that has been with him from the beginning of history. In its nature the escapism of free trade is not different from the escapism of world government or of the United Nations or of disarmament or of other mechanical devices whereby since the First World War men have tried to escape the combination of modern technology and the lust for power, which threatens to engulf and destroy them.

The fourth type of escapism we call totalitarianism, meaning by totalitarianism not merely the particular historic phenomenon which occurred in the twenties and thirties in Italy and in the thirties in Germany and after 1917 in Russia but a state of mind which is the exact opposite of perfectionism. Whereas perfectionism creates an abstract ideal to which it tries to elevate political life through force or exhortation or reform, totalitarianism, that is, the totalitarian state of mind, identifies the ideal with the facts of political life. What is, is good because it is, and power is to the totalitarian not only a fact of social life with which one must come to terms but also the ultimate standard for judging human affairs and the ideal source of all human values. He says "Yes" to his lust for power, and he recognizes no transcendent standard, no spiritual concept which might tame and restrain the lust for power by confronting it with an ideal alien and hostile to political domination.

So the gap between the political ideal and political reality, which perfectionism tries to resolve in favor of the ideal by elevating political reality to the level of the ideal, totalitarianism also tries to eliminate but by the opposite procedure, that is, by tearing the ideal down to the level of the brutal facts of political life. The excesses of power politics, the barbarities and evil propensities of the Bolshevist and Nazi regimes are foreordained in this identification of the realities of political life with the ideal of human life as such.

The totalitarian state of mind is a universal phenomenon. In its Fascist manifestation, it has lost its empires but won many souls. The Western democracies have widely accepted the Fascist standards without knowing it.

They, too, tend to equate and identify political success with moral superiority, thus seeking to eliminate the gap between the moral ideal and the facts of political life. They, too, try to resolve the tension between the two in favor of the political facts. This is perhaps the most dangerous manifestation of political escapism; for, while here the political facts as facts are recognized, their moral significance is obscured. Power is glorified as the source of all material and moral good, and those transcendent concepts by which power must be tamed, restrained, and transformed are denied an independent existence.

21 *The Moral Dilemma of Political Action*

On the plane of political action, the most common escape, especially in the United States, from the autonomy of politics has taken the form of moralism, that is, the substitution of what is popularly believed to be moral principles for the rules of politics. In the domestic sphere, the opportunities for the consistent substitution of moralism for politics are limited; for here failure, swift and obvious, is the punishment for violating the political rules. The situation is different in the international sphere; for success and failure in foreign policy are ambiguous terms, and the causal nexus between them and the actions seemingly leading up to them is often hard to establish. Since it is not always obvious what constitutes failure and what is responsible for it, false doctrines and practices have here a good chance to survive failure. Thus it is not by accident that foreign policy has provided the main opportunity for the moralistic attack upon the autonomy of the political sphere.

Dominant elements in Western culture, and American culture in particular, have consistently misunderstood the nature of foreign policy, and they have done so in the name of morality. In the process, our culture has deformed its understanding of morality and corrupted its moral judgment as well. It has imagined that the tension between foreign policy and morality, given in immediate experience, could easily be made to disappear in one of two ways. Either there could be a kind of reconciliation, a compromise by which foreign policy would be made moral, at least up to the point of non-violence and harmonious co-operation, and the moral law would be adapted to the exigencies of politics; perhaps there might even be two different kinds of moral law, one for man as such and as citizen of his nation and one for the relations among nations. Or else men would have a choice between power politics, morally bad, and another kind of foreign policy not tainted with the lust for power. In any event, there was presumed to be a way out of the dilemma with which the demands of foreign policy appear to confront the moral conscience.

From the *Year Book of World Affairs*, 1951; *American Perspective*, Winter, 1950; and the Introduction to Ernest Lefever's *Ethics and United States Foreign Policy* (1957).

The truth is that there is no way out. The moral dilemma of foreign policy is but a special and—it is true—particularly flagrant case of the moral dilemma which faces man on all levels of social action. Man cannot help sinning when he acts in relation to his fellow men; he may be able to minimize that sinfulness of social action, but he cannot escape it. For no social action can be completely free of the taint of egotism which, as selfishness, pride, or self-deception, seeks for the actor more than is his due. What is true of all social action is particularly true of political action and, within the latter, of foreign policy. For man's aspiration for power over other men, which is of the very essence of politics, implies the denial of what is the very core of Judeo-Christian morality—respect for man as an end in himself. The power relation is the very denial of that respect; for it seeks to use man as means to the end of another man. This denial is particularly flagrant in foreign policy; for the civilizing influences of law, morality, and mores are less effective here than they are on the domestic political scene.

How was it possible for our culture to misunderstand this moral dilemma of foreign policy and, turning its gaze from it, try to smooth and gloss over the conflict, thus doing justice neither to the responsibilities of foreign policy nor to the majesty of the moral law? This escape from both power politics and true morality stems in the main from three factors: man's ambivalent relationship to power and morality, the illusions of nineteenth-century liberalism, and the misunderstanding of the American experience.

The objective position of man on the political scene is always and of necessity ambivalent. While he seeks power over others, others seek power over him. His intellectual and moral attitudes toward power reflect this ambivalence of his objective position. While he takes the power drives of others for what they are or worse, he will close his eyes to his own aspirations for power, which appear to him as something different and nobler—justified by necessity and ethics —than they actually are. Thus ideological concealments, rationalizations, and justifications of necessity blind us both to the ubiquity and the moral deficiency of the aspiration for power. As John Adams put it:

Power always thinks it has a great soul and vast views beyond the comprehension of the weak and that it is doing God's service when it is violating all His laws. Our passions, ambitions, avarice, love and resentment, etc., possess so much metaphysical subtlety and so much overpowering eloquence that they insinuate themselves into the understanding and the conscience and convert both to their party.

Two historic experiences strengthened this ideological misunderstanding and depreciation of power. One was the experience of the Victorian age, as interpreted by liberal philosophy; the other, the experience of the first century of American history, as interpreted by a humanitarian, pacifist philosophy. To both, the struggle for power, especially on the international scene, appeared as the passing product of an ephemeral historic configuration. The liberals identified power politics with the rule of the aristocracy, a historic accident bound to disappear with the disappearance of autocratic government and its manifestations, such as trade barriers and colonialism.

The American experience seemed to provide experimental proof for the assumption that nations have a choice between power politics and a foreign policy not tainted by the lust for power. The Founding Fathers decided that the United States could not afford to get involved in the power politics of the European nations. Yet, to quote Washington, "The toils of European ambition, rivalship, interest, humor, or caprice," with which the United States should have nothing to do, were the only manifestations of power politics before the eyes of America. Abstention from European power politics could, therefore, be taken to mean abstention from power politics as such. This aloofness from European power politics remained a political fact at least until the end of the nineteenth century, if not until the intervention of the United States in the First World War in 1917. While in fact this isolation was the result of a complicated interplay of political and military forces, it was interpreted primarily, if not exclusively, as the result of a deliberate choice. The United States had turned her back on power politics and was applying to her foreign relations the same humanitarian principles of human betterment and peaceful competition which had worked so well at home and had made her both unique and great as a nation among nations.

The experiences of two world wars and of the aftermath of the Second have disabused many of us of these illusions. We have learned that we cannot escape the temptation and liabilities of power politics by an act of will. We must learn to live with them and still remain civilized; that is, we must make the best of them. Yet even at best, we cannot afford to forget that they are ever with us. These historic experiences have reawakened both our understanding of politics and our moral sensibilities. We have begun to resurrect from the rubble of false philosophies which did not stand the test of experience the great perennial truths about politics and morality of which Western civilization is the record. In this task political thinkers and theologians have joined. And it reveals as much about the nature of religious thought as about politics that many of the most important modern insights about politics have come from the pens of theologians.

Yet the illusions of the past are still with us. In *Speaking Frankly*, the account of his tenure as Secretary of State, Mr. James F. Byrnes reports an episode which occurred at the Paris Peace Conference in 1946:

> After a heated session in Paris one afternoon, Chip Bohlen [then adviser to the American delegation] remained behind talking to a member of the Soviet delegation. The Soviet representative said it was impossible for him to understand the Americans. They had a reputation for being good traders and yet Secretary Byrnes for two days had been making speeches about principles—talking, he said, like a professor.
>
> "Why doesn't he stop this talk about principles, and get down to business and start trading?" the Soviet representative asked Chip in all sincerity.
>
> Chip attempted most unsuccessfully to explain that there were some questions which, in the opinion of Americans, involved principle and could not be settled by bargaining.[1]

This episode is significant not only for the pathetically honest lack of understanding between East and West that it reveals but more particularly for the light it sheds upon two diametrically opposed conceptions of foreign policy. On the one side, there is the political realist, the Machiavellian bargainer, who conceives of foreign policy exclusively in terms of power and for whom the end of power justifies all—or almost all—means employed; on the other side, there is the moralist, "talking like a professor"—or should one rather say "like a preacher"?—whose ability to bargain is strictly circumscribed, both in width and in depth, by his insistence upon principles which must be reflected in the bargain but cannot be made its object.

[1] (New York: Harper & Bros., 1947), pp. 280–81.

It is as tempting as it would be false to conceive of the opposition between these two schools of foreign policy as yet another example of the struggle between good and evil, between a noble and benevolent philosophy and practice of politics and a base and nefarious one. Such juxtapositions are tempting, for they fit quite naturally into the black-white pattern in which the struggle between East and West presents itself to the popular mind. Yet they are false just the same. They are false not only because any black-white pattern, conceived in moral and intellectual terms, is by definition inadequate to do justice to a political situation in which on either side good and evil, wisdom and error, are inextricably blended and intertwined. They are false also, and primarily, because what in Mr. Byrnes's episode is presented by implication as a typical expression of Russian realism, or Bolshevist lack of principle, or Soviet amoralism, can in fact look back on a respectable ancestry in the Western practice of foreign policy.

That member of the Soviet delegation, if he had known it and if he had dared to, might well have reminded Mr. Bohlen of Richelieu and Mazarin, of Cromwell and the two Pitts, of Hamilton and Jefferson the statesman, of Castlereagh and Canning, of Cavour, Disraeli, and Bismarck. And Mr. Bohlen, in turn, might have summoned to Mr. Byrnes's defense the shades of Fox and Burke, of Madison and Jefferson the philosopher, of Gladstone and Wilson. If they had felt in need of living witnesses, the Russian might have cited Winston Churchill; the American, Cordell Hull. In one word, then, what stood between the United States and the Soviet representatives in Paris in 1946 was the issue of moral principles versus the reason of state—the issue which Machiavelli had raised into the full consciousness of the Western world and which since then has never ceased to trouble its conscience and to transform into problems those acts of politics which in pre-Machiavellian times had been performed as a matter of course.

It is one of the glories of the political tradition of the English-speaking peoples, unrivaled in any other civilization, that their political theory, as their law, has in the main been developed not in comprehensive systematic efforts but in a series of debates concerned with the practical merits of limited, concrete issues. Three factors have fortuitously co-operated in making the political theory of the

English tongue a succession of "cases" debated in the forum of public opinion: an empirical bent of mind, aiming at immediate practical results rather than theoretical consistency; the ability to see in the concrete issue the particular instance of a general proposition rather than empirical proof for a priori abstractions; and, finally, the institution of public debate which is supposed to determine the decision in view of the rational merits of the case. Thus it has come about that while the issue of reason of state versus moral principles has on the Continent been fought out in the philosophic polemics of the Machiavellians and the anti-Machiavellians, leaving the issue in the end where they found it, in the English-speaking world the issue was always settled, at least for the moment; for, rising as it did from a concrete situation which demanded a decision, it had to be decided one way or the other. That decision, it is true, was, like the decision of the judge, only provisional and decided the issue only within the narrow confines of the situation within which it had arisen. It never purported to offer an abstract proposition settling the issue once and for all. It lacked in generality what it possessed in definiteness.

Thus it follows from the way the English-speaking peoples think in political matters that their political thought must be distilled from the debates through which the political issues of the day were settled. The problem that confronts us here has troubled the thought and life of the Anglo-American world before. To understand its nature and to assess its bearing upon the political issues of our day, the debates on great issues of the past can give us guidance. The problem has perhaps nowhere been stated with greater elemental simplicity, undiluted by side issues and undisguised by ideological rationalizations, than in the debate between Disraeli and Gladstone on the occasion of the "Bulgarian Atrocities." Disraeli made the case for the national interest in his speech in the House of Lords of July 18, 1878, on his return from the Congress of Berlin:

> But I must make this observation to your lordships. We have a substantial interest in the East; it is a commanding interest, and its behest must be obeyed. But the interest of France in Egypt, and her interest in Syria, are, as she acknowledges, sentimental and traditionary interests; and, although I respect them, and although I wish to see in Lebanon and Egypt the influence of France fairly and justly maintained, and although her officers and ours in that part of the world—and especially in Egypt—are acting together with confidence and trust, we must remember that our connection

with the East is not merely an affair of sentiment and tradition, but that we have urgent and substantial and enormous interests which we must guard and keep. Therefore, when we find that the progress of Russia is a progress which, whatever my be the intentions of Russia, necessarily in that part of the world produces such a state of disorganisation and want of confidence in the Porte, it comes to this—that if we do not interfere in vindication of our own interests, that part of Asia must become the victim of anarchy, and ultimately become part of the possessions of Russia.

. . . We do not, my lords, wish to enter into any unnecessary responsibility; but there is one responsibility from which we certainly shrink; we shrink from the responsibility of handing to our successors a weakened or a diminished Empire. Our opinion is, that the course we have taken will arrest the great evils which are destroying Asia Minor and the equally rich countries beyond. We see in the present state of affairs the Porte losing its influence over its subjects; we see a certainty, in our opinion, of increasing anarchy, of the dissolution of all those ties which, though feeble, yet still exist and which have kept society together in those countries. We see the inevitable result of such a state of things, and we cannot blame Russia for availing herself of it. But, yielding to Russia what she has obtained, we say to her—"Thus far, and no farther." Asia is large enough for both of us. There is no reason for these constant wars, or fears of wars, between Russia and England. Before the circumstances which led to the recent disastrous war, when none of those events which we have seen agitating the world had occurred, and when we were speaking in "another place" of the conduct of Russia in Central Asia, I vindicated that conduct, which I thought was unjustly attacked, and I said then—what I repeat now—there is room enough for Russia and England in Asia.

But the room that we require we must secure. We have, therefore, entered into an alliance—a defensive alliance—with Turkey, to guard her against any further attack from Russia.

The case for the other side was clearly stated in Gladstone's pamphlet, *Bulgarian Horrors and Russia in Turkestan*, which, in 1876, touched off the controversy:

My hope, therefore, is twofold. First, that, through the energetic attitude of the people of England, their Government may be led to declare distinctly, that it is for purposes of humanity alone that we have a fleet in Turkish waters. Secondly, that that fleet will be so distributed as to enable its force to be most promptly and efficiently applied, in case of need, on Turkish soil, in concert with the other Powers, for the defence of innocent lives, and to prevent the repetition of those recent scenes, at which hell itself might almost blush.

For it must not be forgotten that the last utterance on this subject was from the Prime Minister, and was to the effect that our fleet was in the

East for the support of British interests. I object to this constant system of appeal to our selfish leanings. It sets up false lights; it hides the true; it disturbs the world. Who has lifted a finger against British interests? Who has spoken a word? If the declaration be anything beyond mere idle brag it means that our fleet is waiting for the dissolution of the Turkish Empire, to have the first and the strongest hand in the seizure of the spoils. If this be the meaning, it is pure mischief: and if we want to form a just judgment upon it, we have only to put a parallel case. What should we say, if Russia had assembled an army on the Pruth, or Austria on the Danube, and Prince Gortschakoff or Count Andrassy were to announce that it was so gathered, and so posted for the defence of Russian, or of Austrian interests respectively?

Perhaps, in these unusual circumstances, before describing what it is that we should seek and should desire, it may be well to consider what we should carefully eschew. In the channel, which we have to navigate, with or without our Government, there are plenty of false lights set up for us, which lead to certain shipwreck. The matter has become too painfully real for us to be scared at present by the standing hobgoblin of Russia. Many a time has it done good service on the stage: it is at present out of repair, and unavailable. It is now too late to argue, as was argued some time back by a very clever and highly enlightened evening journal, that it might be quite proper that twelve or thirteen millions of Christians in Turkey should remain unhappy, rather than that (such was the alternative hardily presented) two hundred millions of men in India should be deprived of the benefits of British rule, and thirty millions more in the United Kingdom made uncomfortable by the apprehension of such a catastrophe.

This very juxtaposition of "power" politics and "moral" politics is fundamentally mistaken. It derives from the assumption that the principles of morality have the same substantive quality as, say, the principles of politics, economics, or law. This assumption leads logically to the conclusion that it is both possible and desirable to replace the principles of politics with those of morality. In truth, this substitution is possible only at the price of political failure and, hence, is neither possible nor desirable on rational grounds.

Morality is not just another branch of human activity, co-ordinate to the substantive branches, such as politics or economics. Quite to the contrary, it is superimposed upon them, limiting the choice of ends and means and delineating the legitimate sphere of a particular branch of action altogether. This later function is particularly vital for the political sphere. For the political actor is peculiarly tempted to blind himself to the limits of his power and thereby to overstep the boundaries of both prudence and morality.

It is not ignorance or misjudgment, that is, intellectual errors, against which the Greek tragedians and biblical prophets warn the powerful of the world but *hubris* and pride. The self-esteem engendered by power, which equates power and virtue, in the process loses all sense of moral and political proportion. Indeed, it is from the moral delusions and corruptions, the poisonous fruits of power, that these intellectual errors receive the strength to lead nations to disaster as though it were truth and not error that led them. The moral corruption of power blinds nations to the distinction between truth and error. Dazzled by the pride of power, they take truth for error, and vice versa, and make ready with unsuspecting confidence to jump into the abyss as if it were the consummation of their dreams.

A nation emerges victorious from a war, and in the exaltation of its supreme power it rejects as unacceptable, if not as outright offensive, the idea that it won the victory because it had better trained and better fed troops, more and better arms, and superior leadership. Providence, either as a personal divinity or as the objective logic of the historic process, has given victory to the nation which deserved it by virtue of its moral superiority. That alleged moral superiority is then taken to be a permanent quality which not only explains past victories but also justifies the national claim to be the lawgiver and arbiter of mankind.

A nation, thus supernaturally endowed, not only has the ability but believes that it has a sacred duty to reform the world in the image of its own supposed superiority. It can and must promote or forestall revolution or reform, as the case may be. It must contain other nations, advance itself, and never retreat. There is nothing it cannot do. What is more, there is nothing it ought not to do. It must and can bring salvation to all the world. By the standards of this national moral delusion, humanity naturally divides into two groups: one all black and the other all white. By definition those who are for you are good, and those who are against you are wicked.

Only future generations will be able to understand fully to what extent in our atomic policy the self-destructive tendencies of power have been at work; how the use of the atomic bomb and our emphasis upon its monopolistic possession and decisive importance have called into existence the very forces that nullify that advantage and turn it against us; how that possession has tempted us from miscalculation to miscalculation, overrating our own and underrating the power of other nations; how the emphasis on secrecy, assuming the permanency of that monopolistic possession, has done more than anything else to destroy the advantage it was intended to preserve; and how, finally, the awareness of such tremendous power has nourished a sense of mission which assumes in its holder an exclusive moral worth and duty of a magnitude commensurate with so much power.

22 *The Military Displacement of Politics*

The autonomy of the political sphere is endangered not only by the misunderstanding of the nature and role of morality but also by the imperialism of other spheres of substantive action, of which in our culture the economic and military are the most important ones. The economic attack upon the political sphere dominated the nineteenth and the first decades of the twentieth centuries. Marxism and liberalism are its outstanding manifestations. When the experience of totalitarianism seemed to have proved conclusively that politics is not a derivation of economics but has an autonomous realm of its own, the Second World War and its aftermath raised the issue of the autonomy of politics again. This time, it was the military which infringed upon it.

The fundamental error behind all the individual blunders committed toward the end of the Second World War, and immediately afterward, was the neglect of Karl von Clausewitz' dictum that war is the continuation of policy by other means. The peaceful and warlike means by which a nation pursues its interests form a continuous process in which, though one means may replace the other, the ends remain the same. We also failed to recognize that foreign policy itself is a continuum beginning with the birth of a state and ending only with its death; isolationists and interventionists alike tended to believe that the "normal" thing for a state was to have no foreign policy at all. What separated the interventionists from the isolationists was the belief that certain crises might require, at least temporarily, an active foreign policy. But even the interventionists felt that after solving the given crisis one could try to return to a position of detachment, though developing and supporting in the meantime international institutions designed to meet the next crisis if and when it should arise. Foreign policy was thus regarded as something like a policeman's night stick, to be used only when it was necessary to bring a disturber of the peace to reason; war, in turn, was like the policeman's gun, to be used only *in extremis* to rid the world of a criminal. But here the analogy ends: the policeman always carries his

From *Commentary*, October, 1952; and *World Politics*, January, 1955.

gun with him, but we threw ours away twice after it had done the job.

War, we could see, did have a necessary connection with what preceded it—that is, with the criminal aggression that provoked it—but it had no organic relation with what followed it. Its purpose was only to eliminate a disturbance by eliminating the disturber; once that was done, the world would presumably settle back into normalcy and order. War, then, was a mere technical operation to be performed according to the rules of military art—a feat of military engineering like building a dam or flattening a mountain. To allow considerations of political expediency to interfere with military operations was unwise from the military point of view and might well be considered an immoral subversion of one self-sufficient department of human action for the sake of another. (It might be added in passing that economic specialists—for instance, administrators of foreign aid—have shown a very similar reluctance, for similar reasons, to let political considerations "violate" the autonomy of economic operations.)

This quality of American thinking emerges clearly from the contrast between the non-political American approach to war and the continuous and generally fruitless insistence of Churchill and his subordinates on the political significance of military action. The British and the Russians knew from long experience that wars are not fought just to bring about the unconditional surrender of the enemy; wars are means to political ends, and military victory, if it is to bear political fruits, must be shaped to those ends.

American military leaders were aware of this difference in outlook, both on the battlefield and afterward. In April, 1945, when the British wanted Patton's army to liberate as much of Czechoslovakia as possible, and Prague in particular, for the sake of the political advantages to be gained thereby, General Marshall passed the suggestion on to General Eisenhower with this comment: "Personally, and aside from all logistic, tactical, or strategical implications, I would be loath to hazard American lives for purely political reasons." Marshall had nothing to worry about in this respect, for Eisenhower replied the next day: "I shall not attempt any move I deem militarily unwise merely to gain a political advantage unless I receive specific order from the Combined Chiefs of Staff." The matter rested there

329

despite repeated and urgent appeals from Churchill and the British chiefs of staff. Similar decisions were made on other occasions. General Bradley in his memoirs has this to say of the British insistence that the Americans take Berlin before the Russians: "As soldiers we looked naïvely on this British inclination to complicate the war with political foresight and non-military objectives."

This concentration on military objectives to the neglect of political considerations has one virtue: it is apt to win wars quickly, cheaply, and thoroughly. Yet such victories may be short-lived, and an enormous political and military price may have to be paid for them later. To win a war without regard for the political consequences of the victory may create political problems as serious as, or worse than, those that the victory was intended to settle; but such a victory leaves a country at least in a position to learn and to try to settle political problems by peaceful means.

Have we learned these lessons? On the face of it, it seems we have. Certainly we have been almost obsessed with the need to fashion our postwar policies so as to avoid the mistakes we and others made during the Second World War. We have learned that a power vacuum will exert a well-nigh irresistible attraction on a great dynamic nation in its vicinity. We have learned that in order to confine such a nation within the limits necessary to our own security it is not enough to show good will and reasonableness and to embody virtuous intentions in legal instruments. We have learned that the balance of power, far from being just an arbitrary device of reactionary diplomats and Machiavellian scholars, is the very law of life for independent units dealing with other independent units—domestic or international—that want to preserve their independence. Independent power, in order to be kept in check, must be met by independent power of approximately equal strength. In the effort to apply these lessons, we have embarked upon a long-range policy of "containment" and rearmament.

We have also learned that an imperialist power confronted with a coalition of powers of varying strength will attempt to eliminate the weaker members one after the other, until the most powerful member is left in the end outmaneuvered and alone. We have therefore developed an intricate system of alliances in the Western Hemisphere, Europe, and Asia, which, whatever the differences of legal language and institutional device, all amount to a declaration that we shall defend the territorial integrity of the members of these alliances as we would our own. We call this system of alliances "collective security" and have put it into operation by defending the Republic of South Korea against aggression by North Korea.

In these ways, we have obviously learned from history. Why, then, are we as uncertain as ever about the success of our policies and still beset by doubts about the course we have been taking in recent years? Have we still missed one of the important lessons of recent history, or have we misunderstood what it seemed to teach us? The answer is not completely reassuring. Though we have learned the lessons of recent history, chapter and verse, though we have memorized them and have never tired of reciting and applying them whenever faced with a problem which seemed to be similar to one of those that we failed to solve during the Second World War, yet we have failed to see that behind the specific lessons of history learned from specific blunders there stands *the* lesson of history, of *all* history, which alone gives meaning to the lessons to be derived from any particular period.

All political action is an attempt to influence human behavior; hence, all political action must be aware of the complexities and ambiguities of the human factor and must itself be ambiguous and complex—and in the right way. The political actor, conscious of history, must be aware of the malleability of the human will; yet he must also be aware of the limits of suasion and of the need for objective barriers to the human will. While he is making use of suasion, he must not be oblivious to the role of power, and vice versa, and of each he must have just the right quantity and quality, neither too much nor too little, neither too early nor too late, neither too strong nor too weak.

He must choose the right admixture, not only in terms of human nature, permanent as such but with the relations of its elements ever changing, but also in terms of the changing historical circumstances under which those elements of human nature confront each other in the form of collectivities called nations. How much suasion and power and what kind is available on my side at a particular moment in history, and how much of it and what kind is likely to be available tomorrow? How much and what kind of susceptibility to suasion and power is present on the other side at a particular moment of history, and how much and what kind is likely to be present tomorrow? And how much and what kind of suasion and power is the other side able to bring to bear upon me and others today and tomorrow? Such are the questions posed by the ever changing social environment.

When, during the closing years of the past war, we thought that Stalin was a somewhat gruff old gentleman who could be charmed into co-operation, we relied on suasion to a greater extent than the teachings of history justified. We think we have learned our lesson from this failure of a policy of suasion pure and simple. Now we seem to have forsworn suasion altogether and seem to rely exclusively upon force as a deterrent to the ambitions of the Soviet Union. We seem to forget that force as the instrument of a foreign policy aiming at the peaceful settlement of international conflicts must be a means to the end of foreign policy, not an end in itself. Force supplements suasion but does not replace it. Mr. Acheson, as Secretary of State, recognized this relation between suasion and force in the abstract when he proclaimed repeatedly that the objective of our foreign policy was the creation of situations of strength from which to negotiate a peaceful settlement with the Soviet Union. In practice, however, our foreign policy, preoccupied as it is with rearmament, seems to have lost sight of this objective. Consequently, it has not faced up squarely to the all-important question of timing: when shall we consider ourselves strong enough in relation to the Soviet Union to be able to negotiate from strength? A positive answer is being postponed to an ever more indefinite future. Trying to learn from history, we have set out on an armament race that must lead to war if it is not subordinated to the professed objective of a negotiated settlement. Here again we have learned but half the lesson and have replaced one error with another.

Most often political blunders consist in this overemphasis of one element in a situation at the expense of others. The twenties and thirties saw the underestimation by the Western world of the uses of power toward moral and legal ends. The Second World War saw but a seeming interruption of that trend, for power was used then in an effort to restore conditions of harmony and "normalcy" under which we could again rely on law and morality and, as it were, forget about power. We seemed at the time to have learned a lesson from our prewar relations with the Axis Powers: we had neglected power; now we would use it without limit until those who had compelled us to do so were forced to surrender their own power unconditionally. With that task accomplished, we would be able to return to the other extreme and build a new world, without power politics, on the foundations of law and morality.

Consistent with this point of view, we treated our wartime allies, including the Soviet Union, with that same disregard of considerations of power which had characterized our behavior toward everybody in the interwar period. Yet the same experience that had forced us into power politics against Hitler was to be repeated in our dealings with the Soviet Union. And here, too, we seem to have learned our lesson now. Having shown good will, we now "get tough." Since one cannot deal with the Soviet Union by legal contract and without regard for the realities of power, we will now use in dealing with her the instruments of power alone, without concern for legal stipulations to be agreed upon through mutual suasion. Just as the only alternative to appeasement of Germany, Japan, or Italy without power had been war, so the alternative to appeasement of the Soviet Union is another kind of war.

We also learned from the experiences of the thirties what a blunder isolationism was, which would let one fight only in defense of one's own country but not in defense of allies. But in learning that lesson we are by way of falling into the opposite error: having realized the error of fighting for nobody but one's self, we are now willing to fight for anybody threatened by the common enemy. Collective security, after all, is as abstract and non-political a principle of action as isolationism, equally impervious to the complexity of all political issues which must be decided not according to abstract principles but by the calculation of opposing interests and powers.

We intervened in Korea because the principle of collective security required it, thus seemingly avoiding the mistake Great Britain and France had made when they refused to defend Ethiopia in 1935–36 and Czechoslovakia in 1938. Actually, as pointed out before,[1] we made exactly the same mistake, only in a different way. In 1950, as

---

[1] See above, pp. 101 ff.

in 1935 and 1938, the issue might better have been decided in terms of the interests involved and the power available as against the interests and power of other nations. Instead, it was resolved in all three instances, either positively or negatively, in the abstract terms of collective security, a principle which could be applied against a major power only at the risk of world war. By substituting an abstract principle of law for the calculation of the concrete conditions of interests and power, we involved ourselves in a war that, in view of these relations of interests and power, we could neither win nor lose. Such are the results of a foreign policy that tries to avoid the mistakes of the past without understanding the principles that should have governed the actions of the past.

We realized what had been wrong with our policies, but in supplying what had been lacking we threw overboard what was no less essential than what we were trying to supply. Thus the very correction of past blunders created new ones. We had seen that diplomacy without power was not enough, so we added power and forgot about diplomacy. We had seen that a nation must stop aggression before it reaches her own shores, and we concluded that we had now to stop all aggression regardless of how our own interests and power were affected. We learned the specific lessons of the last two decades, but in the process we came to neglect the broad lesson of history: that political success depends upon the simultaneous or alternative use of different means at different times and the moderate use of all of them at all times.

Man is never able to look at history with the same objectivity as at inanimate nature. The moral limitation upon his understanding of history is pride: pride in his intellect, pride in his goodness, pride in the collectivity with which he identifies himself as against other collectivities.

Pride in intellect shows itself in the persistence with which ideas once adopted are applied time and again, regardless of the fact that they have been discredited by experience. A general whose strategy brought victory in one war finds in success an additional reason for using the same methods in the next war. He did it once, and he is going to do it again. What General MacArthur was able to do to the Japanese in the Second World War he must be able to do to the Chinese in the Korean War.

Even if a certain strategy has been unsuccessful, there is a strong tendency to try it out again, especially if the general sluggishness of the human mind encourages it. The Maginot line was a disastrous failure in the Second World War. But man is almost irresistibly attracted by the image of a wall behind which he will be safe from the enemy. Since the Maginot line was a failure, as was the Chinese Great Wall before it, why not build a bigger and better Maginot line? Or perhaps a bigger and better general will do what General Gamelin was unable to do with the Maginot line in 1940. The most subtle perversion of the lessons of history is that which appears to heed the experiences of the past and discard its faulty methods, while continuing nonetheless to think in terms of the past. To build a line of static fortifications parallel to the Rhine was certainly a mistake that we shall not emulate. Instead, we shall create a western European army that will defend Europe at the Elbe, at the Rhine, or wherever else it may be. We seem to have learned a lesson from history; but, in view of the novel requirements of global strategy and the numerical superiority of the Russian land armies, have we really?

Pride in intellect is joined by pride in virtue. All individuals and collectivities like to see their conflicts with others not in terms of interest and power determined by circumstances but in terms of moral values determined by abstract principles. When our policies fail, as they did in relation to the Soviet Union after the Second World War, the explanation cannot lie in our having miscalculated our interests and power in relation to the interests and power of the other side. Our failure must be the result of the wickedness of the other side, which took advantage of our guileless trust. We trusted once and were deceived; from now on we shall be on our guard and see the enemy for what he is. Yalta then becomes a symbol, not of the legal ratification of errors of political and military judgment, but of a moral deception that the wicked perpetrated upon the good.

While such one-sidedness, which impairs historical judgment and thus our ability to learn from history, seems inevitable in even the greatest of historians, there are specific manifestations of it that, as great statesmen have shown, can be controlled by moral discipline. One such manifestation is the habit of overestimating one's own power and underestimatng the other side's. The history of the relations between the Western world and the Soviet Union since 1917 could be written in terms of the underestimation of Russian power. From the Allied intervention in the Russian civil war through the debates on the implementation of the Franco-Russian alliance of 1935, the Russian offer of support to Czechoslovakia in 1938, the Anglo-French military mission to Moscow in 1939, the German attack upon the Soviet Union in 1941, the first atomic explosion in Russia in 1949, up to the very present, we have always underestimated the power of the Soviet Union. We have done so because we are inflexibly opposed on moral grounds to both communism and Russian imperialism. Thus our moral sentiment stands in the way of a correct appraisal of the realities of power. To separate our pride in our own moral superiority from our historical judgment, which might lead us to recognize the political and military superiority of the Soviet Union in certain respects, requires an effort at moral detachment which few are willing to make. It is easier and more satisfactory to conclude that political and military superiority necessarily go hand in hand with moral superiority. Yet the monopoly of the atomic bomb may have been, but was not of necessity, concomitant with a monopoly in virtue. Here again moral pride stands between our judgment and historical experience.

The classic example of this kind of pride, and of its disastrous political and military consequences, is Hitler's. Since Bismarck, it had been the basic axiom of German strategy that Germany could not win a two-front war. However, it was exactly such a war that she deliberately embarked upon both in 1914 and 1941. Hitler himself was resolved not to make this blunder, but he could not help making it, for he believed firmly that it was Germany's "mission" to triumph over her enemies. Holding such a faith, he was led to assume that Germany had already won the war against the West when she had not yet done so, and could therefore safely invade the Soviet Union.

If we find it so difficult to learn from history, the fault is not with history but with the pride and the intellectual limitations of men. History, in the words of Thucydides, is philosophy learned from examples. Those who are morally and intellectually inferior to its teachings, history leads to disaster. Those who are philosophers in the moral and intellectual sense, it teaches.

Of this ability to learn from history that the autonomy of the political sphere must be protected against encroachments of the mili-

tary, Sir Winston Churchill provides the greatest contemporary example. Its literary manifestation is *Triumph and Tragedy*.[2] The
range of this book is narrow in every respect—in subject matter, in
style, and in purpose. It covers the period from the invasion of Nor-
mandy in June, 1944, to the Potsdam Conference of July, 1945. Its
theme is, in the words of the author, "How the Great Democracies
Triumphed, and So Were Able To Resume the Follies Which Had
So Nearly Cost Them Their Life." Its central problem is simple:
military strategy and its relation to foreign policy.

The style is of the same classic simplicity as the problem. As the
problem raises a perennial issue of statecraft, so the mode of thought
which the author brings to bear upon the problem moves within the
perennial categories of political thought. Sir Winston Churchill's
mind is not that of an intellectual who loves to think and know for
the sake of thinking and knowledge. His is the intellect of a man of
action who relives in thought past action and what preceded and
followed it. Sir Winston thinks with a purpose which transcends
thought. His purpose as a thinker is that of the man of action and,
hence, is intensely personal; it is so in three different respects.

Its most personal purpose is to enable the author to relive in remi-
niscence his part in the drama of history, enjoying its victories,
mourning its defeats. Yet this process of recollecting and reflective
reliving is also one of simplification, of seeing, and of making others
see, perhaps for the first time, the essence of one's action and its purpose, aside from what is but pretense and byplay. The first purpose,
then, is autobiographical in the strict, classic sense of the term.

The second purpose is autobiographical in what one might call the
political sense. It is to justify the author as past actor on the political
scene. It is to prove that the author was right when he did what he
did and when he gave advice that was not heeded. When the author
must admit that he was wrong in action or advice, he at least evokes
the sympathetic companionship of the reader, who learns to his satisfaction that the great and the powerful share in the human fallibility of all. Thus the author assigns himself the place in history
which he deems his due or, at the very least, helps future historians
to assign it to him.

Finally, the book teaches a lesson. By contrasting the mistakes of

[2] Boston: Houghton Mifflin Co., 1953.

the past with the principles of right action, the author calls our attention, by implication, to opportunities in the more recent past and in the future of making the same mistakes by neglecting the same principles. It is this contribution to political wisdom which makes this book important, particularly for us and at this time. What, then, transforms this autobiographical account of history into a source of political wisdom? With this question we approach the secret of Sir Winston's greatness.

That secret cannot be explained in this space, if it can be explained at all; it can only be adumbrated. It seems to lie in the conjuncture of three qualities, one intellectual, one practical, and one moral. These qualities are the intellectual grasp of statesmanship, the ability to act according to the requirements of statesmanship, and the subordination of all other considerations to these requirements. Others are as wise as Sir Winston; others again are as effective in action; and others still have dedicated themselves as single-mindedly to a purpose. Yet nobody alive combines to such a degree intellectual excellence with ability in action and dedication to a cause.

What John Stuart Mill said of Bentham applies also to Churchill: "The field of [his] labours was like the space between two parallel lines; narrow to excess in one direction, in another it reached to infinity." The field of Sir Winston's labors, of his interests, and of his understanding is narrow. Yet one is also struck with the enormity of the purposeful intellectual and moral force that sweeps through the narrow confines of his cause: to remember the past in order to learn how to act aright in matters political and military.

The outstanding quality of that intellectual force is the ability to see a problem in its true proportions, by not allowing the involvement of will and emotion to interfere with understanding. What is required of the statesman is, first of all, to see clearly: himself, the enemy, and then himself again as the enemy sees him. To see clearly means to see without passions, without the passion of pride, of hatred, and of contempt. The statesman must master the paradox of wanting passionately to win over an enemy to whom he feels passionately superior, and of having to view his relations with the enemy with the detachment and objectivity of the scholar. This book provides proof of the extent to which Sir Winston has mastered this paradox. His most spectacular failures are his support of "unconditional surrender" and his inability to reconcile Great Britain's moral and legal commitment to the independence of Poland with the political and military realities which the Russian conquest of eastern Europe had created.

The moral counterpart of the intellectual ability of mastering this paradox of passion and understanding is humility toward one's self and generosity toward others. As such, this moral attitude is not only a moral virtue in itself but one of the conditions for political success as well. The extent to which this book reveals these qualities is another measure of Sir Winston's greatness as a statesman. He deplores President Truman's decision to withdraw the American troops, on the eve of the Potsdam Conference, to the zonal borders agreed upon at Quebec and Yalta, a step against which he had repeatedly warned; and there is no doubt in his mind now, as there was none then, that he was right and Truman wrong. Yet he enumerates all the mitigating circumstances which can be cited in explanation and support of Mr. Truman's decision and adds: "Those who are only wise after the event should hold their peace." And, while he bends every effort to forestall Stalin's designs, with what understanding does he speak of Russian interests, and with what respect does he pay tribute to Stalin's qualities!

If the cause to which Sir Winston brings these qualities were less challenging intellectually, less demanding morally, and less vital for all of us, we would think less of Sir Winston's greatness. As it is, upon our ability to learn Sir Winston's lessons the survival of the West may well depend. That, then, completes Sir Winston's greatness: that he brings a great intellectual and moral force successfully to bear upon the greatest of all contemporary causes.

What are the lessons we can learn from Sir Winston's book? The relationships between political and military policy being its main theme, this book is a study in contrasts, the contrast between British and American policies, between Churchill's and Roosevelt's strategy and statecraft. That contrast can be defined in two fundamental and interrelated propositions. For Sir Winston, the war was a military means to a political end, and the influence of the political end upon the military means was to increase with the speed with which the armies of the Allies were approaching military victory. For the United States, the war was essentially a self-sufficient technical operation to be performed as quickly, as cheaply, and as thoroughly as the technical rules of warfare would allow. The political issue with which Sir Winston's strategy and statecraft were primarily concerned during the last year of the Second World War was no longer German and Japanese imperialism but the imperialism of the Soviet Union. For the American government, the approaching defeat of German and Japanese imperialism signified the elimination of the major political problem that faced the Western world, and what remained could safely be left to mutual good will, especially toward the Soviet Union, and to the United Nations.

In one word, Sir Winston's was a historic concept of the war, while the American was apocalyptic. Sir Winston viewed the war as part of a historic continuum, as a product of historic forces not in essence different from those that had preceded it and were likely to follow it, subject to historic laws, which are of the timeless essence of politics itself and for whose disregard a nation must pay a heavy price. Our government looked at the war as the catastrophic interruption of a normalcy which the victorious conclusion of the war would almost automatically restore. For us the war was like a thunderstorm darkening a peaceful scene; its passing would by itself restore peace. For Sir Winston the war—in its causes, manifestations, and consequences—was, as it were, part of the natural environment of nations, and its consequences would be determined by the policies carried on during the war.

In Sir Winston's thought and argument, as revealed in this book, one concern took precedence over all others: to meet the Russians as much to the east as possible. Whenever a military decision had to be made, small or great, Sir Winston hammered on this concern to the point of obnoxiousness. During the Italian campaign, he was obsessed with the opportunity to occupy Vienna before the Russians and urged that the invasion of southern France be sacrificed to the exploitation of this opportunity. After the Allied armies had crossed the Rhine, he urged striking directly at Berlin rather than southward, in order not to leave Berlin to the Russians. It was for similar reasons that he advised occupying as much as possible of Czechoslovakia, and more particularly Prague, and keeping what had been occupied. And when the war in Europe had ended with the surrender of Germany, he continued to view military operations in the light of their political consequences: he urged an over-all settlement with the Soviet Union while the armies of the United States were still intact and in Europe.

Sir Winston was defeated on every major issue. The only important exception was Greece, where he was able to act on his own, subordinating military to political considerations. When Greece was about to be conquered by communism and, through it, by Russian imperialism, he sent British forces to Greece to defeat that very underground army which had just been successfully fighting the Axis. It was argued then, as it is being argued now, that his advice was militarily unsound. However, this is not the point which Sir Winston's book raises. Sir Winston's concern—and ours—is not with the military soundness of this particular action or that but with the political quality of thinking which led to military action, however sound or unsound it might have been in its own military terms. It is the contrast between his own thinking and that of his American counterparts, and the political superiority of his to theirs, which is the main revelation of the book.

It would be as comforting as it would be false if one were to conclude that the main lesson of Sir Winston's book has been learned. Looking at Asia, the Middle East, and Europe—let alone at Washington—one cannot escape the conclusion that it has not been learned. Everywhere the requisite primacy of foreign policy over military policy is at best tenuous or ineffectual, if it exists at all. This book, then, is not only a repository of perennial wisdom; it also carries a very timely warning.

23 *Traditional and United Nations Diplomacy*

When Metternich was informed of the death of the Russian ambassador at the Congress of Vienna, he is supposed to have exclaimed, "Ah, is that true? What can have been his motive?" The great diplomatist of the post-Napoleonic era was not alone in this moral depreciation of diplomacy. From the anti-Machiavellian writers to our time, the diplomat has been held in low esteem, and while his professional competence and even his ordinary intelligence have frequently been questioned, his moral qualities have always been under a cloud.

It is, however, one thing to have a low opinion of the intellectual and moral qualities of a group of professional men, and it is quite another to believe that they and their work fulfill no useful function, that they have become obsolete, and that their days are numbered. While the former opinion is as old as the profession of diplomacy itself, the latter belief has its roots in the liberal philosophy of the nineteenth century. In the Wilsonian conception of foreign affairs and the philosophy of the League of Nations it bursts forth in full bloom, and today we witness in the theory and practice of the United Nations and the movement for world government a second flowering of the same thought.

While the spokesmen of public opinion seem to be unanimous in opposition to traditional diplomacy, they split into two schools of thought on the question, What, if anything, shall replace the discarded method of conducting foreign affairs? There are those who believe that foreign policy itself is a relic of a prescientific past which will not survive the coming of the age of reason and good will; when foreign policy disappears, diplomacy as the technique by which foreign policy is effectuated will disappear, too. There are others who would substitute for power politics another type of foreign policy based on international law and consequently would replace the "old" diplomacy by a "new" one, the diplomat of national power by the advocate of international law.

From the *Yale Law Journal*, Vol. LV, No. 5, August, 1946.

The former school, which one might call perfectionist in contradistinction to the legalistic one, has found its typical representatives among nineteenth-century liberals, some Wilsonians, and contemporaneous adherents of world government. The liberals of the nineteenth century saw in foreign policy a residue of the feudal age, an aristocratic pastime bound to disappear with the application of liberal principles to international affairs. According to Bentham,[1] "Nations are associates and not rivals in the grand social enterprise." "At some future election," said Cobden,[2] "we may probably see the test of 'no foreign politics' applied to those who offer to become the representatives of free constituencies." "The idea of conscious planning," says Paul S. Reinsch,[3] "or striving to subject national and economic facts and all historic development to the conscious political will—that conception of diplomacy is synonymous with the essence of *politics* and will stand and fall with the continuance of the purely political state. Manipulative, and hence secret, diplomacy is in fact the most complete expression of the purely political factor in human affairs. To many, it will seem only a survival of a hyper-political era, as human society now tends to outgrow and transcend politics for more comprehensive, pervasive, and essential principles of action. . . . But if it should be achieved, then plainly the old special functions of diplomacy will fall away and administrative conferences will take the place of diplomatic conversations. When Portugal became a republic, the proposal was made to abolish all diplomatic posts and have the international business of Portugal administered by consuls. That would eliminate politics from foreign relations."

Here, the disappearance of foreign policy and, with it, of diplomacy is expected as a by-product of the ascendancy of liberal principles over the feudal state, and this expectation is indeed in harmony with the laissez faire philosophy of nineteenth-century liberalism. The twentieth-century opponents of any foreign policy and any kind of diplomacy have found in the conception of world gov-

---

[1] *Principles of Penal Law*, in *The Works of Jeremy Bentham* (Edinburgh: W. Tait, 1843), I, 563.

[2] Quoted in Walter Lyon Blease, *A Short History of English Liberalism* (New York: G. P. Putnam's Sons, 1913), p. 195.

[3] Reinsch, *Secret Diplomacy* (New York: Harcourt, Brace & Co., 1922), pp. 13, 15.

ernment a positive instrumentality which will make foreign policy and diplomacy superfluous. "The United Nations," declares a group of distinguished members of the American Bar Association,[4] "cannot be saved by the process of shunting all the major controversies between its members back for solution by diplomacy. It can only be saved . . . by transforming the present league structure into a general government to regulate and promote the common interests of the people of the States. The American Bar can dedicate itself to no greater responsibility nor higher aim than that of world government to make world laws for the control of world affairs so as to assure world peace."

The adherents of the legalistic school, too, believe in law as the alternative to power politics. They expect, however, the preservation of peace not from a world law enacted by a world government, but from international law agreed upon by sovereign nations organized in a Holy Alliance, a League of Nations, or the United Nations. Traditional foreign policy pursuing the national interest is superseded by a new conception of international affairs, the essence of which is respect for international law as embodied in the fundamental law of an international organization. According to this school, the League of Nations and the United Nations supersede the methods by which foreign policy has been conducted in the past. The period of power politics, spheres of influence, alliances, and secret diplomacy has come to an end; a new conception of international affairs, recognizing the solidarity of all nations, based upon the respect for international law and operating through the instrumentality of the new organization, has come into being. Consequently, traditional diplomacy, too, must give way to a new conception of diplomatic intercourse appropriate to the new relations established between nations. If the end of the state is power, the character of its diplomacy will be adapted to that end. If the end of the state is the defense of international law, a different type of diplomacy will serve that end.

Woodrow Wilson is the most eloquent apostle of the new diplomacy of the League of Nations. It is true that sometimes Wilson seemed to join hands with the opponents of any diplomacy whatsoever, as when he wrote in his letter to Senator Hitchcock of March

[4] *American Bar Association Journal*, XXXII (1946), 270.

8, 1920, "For my own part, I am not willing to trust to the council of diplomats the working out of any salvation of the world from the things which it has suffered." However, he saw more clearly than anybody else the intimate connection between the new conception of international affairs as embodied in the League of Nations and a new diplomatic technique by which that new conception was to be realized. The preamble to and the first of the Fourteen Points are still the most persuasive statement of the new philosophy of international affairs.[5]

The philosophy of the United Nations has added nothing to Wilson's program. While it equals the Wilsonian philosophy in its opposition to traditional diplomacy, it is much less outspoken as to the alternative. Thus, the former Secretary of State, Cordell Hull, said on his return from the Moscow Conference[6] that the new international organization would mean the end of power politics and usher in a new era of international collaboration. Mr. Philip Noel-Baker, British Minister of State, declared in the House of Commons[7] that the British government was "determined to use the institutions of the United Nations to kill power politics, in order that, by the methods of democracy, the will of the people shall prevail." Mr. Ernest Bevin, the British Secretary of Foreign Affairs, in his speech of March 30, 1946,[8] expressed in somewhat more cautious language the expectation that while "you cannot change a policy that has been

---

[5] The Preamble to the Fourteen Points states, "It will be our wish and purpose that the processes of peace, when they are begun, shall be absolutely open, and that they shall involve and permit henceforth no secret understandings of any kind. The day of conquest and aggrandizement is gone by; so is also the day of secret covenants entered into in the interest of particular governments, and likely at some unlooked-for moment to upset the peace of the world. It is this happy fact, now clear to the view of every public man whose thoughts do not still linger in an age that is dead and gone, which makes it possible for every nation whose purposes are consistent with justice and the peace of the world to avow, now or at any other time, the objects it has in view." The first point reads, "Open covenants of peace, openly arrived at, after which there shall be no private international understandings of any kind, but diplomacy shall proceed always frankly and in the public view." Albert B. Hart (ed.), *Selected Addresses and Public Papers of Woodrow Wilson* (New York: Boni & Liveright, Inc., 1918), pp. 247–48.

[6] *New York Times*, Nov. 19, 1943, p. 1, col. 6.

[7] 419 House of Commons Debates (5th ser.) 1262 (1946).

[8] *New York Times*, March 31, 1946, p. 22, col. 1.

pertaining for three or four hundred years among different powers in a moment," the United Nations would put an end to the imperialistic methods of the past. Secretary of State Byrnes declared in his address of February 28, 1946,[9] that "we have pinned our hopes to the banner of the United Nations. . . . We have joined with our allies in the United Nations to put an end to war. We have covenanted not to use force except in the defense of law as embodied in the Purposes and Principles of the Charter. We intend to live up to that covenant."

Since the philosophy underlying these statements proclaims respect for international law and, more particularly, for the Charter of the United Nations as the alternative to traditional power politics, it is safe to assume that it favors a diplomacy commensurate with the new foreign policy. Indeed we have already seen this new legalistic diplomacy in action when the Security Council of the United Nations dealt on the basis of international law with the Greek, Syrian, Indonesian, Iranian, and Spanish situations.

Even those, however, who, like Mr. Noel-Baker, are out "to kill power politics" through the instrumentality of the United Nations must by implication admit that power politics, as of today, is still alive. Even those who, like the nineteenth-century liberals and their twentieth-century heirs, see in power politics nothing but an irrational atavism, cannot deny that the end of power politics is yet to come. They welcome the new legalistic diplomacy of the United Nations as a step toward the ultimate victory of law over politics. They expect that the persisting dualism between traditional and legalistic diplomacy will gradually transform itself into the monism of the latter. Though the heads of state still meet in secret conferences and the foreign ministers discuss the most important postwar problems according to the procedures of traditional diplomacy, future negotiations of this kind will be carried out within the United Nations and according to the procedures of the new diplomacy. President Truman gave voice to this expectation when he told his press conference of March 21, 1946 that "the United Nations Organization is supposed to take over the questions formerly discussed in Big Three meetings, and it was time it assumed that responsibility if

[9] *New York Times,* March 1, 1946, p. 10, col. 1.

there was to be peace in the world. . . ."[10] The same philosophy, aiming to superimpose the new legalistic diplomacy of the United Nations upon the traditional diplomatic methods, is at the foundation of the proposal advanced by Secretary of State Byrnes to charge the Assembly of the United Nations with the task of writing the peace treaties with the powers defeated in the Second World War.[11]

This philosophy of legalistic monism is, however, contradicted by the Charter of the United Nations itself, which, explicitly and implicitly, recognizes a dualism between the methods of traditional diplomacy and the new diplomacy of the United Nations.

It should be noted in passing that this dualism between the old and the new methods of settling international disputes was expressly recognized in Article 13 of the Covenant of the League of Nations, which provides that certain disputes "which cannot be satisfactorily settled by diplomacy" shall be submitted to arbitration. This dualism was likewise recognized in the debates of the League of Nations. Thus, in the face of certain Iranian complaints submitted to the Sixth Committee of the Assembly of 1928, its president declared, "Every country had diplomatic difficulties. If all these difficulties were discussed before the League of Nations, it would be overwhelmed with work. Each Government must try to solve its own difficulties by direct negotiations, and not refer them to the League unless the negotiations failed."[12]

The dualism between the procedures of the League and those of traditional diplomacy became a manifest problem, however, mainly in the interpretation of Article 11, Paragraph 2, of the Covenant. Article 11, Paragraph 2, stipulated "the friendly right of each Member of the League to bring to the attention of the Assembly or of the Council any circumstance whatever affecting international relations which threatens to disturb international peace or the good understanding between nations upon which peace depends." Its function within the system of the Covenant was similar to that which Article 35, Paragraph 1, fulfills in the Charter of the United Nations.

The non-exclusive and supplementary character of the procedures under Article 11, and hence the dualism between the latter and the

[10] *New York Times*, March 22, 1946, p. 1, col. 5.

[11] *New York Times*, May 21, 1946, p. 1, col. 8.

[12] League of Nations Official Journal, Spec. Supp., No. 70, at 29 (1928).

traditional procedures of diplomacy, was stressed in theory[13] and practice.[14] With an incisiveness and maturity of political judgment justifying extensive quotation, Mr. Jean Ray, the leading commentator of the Covenant of the League, pointed out under the heading of "Possible Abuses of Article 11" that

there are in international relations a great number of delicate or irritating questions: it is the function of diplomacy to resolve them. Any document which organizes an international agency creates a risk: the one of accentuating differences of opinion. This risk is increased when the document is very vague, and that is exactly the case of the second paragraph of Article 11. What is the circumstance which is not, more or less indirectly, of such a nature as to "affect international relations" and which does not threaten therefore to "disturb," one day or another, the good understanding between nations? One must therefore wish that this provision be applied with great zeal perhaps in certain exceptional cases but with great moderation in ordinary ones.

Let us say, first of all, that it is not very fortunate that the eventual recourse to the League of Nations be presented, in the course of a negotiation, as a kind of threat. It is natural and excellent that this supreme remedy be envisaged, that it be taken into account beforehand, that it be raised in diplomatic conversations; but it seems to us a practice which ill prepares the League for its conciliatory function to mention the eventual appeal to the League in an official step in order to exert pressure upon the other side. . . . But in a certain number of cases states have submitted to the Council secondary questions which without doubt could have been settled by diplomatic means; in such cases the Council has adopted the wise policy of inviting the parties to come to an understanding outside the League.[15]

13 See, e.g., the Rutgers Memorandum on Articles 10, 11, and 16 of the Covenant, submitted in 1928 to the League's Committee of Arbitration and Security. The Memorandum declared, ". . . in certain cases it may be expedient to resort to all possible means of direct conciliation, and to the good offices of third Powers, before bringing a dispute before the Council. . . . If efforts of conciliation are to be successful, it may be essential that the question should be discussed by a very small number of Powers . . . [with] full latitude to decide whether the Council should be kept informed. . . ." League of Nations Official Journal, 9th Ass. 670, 675–76 (1928).

14 See, e.g., Politis' objection that Albania's bringing a complaint against Greece before the Council while direct diplomatic negotiations were in progress constituted "pressure" and "abuse" of Council procedure. Ibid. at 873. The Zaleski report on this dispute endorsed "friendly agreement" by "direct negotiation." Ibid. at 942. And see the debates on the applicability of Article 11, Paragraph 2 to the Swiss war claims and Finnish ships cases, ibid., 15th Ass. 1436 f., 1454 (1934).

15 Ray, Commentaire du Pacte de la Société des Nations (Paris: Librairie du Recueil Sirey [société anonyme], 1930), pp. 380–81.

The theory and practice of the League of Nations had to develop this general dualism between the procedures of the League and of traditional diplomacy out of the interpretation of Article 11, Paragraph 2, of the Covenant and the explicit formulation of Article 13 which allowed, however, of only limited application. The over-all importance of this dualism is implicit in the structure of the Covenant and only the decay of the League of Nations in the thirties made it fully obvious. The Charter of the United Nations, on the contrary, makes this dualism explicit from the very outset in the words of its provisions. On the one hand, Article 24 establishes as a matter of principle the Security Council's "primary responsibility for the maintenance of international peace and security." On the other hand, in the specific provisions of Chapter VI the Charter makes explicit not only the general character of this dualism but also, as a matter of practical application, the primary importance of the traditional methods of diplomacy. At the very beginning, Chapter VI stipulates in Article 33 that the parties shall "first of all" try to settle their disputes "by negotiation, enquiry, mediation, conciliation, arbitration, judicial settlement, resort to regional agencies or arrangements, or other peaceful means of their own choice." Paragraph 2 gives the Security Council the right at its discretion to refer the parties to such traditional means of diplomatic and judicial settlement. Article 36 elaborates this right by empowering the Security Council to make recommendations and stresses, in Paragraph 2, the primary importance of the traditional procedures of diplomacy by stipulating that "the Security Council should take into consideration any procedures for the settlement of the dispute which have already been adopted by the parties." While Articles 34 and 35 establish the discretionary competency of the United Nations, concurrent with the traditional methods of peaceful settlement, Article 37 reaffirms the primary character of the traditional methods and at the same time establishes the supplementary character of the procedure under the Security Council by obligating the parties who have failed to settle a dispute by the traditional means enumerated in Article 33 to refer it to the Security Council.

The same dualism is again explicitly recognized in Articles 51 and 52. Article 51 is in this respect important, as it stipulates "the inherent right of . . . Collective self-defense," especially under the conditions of modern warfare, is impossible without political and military understandings anticipating military eventualities that might make collective military measures desirable. In other words, "the inherent right of . . . collective self-defense" involves the inherent right to conclude political and military alliances against a prospective aggressor.

The qualifications of this right in the remainder of Article 51 are of a verbal rather than of a substantive nature. These qualifications are three-fold. First, the right of collective self-defense shall remain unimpaired only "until the Security Council has taken the measures necessary to maintain international peace and security." Yet the Security Council can act only through its member states, and when, as will be regularly the case, one of the permanent members of the Council is a party to collective self-defense, the requirement of the unanimity of the permanent members according to Article 27 will vouchsafe the identity of any measures taken by the Security Council with the measures taken in collective self-defense. Second, measures taken in collective self-defense have to be reported immediately to the Security Council, whose information through press, radio, and ordinary diplomatic channels will thus be duplicated. Finally, such measures shall not affect the authority and responsibility of the Security Council to take appropriate action itself. Here again, however, the Security Council is but another name for the five permanent members acting in unison, and the measures which one or the other of these members has taken by virtue of the right of self-defense will of necessity be in harmony with the measures to which these members are willing to agree by virtue of the Charter of the United Nations. Thus, while the wording of Article 51 seems to subordinate the traditional methods of international intercourse to the new diplomacy of the United Nations, its actual effect reverses this relationship.

It is in the light of this structure of Article 51 that one must read Articles 52 and 53. Article 52 stipulates not only the right but also the obligation of member states to use regional arrangements or agencies for the settlement of regional matters before they are referred to the Security Council. The latter, in turn, is charged with encouraging regional settlements and, in Article 53, with utilizing regional arrangements and agencies for enforcement actions. Such arrangements and agencies, however, must be created and maintained by the traditional methods of diplomacy. Since it is difficult to visualize an international dispute or situation which would not have a geographical focus, and therefore a regional character, Articles 52 and 53 not only reaffirm for practically all international situations and disputes the dualism between traditional and United Nations diplomacy but also establish the precedence of the former over the latter as both a right and a duty of all concerned. It is true that according to Article 52, Paragraph 4, Article 52 must be read in the light of Articles 34 and 35. But it is no less true, even though it is not expressly stated, that, in point of practical application, Articles 34 and 35 must be read in the light of Articles 51, 52, and 53.

This dualism between traditional diplomacy, conceived in terms of regionalism, and the new diplomacy of the United Nations suffers only one exception provided for in Article 53. Enforcement actions under regional arrangements or by regional agencies are subordinated to the United Nations; they can be taken only with the authorization of the Security Council. Here again, however, the subordination is verbal rather than actual, for the likelihood that one of the nations instrumental in regional enforcement will be identical with one of the nations without whose consent the Security Council cannot act, will make it unlikely that the action which the Security Council is willing to authorize will diverge from the regional enforcement upon which that particular nation has decided.

Even this exception is, however, limited, at least for the time being, to enforcement actions which would be taken on a regional basis against states which have not been enemies of any signatory of the Charter. According to Articles 53, 106, and 107, any action, regional or otherwise, taken or to be taken against an enemy power as a result of the war or for the purpose of forestalling renewed aggression on the part of such power, is for the time being not subject to the limitations of the Charter. Here the dualism between traditional and United Nations procedures is replaced, at least temporarily, by the monism of the traditional methods of international intercourse. Traditional methods become here a substitute for United Nations procedures until the latter are available for the purpose of preventing aggression by an enemy state.[16] Article 106 in particular establishes for the five big powers, as well as for other members of the United Nations, the obligation to consult outside the framework of the new organization, and reference to Paragraph 5 of the Moscow Declaration,[17] whose purport is identical with that of Article 106, only serves to underline the monistic conception of this provision.

The dualism between traditional and United Nations diplomacy, explicitly stated or implicitly contained in the individual provisions of the Charter, reveals itself also in the over-all structure of the new organization. The United Nations, in the performance of its functions according to the purposes of its Charter, is predicated upon the continuing unity of the permanent members of the Security Council. In the scheme of the Charter these members are, as it were, the nucleus of a world federation, a Holy Alliance within a Holy Alliance, without whose consent the Security Council can make no binding decision in substantive matters. Under Article 27, Paragraph 3, the United Nations cannot exist as a functioning organization without the consent of all permanent members to decisions in substantive matters. This general rule is inapplicable only to the pacific settlement of disputes to which permanent members are party, their consent in this case not being required to make the decision of the Security Council legally binding. Yet their consent is required to enable the Security Council to enforce the pacific settlement through sanctions under Chapter VII. If the Security Council should try to enforce its decision despite the dissent of one or the other of its permanent members, the United Nations would lose its function for "the maintenance of international peace and security" and at the

[16] It might be mentioned in passing that the same dualism is also made explicit in Article 79 of the Charter, where the agreement on the terms of trusteeship is referred to the states directly concerned and where the agencies of the United Nations are only called upon for approval of the agreements arrived at in traditional diplomatic negotiations.

[17] Paragraph 5 of the Moscow Declaration reads as follows: "That for the purpose of maintaining international peace and security pending the re-establishment of law and order and the inauguration of a system of general security, they will consult with one another and as occasion requires with other members of the United Nations with a view to joint action on behalf of the community of nations." "Official Documents," *American Journal of International Law,* XXXVIII (Supp.), 5.

same time its legal identity; it would at best become a political and military coalition against the dissenting permanent member or members. The United Nations would break up into warring camps, and only through total victory in war would the Nations be re-United.

The consent of the permanent members, which is but the outward manifestation of their continuing political unity, the Charter does not create but presupposes. How is this unity to be created and maintained? The Charter does not say. Its silence refers by implication to those methods by which political unity among nations has traditionally been established and maintained, that is, the traditional methods of diplomacy. As the continuing political unity of the great powers (who are permanent members of the Security Council) is the foundation upon which the edifice of the United Nations rests, so is the successful operation of traditional diplomacy the cement which keeps that foundation together. The successful operation of the old methods gives the new diplomacy of the United Nations a chance to operate.

This dualism between old and new diplomacy and the dependence of the latter upon the success of the former are implicit in the structure of the United Nations. This dualism, however, if not the fundamental importance of the successful operation of traditional diplomacy, is expressly recognized by the Report of the Crimea Conference.[18] Under the heading "Meetings of Foreign Secretaries" this report states:

These meetings have proved of the utmost value and the Conference agreed that permanent machinery should be set up for regular consultation between the three Foreign Secretaries [of the United States, Great Britain, and the Soviet Union]. They will, therefore, meet as often as may be necessary, probably about every three or four months. These meetings will be held in rotation in the three capitals, the first meeting being held in London, after the United Nations Conference on World Organization.

Here we are in the presence of a legal understanding establishing a concert of the great powers not for a limited purpose as envisaged in Article 106 of the Charter but, in view of its proved usefulness, on a permanent basis. In order to realize fully the import and the potentialities of this provision, it is useful to compare it with the text of

[18] 12 Department of State Bulletin 213 (1945).

Article 6 of the Treaty of Paris of November 20, 1815, which established the "diplomacy by conference" of the Holy Alliance:

To facilitate and to secure the execution of the present Treaty, and to consolidate the connections which at the present moment so closely unite the Four Sovereigns for the happiness of the world, the High Contracting Parties have agreed to renew their Meetings at fixed periods, either under the immediate auspices of the Sovereigns themselves, or by their respective Ministers, for the purpose of consulting upon their common interests, and for the consideration of the measures which at each of those periods shall be considered the most salutary for the repose and prosperity of Nations, and for the maintenance of the Peace of Europe.[19]

Since it is not likely that the authors of the Report of the Crimea Conference had this article of the Treaty of Paris in mind when they phrased their document, the coincidence between the two provisions reveals a striking similarity in the underlying political situations.

The provision that this permanent machinery of traditional diplomacy should operate for the first time after the permanent machinery of the new diplomacy of the United Nations had been established makes the dualism between the two methods of international intercourse most emphatic. The quoted paragraph from the Report of the Crimea Conference has the same fundamental importance for traditional diplomacy which Article 24 of the Charter has for the new diplomacy of the United Nations. The organic link between both is provided by the structure of the United Nations, which presupposes the continuing political unity of the great powers without being able to create and maintain it. It is for the achievement of the latter task that the Crimea Conference has called upon the traditional diplomacy of the foreign offices.

The monism of the new diplomacy of the United Nations, proclaimed by the spokesmen of public opinion, finds no suport in the Charter and structure of the new organization. Since the latter's inception, diplomatic procedure has been dualistic in practice. On the one hand, the chief executives and foreign ministers of the great powers have tried to solve by the traditional methods of diplomacy the fundamental political issues of the postwar world. On the other

[19] Frank Maloy Anderson, *The Constitutions and Other Select Documents Illustrative of the History of France, 1789–1901* (Minneapolis: H. W. Wilson Co., 1904), pp. 484–85.

354

hand, the Security Council of the United Nations has attacked by the new methods of legalistic diplomacy certain secondary issues, such as the Greek, Syrian, Indonesian, Iranian, and Spanish situations. The question arises as to which of the two methods is more appropriate to the problems dealt with and therefore more promising of success. For while it is obvious that the monism of United Nations diplomacy does not exist in actuality, it might be that it ought to exist by virtue of the superiority of United Nations diplomacy over the traditional diplomatic methods, and that therefore an ever greater number of ever more important international issues ought to be dealt with by the former rather than by the latter. Conversely, it is also possible that the legalistic approach to essentially political problems is but an aberration from the true laws of politics and that, far from increasing the scope of the new diplomacy, our statesmen ought to return to the traditional principles of diplomacy, which, truly understood, reflect the nature of man, the nature of politics, and the conditions for successful political action. I shall try to prove that this latter conception is indeed correct.

The legal decision, by its very nature, is concerned with an isolated case. The facts of life to be dealt with by the legal decision are artificially separated from the facts which precede, accompany, and follow them and are thus transformed into a "case" of which the law disposes "on its merits." In the domestic field this procedure is not necessarily harmful, for here executive and legislative decisions, supposedly taking into account all the ramifications of a problem, together with the "spirit of the law" manifesting itself in a judicial tradition of long standing, give the isolated legal decisions a coherence which they cannot have standing alone.

On the international scene, however, these regulating and integrating factors are absent; for that reason the social forces operate on each other with particular directness and spontaneity, and the legal decision of isolated cases is particularly inadequate. A political situation presenting itself for a decision according to international law is always one particular phase of a much larger situation, rooted in the historic past and extending far beyond the issue under legal consideration. There is no doubt that the League of Nations was right, according to international law, in expelling Russia in 1939 because of her attack upon Finland. But the political and military problems with which Russia confronted the world did not begin with her attack on Finland and did not end there, and it was unwise to pretend that such was the case and to decide the issue on that pretense. History has proved this, for only Sweden's refusal to allow British and French troops to pass through Swedish territory in order to come to the aid of Finland saved Great Britain and France from being at war with Germany and Russia at the same time. Whenever the League of Nations endeavored to deal with political situations presented as legal issues, it could deal with them only as isolated cases according to the applicable rules of international law and not as particular phases of an over-all political situation which required an over-all solution according to political principles. Hence, political problems were never solved but only tossed about and finally shelved according to the rules of the legal game.

What was true of the League of Nations has already proved to be true of the United Nations. In its approach to the Greek, Syrian, Indonesian, Iranian, and Spanish situations, the Security Council has remained faithful to the legalistic tradition established by the Council of the League of Nations. These cases have provided opportunities for exercise in parliamentary procedure and for just that chicanery for which traditional diplomacy has so often been reproached, but on no occasion has even an attempt been made to face the political issues of which these situations are the surface manifestations. What would have happened to Europe and to the world if the very similar conflicts which separated Great Britain and Russia in the seventies of the last century had been handled in 1878 by the Congress of Berlin in a similar manner?

Conflicts of this kind cannot be settled on the basis of established rules of law, for it is not the established law, its interpretation and application, that is in doubt. The parties to the conflict were well aware of the law in the Ethiopian case of 1935, and in the cases of the Sudetenland in 1938, of Danzig in 1939, and of Iran in 1946. What they wanted to know was whether and how the law ought to be changed. Hence, what is at stake in conflicts of this kind is not who is right and who is wrong but what ought to be done to reconcile the particular interests of individual nations with the general interest in peace and order. The question to be answered is not what the law is but what it ought to be, and this question cannot be answered by the lawyer but only by the statesman. The choice is not between legality and illegality but between political wisdom and political stupidity. "The question with me," said Edmund Burke, "is not whether you have a right to render your people miserable, but whether it is not your interest to make them happy. It is not what a lawyer tells me I *may* do, but what humanity, reason and justice tell me I ought to do."[20] "Lawyers, I know," the same author said, "cannot make the distinction for which I contend, because they have their strict rule to go by. But legislators ought to do what lawyers cannot; for they have no other rules to bind them, but the great principles of reason and equity, and the general sense of mankind."[21]

Law and political wisdom may or may not be on the same side. If they are not, the insistence upon the letter of the law will be inexpedient and may be immoral. The defense of the limited interest protected by the particular rule of law will injure the larger good which the legal system as a whole is supposed to serve. Therefore, when basic issues, on the national scene, in the form of economic, social, or constitutional conflicts demand a solution, we do not as a rule appeal to the legal acumen of the judge but to the political wisdom of the legislator and of the chief executive. Here we know that peace and order do not depend primarily upon the victory of the law with the aid of the sheriff and of the police but upon that approximation to justice which true statecraft discovers in, and imposes upon, the clash of hostile interests. If sometimes in our domestic affairs we are oblivious to this basic truth of statesmanship, we pay with social unrest, lawlessness, civil war, and revolution.

On the international scene we have not stopped paying for our forgetfulness since 1914, and we seem to be resolved to pay with all we have for the privilege of continuing to disregard the lessons of history. For here our first appeal is always to the law and to the lawyer, and since the questions which the law and the lawyer can answer are largely irrelevant to the fundamental issues upon which the peace and welfare of nations depend, our last appeal is always to the soldier. *Fiat justitia, pereat mundus* becomes the motto of a decadent legalistic statecraft. But this alternative to our legalism we do not

[20] Burke, "Speech on Conciliation with the Colonies" (1775), in *The Works of Edmund Burke* (Boston: Little, Brown & Co., 1865), II, 140.

[21] Burke, "Letter to the Sheriffs of Bristol" (1777), in *ibid.*, pp. 196–97.

357

dare face as long as we still can choose. Thus, an age which seems to be unable to meet the intellectual and moral challenge of true statesmanship, or to face in time the cruel alternative to its political failure, takes refuge in the illusion of a new diplomacy. The old diplomacy has failed, it is true, but so has the new one. The new diplomacy has failed and was bound to fail, for its legalistic tools have no access to the political problems to be solved. The old diplomacy has failed because the men who used it had forgotten the rules by which it operates. Blending misplaced idealism with misunderstood power politics, our statesmen vacillate between the old and the new, and each failure calls forth an ever stronger dose of an illusory remedy. Whether they swear by Wilson or follow Machiavelli,[22] they are always utopians pursuing either nothing but power or nothing but justice, yet never pausing to search for the rules of the political art which, in foreign affairs, is but another name for the traditional methods of diplomacy well understood.

[22] Compare Morgenthau, "The Machiavellian Utopia," *Ethics,* LV (1945), 145.

PART V

THE INTEGRITY

OF POLITICAL

ACTION

As the autonomy of the political sphere must be protected from the encroachments of other spheres of action, so must
its integrity be safeguarded against corruption from within. This
conflict between integrity and corruption creates the classic dilemma
of democratic politics. The democracy of ancient Greece fell victim
to it, and we suffer from it, unwilling to face it and, if for no other
reason, unable to cope with it. Stripped to their essentials, the two
horns of the dilemma are the demands of right political action in
terms of the action's justice and success and the demands of political
power in terms of the actor's personal success, which depends in
good measure upon the approval of a largely ignorant and emotional
public. In one word, this is the dilemma between statesmanlike and
demagogic action.

It is the essence of the dilemma that in a democracy it is at the
very best difficult and hazardous to satisfy these two demands simultaneously and that, especially in the short run, it is frequently impossible to do so. The right political action—right in terms of the
justice of ends and means and of the expediency of means—is likely
to be unpopular and, hence, endanger the actor's political power, and
the latter requires to be safeguarded by action which, while popular,

is likely to be unsound. Furthermore, the soundness of a policy, in so far as it is revealed by its success, frequently becomes apparent only in the long run, while the demands of personal power must be satisfied in the short run. As Machiavelli put it:

> Here we have to note two things; first, that the people often, deceived by an illusive good, desire their own ruin, and, unless they are made sensible of the evil of the one and the benefit of the other course by some one in whom they have confidence, they will expose the republic to infinite peril and damage. And if it happens that the people have no confidence in any one, as sometimes will be the case when they have been deceived before by events or men, then it will inevitably lead to the ruin of the state. Dante says upon this point in his discourse "On Monarchy," that the people often shout, "Life to our death, and death to our life!" It is this want of confidence on the part of the people that causes good measures to be often rejected in republics. . . . If we consider now what is easy and what difficult to persuade a people to, we may make this distinction: either what you wish to persuade them to represents at first sight gain or loss, or it seems brave or cowardly. And if you propose to them anything that upon its face seems profitable and courageous, though there be really a loss concealed under it which may involve the ruin of the republic, the multitude will ever be most easily persuaded to it. But if the measure proposed seems doubtful and likely to cause loss, then it will be difficult to persuade the people to it, even though the benefit and welfare of the republic were concealed under it.[1]

The actor, having to strike a balance between two demands, none of which he is able to satisfy fully, is forced by the very logic of the democratic process, if he were not already by the propensities of his human nature, to yield to the demands of personal power more than to those of right political action. For if he were to act otherwise he would thereby jeopardize his very ability to act at all on the political stage: his personal power. Starting out with a compromise between the demands of sound policy and the demands of personal power, he is tempted to follow what appears in the short run to be the line of least resistance, by sacrificing more and more of the substance of sound policy to considerations of personal power. This process of corruption, particularly far advanced in foreign policy, puts into question the very survival of democratic government.

[1] *Discourses on Livy* i. 53.

24 *The Great Betrayal*

The Van Doren case is a great event in American history. It is the Hiss case of the academicians and the Dreyfus case of America. As the Hiss case pointed to the possibility of treason where it could least be tolerated—that is, in the foreign office—so the Van Doren case confronts America with the fact of mendacity where it can least be tolerated—that is, among the academicians—the professional guardians of the truth. Both cases, by bringing American society face to face with intolerable evil, test the moral judgment and fiber of America. As the Hiss case raised the specter of defenseless exposure to a foreign peril, so the Van Doren case presents us with the actuality of moral disintegration from within. As the Dreyfus case confronted French society with an inescapable moral choice, so does the Van Doren case American society, and as it was France and not Captain Dreyfus which was really on trial, so it is now America and not Professor Van Doren. Here, however, the analogy ends. For while the French institutions condemned an innocent man to be acquitted belatedly by public opinion, the American institutions have condemned a guilty man whom the preponderance of public opinion appears to acquit without further ado.

Thus the Van Doren case is a great event in the history of America in a dual sense. It brings to the fore certain qualities of American society, known before but perhaps never revealed with such poignancy, and it poses a moral issue which goes to the very heart of American society. The confrontation of Van Doren with America illuminates with a sudden flash the social landscape: it makes the familiar intrude into the senses with a novel sharpness; it reveals the presence of things hidden and unsuspected; it proves the inescapable reality of things suspected but hopefully obscured. It poses a general moral problem in a peculiarly American context and, by doing so, confronts America with a fundamental moral choice and puts the moral sensitivity of the nation to a crucial test. The American reac-

From the *New York Times Magazine*, November 22, 1959.

tion to the Van Doren case bears eloquent testimony to the moral values of America. In what America says about Van Doren, the moral fiber of America itself stands revealed. By judging Van Doren, America bears judgment upon itself.

This is not a case of political or commercial corruption, such as Tweed, Teapot Dome, or Insull. Pecuniary corruption in the political and commercial spheres must be expected. For since the ultimate values of these fields are power, and wealth is a source of power, the abuse of wealth in the form of corruption is, as it were, foreordained by the very structure of these spheres; the ever present possibility of pecuniary corruption is built into them, however great or small the incidence of actual corruption may be in a particular period of history. Many politicians and businessmen are uncorrupted and fewer are uncorruptible, but they are all, by the very nature of their occupations, on familiar terms with corruption, encountering and skirting it even if they do not touch it.

Public reaction to political and commercial corruption is as predictable as the incidence of corruption itself. The familiarity of the fact evokes complacency, especially since many an onlooker preserves his virtue only for lack of opportunity to sin. The public rises in indignation only when the magnitude of the outrage exceeds the customary, when corruptive practices run counter to the political and commercial mores which are indifferent to some, such as implicit bribery, and condemn others, such as open blackmail, or when a prominent member of the other party or of the competition has been caught. The moral issue which political and commercial corruption poses is but the general issue of human fallibility. That fallibility was brought into the world by Eve and will be with us to the end of time. The best we can hope and strive for is to restrict its manifestations and mitigate its evil. In one form or other, we must live with it.

The Van Doren case raises an issue different from and more profound than political or commercial corruption. It arose in a sphere whose ultimate value is neither power nor wealth but truth. The professor is a man who has devoted his life to "professing," and what he is pledged to profess is the truth as he sees it. Mendacity in a professor is a moral fault which denies the very core of the professor's calling. Power and corruption go together, as do wealth and corruption;

pecuniary corruption is, as it were, their illegitimate offspring, pre-
formed in their nature. Yet mendacity is the very negation of truth,
the enemy which seeks its death. A mendacious professor is not like
a politician who subordinates the public good to private gain or like
a businessman who cheats. Rather he is like the physician who,
pledged to heal, maims and kills, or like the policeman who, pledged
to uphold the law, assists the criminal in breaking it. He is not so
much the corrupter of the code by which he is supposed to live as
its destroyer. This is the peculiar enormity of his outrage, which
sets his deed apart from the common corruption of power and
wealth.

It is in view of the nature of the deed that the reaction of American society must be judged. There is nothing extraordinary in the
deed itself. The truth is being betrayed every day by those who are
supposed to uphold it. What is extraordinary in the Van Doren case
is the spectacular and stark simplicity with which the issue has been
presented to the moral forum of America. The issue, thus presented,
must be met head on. The verdict must be "guilty" or "not guilty";
there is no room for a hung jury or for a Pontius Pilate washing his
hands in skeptical abstention.

The two institutions concerned—Columbia University and NBC—
have acted honorably, appropriately, and expeditiously. NBC put
the finger on the crux of the matter when it cited as grounds for
dismissal, aside from the original deception, the subsequent series of
deceptions masking the original one. Yet the reactions of the public
contrast strikingly with those of the institutions. Of the nine members of the House of Representatives who heard the testimony, five
addressed Van Doren in laudatory terms, "commending" and "com-
plimenting" him and expressing their "appreciation." Two Congress-
men expressed the hope that he would not be dismissed from his
positions at Columbia University and NBC, and the chairman of the
committee delivered a peroration predicting "a great future" for
him. Only one member of the committee openly disagreed with the
commendation of his colleagues. But even he did not convey awareness of the real issue, the scholar's special commitment to the truth.

Nor did the comments of most of Van Doren's students as reported by the press. One expressed "faith in him as a man" and
called him "a fine gentleman," another thought that "what he did

was not wrong," a third called the acceptance of his resignation "very unfair." The two students who are quoted as having approved of the acceptance justified it with the embarrassment Van Doren's continued affiliation would have caused the University. As one of them put it: "If Mr. Van Doren had remained, the school would have become associated with everything he had done." And a petition bearing the signature of 650 students demanded that he be rehired. None of the students whose reactions were recorded showed the slightest inkling of the moral issue raised by the case. And but a small minority of editorial comment and letters to newspapers did so.

How is this perversion of moral judgment, praising what deserves to be condemned and even at best remaining indifferent to the real issue, to be explained? The explanation of Congressional reaction is simple. The five members of Congress who approved Van Doren applied the standards of political behavior to the academic sphere. What they would have found pardonable and even praiseworthy in the politician they were unable to condemn in the scholar. Theirs was the fault of parochialism, which elevates the standards applicable to a particular sphere into absolutes applicable to all men regardless of circumstances. They dealt with the Van Doren case as though it were just another case of political corruption to be dealt with tolerantly, understandingly, and even approvingly after the culprit had come clean and returned to the fold of fairly honest politicians.

However, the complacency of the politicians points to a more profound issue, a moral dilemma built in, as it were, to the very fabric of American democracy. This is the dilemma between objective standards of conduct and majority rule, between the compliance in thought and deed with standards which are true regardless of time and place, and accommodation to the standards prevailing in a particular society in a particular time and place. America was founded upon the recognition of certain self-evident truths which men do not create but find in the nature of things. Yet American society and, more particularly, American democracy have lived in good measure, and in even greater measure as time went on, by conformity to whatever values appeared to be accepted by the elite or the majority of the moment.

At the beginning of American history and in its great moments of heroic dedication, the moral relativism, if not agnosticism, of that conformist attitude was mediated and even at times overwhelmed by the intellectual awareness of those eternal verities and the compliance with them in deeds. Yet in our day-to-day collective life that tension between objective standards and the ever changing preferences of society tends to be resolved in favor of the latter. Mr. Justice Holmes's famous dictum, "I have no practical criticism [with regard to laws] except what the crowd wants," is the classic expression of that resolution. It is also expressed in one Congressman's hope that Columbia University would not act "prematurely" and would at least wait to judge public reaction to Van Doren's statement.

The objective standards which constitute, as it were, the moral backbone of a civilized society are here dissolved into the ever changing amorphousness of public opinion. What a man ought or ought not to do is here determined not by objective laws immutable as the stars, but by the results of the latest public opinion poll. What is expected of a man is not compliance with those laws, but conformity to the demands of society, whatever they may be. A man who has gotten into trouble because he is temporarily out of step with public opinion needs only to slow down or hurry up, as the case may be, in order to get back into line, and all will be all right again with him and the world. Moral judgment thus becomes the matter of a daily plebiscite, and what is morally good becomes identical with what the crowd wants and tolerates. The Congressional reaction to the Van Doren case, then, is easily understood in terms of the trend, deeply ingrained in American society, toward making conformity with prevailing opinion the final arbiter of moral worth.

The moral illiteracy of the student is less easily explained. For the students, so one would like to think, are apprentices in that noble endeavor of discovering and professing the truth, not yet compelled by the demands of society to compromise their convictions; they behold truth in all its purity; and they must look at a mendacious professor as a student of the priesthood looks at a priest who blasphemes God. How is it possible for a young man of presumably superior intelligence and breeding, predestined to be particularly sensitive to the moral issue of truth, to be so utterly insensitive to it? These men were not born morally blind; for, as I have said elsewhere, man "is a moralist because he is a man." These men were born with a moral sense as they were born with a sense of sight; they were no more morally blind at birth than they were physically blind. What made them lose that moral sense? Who blinded them to the moral standards by which they—at least as students—are supposed to live?

The answer must be in the same sphere which produced Van Doren himself: the academic world. There is profound meaning in the solidarity between Van Doren and his students, and that meaning is found in the academic sphere which made them both what they are as moral beings. While public opinion has pinned responsibility on television, advertising, business, or low teachers' salaries, nobody seems to have pointed to the academic system which taught both teacher and students.

A system of higher education, dedicated to the discovery and transmission of the truth, is not a thing apart from the society which has created, maintains, and uses it. This is especially true of a decentralized and largely private system such as ours. The academic world partakes of the values prevailing in society and is exposed to the social pressures to conform to them. Its very concept of what truth is bears the marks of the relativism and instrumentalism dominant in American society; and by teaching that kind of truth, it strengthens its dominance over the American mind.

Yet even its commitment to this kind of truth is bound to come into conflict with the values and demands of society. The stronger the trend toward conformity within society and the stronger the commitment of the scholar to values other than the truth, such as wealth and power, the stronger will be the temptation to sacrifice the moral commitment to the truth for social advantage. The tension between these contradictory commitments typically issues in a compromise which keeps the commitment to the truth within socially acceptable bounds—exempting, for instance, the taboos of society from investigation—and restrains social ambitions from seriously interfering with the search for a truth cautiously defined. In the measure that truth is thus limited and defined, the search for it is deflected from its proper goal and thereby corrupted. On either end of the spectrum, one finds a small group which either is subversive of the truth by telling society what it wants to hear or else is subversive of society by telling society what it does not want to hear.

Contemporary American society offers enormous temptations for the academic world to follow the former path—that is, not only to corrupt the truth, but to betray it. In the process, the academic world tends to transform itself into a duplicate of the business and political worlds, with the search for truth subordinated to the values of these worlds. To the temptations of wealth and power held out by government, business, and foundations, the scholar has nothing to oppose but his honor committed to a truth which for him, as for society, is but a doubtful and for most of them at best a relative thing. He has his feet on an island of sand surrounded by the waves of temptation. The step from corruption to betrayal is big in moral terms but small in execution. What difference is there between receiving $129,000 under false pretenses from government, business, or a foundation, which has become almost standard operating procedure, and receiving the same amount under false pretenses from Revlon? The difference lies not in moral relevance but in the technique, which in the former case is discreet and elegant and remains within the academic mores, while in the latter it is blatant, vulgar, and obvious. Van Doren and his students were formed by a world which makes it easier for some of its members to receive money than reject it and condones the betrayal of truth for the sake of wealth and power, provided the academic amenities are preserved. Van Doren is indeed a black sheep in the academic world, but there are many gray ones among the flock.

In the world of Van Doren, American society beholds its own world, the world of business and politics, of wealth and power. It cannot condemn him without condemning itself, and since it is unwilling to do the latter, it cannot bring itself to do the former. Instead, it tends to absolve him by confusing the virtues of compassion and charity for the actor with the vice of condoning the act. Yet by refusing to condemn Van Doren, it cannot but condemn itself. For it convicts itself of a moral obtuseness which signifies the beginning of the end of civilized society. The Van Doren case is indeed the Dreyfus case in reverse. As France, by acquitting Dreyfus, restored itself as a civilized society ordered by the moral law, so must America by condemning Van Doren. Otherwise it will have signed the death warrant of its soul.

25 Epistle to the Columbians on the Meaning of Morality

Some of you, students of Columbia University, have written me, commenting on an article on the Van Doren case which was published in the *New York Times Magazine* of November 22, 1959. Since your letters either raise identical points or express the same general philosophic position, I am addressing you collectively. By doing this in public, I am already establishing an important difference between your and my position. For all of you request that, if I should write on this topic again, I not reveal your names; and one of you asks that the content of his letter not be revealed either. You appear to shun the public debate of public issues and prefer to drop opinions into the confidential darkness of the mailbox. I believe that in a democracy which still possesses its vitality public issues must be debated in the public forum and that the citizens must be seen, heard, and counted in the interchange of ideas and the interplay of interests, out of which a new consensus will arise.

But what are you afraid of? Why do you feel you must hide your faces and muffle your voices? Your letters are courteous, decent, intelligent, literate, and moving in their concern about the moral problem and their anxiety to be on the right side of it. The opinions you express are eminently respectable and even conformist to a fault. You say what almost everybody says and you say it better and with greater erudition than most, but there is not a rebel among you. The only deviation which you allow yourselves is a criticism of the trustees of your university for having acted hastily in accepting Van Doren's resignation; but that indiscretion you had already committed when you signed the petition asking that Van Doren be rehired. If your letters were published and the identity of the writers revealed, it is inconceivable that you would suffer in even the slightest degree, for you have done nothing to be ashamed of, you have

From the *New Republic*, December 22, 1959.

368

violated none of the mores of society, and you have much to be proud of by way of intellectual accomplishment and moral aspiration. Why, then, are you afraid?

I will tell you what frightens you. You are afraid of your shadows in the sunlight. You are afraid of the sound of your voices in the silence of the crowd. You are afraid of yourself. You are afraid to speak what is on everybody's lips as long as it is only you who would speak. Only when your voices merge into the chorus of the mass do you cease to be afraid. It is the protective anonymity of the crowd which gives you courage. To sign a petition in the company of 650 of your fellows, then, is one thing; to speak without assurance that you are not alone is quite another.

But imagine for a moment where man would be if his most intelligent, best educated, and most secure children had throughout history hidden their faces and spoken only in whispers. The great men whose lives and works you study are remembered exactly because they were not anonymous, because they showed their faces above the crowd and spoke in a loud voice all by themselves. What they spoke was more often than not the opposite of what the crowd believed and wanted to hear, and many of them lived in prison or in exile and died in disgrace or on the cross. Have you ever heard of two German students by the name of Scholl, brother and sister, who openly defied Hitler in the University of Munich and were hanged? Do you not remember the Hungarian, East German, Polish, and even Russian students who risked everything for their convictions and many of whom paid for them with their freedom and their lives? And you, risking nothing at all, refuse to speak above an anonymous whisper! Why are you so frightened by your own faces and your own voices? The answer to that question will become clear at the end of this letter; for it is intimately connected with the moral problem, to which we are turning now.

You are stung by my assertion that you are unaware of the moral problem posed by the Van Doren case, and you assure me that you disapprove of his conduct. But my point is proven by the very arguments with which you try to reconcile your disapproval of Van Doren's conduct with your petition to rehire him. The issue is for you confined in a three-cornered relationship between Van Doren, yourself, and Columbia University. Your concern is primarily with the misfortune of an attractive teacher, your regret in losing him, and the rigor of the university's decision. You support your position by five main arguments: the confession has swept the slate clean, Van Doren will not do it again, his teaching was above reproach, academic teaching is not concerned with substantive truth, and the university acted with undue haste. These arguments, taken at face value and erected into general principles of conduct, lead of necessity to the complete destruction of morality.

If confession, especially one which, as some of you conveniently forget, was not rendered by free moral choice but extracted by sheer necessity, can undo the deed, no evil could ever be condemned and no evildoer ever be brought to justice. If wrong could be so simply righted and guilt so painlessly atoned, the very distinction between right and wrong, innocence and guilt would disappear; for no sooner would a wrong be committed than it would be blotted out by a confession. Confession, even if freely rendered as an act of contrition and moral conversion, can mitigate the guilt but cannot wipe it out.

The argument that the morally objectionable act is not likely to be repeated assumes that the purpose of moral condemnation is entirely pragmatic, seeking to prevent a repetition of the deed; if what has been done once is not likely to be done again, we might as well forget it. Yet while it is true that according to the common law a dog is entitled to his first bite, it is nowhere written that a man is entitled to his first murder, his first fraud, or his first lie. The moral law is not a utilitarian instrument aiming at the protection of society, even though its observance has this effect, but its commands are absolute and must be obeyed for their own sake. Oedipus did not think that it was all right to marry his mother once since he did not do it again. Or would you suggest that Leopold and Loeb should have gone free because it was most unlikely that they would repeat what they had done?

The arguments of the good teacher and of teaching not being concerned with substantive truth go together. You assume, and some of your academic experience may well support your assumption, that the teacher is a kind of intellectual mechanic who fills your head with conventionally approved and required knowledge, as a filling-station attendant fills a tank with gas. You don't care what the teacher does from 10:00 A.M. to 9:00 A.M. as long as he gives you from 9:00 to 10:00 A.M. the knowledge which he has been paid to transmit. You recognize no relation between a teacher's general attitude toward the truth and his way of transmitting knowledge because you do not recognize an organic relation between transmitted knowledge and an objective, immutable truth. Yet the view that knowledge is but conventional—one conception of truth to be superseded by another—while seemingly supported by the radical transformation of physics, finds no support in the fields of knowledge dealing with man. If it were otherwise, Plato and Aristotle, Sophocles and Shakespeare, Montesquieu and Locke could mean nothing to us, except as objects for antiquarian exploration.

There is, then, in these fields an accumulation of knowledge, old knowledge being refined and added to, but not necessarily superseded, by new insights. The teacher of such knowledge is not only the recorder and transmitter of what goes by the name of knowledge in a particular time and place, but he is also and foremost the guardian and augmenter of a permanent treasure. This is not a part-time job to be performed during certain hours without relation with what goes on before and after. Quite to the contrary, this is a profession which requires the dedication and ethos of the whole man. Of such a man, it must be expected that he be truthful not only between 9:00 and 10:00 A.M. when he teaches, but always.

The last argument that the trustees of the university acted with undue haste is the most curious of all, and it gives the show away. One of you says that the trustees could not have evaluated the evidence during the four hours of their deliberations. Another mentions that the trustees acted before all the evidence was in. Still another argues that they wanted to wash their hands quickly of the whole business for fear of public opinion. And one advances the ingenious proposition that the students would not have protested if the trustees had waited a month or so with the acceptance of the resignation, pretending "however untruthfully," that they were investigating the case!

In truth, you do not mean any of these things, which are either patently at odds with the obvious facts or else absurd on their face. You look for reasons which justify your unwillingness to transcend that three-cornered relationship between yourself, your teacher, and your university and to judge the obvious facts by the standards of morality rather than adjust them for your and your teacher's convenience. You are sorry about losing an attractive teacher and you hate to see that teacher suffer; nothing else counts. But there is something else that counts and that is the sanctity of the moral law. Your dean, in an admirable statement, which I have seen quoted only in your student paper, has formulated it thus:

The issue is the moral one of honesty and the integrity of teaching. Appearing as a teacher, Mr. Van Doren engaged in an act of deception in professing to know what he did not know, and of dishonesty in accepting answers in a test of knowledge against an opponent he believed to be honest. Thereafter, he continued to act out the deception and continued to lie about his actions, even under oath, until after he had been subpoenaed by a committee of Congress. This behavior seems to me to have been contrary to the principles that a teacher stands for and undertakes to instill in his students. If these principles are to continue to have meaning at Columbia, Mr. Van Doren's ultimate offer to resign had to be accepted.

Here is indeed the nub of the matter.

You must have smiled indulgently or shrugged with impatience when you saw me refer to the sanctity of the moral law. Is not morality, so you might ask, a relative thing, the ever changing result of environment and circumstances? If this were so, let me ask you, how do you explain that we cannot only understand the moral relevance of the Ten Commandments, originating in a social environment and circumstances quite different from ours, but also make them the foundation for our moral life? How do you explain that the moral ideas of Plato and Pascal, of Buddha and Thomas Aquinas are similarly acceptable to our intellectual understanding and moral sense? If the disparate historic systems of morality were not erected upon a common foundation of moral understanding and valuation, impervious to the changing conditions of time and place, we could not understand any other moral system but our own, nor could any other moral system but our own have any moral relevance for us. It is only because we as moral beings have something in common with all other men—past and present—that we are able to understand, and make our own, the core of the moral systems of others. What is it that all men have in common as moral beings?

All men—civilized and barbarian—in contrast to the animals, are born with a moral sense; that is to say, as man is by nature capable of making logical judgments, so is he capable by nature of making moral judgments. As I have said in the *New York Times Magazine* article and elsewhere, man "is a moralist because he is a man." You in your groping for a tenable moral position, in your anxiety to justify yourself in moral terms, bear eloquent testimony to the innate character of that moral faculty. Civilized man shares with the barbarian the faculty of making moral judgments, but excels him in that he is capable of making the right moral judgments, knowing why he makes them. He knows—as Socrates, the Greek tragedians (to whom one of you rather wistfully refers), the Biblical prophets, and the great moralists and tragedians of all the ages knew—what is meant by the sanctity of the moral law.

The moral law is not made for the convenience of man, rather it is an indispensable precondition for his civilized existence. It is one of the great paradoxes of civilized existence that—in contrast to the existence of the animals and barbarians—it is not self-contained but requires for its fulfillment transcendent orientations. The moral law provides one of them. That is to say, human existence, not in its animal but in its civilized qualities, cannot find its meaning within itself but must receive it from a transcendent source.

You are still in all likelihood closer to your birth than to your death; yet in the measure that your life approaches its natural limits, you will become aware of the truth of that observation. For when you look back on your life in judgment, you will remember it, and you will want it to be remembered, for its connection with the things that transcend it. And if you ask yourself why you remember and study the lives and deeds of great men, why you call them great in the first place, you will find that they were oriented in extraordinary ways and to an unusual degree toward the things that transcend their own existence. That is the meaning of the passage from the Scriptures, "He that findeth his life shall lose it; and he that loseth his life for my sake shall find it."

This connection between our civilized existence and the moral law explains the latter's sanctity. By tinkering with it, by sacrificing it for individual convenience, we are tinkering with ourselves as civilized beings, we are sacrificing our own civilized existence. As

Kant put it: "If justice should perish, man's existence on earth would have lost its meaning."

The issue before you, when you were asked to sign that petition, was not the happiness of a particular man or, for that matter, your own, but whether you and your university could afford to let a violation of the moral law pass as though it were nothing more than a traffic violation. Socrates had to come to terms with that issue, and he knew how to deal with it. You did not know how to deal with it. And this is why you hide your faces and muffle your voices. For since your lives have lost the vital contact with the transcendence of the moral law, you find no reliable standard within yourself by which to judge and act. You are frightened by the emptiness within yourself, the insufficiency stemming from a self-contained existence. And so you flee into the protective cover of the anonymous crowd and judge as it judges and act as it acts. But once you have restored that vital connection with the moral law from which life receives its meaning, you will no longer be afraid of your shadow and the sound of your voice. You will no longer be afraid of yourself. For you will carry within yourself the measure of yourself and of your fellows and the vital link with things past, future, and above.

26 *Christian Ethics and Political Action*

The conflict between the demands of Christian ethics and the way man must live is the overriding moral experience of Western civilization. That conflict is foreordained in the nature of Christian ethics and the nature of man. It is the very function of Christian ethics to call upon man to comply with a code of moral conduct with which, by virtue of his nature, he cannot comply. This function, it should be added in passing, is not only moral but also—and probably primarily—theological. For if that unbridgeable gap between the demands of Christian ethics and human nature did not exist, if, in other words, man could become a perfect Christian by his own unaided efforts here and now, the grace of God would have no object for its work and would have no organic place in a theological system.

The moral function of Christian ethics is to hold up to man a code of moral conduct both unattainable and approachable. Man cannot attain moral perfection in this world; the best he is capable of is to conceive its meaning, to achieve through an isolated act of goodness a tiny fragment of it, and make aspiration toward it the guiding principle of a whole life. Those who conceive the perfection of Christian ethics with their mind's eye are theologians and philosophers; those who from time to time do deeds conforming to the demands of Christian ethics are what we call good men; those who orient their whole life toward that perfection are saints.

Few are the true theologians, philosophers, good men, and saints among us. Most of us try to escape the conflict between what is demanded of us and what we can do. For to face that conflict squarely places an intolerable burden either upon our actions or our consciences....

It is against this background of the conflict between Christian teaching and human action . . . that one must put the Quaker attitude toward foreign policy. This attitude bears three distinct qualities. The

The Foreword to Robert O. Byrd's *Quaker Ways in Foreign Policy* (1960).

Quakers have not endeavored to escape that conflict but have had the courage to face it. They have had the still greater courage of trying to overcome that conflict through action which is both politically relevant and morally tenable in the light of Christian teaching. Finally, they have endeavored to elevate the political sphere to the level of Christian ethics not by superimposing upon that sphere a rigid dogma but rather by penetrating it with a pragmatic goodness inspired by the "Inner Light." The Quaker approach to foreign policy is not so much a doctrine as a disposition of the soul translated into action. It is truly political in its adaptability to circumstances; it approaches Christian moral excellence in being consistently informed by the pure demands of Christian ethics.

The history of the unfolding of this approach is moving, and is so on three counts. It moves as human excellence in all spheres of human endeavor moves. We are moved whenever we see a man perform a deed seeking with singlemindedness the perfection of its realm. We are moved to an even higher degree when that perfection is sought by a group of men who have been tied together over the centuries through a pledge of voluntary allegiance to the seeking of perfection in the realm of religious practice. For no human enterprise has been more consistently debased than this most noble of all by having been made the servant and the shield of the seekers after power and wealth, the money changers and the Pharisees. I am reminded of the fictional account of Martin Luther, whom Strindberg makes say of a rabbi that he was the only Christian in Rome and that it was too bad that he was of the wrong faith. In a world which uses Christian ethics for unchristian ends, it is indeed moving to follow the historical trail of a Christian sect which seeks to transform itself and political society in the image of Christian teaching. Finally, there is something moving in the success of the endeavor on the individual level and its consistent failure on the political plane. The persistent effort, doomed to ever renewed failure, carries within itself an element of tragedy. In their convictions, achievements, and sufferings the Quakers bear witness to the teachings of Christianity, in their failures they bear witness to the insuperable stubbornness of the human condition.

27 *The Nuremberg Trial*

I fully agree with Professor Gustav Gundlach's basic premise "that the Nuremberg trial was first and last a *punitive* trial," and that this is its core: "that is what we are to subject to moral scrutiny."[1] I should add that the moral doubts to which the trial has given rise, and which I share, concern primarily the first count of the indictment, that is, the planning and waging of a war of aggression and of a war in violation of international law. These moral doubts are not founded, in the words of Professor Edmund A. Walsh, in "controversy over the minutiae of the procedure at Nuremberg." Nor are they concerned with the alleged "subjectivity" of the judges.[2] They arise from their complicity.

If the leaders of Nazi Germany are guilty of conspiring to wage, and of planning and waging, a war of aggression and a war in violation of international law, so are the leaders of France, Great Britain, and Russia. It is a matter of historic record that from 1935 onward the main objective of British, French, and Russian diplomacy was not to make German aggression impossible but to deflect it from their respective territories. German aggression and lawlessness were not morally obnoxious to France and Great Britain as long as they were directed against Russia. If one can believe Ribbentrop's last plea, Stalin wired congratulations to Hitler upon the starting of the Second World War, which became morally reprehensible in Russian eyes only on June 22, 1941. And, lest the truth be drowned in a flood of moralizing legend, it was not moral indignation at German aggression and lawlessness but the mortal peril of the British Isles and the resulting danger for its own national security which drew the United States to the side of Great Britain; and it was not Coventry, Rotterdam, or Warsaw, but Pearl Harbor which made the United States an active belligerent in the Second World War.

From *America*, December 7, 1946.

[1] "A Moral Estimate of the Nuremberg Trial."

[2] "Comments and Corollaries."

Thus it was a mere coincidence, engendered by Hitler's madness, that at the end of the Second World War France, Great Britain, Russia, the United States, and nineteen other nations found themselves united as actual and prospective victims of German aggression and, hence, also united in moral indignation at the defeated aggressor. Whether or not the rule of international law by virtue of which the Nazi leaders were punished for planning and waging aggressive war was *ex post facto* may be an open question; there ought, however, to be little doubt that the universal moral condemnation of German aggression as such, without regard to its victim, is very much *ex post facto*. It is a mere by-product of a passing historic constellation. Four judges, as it were, sat in judgment over a criminal, of whose crimes they all had been the victims and three of them, at one time or another, the accomplices. The Second World War was a war for survival, undertaken by individual nations in their own national interest, not the punitive war of a morally united humanity for the purpose of making eternal justice prevail.

In the compass of a brief comment, it is impossible to show in the light of scholastic doctrine the doubtful moral validity of the Nuremberg trial, in so far as its foundation is the immorality of aggressive war. It must suffice here to point out that the moral unity of Christendom is the indispensable precondition for the distinction between *bellum justum* and *bellum injustum*, that aggressive war is not identical with *bellum injustum* (in other words, there can be aggressive wars that are just), and that the indirect power of the Pope *in temporalibus* limited and qualified the authority of the princes to pass judgments on the justice of the cause of their enemies in war.

There is a great temptation for the victors in war to flatter themselves with the delusion that they have the last word in history because they had the last word in war; to believe that a monopoly in a weapon of war implies a monopoly in virtue; and to mistake the voice of the victor for the voice of Divine Justice. It is a temptation to which the heathens of the ancient world yielded without misgivings. Yet we who have heard the voice of Isaiah and St. Augustine ought to be on our guard against identifying too easily a fortuitous result of the complexities of history with the plans and judgments of Providence. The eighteen men convicted at Nuremberg were guilty of many crimes, and they were justly condemned and punished. To make the condemnation the occasion for the revival of the institution of punitive war is morally unwarranted and fraught with moral and political danger. It is but a symptom of the moral and intellectual confusion of our times. The moral philosophy of the Nuremberg trial confounds that confusion.

28 *The Decline of the Democratic Process*

The crisis of American politics, domestic and international, and the prevailing unawareness of its gravity and of its very existence are rooted in two misunderstandings and misuses of American democracy. They affect the very essence of democratic government. One concerns the position and functions of the President; the other, the relationship between the requirements of sound policy and the will of the majority. The major weaknesses of American policies can be traced to one or the other or both of these misunderstandings and misuses.

Democratic government is government by popular choice—choice of men and, through it, choice of policy. A government that can keep itself in power regardless of the preferences of the people is not democratic at all; a government whose choice by the people does not also imply a choice of policy is but imperfectly so. It follows that a perfectly democratic system of government must be partisan government in the sense that those who have been elected to govern stand for one set of policies and those who have been rejected at the polls are committed to another set of policies. The candidates for office have been judged by the policies with which they are identified and by their ability to carry them through, and at the next elections they will again be judged by these criteria.

The government of the United States, as presently constituted on its highest level, is not perfectly democratic. The President was re-elected in 1956, not because he stood for specific policies which the electorate preferred to those of his opponent, but because he was committed only to general aspirations shared by all men of good will. It is exactly this lack of partisanship, this commitment to unexceptional generalities which imply no commitment to anything concrete in terms of policy, which made him into the incarnation of the nation's better self, the symbol of its nobler longings. Thus he was re-elected, not on the strength of particular foreign policies executed or proposed, but as a symbol of the nation's longing for

From the *New Republic*, December 17, 1956.

peace, as the man who had brought peace to Korea and would preserve it elsewhere.

This popular image of the President reflects Mr. Eisenhower's own conception of the Presidency in theory and practice. Supported by an optimistic philosophy, unaware of man's propensities for evil and the tragic dilemmas of human existence, he has limited himself, by and large, to the enunciation of general principles, leaving the political task of their implementation to subordinates or to nobody in particular. His interest in factual information and day-by-day administration has been sporadic, and his intervention in the formation of policy has generally been reserved for crisis situations. Thus the President, by divorcing his person and his office from the partisanship of politics, has transformed the character of politics itself. Politics has lost its fanatical partisanship and bitter animosities, and the warming benevolence of a President who appears to be above politics envelops the nation as in a *union sacrée*.

It is the fatal weakness of Mr. Eisenhower's contribution to the substance of American foreign policy that it is informed by the same philosophy of abstention, conciliation, and pacification as is his domestic one. Conciliation and pacification as ends in themselves can, under certain circumstances, be virtues at home; they are, except under the rarest of circumstances, vices abroad. And one may well speculate whether the price the nation will have to pay in the long run even for its present domestic tranquillity in terms of moral stagnation, intellectual sterility, issues unrecognized, and problems unsolved will not turn out to be vastly excessive.

The price we must pay for international tranquillity as an end in itself is not a matter of speculation but of historic experience. Optimistic assumptions about human nature may be able to support for a while domestic policies carried on in a civilized Western society. They are bound to be disappointed on the international scene. For here conciliation and peace can hardly ever be ends in themselves but must be sought as the by-product of a political settlement which actually reconciles antagonistic interests and thereby deprives the parties concerned of the incentive to seek redress by force. At home and abroad, the President's philosophy spells avoidance of problems, abstention from action, tranquillity as an end in itself. Yet what can be tolerated in the short run at home—for here the agencies for thought and action other than the President continuously operate on behalf of the United States—becomes a mortal danger abroad. For if the United States does not reflect on the problems that concern it and does not try to solve them on its own terms, the enemies of the United States do so reflect and act. International peace and tranquillity achieved at the price of abstention from thought and action, then, are tantamount to retreat and surrender.

The new conception of the Presidency not only impairs the freedom of choice at democracy's decisive moment—the presidential elections—and leads to impotence in its application to foreign policy but it also impairs the day-by-day democratic processes by destroying the functions of the opposition. Historically, that destruction has manifested itself as the corruption of bipartisanship in foreign policy. Bipartisanship, as originally conceived at the end of the Second World War, carried the negative implication that a foreign policy ought not to be opposed by one party for the sole reason that the President and Secretary of State belonging to the other party were carrying it out. In positive terms, bipartisanship implied that the opposition party should support sound foreign policies and oppose unsound ones, regardless of the party affiliation of those carrying them out. Conceived in these terms, bipartisanship recognized the elemental fact that the consequences of foreign policy are not limited, as are those of many domestic ones, to a particular segment of the population identified with one or the other party, but affect the whole nation for generations to come. Bipartisanship drew from this fact the sound and indispensable conclusion that party strife for its own sake must stop at the point where the whole nation meets other nations in defense of its interests and its very existence.

However, bipartisanship, as originally conceived, never did imply that the opposition should not oppose when opposition appeared justified by the demerits of the foreign policy pursued. Nor did it imply that the opposition should forego what is not only its privilege but also its mission, whose fulfilment is indispensable for the proper functioning of the democratic process: to submit alternative policies for the administration to adopt or else for the people to support by changing the administration. An opposition that does not perform these two functions deprives the people in yet another way of that choice of policies essential to democracy.

This is indeed what the opposition was doing during Mr. Eisenhower's first term. It abdicated its mission, confounding bipartisanship with conformity. What did its titular head and its leaders in Congress contribute to public enlightenment, to the clarification of the issues, to intellectual and political pressure upon the administration? What the policy of the British Labour party was in successive international crises we know. But what was the policy of the Democratic party of the United States? The answer is simple and disquieting: there was no such policy. Nor is the picture that the mass media of communication present much more reassuring. A very few notable exceptions notwithstanding, the abdication of judgment and will of the political opposition was duplicated here. Everybody seemed to emulate the President's example and rise above politics, sharing in the nobility of his sentiments and general objectives. The result is national unity, paid for with the lifeblood of the democratic process. For this is not the unity of a people who, after weighing the alternatives, have decided what they want and how to get what they want. It is rather like a fog that makes us all brothers in blindness.

Yet among those whose duty it is to lead by criticizing and proposing—the public officials, politicians, correspondents, columnists, commentators, academicians—the failure is one of will rather than of judgment. Of those who keep silent or speak only by indirection so great as to confuse the ignorant and to be intelligible only to the informed, the great majority know the awful truth. Why is it that during Mr. Eisenhower's first term none of the policy-makers who express their misgivings and forebodings freely in private raised his voice in anguish or resigned in protest? And what of all the others who have to risk much less? They have all become the victims of the official conception of the Presidency, which allows only of whispered hints as some isolated deficiency here and there and must regard political attack and even frank debate, the very dynamics of democracy, as a sacrilege against the spirit of the nation, incarnate as it is in the person of the President.

The debilitating effect which a new conception of the Presidency and the corruption of bipartisanship reflecting it has had upon the foreign policy of the United States is, in turn, reflected and aggravated by a new conception of the office of the Secretary of State and a new method of gaining public and, more particularly, congressional support in the conduct of foreign policy.

Mr. Dulles' conception of his office in one respect curiously duplicates Mr. Eisenhower's conception of the Presidency: both conceive of their offices as being divorced from the day-by-day operations of policy formation and execution. What Gettysburg and Augusta are for the President, all the capitals of the world are for the Secretary of State: respectable escapes from the daily responsibilities of government. Here, however, the analogy ends. For while Mr. Dulles has shut himself off from the regular departmental channels of information and advice, he has kept a monopoly on major policy decisions and has taken an unprecedentedly large part in certain phases of their execution, so large a part as to keep him from his desk for about one-third of his tenure of office. The results have been unfortunate in four different respects.

The Secretary of State has been unable to perform adequately the very functions of policy formation which he considers his exclusive prerogative. Not even the wisest and most experienced of secretaries of state can afford to dispense with the information and advice of his subordinates; and the most traveled of secretaries of state can afford it even less. The great abilities and greater self-confidence of Mr. Dulles have not compensated for this deficiency. In consequence, Mr. Dulles has not had the time or the incentive, in terms of new knowledge and new ideas, to deal constructively with the drastic changes that have occurred in recent years on the international scene. This is one of the reasons why his tenure of office has been outstanding not for bold initiative and innovation in policy but rather for the virtually mechanical continuation of established routines long after they had served their purpose.

Mr. Dulles' assumption of the role of roving ambassador and ubiquitous negotiator has impaired the performance of his functions in yet another way. There is great wisdom, reflecting the nature of things, in the tradition that requires the head of the foreign office to stay at home and reflect and decide, and the ambassadors to go abroad and negotiate. This division of labor not only frees the head of the foreign office from preoccupation with details obstructing his over-all view of foreign relations but also protects him from involvement in the intrigues, indiscretions, and commitments inseparable from the routine of diplomacy. Mr. Dulles, by doing what ambassadors are supposed to do, has not been able to do the job only he could have done. Furthermore, he has wasted the prestige of his office on a multitude of minutiae, magnifying them far beyond their intrinsic importance. He owes his unpopularity abroad and the foreign mistrust of his word in good measure to that assumption of functions which no Secretary of State ought to assume.

The Secretary of State has also been unable to exert effective control over his department on behalf of his own policies. Mr. Dulles has sought to carry the formation of policy in his own head and leave the implementation of the policy through day-by-day administration and execution to subordinates. Yet in actual performance policy formation cannot be so neatly separated from implementation, and those who control the day-by-day operations of the Department uncontrolled by the Secretary become, by the very logic of their functions, makers of policy on their own. The permanent functional and frequent physical separation of the Secretary from the Department has transformed the top echelon of his subordinates into a sort of collective leadership performing the institutional functions of the Secretary without his permanent control and without his authority. Thus the undersecretary of state, the counselor, the legal adviser, certain deputy undersecretaries and assistant secretaries, severally or collectively, have been carrying out functions which only the Secretary should perform and can perform successfully.

Such a state of affairs is fraught with danger under the best of circumstances, that is, when the Secretary and his immediate subordinates see eye to eye on policy; for it is bound to result in misunderstandings, misinterpretations, disorganization, and the incoherence of policies. However, the circumstances under which Mr. Dulles' system has operated were never of the best. For reasons that shall be discussed in a moment, Mr. Dulles frequently appointed to key positions in his department men who were out of sympathy with his own policies. This being so, it is but natural that in the process of execution the Secretary's policies were often infused with the spirit of their opponents. The Secretary's policies were sometimes so completely perverted by his subordinates that deliberate sabotage provides the only plausible explanation.

The effects of this situation were clear to see in the Suez crisis of

November, 1956. The Department of State ceased to function as the instrument of a viable American foreign policy. It split into two factions, committed to radically different and mutually exclusive policies. One faction looked at the trend of American foreign policy with alarm and despair. The other faction welcomed that trend, being in good measure of its own making, with enthusiastic expectations. One day, one faction seemed to prevail; another day, the other, and there was nobody above them to mold out of the welter of opinion a foreign policy capable of execution and promising success.

These weaknesses were compounded by the revival of a propensity, which has at times exerted a strong influence upon the conduct of American foreign policy, to look at foreign policy with a lawyer's eye and to manipulate it with a lawyer's tools. It would certainly be preposterous to suggest that lawyers cannot make great statesmen and diplomatists; the pages of history are full of them. But those lawyers were transformed by their political experience into something more than lawyers; they were able to transcend the limits of their craft. It is the strength and weakness of Mr. Dulles that he has brought to his office a first-rate legal mind which excels in negotiations and in deft maneuver but fails in the constructive tasks of statesmanship. For the lawyer's mind is uncongenial to these tasks.

The lawyer sees reality dissolved into a sequence of isolated "cases," each to be dealt with on its "merits." Thus Great Britain and France committed "aggression" against Egypt and must not be allowed to get away with it. Little does it matter that this "case" has a history which antedates the invasion of Egypt and that it will make history long after the last British and French soldiers have left Egyptian territory. Let us first close this "case" by restoring the pre-invasion status quo, and we shall then turn to the next "case" if and when it arises. The subject matter with which the lawyer thus endeavors to deal being a continuum of which the particular "case" is an organic and inseparable element, the lawyer's method is singularly inadequate to deal with it. Its political manifestations are the conception of policy as the reaction to the initiative of others; improvisation, since before a "case" arises there is nothing to be done; aversion to long-range planning, since the scope of action is limited by the dimensions of the "case" and when the "case" is settled action must await another "case."

The lawyer is particularly averse to long-range planning that entails risks and requires daring because he has been conditioned in dealing with his clients—and is not the government just another client?—to chart a course that avoids trouble, minimizes risks, and is plainly calculable. He plans foreign policy as he would plan an estate. Examining a plan for action, he sets himself the task of finding its faults in terms of these criteria, and he cannot help finding them in any plan for international action. For such is the nature of foreign policy that success must be paid for with troubles, risks, and the threat of the unknown. To be fearful of that price means to do nothing, and the lawyer's caution becomes the paralysis of the statesman.

These deficiencies which have sapped the strength of American foreign policy are overshadowed in lasting importance by a dilemma which is, as it were, built into the constitutional and political system of the United States: how to reconcile the requirements of sound foreign policy with the requirement of popular and, more particularly, congressional support. The problem of how to reconcile these two factors which in the nature of things cannot be fully reconciled has bedeviled the conduct of American foreign policy since Washington's day. For, if American statesmen go too far in complying with the requirements of sound foreign policy, they are likely to lose the support of opinion at home; if they go too far in accommodating that opinion at the expense of what sound foreign policy requires, they risk jeopardizing the interests of the country and thus in the long run the support of opinion as well.

The task of the statesman, then, is twofold: to impress upon the people the requirements of sound foreign policy by telling them the facts of political life and what they require of the nation, and then to strike a compromise which leaves the essence of a sound foreign policy intact. It must be said, and it is being said with deep regret by one who expected great things in this regard from the co-operation between an immensely popular President and an experienced and skilful Secretary of State, that the Eisenhower administration has failed in both tasks. It is this failure which is in good measure responsible for the sterility of American foreign policy, for the disasters which have befallen and threaten it, and for the popular ignorance of the bearing of these disasters upon the future of America and of the world.

That the administration has failed to educate the people hardly needs to be argued. Official statements have been consistently at odds with the facts and their import for the interests and policies of the United States. Let anyone make a compilation of the official statements about the Suez Canal crisis and compare them with the facts as reported by the same newspapers! Let anyone undertake a history of world affairs since 1953, using only official statements and forgetting everything else he knows, and what a mélange of fiction and caricature we would get! In one word, the public relations expert has taken over from the statesman.

In the task of fashioning a compromise between the requirements of foreign policy and the preferences of public opinion, the administration has likewise failed. The Secretary of State has been haunted by the memory of his able and high-minded predecessor who failed in this task because he failed to marshal public opinion in support of sound policies and compounded his failure when in the end he even embraced unsound ones without gaining popular support. Mr. Dulles resolved not to repeat that failure. Instead of heeding Sir William Harcourt's advice that "political heads of departments are necessary to tell the civil service what the public will not stand," thus approaching the public with a sound and settled policy, he would first get popular and, more particularly, congressional support at whatever cost in policy commitments and then, with the home front secure, face the nations of the world with the right policies. The plan was ingenious but doomed to failure on two counts. Its success was predicated upon the possibility of appeasing the opponents of American foreign policy as it had developed since 1939, and that possibility never existed. No concession could reconcile these men to the active involvement of the United States in the affairs of the world, to its risks, liabilities, opportunities, and rewards. They had to be disarmed and neutralized, not appeased. Yet by trying to appease them, Mr. Dulles destroyed the very instrument without which no foreign policy could be successfully pursued, his own department, and narrowed his freedom of action to such an extent as to foreclose any fresh initiative, any creative response to novel situations.

The destruction of the Department of State proceeded in two stages: the elimination of most of the able and experienced members of its higher ranks and the appointment to key positions of men whose main qualification was sympathy with the philosophy and policies of the irrreconcilable opposition. Thus foreign aid was administered by a man who did not believe in foreign aid; the Refugee Act was administered by a man who did not believe in immigration; some key men in the Far Eastern Division do not believe in negotiations with Communist China; and the only visible qualification of one undersecretary of state for his eminent position was the Hoover name which evokes memories dear to the opposition. The purpose of these appointments was to commit the opposition to the support of the foreign policies of the administration. Actually they committed a powerful group within the Department to the support of opposition policies. The opposition, far from giving hostages to Mr. Dulles, imprisoned him in a cell of old ideas and old policies from which he could not move when momentous opportunities for fresh initiatives—the atomic stalemate, the new Soviet policies, the stirrings of Asia and Africa, the disintegration of the alliances, the rise of Germany and Japan—knocked at the door.

What of the remedy? What of the cure? The cure is as grand and simple as the disease is stark and simple.

It is for the President to reassert his historic role as both the initiator of policy and the awakener of public opinion. It is true that only a strong, wise, and shrewd President can marshal to the support of wise policies the strength and wisdom latent in that slumbering giant—American public opinion. Yet while it is true that great men have rarely been elected President of the United States, it is upon that greatness, which is the greatness of its people personified, that the United States, from Washington to Franklin D. Roosevelt, has had to rely in the conduct of its foreign affairs. It is upon that greatness that Western Civilization must rely for its survival.

Those words we addressed in 1949 to Mr. Eisenhower's predecessor. If they were true then they are true today. Will Mr. Eisenhower heed their truth? Will he ever know that it exists?

29 *The Corruption of Patriotism*

Of the surrender of sound principles of policy to
the pressures of demagogic politics and the resulting corruption of
the democratic processes, the security policies of the United States,
culminating in the years 1953–55, provide an extreme example. It is
possible to explain the security system of the President's Executive
Order 10450 of April 27, 1953—which incidentally the Eisenhower
administration inherited and perfected but did not create—psychologically as a reaction to the laxity preceding it; it is impossible to
defend it on rational and empirical grounds. We are faced with the
stark fact, which the scholar cannot evade, that well-meaning and
otherwise intelligent men were joined by the great majority of the
people in embracing a philosophy of security, which is in truth a
mythology, and a policy of security, which is in truth a series of
ritualistic performances requiring human sacrifices, both completely
divorced from reality and reason.

A critical analysis of the security regulations, as applied to the
Department of State, must answer four basic questions. What is to
be secured? Against whom is it to be secured? By what means is it
being secured? What is the cost of security in terms of other goals
to which the nation is equally committed?

A security system, in so far as it concerns the Department of State,
must protect the integrity and secrecy of foreign policy. It has to
assure, first of all, that the foreign policy of the United States is not
determined by persons who owe primary loyalty to a foreign power
and, hence, put its interests above those of the United States. Or, to
put it in positive terms, it has to assure that those who determine
American foreign policy are loyal to the United States. If there had
ever existed, as is widely but falsely believed, in the Department of
State a pro-Communist clique who deliberately worked for the triumph of communism in China, a security system would have to
prevent such a situation from repeating itself.

It must, however, be said that the very mechanics by which the

From the *Bulletin of the Atomic Scientists*, April, 1955; and the *New Republic*, April 18, 1955.

foreign policy of the United States is conducted make it extremely unlikely that such a situation could ever arise. The formation of American foreign policy is characterized by a diffusion so extreme as to border on chaos. The determination of American foreign policy is subject to a multitude of influences, not only from within the Department of State, but also from a great number of executive agencies which are directly or indirectly concerned with the conduct of foreign policy. To them must be added the—often decisive—influence that both houses of Congress exert upon the conduct of American foreign policy. A multitude of people, typically organized in committees, on all levels of the governmental hierarchy are continuously called upon to analyze a certain political situation and to propose a policy dealing with it. Out of that welter of divergent opinions, certain basic propositions are slowly distilled which are submitted to the President for final approval. It is only when the President has spoken with the ultimate authority of his office, not infrequently choosing among alternative policies, that the foreign policy of the United States has been determined.

Given this diffuse process of policy formation, no one foreign agent, however highly placed, could deflect the foreign policy of the United States from its national course. For his advice favoring a foreign power would be counteracted by the multitude of loyal officials who also participate in the process of policy formation. For a foreign power to subvert the foreign policy of the United States, a network of agents is needed strategically located not only in the Department of State but also in the other governmental establishments, such as the White House and the National Security Council, which are directly concerned with the determination of American foreign policy. No foreign power was able to establish such a network when American public opinion was hardly aware of the problem of security and when security regulations were extremely lax. It is important in this context to remind ourselves that there is no evidence to suggest that any of the officials who were concerned with the conduct of American foreign policy and whose pro-Communist sympathies have been proven have been able, or have even attempted, to influence American foreign policy in favor of a foreign nation.

The classic activity of the foreign agent, at least in popular imagination, is indeed not the determination of policy but the transmission of secrets. The prototype of the foreign agent is the spy. Not only public opinion but all governments assume that espionage is an enterprise worthwhile for all. Hence, they embark upon espionage for themselves and endeavor to protect themselves against the espionage of others. However, this assumption, at least as it concerns foreign policy in contrast to military dispositions and planning, is open to radical doubt.

It stands, of course, to reason that genuine military secrets must be protected. The quality and quantity of weapons, the disposition of the armed forces, war plans, and codes fall into that category. In so far as the operations of the Department of State deal with such military secrets, they require protection on military grounds. Secret-service operations with which the Department of State concerns itself must be protected on similar grounds. The considerations of the problem of secrecy in the Department of State that follow, then, apply exclusively to foreign policy proper.

I was once told by an official of the Department of State that from his long experience he could remember only two documents the transmission of which would have been advantageous to a foreign power. From my own much more limited experience, I do not remember a single top-secret document, let alone any document of a lower security classification, the knowledge of which would have been advantageous to a foreign power. I would go so far as to say that if a foreign power would gain knowledge of all the classified documents I have seen or written, such knowledge might be advantageous to the United States rather than to that power, provided it would be advantageous to the United States to confound a foreign power as to the nature of our foreign policy and its future course. As concerns espionage with regard to foreign policy in general, it is hardly more than a racket, engaged in by shady characters frequently working both sides of the street. The typical information thus obtained is either phony, irrelevant, or public property.

That this cannot be otherwise, a consideration of foreign policy, especially as it must be practiced under present world conditions, will make obvious. The great lines of action which the foreign policies of the great powers are likely to take are predetermined by their respective national interests as they are rationally defined by the small group which ultimately decides upon the course of action. This has always been so and is so today. The Cold War has, however, imposed a peculiar rigidity upon the foreign policies of the great powers, which leaves very little room for maneuver in the implementation of their respective national interests. Given this situation, there can be hardly any secrets which rational analysis could not detect but which espionage would be able to uncover. In order to know what Chinese policy with regard to Korea or Formosa is likely to be, it is not necessary, and probably not even expedient, to pilfer the secret files of the foreign office in Peiping; it is only necessary to ask one's self what the national interest of China has been with regard to these two regions and what it is likely to be as interpreted by the present rulers of China. In order to know what the Soviet Union is up to with regard to Germany, and vice versa, it is not necessary, and will avail little, to have secret agents in the foreign offices of Bonn and Moscow. If rational analysis cannot answer our quest, nothing else will.

The security regulations, as applied to the Department of State, completely misunderstood the nature of foreign policy and the problem of security with regard to it. Executive Order 10450 distinguishes among different positions in view of their different relevance for security but leaves the actual determination of that relevance to the officers charged with the enforcement of the executive order [Sec. 3 (A) par. 2, (B) par. 1; Sec. 8 (A) 1]. In its application to the Department of State that distinction between different degrees of sensitivity disappeared. The security policy of the Department of State conceived of foreign policy as one vast operation, all elements of which, from the determination of policy to the washing of windows, are equally important in view of their bearing upon integrity and secrecy.

In truth, what needs protection from foreign subversion is not the whole process of foreign policy in all its ramifications but only those elements of it that, in the nature of things, are capable of being subverted, that is, that small area where decisions are actually made and which has access to military secrets and secret-service operations. Secrecy in foreign policy serves not so much the security of the United States in terms of concealment of its plans and operations as it protects its officials who must be free to express their opinions without concern for the favorable or unfavorable reaction of outsiders. If the officials who are engaged in the conduct of foreign policy could not rely upon their official actions and expressions of opinion being made in confidence, they would at the very least be tempted to surrender their own professional judgment of the merits of the case to outside pressures, domestic and foreign. In the absence of secrecy, an official could not be expected to express his opinions about the personnel and policies of a foreign government without anticipating the reactions of that government. Nor could he be expected to express his opinions about the policies of his own government without regard for domestic political reactions.

The main purpose of secrecy, then, is the protection of the professional integrity of the Foreign Service and affiliated agencies. Security regulations which seek to protect that professional integrity must obviously be different from those which seek to protect the United States against the betrayal of official secrets. Security regulations which are completely unaware of the former function but animated by an unrealistic assessment of the need for the performance of the latter are likely to fail in both. More will have to be said on this point later on.

Against whom are the integrity and secrecy of American foreign policy to be secured? How can we determine beforehand who is likely to be disloyal if participation in the conduct of American foreign policy should be intrusted to him? How does, in one word, the mark of Cain look, which is supposed to set the prospective traitor apart from the mass of loyal citizens? Section 8 of Executive Order 10450 undertakes to answer that question. It enumerates close to one hundred characteristics, any one of which excludes a man from government employment as a security risk, his employment being not "clearly consistent with the national security." Yet that list of characteristics, according to the preamble of Section 8, is not intended to be exhaustive but rather to establish general categories to which the security officials may add other related ones.

These characteristics fall into three different categories:

1. Those which make a person unfit for government service on obvious security grounds, such as "commission of any act of sabotage, espionage, treason or sedition . . ." [Sec. 8 (A) 2].

2. Characteristics which make a person unfit for government

service in general, without any special reference to security, such as "An adjudication of insanity, or treatment for serious mental or neurological disorder without satisfactory evidence of cure" [Sec. 8 (A) 1. IV].

3. Characteristics the absence of which in the composite reveal a picture of the "normal" good American, who alone is worthy of government employment, such as "any criminal, infamous, dishonest, immoral, or notoriously disgraceful conduct, habitual use of intoxicants to excess, drug addiction, or sex perversion" [Sec. 8 (A) 1. III].[1]

Here is indeed the crux of the matter. What the security regulations are trying to do in the third category is to localize treason as an outstanding but surreptitious evil by making it a function of other outstanding but patent evils. In this philosophy a man who has deviated drastically in other respects from the moral standards of society is more likely to deviate from those moral standards by committing treason than one who has not so deviated. This assumption is illogical to begin with, and there is not a shred of empirical evidence to support it. Its illogical character stems from the very nature of treason which is an act of disloyalty committed by a person who, in view of his revealed qualities, appears to be deserving of trust. If it were possible to identify the prospective traitor by some outward quality, the commission of treason would by definition become impossible. That the assumption of a necessary relationship between general immorality and the particular immorality of treason also is untenable on empirical grounds can be shown by putting the following two questions to the empirical test: Are people who deviate in a particular respect from the moral standards of society more likely to commit treason than others, and are traitors as a type likely to be immoral in other respects as well?

In order to answer the first of these two questions, let us take the type of immorality which not only constitutes a particularly radical and repulsive violation of "normal" moral standards but by general consensus is also most obviously conducive to treason: sexual perversion. That the homosexual is peculiarly prone to commit crimes

[1] Some of these characteristics taken in isolation, such as drug addiction, disqualify a person for government service in general and, hence, belong to the second category.

under the threat of blackmail is hardly doubted by anyone who faces the problem for the first time. Yet neither the histories of diplomacy and of treason nor the recollections of practitioners of diplomacy, in so far as I could ascertain, contain an instance of a homosexual having committed an act of treason under the threat of blackmail.

Nor is there any such evidence with regard to a very mild "deviation," completely devoid in itself of any negative moral connotation: that of having relatives behind the Iron Curtain. That an official who has relatives living behind the Iron Curtain is particularly susceptible to committing treason under blackmail sounds on the face of it so plausible that it is virtually accepted as self-evident. But who knows of an official who has violated security regulations under such circumstances? Here again, what on the face of it looks like common sense reveals itself on closer examination as superstition which unchallenged repetition has vested with the plausibility of truth.

Executive Order 10450 assumes the existence of two easily discernible types of men, one likely to commit treason, the other not. The composite picture of the latter, which emerges from Executive Order 10450 and its application to the personnel of the Department of State, is the ideal type of a Babbitt with strong pseudopuritanical connotations. He is a person who is "normal" in every respect, that is, who conforms to certain requirements which a "good" American is supposed to possess. In their application to the Department of State, these requirements run the whole gamut of actions, associations, attitudes, and opinions with which a person might identify himself. It is significant for the concern with conformity rather than with security that much emphasis has been put upon conformity with a conservative ideal in the field of political opinion and attitudes and with a pseudopuritanical ideal in the sphere of sexual behavior. In the course of security investigations, officials of the State Department have been asked about their attitude toward Franklin D. Roosevelt, the New Deal, and the recognition of the Communist government of China. Investigators have also shown an almost obsessive curiosity about the pre- and extramarital sexual activities of public officials.

It stands to reason that this ideal of the "good" American is at odds in one or the other respect with the actual behavior of most men who have ever lived and are now living. Hardly an American statesman from Franklin and Washington to Dulles and Eisenhower has, and could have, lived up to it, and most of them would fail the test on multiple grounds. And it is not by accident that men of undoubted loyalty and merit have been dismissed from the Foreign Service as security risks under Executive Order 10450. For that executive order makes virtually everybody a security risk and for two reasons. First of all, as already pointed out, few men will correspond in every respect to the ideal picture of the "good" American which is implicit in Executive Order 10450 and its application (and it may be doubted that those who do make desirable public servants). More importantly, few men will be so transparently good, approaching saintliness, that it can be said of them that their employment is "clearly consistent with the interests of the national security," which is the general standard repeated again and again by the executive order.

I am myself indifferent honest; but yet I could accuse me of such things, that it were better my mother had not borne me: I am very proud, revengeful, ambitious; with more offenses at my beck than I have thoughts to put them in, imagination to give them shape, or time to act them in. What should such fellows as I do crawling between earth and heaven? We are arrant knaves all; believe none of us.

These words of Hamlet all men can say of themselves and of each other. Even the best man's goodness is darkened at least by the shadow of a doubt, and thus he is a security risk within the meaning of Executive Order 10450.

The security regulations, as applied to the Department of State, operated essentially through three instrumentalities: security investigations, police supervision, and political pressure.

That a person be subjected to a security check before he is employed in a sensitive position by the Department of State is an obvious necessity. Yet in the eyes of the Department of State a man's loyalty is never settled once and for all (as actually it cannot be, in view of what we have said above). Since no man can ever be fully trusted, all men are forever suspect on grounds of security and, hence, are at àll times subject to renewed security investigations. The case of Mr. John Paton Davies, Jr., who underwent nine security investigations, has gained nationwide attention; yet his case is but an extreme example of a fairly typical situation. Hundreds of officials of the Department of State have been subjected to multiple security investigations by different agencies, for different purposes, and on different grounds. A patently scurrilous denunciation can call forth a new security investigation, proceeding as though nothing at all were known of the individual's record as a private citizen and public official.

This multiplication of security investigations is institutionalized by the requirement that the personnel file of every official of the Department of State in whose personnel status a change, such as a new assignment or promotion, is contemplated be checked for security. In the course of such a check any old incident which has been satisfactorily explained in preceding security investigations can jeopardize the official's career and destroy his reputation. An official who has been suggested for a promotion by virtue of his professional competence (of which compliance with security regulations is obviously a part) may be suspended for months as a security risk because ten years ago, on the instigation of the government, he joined an organization infiltrated by Communists in order to combat their influence. Never mind that this incident was a matter of record from the very beginning, that it has been explained to the satisfaction of all concerned time and again; now it must be explained again and with it the whole life of the official, private and public, from the day of his birth to this, and it is he who must prove that the continuation of his employment is "clearly consistent with the interests of the national security," by collecting affidavits from public and private acquaintances testifying that they found nothing wrong with him. By requiring the official to disprove the suspicion of being a security risk, it eliminates for all practical purposes from the evidence to be weighed the positive record of his accomplishments. A man may have given outstanding service over a long period of time in the most sensitive positions. Let him have had dinner with somebody who is suspected of having once been a Communist, and he will be unable to prove that he is not a security risk.

The assumption that all men are really security risks and that this defect, shared by all men, can somehow be neutralized, if not eliminated, through the proper social arrangements cannot but give rise to a psychology which is indistinguishable from that of the police state. For given these two assumptions, eternal vigilance becomes the price of security. Treat everybody as though he were a traitor, and you will be safe from treason.

The Department of State acted upon these assumptions and established a system of supervision which in good part is supposed to operate covertly but of which everybody within the Department is—jokingly or indignantly—aware. The Bureau of Security of the Department of State employs, of course, a staff whose personnel and functions are officially known. Aside from this official staff, it employs a network of agents (both categories estimated to total more than a thousand) whose identity and functions are not supposed to be known. Individuals have been placed in the different functional and geographic units of the Department of State for the ostensible purpose of performing the substantive functions of these units, yet for the actual purpose of supervising and reporting on their colleagues. Delegations to international conferences are accompanied by individuals who perform similar functions, traditionally associated with a GPU or Gestapo. The Secretary of State himself has invested this system with the authority of his office by imposing, through Department Circular 95 of April 15, 1954, upon all officials of his Department the duty to be informers.

I am aware that no agency of the government can improve, or even maintain, its level of effectiveness unless it is receiving a stream of new ideas and constructive criticisms. I hope that the inspection operation will be the focal reception point of that stream. I have told Mr. McLeod that in his capacity as administrator of the inspection operation he should be available at any time to receive personally from any of our people the benefit of their thinking on improving operations and procedures or on other problems, official and personal.

In brief, I regard the internal inspection operation of the Department as one of its most important concerns. Its success will depend upon the cooperation and aid received generally from employees of the Department.

There have been persistent rumors, in the nature of things hard to verify, of tapped telephones, hidden microphones, steamed-open letters, and special rooms and devices for the grilling of suspects. But regardless of whether or not there is any evidence to support these rumors, the very fact that they could be spread and widely believed reveals a spirit vastly different from that which is supposed to prevail in an agency of a democratic government.

This emphasis upon the vital importance of investigation and supervision for purposes of security, institutionalized in a special bureau within the Department of State, inevitably led to a shift—lasting through most of Mr. Eisenhower's first term—of effective control over the operations of the Department from the Secretary and Undersecretary of State and the heads of the functional and geographic units to the Bureau of Security. This shift has occurred in all modern totalitarian states and has given rise to a phenomenon which has been aptly called the "dual state." It is characteristic of the "dual state" that in it, as a matter of law, the power of making decisions remains with the authorities charged by law with making them while, as a matter of fact, by virtue of their power over life and death, the agents of the secret police—co-ordinated to, but independent from, the official makers of decision—at the very least exert an effective veto over the decisions. Once the secret police has established itself firmly in an agency of the government, it will have less and less need for intervening drastically in day-by-day operations; for its omnipresence and reputed omnipotence will generally be sufficient for the constituted authorities to avoid any action which might displease the secret police.

The Bureau of Security in the Department of State, as originally constituted, was combined with, and hence had direct control over, four areas of operation: security, consular affairs, personnel, and inspection of United States missions abroad. While the administrator of the Bureau of Security has been deprived of direct responsibility for the two latter functions, it is generally believed that the first incumbent of the office retained effective control over personnel because the office of personnel continued to be administered in the spirit of, and in close co-operation with, the Bureau of Security. For the powers of the Bureau of Security by themselves are all-pervading in so far as the hiring, assignment, promotion, and firing of personnel are concerned.

The powers which the Bureau of Security assumed over the operations of the Department of State flowed only in part from its police functions as such. As in fully developed totalitarian systems the power of the secret police is in good measure the reflection of the political power of its head, a Himmler or a Beria, so did the power of the Bureau of Security over the Department of State reflect in good measure the political power of those whose political philosophy its leading officials represented, to whom they owed their positions and their primary loyalties as well. Those were not the President of the United States or the Secretary of State but certain members of Congress and, more particularly, of the Senate. The police system which was established in the Department of State was their secret police in a more profound sense than it was the secret police of the executive branch. It was through it that these members of Congress were kept informed about the—presumably secret— operations of the Department of State, and it was through it that they exerted a direct or indirect influence upon its operations. To an extent which changes with the ebbs and tides of political fortune, it was these members of Congress, and not the President or the Secretary of State, who determined the operations of the Department of State and its affiliated agencies.

The most spectacular instance of this extra-constitutional influence to have come to light thus far is provided by the International Information Administration. The report which the chief consultant to its director has published[2] leaves no doubt but that, at least from February through July, 1953, Senator McCarthy and his friends in Congress had taken over the functions which, according to the Constitution, the President and the Secretary of State are supposed to perform. These members of Congress determined the policies of the International Information Administration as concerns both personnel and substance. It was to them that the top officials of the agency reported; it was their approval which they had to seek; and it was their orders which they were supposed to execute. And when they finally incurred the displeasure of their congressional masters, they had to resign.

For these members of Congress, all men were suspect as traitors, but diplomats in particular were so. For they deviate in certain obvious respects from the ideal type of the "normal" good American: they know foreign languages, spend much of their lives abroad, have many contacts with foreigners, concern themselves professionally

[2] Martin Merson, *The Private Diary of a Public Servant* (New York: Macmillan Co., 1955).

with foreign countries—and they tend to be intellectuals, committing their brains rather than their passions to the conduct of foreign policy. Thus it is not by accident that an enterprise which started out to protect the integrity and secrecy of American foreign policy transformed itself, as we have seen, in an undertaking to assure conformity and ended in an attempt to make the United States safe from foreign policy as such. What began as a technical operation to improve the protection of the United States against subversion and espionage matured into an onslaught—"know-nothing" in its philosophy and isolationist in its implicit purpose—against the very existence of an active American foreign policy.

Obviously, to preserve the integrity and secrecy of foreign policy is only one among many objectives to which the United States is committed. A policy, however sound and successful in its own terms, must be evaluated in terms of the impact it has upon other national objectives, as important or even more important than its own. Such scrutiny is particularly required for a policy which is so unsound and unsuccessful as we believe the security policy of the Department of State to have been. What, then, has been the price in terms of equally or more important objectives we have had to pay for the security policy of the Department of State? That price is being paid primarily in three areas: the effectiveness of American foreign policy, the prestige of the United States abroad, and the security of the United States.

In the *New York Times* of January 17, 1954, five of the most distinguished older diplomatists of the United States, four of whom have been ambassadors and an equal number under or assistant secretaries of state, summarized the "sinister results" of the security policy of the Department of State in these words:

The conclusion has become inescapable, for instance, that a Foreign Service officer who reports on persons and events to the very best of his ability and who makes recommendations which at the time he conscientiously believes to be in the interest of the United States may subsequently find his loyalty and integrity challenged and may even be forced out of the service and discredited forever as a private citizen. A premium therefore has been put upon reporting and upon recommendations which are ambiguously stated or so cautiously set forth as to be deceiving.

When any such tendency begins its insidious work it is not long before accuracy and initiative have been sacrificed to acceptability and conformity. The ultimate result is a threat to national security. In this connection the history of the Nazi and Fascist foreign services before the Second World War is pertinent.

The forces which are working for conformity from the outside are being reinforced by the present administrative set-up within the Department of State which subordinates normal personnel administration to considerations of security.

It is obvious, of course, that candidates for the Foreign Service should be carefully investigated before appointment and that their work should at all times be under the exacting scrutiny of their professional superiors. But when initial investigation attaches undue importance to such factors as even a temporary departure from conservative political and economic views, casual association with persons holding views not currently in fashion or subscription to a periodical labeled as "liberal"; when subsequent investigation is carried to the point of delaying a promotion list for a year and routine transfers from one post to another; when investigations of individual officers must be kept up-to-date to within ninety days; when an easy path has been opened to even the anonymous informer; and when the results of these investigations are evaluated not by persons experienced in the Foreign Service or even acquainted at firsthand with conditions abroad, but by persons of quite different experience, it is relevant to inquire whether we are not laying the foundations of a Foreign Service competent to serve a totalitarian government rather than the government of the United States as we have heretofore known it.

Fear is playing an important part in American life at the present time. As a result the self-confidence, the confidence in others, the sense of fair play and the instinct to protect the rights of the nonconformist are—temporarily, it is to be hoped—in abeyance. But it would be tragic if this fear, expressing itself in an exaggerated emphasis on security, should lead us to cripple the Foreign Service, our first line of national defense, at the very time when its effectiveness is essential to our filling the place which history has assigned to us.

For an impartial professional observer, the conclusion is inevitable that more than a year after this letter was written the Department of State was hardly competent to serve any government, totalitarian or otherwise. Not only the morale but also the professional competence and capacity for teamwork of its members had drastically declined. The Department of State which the Eisenhower administration inherited was, to say the least, a useful instrument of foreign policy. Its obvious administrative weaknesses were compensated for by the intellectual ability, technical competence, and devotion of most of its top and middle layer officials. Many of these officials have either been dismissed or have voluntarily resigned. Of the officials of this type with whom the American High Commission in Germany was staffed in 1953, not a single one was left two years later. They could not have been replaced even under the best possible circumstances with a new team of equal competence and experience. For no nation is rich enough in diplomatic talent, demanding a rare combination of extraordinary qualities of mind and character, to be able to afford taking one team out of the game and replacing it with another one equally good. What is possible in football cannot be done in diplomacy.

The United States could not have afforded the loss of its ablest diplomatists even under the best of circumstances. Yet the circumstances under which the United States had to make good this loss were far from being the best. A system that makes security the overriding consideration gives a golden opportunity for advancement to the incompetent, the time server, and the informer, who has never uttered a wrong thought and who has never associated with the wrong person. A system that not only does not require professional competence but actually suspects it cannot help using standards of selection congenial to that point of view. But it goes without saying that those standards are incompatible with the standards by which diplomatists ought to be selected.

Not only has there been deterioration at the top and in the middle layers of the departmental hierarchy, but there has also been starvation at the bottom. A system characterized by repeated security investigations, police supervision, and political pressure has depleted the lower ranks of the Foreign Service. Many younger officials have been dismissed as security risks, and many more have resigned of their own volition. What is worse is that such a system must act as a deterrent upon both application for employment and employment itself. The number of graduates of our institutions of higher learning who in 1954 or 1955 chose to make the Foreign Service their career was small as compared with that of three or four years earlier. The few who applied then may have been the bravest and the most desperate, but they could hardly have been the best; and those who were able to pass the security test and were actually hired were not necessarily the best of them, and even many of them resigned soon in disgust.

This decline in the quality and quantity of the personnel of the Department of State was matched by the decline in the quality of its operations. The premonitions of the five diplomatists which we have quoted above were fully borne out by events. Objective analytical reporting, the prime function of diplomacy, fell to a low ebb in the Foreign Service. Diplomatic reports were no longer as regularly read by the officials at the respective geographic desks in Washington as they were in times past; for they contained frequently nothing more than digests of the newspapers of the countries concerned, which the official in Washington can and does read himself. Heads of missions refused to allow the transmission to Washington of reports painting a picture of the local situation at variance either with reports of other agencies or with the estimate of the situation prevailing in Washington.

This abdication of independent judgment is, of course, the result of the fear that deviation from the "official line" might jeopardize one's chances for advancement, if not one's very livelihood and reputation. Yet this fear is more than the subjective anticipation of an evil which is largely imaginary, as is much of the fear of being "controversial," so prevalent in academic life. That fear is, indeed, the fruit of bitter experience. Officials were dismissed for having reported facts that they were not supposed to report and for having advocated policies that they were not supposed to advocate; and officials were subjected to still another security investigation on the complaint of a foreign government which did not approve of the policies they advocated.

Under the impact of all these influences, the Department of State probably did not become more immune to subversion and treason than it was before. A case could even be made for the proposition that an official whom the "dual state" constantly subjects to the moral stress of having to reconcile his own professional judgments and moral principles with those of the organization in which he works may become particularly prone to laxity and failure of judgment in matters of security. In any event, the Department of State ceased to be the eyes, ears, and brains of the foreign policy of the United States. Its eyes became blind; its ears, deaf; and its brains, dull. Yet a foreign policy that makes itself incapable of knowing the facts with which it must deal and of understanding the problems it must solve can rely for success upon nothing but the vagaries of luck.

It must, however, be said that this dark picture is brightened by a few light spots. Through luck, personal connections, or the inefficiency of the security system, there remained in the Department of State a few officials who did not yield to the pressures which incessantly bore upon them. Forsaken from above, spied upon from below, surrounded by all manner of opportunists and worse, they risked their careers, their positions, and their honor in maintaining for themselves and in defending in their subordinates the traditional standards of intellectual integrity, professional competence, and devotion to duty. If and when out of the ruins of today a new foreign service will be built, worthy of the traditions and the mission of America, the nation will owe a great debt to these brave, able, and devoted men who defended in obscurity and against great odds the pitiful remnants of a fine tradition.

This disintegration of the Foreign Service of the United States is better known abroad than it is at home. The governments and the public of foreign countries have seen with amazement officials, of whose competence and loyalty they have had tangible evidence, investigated, dismissed, or forced to resign as security risks. Continuous contacts with our representatives abroad provide them with unmistakable evidence of the diminution of their professional competence. In consequence, the influence the United States should be able to exert by virtue of its material strength and of the mission it has assumed for the free world has drastically declined. The word of the United States is no longer listened to with respect. What is worse, the very image of the United States as the champion of justice and freedom against totalitarian oppression has been obscured. If the United States owed its position in the world to nothing but its material power, such foreign reactions would be of little consequence. In truth, however, the United States has been able to command the sympathies of millions of people abroad, not because it has more atomic bombs than the Soviet Union, but because it was founded upon, and has tried to live up to, certain principles of government to which those millions of people are also committed. Seeing the last best hope of the free world forsake these principles and even seemingly be proud of a security system that the London *Economist* has called a "vicious stupidity,"[3] many of our friends abroad began to doubt whether there is much to choose between East and West.

This loosening of the bonds of sympathy that unite America to its friends abroad raises a specter more ominous still: the loosening of the bonds of loyalty which tie the citizens of the United States to their own government. The United States was founded upon loyalty, not to a king or piece of territory, but to an ideal of political justice. We pledge allegiance to a flag which is a symbol of "liberty and justice for all." Loyalty which attaches to a man or a territory may not be affected by injustice perpetrated by that man or within that territory. A nation which was built on a common belief in certain principles of justice, whose citizens have voluntarily come together from all over the world to share in the practice of those principles, which owes its very existence to a revolt against injustice—such a nation stands and falls, as a nation, with its loyalty to those principles.

The loyalty of its citizens presupposes the loyalty of its government, not as a matter of verbalization but of policy, to those principles of justice. The government of such a nation cannot help committing injustices by sacrificing some of the freedom and interests of individuals to a higher good. The government of such a nation will be forgiven sporadic injustices not justified by the achievement of such a higher good. The government of such a nation will embark upon a deliberate policy of injustice only at the risk of weakening the very foundation of loyalty which supports its voluntary acceptance by its citizens.

A citizen, unjustly accused of disloyalty, condemned and ostracized, may well be tempted to conclude that if he is to be treated as disloyal he may as well act the part.[4] To the government's severance of the ties which unite government and citizen, he might want to respond in kind. The man whom his government has cast into the

---

[3] Jan. 8, 1955, p. 110.

[4] This psychological process is strikingly revealed in this statement by the leader of a juvenile gang, reported in the *New York Times* of March 25, 1958, p. 26: " 'That's the way it starts,' Vincent says, 'I've seen it happen many times. The police blame you for something you didn't do. You get a record. They send you away. So, then, the kid comes back and he says, "Well, I'm going to do something and get a record of my own. At least then if I'm sent up it will be for something I did myself." ' "

outer darkness may make common cause with the forces of darkness. The alienation of the government from the principles upon which it was founded and, in consequence, from some of its citizens may well have brought in its wake the alienation of some citizens from the government. Thus a policy which sought to protect the government from disloyalty may well have corrupted, by dint of its own corruption, if not the actions so at least the minds of some of the citizens upon whose loyal services the government could otherwise have counted. A policy intended to protect the country from treason is likely to have actually increased if not the actuality so at least the risk of treason.

Such, then, is the price we were paying for Executive Order 10450, as applied to the Department of State. It is a high price to pay. Paid for what? For nothing.

30 *The Subversion of Foreign Policy*

The destruction of the Foreign Service of the United States, in order to take the wind out of the sails of the domestic opposition, is paralleled by the paralysis and the distortion of the foreign policy of the United States. The first two years of Mr. Eisenhower's foreign policy provide a case study of the corrupting effects that considerations of domestic politics can exert upon the conduct of foreign policy. An attempt to assess this period of American foreign policy must overcome three formidable obstacles. One, the nature of the standards of evaluation, is inherent in the nature of all foreign policy; the second, the conduct of foreign policy in view of popular preferences, is peculiar to democratic foreign policy; the third, the utter contrast between the presentation and the substance of foreign policy, seems to be inherent in the nature of Mr. Eisenhower's foreign policy.

What is the standard by which we judge the quality of foreign policy? Is it success? If so, then inevitably the incompetent heir will reap the fruits of his wise predecessor's labors and take credit for the results of what was actually somebody else's achievement. Conversely, the great statesman to whom it has fallen to dispose of the bankrupt estate of the preceding government must take the blame for a failure which is not his own. The verdicts of popular history are indeed permeated with misjudgments of this kind.

Yet, how do we determine success and failure in foreign policy? Surveying the centuries, history is able to assess the contribution of a particular move at a particular time to the ultimate success or failure of a nation's foreign policy. The contemporary observer is handicapped by his ignorance of the consequences of contemporary policies. Judged by success alone, Hitler's foreign policy, if viewed in the perspective of 1938–40, made Bismarck's look like a mere preparation for greater things to come. But how did it look but five years later? Who did not think in 1929 that the Kellogg-Briand Pact was a great success, and who did not think so of the Teheran, Yalta,

From the *Year Book of World Affairs,* 1955.

and Potsdam agreements at the time of their conclusion? But who would think so now?

However, we do not object to the Kellogg-Briand Pact and the wartime agreements with the Soviet Union solely or even primarily for their lack of success. What we are critical of is the cause of their failure, that is, the wrong way of thinking about foreign policy which made the framers of these agreements expect success when failure could have been avoided only by fortuitous circumstances lying beyond the ken of their intentions and control. What makes foreign policy deserving of praise or blame is, then, not success or failure per se but a way of thinking about foreign policy which by virtue of its inherent qualities is likely to lead to success or failure. A foreign policy based upon correct thinking deserves to be called "good" even though it fails for reasons that have nothing to do with the quality of thought that went into it, and a foreign policy derived from wrong thinking must be called "bad" even though it succeeds in spite of the deficiences of the reasoning from which it stems.

What do we mean when we speak of correct thinking and the quality of reasoning on matters of foreign policy? We assume, as pointed out elsewhere in greater detail,[1] that there exists an objective rational standard by which the quality of political action can be judged. This assumption derives from the rational nature of man which the actor on the political scene cannot help bringing to bear upon his action to a greater or lesser degree. It is the degree of conformity between political action and rational requirements which determines the quality of the action. The active participant in politics as well as the detached observer of the political scene cannot but proceed on this assumption. For they would not be able to judge political action at all, beyond the crudest statements about success or failure, if they did not carry in their minds a picture of what a certain political action ought to have been. Actors and observers alike cannot help sharing in the assumption of the rationality of this picture; for otherwise they would have no common ground for correlating each other's thoughts and actions.

It is no argument to say that the rational requirements of foreign policy are difficult to ascertain and ambiguous in nature and that

[1] *Politics among Nations* (2d ed.; New York: Alfred A. Knopf, 1954), pp. 7–8.

their application to concrete problems is even more so. The fact remains that the assumption of the possibility of judging foreign policy rationally, in terms of the quality of reasoning underlying it, is the precondition for both the intellectual comprehension of foreign policy and for its objective evaluation.

This task of evaluation is even more complicated when foreign policy is carried on under the conditions of democratic control. Two factors make it so. First of all, a democratically conducted foreign policy, as pointed out in chapter 17, is of necessity a compromise between the rational requirements of good foreign policy and the emotional preferences of public opinion. If one wanted to overstate the case, one might say that a democratically conducted foreign policy is of necessity bad foreign policy. In any case, a foreign policy carried on under democratic control must fall short of the rational requirements of good foreign policy; for it must satisfy emotional preferences whose satisfaction is incompatible with meeting those requirements. It would, therefore, be unjust to judge a democratic foreign policy exclusively by its compliance with these requirements; such judgment must be qualified by the need, greater or lesser as the case may be but always present, to compromise with the emotional preferences of public opinion.

The ultimate judgment on a democratic foreign policy will then be composed of two specific judgments: one establishing the degree to which a foreign policy meets the rational requirements of good foreign policy, and the other assessing the need for compromise with public opinion and the degree to which foreign policy has met that need. Did it yield not enough and thus destroy the foundation of public opinion on which democratic foreign policy must operate? Or did it yield too much, deviating from rational requirements to such an extent as to condemn foreign policy to failure? It is answers to questions such as these which will determine the ultimate verdict. It is with them that we are here concerned.

The other factor complicating the evaluation of democratic foreign policy results from the one just discussed. Not only must democratic foreign policy make concessions to public opinion, but it must also present its foreign policy in terms acceptable to public opinion. That is to say, it must make it appear as though it responds to the emotional preferences of public opinion to a greater extent than it actually does. It must cover those of its rational elements that are least likely to find favor with public opinion with a veil of emotional pronouncements which are intended to conceal its true nature from the public eye. It is for the objective observer to distinguish between public pronouncements on foreign policy that reveal and those that conceal the true nature of the foreign policy actually pursued, by correlating pronouncement with action.

This is a very difficult task at best. It has been made even more difficult by the way United States foreign policy has been traditionally conducted and the particular way the Eisenhower administration has been conducting its foreign policy. The processes by which decisions on foreign policy are arrived at in the United States are chaotic in the extreme. The writer has endeavored elsewhere to analyze the constitutional and political factors that make them so.[2] It is a further peculiarity of the American system that this business of institutionalized chaos is carried on on the public stage. Given the importance of public opinion for the determination of foreign policy, this can hardly be otherwise; for that course of action which can mobilize public opinion in its support has gained a great advantage in the struggle for the ultimate determination of United States foreign policy. Thus it is possible, and has almost become customary, that on any pending question of foreign policy any member of the executive or legislative branches of the government, be it the Vice-President, the Secretary of State, the Chairman of the Joint Chiefs of Staff, the party leaders in Congress, or a ranking member of the foreign affairs committee of either house formulates his own foreign policy in public speech. Thus on United States over-all relations with the Soviet bloc as well as on more specific questions, such as American policies toward Communist China and the problems raised for American policy by the Indochina War, prominent members of the Eisenhower administration and of the Republican party in Congress have publicly advocated policies that did not become the policies of the United States. It was only from subsequent action, taken upon the responsibility of the President, that it was possible to determine in retrospect what the policy of the United States actually had been.

[2] "The Conduct of Foreign Policy," in S. D. Bailey (ed.), *Aspects of American Government* (London: Hansard Society, 1950), pp. 99 ff.

To complicate matters still further, action taken on the responsibility of the President has sometimes belied the President's own words. For it is a peculiarity of the Eisenhower administration that it is the first democratic government whose relations with the public imitate on a large and institutionalized scale the techniques of public relations experts and commercial advertising. This is so with regard to form and content. Mr. Robert Montgomery, a movie actor, has the official title of White House adviser on radio and television. The President on television conveys the impression that he smiles and raises his voice or hand not on an impulse of his own but rather on somebody else's cue. The first cabinet meeting ever televised, in which the Secretary of State reported on the London Conference of 1954, conveyed the impression of a performance staged by experts and executed by amateurs. In the words of Mr. Alistair Cooke:

The whole show had a relaxed, closed-door air, almost like a Cabinet meeting. In the lead part . . . Mr. Dulles gave a naturalistic performance of great ease and articulateness. Mr. Henry Cabot Lodge made the most of a single-sentence tribute to the President for his peaceful atomic energy proposals. Cast as the unsleeping watchdog of the people's purse, Mr. Secretary of the Treasury Humphrey expressed with moving verisimilitude his concern that the Paris Agreement should not cost the American taxpayer one extra nickel. Mrs. Hobby conveyed an intelligent anxiety over the Saar.

Only Secretary of Agriculture Ezra Benson, an artless man from the West, had to be prodded into his line by Mr. Dulles, who suggested after an anxious pause that some of them might now be wondering "how the Soviet Union is taking this." Mr. Benson was indeed wondering just that, and made an alert retrieve. It was the only missed cue in an otherwise flawless performance, surely an enviable record for any amateur dramatic company.[3]

The ascendancy of the public relations expert over the responsible political leader has also been marked in the substance of what the leaders of the Eisenhower administration have told the people about the foreign policy they are pursuing. Here, too, the methods of salesmanship have largely replaced the principles of responsible democratic leadership, and, in consequence, it has become a principle of government to impress the public favorably at any price, even that of truth, rather than to inform it. Spectacular announcements have

---

[3] *Manchester Guardian Weekly,* Oct. 28, 1954, p. 2.

been made carrying the impression of momentous decisions in foreign policy which turned out to be meaningless in view of the actual policies pursued. Five major announcements of this kind, creating a great deal of public comment and controversy but no policies even faintly reflecting them, were made during the first two years of the Eisenhower administration: liberation, the unleashing of Chiang Kai-shek, agonizing reappraisal, the "new look," and intervention in Indochina.

During the election campaign of 1952 and during the first months of its tenure of office, the spokesmen for the Eisenhower administration announced that the old policy of containment was to be replaced by a policy of liberation. Yet as the London *Economist* put it as early as August 30, 1952, "Unhappily 'liberation' applied to Eastern Europe—and Asia—means either the risk of war or it means nothing . . . . 'Liberation' entails no risk of war only when it means nothing." Yet the Eisenhower administration has shied away from the risk of war at least as much as did its predecessor. And when the East German revolt in June, 1953, and the Hungarian revolution of October, 1956, coming closer to success than anybody had dared to expect, put the policy of liberation to the test of actual performance, it became obvious that in actuality the policy of liberation was indistinguishable from the policy of containment.

In his State of the Union message of February 2, 1953, President Eisenhower declared, "In June, 1950, following the aggressive attack on the Republic of Korea, the United States Seventh Fleet was instructed both to prevent attack upon Formosa and also to insure that Formosa should not be used as a base of operations against the Chinese Communist mainland." In view of the Chinese intervention in the Korean War, the President declared that he was "issuing instructions that the Seventh Fleet no longer be employed to shield Communist China." This announcement implied a fundamental change in the Far Eastern policies of the United States from the preservation of the status quo to the active attempt to restore Chiang Kai-shek's rule on the Asiatic mainland. In actuality, no such change occurred. Quite to the contrary, the Eisenhower administration seems to have been at least as anxious as its predecessor to limit the military activities of Chiang Kai-shek to strictly defensive measures. By making this limitation part of agreements with Chiang Kai-shek negotiated at the end of 1954, the Eisenhower administration went even beyond the unilateral declaration of policy contained in President Truman's instructions to the Seventh Fleet of June, 1950.

On December 14, 1953, Secretary of State Dulles declared at the meeting of the North Atlantic Council, "If, however, the European Defense Community should not become effective, if France and Germany remain apart, so that they would again be potential enemies, then indeed there would be grave doubt whether Continental Europe could be made a place of safety. That would compel an agonizing reappraisal of basic United States policy."[4] This statement implied the threat that in certain contingencies the United States might lose its interest in the military defense of Europe and leave it to its fate. This threat called forth much comment and little anxiety in Europe and elsewhere. As an incentive for France to ratify the European Defense Community, it was ineffective. For in order to take this threat seriously one would have had to assume that the United States had committed itself to the defense of western Europe, not because it deemed its own defense dependent upon it, but because it happened to approve of the policies of certain European nations. Few observers were, and no responsible statesman was, willing to make so fantastic an assumption.

However, the most far-reaching and most widely commented upon announcement of this kind was the Secretary of State's speech of January 12, 1954, proclaiming the "new look" in American foreign policy as the result of "some basic policy decisions" which the President and the National Security Council had taken. Mr. Lester Pearson, then Canadian secretary of state for external affairs, thought as late as March 15, 1954, that this speech "may turn out to be one of the most important of our times." The present writer, on March 29, 1954, published an article in the *New Republic* interpreting and evaluating this speech as if it meant what it said. Yet Mr. Walter Lippmann could say on March 18 that "The official explanations of the new look have become so voluminous that it is almost a career in itself to keep up with them" and characterize it as "a case of excessive salesmanship," concluding that "there is no doubt that the words of the text convey the impression that something momentous and novel has been decided. But everything that has been said since then

[4] *New York Times,* Dec. 15, 1953.

by the Chiefs of Staff, notably by Admiral Carney, and no less so by Mr. Dulles himself, make it plain that there has been no radical change in our strategic policy."

On the same day, the *Manchester Guardian* summed it all up by saying, "The 'new look' in American military strategy is mainly old merchandise in a new package. There is really nothing new in relying on 'massive mobile retaliatory power' as the principal safeguard of peace—nothing new, that is, except the sales campaign by which the Administration is trying to persuade the American people that some small changes make the strategy of 1954 fundamentally sounder than the strategy of 1953." On March 19, the Senate Committee on Foreign Relations was the scene of the following dialogue between Senator Mansfield and Mr. Dulles, who for all practical purposes buried the "new look" under the cover of military secrecy:

SENATOR MANSFIELD: Do you consider this new policy a new policy?
SECRETARY DULLES: It certainly has new aspects.
SENATOR MANSFIELD: What are they?
SECRETARY DULLES: Well, I am sorry I cannot go into that here. All I can say to you, and you will have to take it on faith, is that a series of new decisions have been taken by the National Security Council and many have been involved, close, and difficult decisions, but there is today on the record a series of decisions which are largely derived from this basic philosophy which were not there a year and a half ago.

While the "new look" was the most spectacular and far-reaching of these announcements, the official declarations concerning the Indochina War were politically the most harmful; for these dealt not with general principles of United States policy but with a concrete situation which required action here and now. On March 25, 1954, the President declared at his news conference that the defense of Indochina was of "transcendent importance." On March 29, the Secretary of State announced: "Under the conditions of today, the imposition on South-East Asia of the political system of Communist Russia and its Chinese Communist ally, by whatever means, would be a grave threat to the whole free community. The United States feels that that possibility should not be passively accepted, but should be met by united action. This might have serious risks, but these risks are far less than would face us a few years from now if we dare not be resolute today." The President and the Secretary of State referred to Indochina as the cork in the bottle of Southeast Asia and as the first in a row of dominoes whose fall would necessarily cause the downfall of the others. Yet no action of any kind reflected even faintly the conception of policy which these words seemed to convey. It was, in the words of the *Economist* of August 21, 1954, this "spectacle of vociferous inaction" which led to "the worst diplomatic disaster in recent American history."

This "foreign policy by hoax" has served to confuse the American people. It has raised doubts in the minds of many about the reliability of public pronouncements on anything and has thus led to the beginnings of a crisis of confidence which endangers democratic government itself. It has raised similar doubts in the minds of friends and enemies alike. The allies of the United States have been fearful lest political action might conform to official utterance. The enemies of the United States must similarly doubt the reliability of official announcements of policy, and they might even doubt it on the wrong occasion when the peace of the world may well depend upon whether or not a warning by the government of the United States is to be believed. The government of a great nation may, or even must, bluff from time to time; but it can afford to bluff only within the framework of a consistent policy understood by all. However, when it erects bluff into a principle of foreign policy, it risks that it would not be believed even if it should. While the spokesmen for the Eisenhower administration have benefited from this "foreign policy by hoax" in that they were able to pose for a fleeting moment as the initiators of new and bold policies, their prestige at home and abroad has suffered in the long run, as has the foreign policy of the United States.

This conduct of foreign policy for the apparent primary purpose of gaining popularity at home results from a misunderstanding of the fundamental relations which must exist between democratic government and public opinion. It also results from a misunderstanding of the conditions which the constitutional and political system of the United States imposes upon these relationships. This misunderstanding the Eisenhower administration has inherited from its predecessor, but it has immensely aggravated it. That aggravation has created a constitutional and political crisis of the first order, which is no less real for being in good measure hidden from the public view by the personal prestige of the President.

The Eisenhower administration assumes correctly that democratic government must be responsive to public opinion, but it errs grievously in the manner in which it tries to bring that response about. Regarding public opinion as the ultimate arbiter of foreign policy, it tries first to ascertain what the preferences of public opinion are and then to comply with them. In the process of bringing its foreign policy into harmony with public opinion, it assumes—and there lies its error—that public opinion with regard to a certain foreign policy pre-exists that foreign policy itself, somewhat in the manner in which a rule of law pre-exists the action to be judged by it. In truth, public opinion is not a static thing to be ascertained and quantified by polls as legal precedents are by the science of law and as the data of nature are by the natural sciences. Rather it is a dynamic thing to be created and continuously re-created by that selfsame political leadership which also creates the foreign policy to be supported by public opinion.

If the executive branch cannot obtain the support of public opinion for a certain policy it would like to pursue, it is not because public opinion—"naturally," as it were—is opposed to this particular foreign policy but because the political leadership of the executive branch has not been effective and has been replaced by political leadership hostile to this foreign policy. In other words, the contest is really not between the foreign policy of the executive branch and public opinion but between the former and other political forces propounding a different foreign policy. The executive branch, by surrendering passively its own initiative to the verdict of public opinion, in truth surrenders to the political opposition which has taken hold of public opinion. In consequence, the executive branch condemns itself to executing the foreign policy of its opponents, which it cannot help doing but half-heartedly and ineffectually; for, knowing better than the opposition and, furthermore, bearing responsibility for the consequences of its acts, whatever it does in order to satisfy the opposition always falls short of the standards which the opposition has erected and the executive branch has accepted as its own. In consequence, the foreign policy of the executive branch will always stand condemned in the eyes of public opinion as having sought and achieved less than public opinion had a right to expect in view of the standards which the executive branch professes as its own.

Of this vicious circle in which the executive branch is caught because it misunderstands the nature of public opinion and, in consequence, surrenders initiative in foreign policy to the opposition, the China policy of the Eisenhower administration is the classic example. There can be no doubt that a majority of the leading officials who advised Mr. Eisenhower on foreign policy during the first years of his tenure of office were opposed to the policies which the President had been pursuing in the Far East. That majority was composed of two groups. By far the larger of these groups wanted to advance toward a more aggressive position, even at the risk of a limited war with Communist China; by far the smaller one would have liked to retreat into less exposed positions. The actual policy of the United States was able to maintain an intermediate position between those two extremes, which followed the line of least resistance by trying neither to advance nor to retreat but to maintain the status quo.

Yet a rational examination of the forces opposing each other in the Far East and their probable dynamics cannot but lead to the conclusion that a policy of the status quo was not likely to be tenable in the long run. Both the United States and Communist China would have to go forward or backward, but they were not likely to remain indefinitely where they were then. Why, then, was the policy of the United States based upon an assumption that cannot be supported by rational argument? The answer is to be found in the surrender, in reasoning if not in policy, to an opposition whose reasoning, contradictory in itself, does not provide the basis for a rational policy, but which has been able to mold public opinion by default of the executive branch.

Public opinion with regard to Communist China was dominated by two strong contradictory emotions: to make somehow good the defeat which the United States suffered through the defection of China to the Communist camp, and to do so without getting involved in a major war on the continent of Asia. The opposition presented a program designed to meet these two emotional preferences. It promised the overthrow of the Communist regime of China and the restoration of Chiang Kai-shek's rule through aerial bombardment and a naval blockade, using Formosa as a springboard. Yet a careful reading of the minutes of the joint congressional committee investigating in 1951 the dismissal of General MacArthur can leave no doubt in the mind of the unbiased reader about the military and political emptiness of the Far Eastern policies of the opposition. For the opposition was not able to devise the policies the United States would have had to pursue short of all-out war if the Communist regime of China should have been able to withstand the limited measures of war proposed, if the conflict should not have been limited to China, and if the Chinese people should not have been waiting to be liberated from their Communist government. In one word, the program of the opposition served as an effective instrument for the demagogue to achieve an illusory reconciliation of policy with popular emotional preferences which cannot be reconciled in action. Hence, that program offered no basis for a rational policy which any responsible government would have been able to pursue.

Nevertheless, the Eisenhower administration, frightened like its predecessor by this specter of public opinion, at least appeared to have accepted the objectives and expectations of the opposition and thus allowed its own policies to be judged by the standards of the opposition. Judged by these standards, its policies could not help being found wanting. For, on the one hand, it was responsible enough not to embark upon military adventures; yet, on the other, it committed itself at least to the defense of Formosa, whose indispensability for the defense of the United States was accepted as a dogma by government and opposition alike. In consequence, the executive branch found itself continuously on the defensive, apologizing, as it were, for not living up to its own standards and feeling compelled from time to time to substitute for policy a momentous announcement or a grandiose gesture suggesting the imminence of forceful action. The executive branch had thus become the prisoner of the opposition. Too responsible to do what the opposition wanted it to do and prevented by its fear of public opinion from substituting a positive policy of its own for that of the opposition, the executive branch was reduced to having no positive policy at all, while trying to make it appear as though it were following in the footsteps of the opposition, however cautiously.

The Eisenhower administration was handicapped not only by its misunderstanding of public opinion, a misunderstanding it shares with its predecessor, but it added to that error one which is peculiarly its own: the misunderstanding of the nature of the "opposition" as it operates under the conditions of the American constitutional and political system. President Eisenhower's thinking on this matter was dominated by two basic assumptions: that of the two-party system in which the President's party supports the executive branch while the other party opposes it, and the assumption of the equality, in separation, of the executive and the legislative branch with regard to the conduct of foreign policy. Both assumptions are completely at odds with the constitutional principles and political practices of the American government. It can safely be said that diametrically opposite assumptions come closer to reflecting the actual facts of American political life.

On any controversial issue of United States foreign policy no Republican President can count upon the support of all members of his party. A Republican President, pursuing a rational foreign policy in a responsible manner, cannot help having at least a third of the Republican party in Congress against him, and on many a crucial issue he cannot count upon the support of even a bare majority. This seeming paradox is the result not of accident but of the political revolution which has transformed the American political scene in the last twenty-five years.

The general political and social outlook and the specific policies which this revolution has pushed to the fore are supported by a solid majority of the people but not by a majority of the Republican party in Congress. It follows that a Republican President, to be elected and to be re-elected, must identify himself with this outlook and these policies supported by the majority of the people. Yet he will have the support of his own party without major defections only between his nomination as a presidential candidate and his election, but neither before nor after. For the revolution which has transformed the political life of the United States has split the Republican party right down the middle. Its left wing has accepted, at least as inevitable, the results of that revolution, while its right wing lives in a prerevolutionary age, pursuing prerevolutionary policies with the fanaticism and irresponsibility of desperation.

The core of the opposition to a Republican President's foreign policies lies here, and it is against that opposition that the President must make his foreign policies prevail. A Republican President who thinks and operates in terms of party discipline and looks at the Republican party as his own and the Democratic party as the opposition confounds the American political system with the British and completely misreads the lines which divide both Congress and the people with regard to foreign policy. When it comes to foreign policy a Republican President has no party of his own to rely on, but must rely upon a bloc composed, at best, of the main bulk of the Democratic and a tenuous majority of the Republican party and, at worst, of a majority of the Democratic and a minority of the Republican party.

A Republican President who, like Mr. Eisenhower, conducts foreign policy with a view to maintaining the unity of his own party can do so only at the price of his own paralysis or of his own surrender. For political compromise is possible among groups that have certain basic assumptions in common and are at one in the desire to reconcile their formulation in a particular instance and to adjust their application for practical purposes. However, there can be no compromise with a group that denies the very assumptions of the foreign policy which the United States has pursued in the last decade and a half and regards the very principles of that foreign policy as an intellectual and moral aberration, if not close or tantamount to treason.

Misunderstanding what "opposition" means in American political life, the Eisenhower administration continuously and vainly tried to appease its real opposition which is within the Republican party, and it at the same time blessed, if not actively participated in, the attempts of that very opposition to stigmatize as the perpetrators and condoners of treason that very group within Congress and within the country which in terms of numbers and conviction provides the most solid support for the foreign policies the Eisenhower administration would have liked to pursue. This misunderstanding was symbolized in the paradoxical position of Senator Knowland who, as majority and minority leader in the Senate, had the official function to rally his party to the support of the President's foreign policies and who by conviction was the most outspoken critic of them. Even the most dexterous of politicians cannot at the same time be the chief spokesman for the executive branch and the leader of the opposition.

As the President has misjudged the meaning of "opposition" within the American political system, so has he misunderstood the relation the Constitution establishes between the President and Congress with regard to the conduct of foreign policy. Here again, the President has thought in terms of peaceful co-operation, while conflict is foreordained in the nature of things. The Constitution nowhere assigns the ultimate responsibility for the conduct of foreign policy to a particular office. It assigns certain functions to the President, others to Congress, and others still to the President and the Senate to be discharged in co-operation. Apart from these specific grants, the Constitution limits itself to an over-all distribution of powers between the President and Congress by vesting in the former the executive power and making him commander-in-chief of the armed forces and by vesting all legislative powers and the power of appropriations in Congress.

This silence of the Constitution as to where the ultimate responsibility for the conduct of American foreign policy rests is, in the words of Professor Corwin, "an invitation to struggle for the privilege of directing American foreign policy." This invitation has been accepted by all Presidents from Washington to Truman; for it could have been declined only at the price of surrendering the powers of the Presidency to a Congress which, in the nature of things, could not have discharged them. President Eisenhower was in large measure willing to pay that price, without, however, buying the peace with Congress he sought. Quite to the contrary, each surrender of executive powers to Congress called forth congressional demands for more, and, when the President retreated, he did not retreat into a prepared position from which to fight back but simply yielded to congressional pressure, waiting for renewed pressure to push him farther back. He resisted those pressures only when the issue of peace or war was directly at stake, not realizing that paralysis or surrender on other issues greatly complicated his task to defend his position against the advocates of war within his own administration and party.

It is at this point that the problem of the "opposition," discussed before, and the problem of the relations between the President and Congress merge. For when it is said that the President surrendered some of the prerogatives of his office in the conduct of foreign policy to Congress, the issue is oversimplified. It is not Congress as such, acting as a collective body by majority rule, which took over functions which by tradition and logic are the President's. It is to the opposition within his own party that the President surrendered them. While the more spectacular raids of the congressional opposition upon the executive preserve abated from 1955 onward, the impact which the opposition made upon both the substantive foreign policies and the personnel of the Eisenhower administration has been lasting and destructive of those very policies.

It stands to reason that a foreign policy which must be carried on under such conditions of domestic politics can leave little room for the initiative of even the greatest of statesmen. One might pause for a moment and imagine Sir Winston Churchill in his policies toward Egypt endeavoring to satisfy not only the military and political interests of Great Britain and the Egyptian aspirations for the evacuation of the Suez Canal Zone but also the opposition within his own party to that evacuation. Confronted with the choice between the national interest of Great Britain and considerations of domestic politics, he did not hesitate to choose the former. Yet the Eisenhower administration, confronted with similar choices, short of the ultimate choice between peace and war, invariably tended to choose the latter. In this it went far beyond those concessions which the requirements of democratic control and the peculiarities of the American constitutional and political system make inevitable.

Yet it is a tribute to President Eisenhower's innate good sense and a manifestation of the narrow limits within which objective circumstances confine initiative in foreign policy that the Eisenhower administration was by and large able, during the first years of its tenure of office, to continue the foreign policies of its predecessor, preserving its strong points, perpetuating and aggravating its weaknesses. It suffered its severest defeat on the plane of the imponderables of moral leadership and political prestige. And their drastic decline during the first two years of the Eisenhower administration can be directly traced to the ascendancy, during that very same period, of a kind of domestic politics that is incompatible not only with good foreign policy but with democratic government itself.

Index

DATE DUE

FEB 3 '75			
JUL 21 '75			